Cornwallis

THE

American Adventure

First Printing w

Library of Congress
Catalog Card Number: 75–91059

Printed in the United States of America

Cornwallis

THE

American Adventure

Franklin and Mary
WICKWIRE

Illustrated with Photographs and Maps

HOUGHTON MIFFLIN COMPANY BOSTON

1970

To Pamela

who enthusiastically

joined our pursuit

. . . without baggage, necessaries, or provisions of any sort for officer or soldier, in the most barren inhospitable, unhealthy part of North America, opposed to the most savage, inveterate, perfidious, cruel enemy, with zeal and with bayonets only, it was resolved to follow Greene's army to the end of the world.

Brigadier General Charles O'Hara
to the Duke of Grafton,
April 20, 1781

Preface

DURING HIS LONG CAREER of public service in the eighteenth and early nineteenth centuries, the first Marquis Cornwallis helped influence the course of history on three continents. His surrender at Yorktown occasioned the end of the American Revolution and ensured the triumph of American independence. His tenure as governor general and commander in chief in India represented a new phase in the history of British government there. He radically altered the traditional system of land tenure in Bengal and introduced some of the better elements of the English common law into the Bengal legal system. He reformed the civil service of India, imbuing it with an *esprit de corps* that fostered honesty and efficiency. Not least important, he fought a successful war against the Sultan of Mysore, thus adding substantially to the territories controlled by the East India Company. Several years later he served as governor general and commander in chief in Ireland, playing an important role in the events which led to its legislative union with Great Britain. Finally, his single venture into the labyrinth of European diplomacy resulted in the only period of peace his country knew during its twenty-year struggle against the imperial pretensions of France.

Yet neither this remarkable man nor his remarkable career has ever been fully chronicled. A person of so much importance to British history, who merits a multivolume study, has never received a comprehensive biography. A few panegyrics published shortly after his death scarcely distinguished fact from fiction in his life. While two lengthy articles — in the *Dictionary of National Biography;* and in Sir Lewis Namier and John Brooke, *The History of Parliament: The House of Commons, 1754–1790* (3 vols.; 1964) — outline well his career, they hardly do him justice. W. S. Seton-Karr, *The Marquis Cornwallis and the Consolidation of British Rule* (Oxford, 1914) is itself little more than a sketch, and it concentrates on India; while A. Aspinall, *Cornwallis in Bengal* (Manchester, 1931) deals only with a portion of Cornwallis' reforms as governor general in Bengal and offers few observations about the man and his personality. Charles Ross in 1859 produced a three-volume edition of Cornwallis' correspondence, an edition which yet stands, after more than a century, as the single best published guide to the first Marquis' life. Yet correspondence does not constitute a biography, and furthermore Ross omitted publishing many letters which today both the historian and the student of history would consider extremely important.

This strange failure to chronicle the career of one of Britain's most important imperial generals and statesmen cannot be explained by a lack of materials. The Marquis' surviving papers, all 281 bundles of them, are available in the Public Record Office to qualified scholars, as are other manuscript records relevant to all phases of his work. The India Office houses masses of material bearing on his administration in India. The British Museum, as well as a number of smaller archives in England, contain several important papers. Indeed, perhaps the plethora, rather than the paucity, of material has turned scholars away from Cornwallis. A man whose career touched three continents and who served as a general, a governor, and a diplomat challenges not only the skill but also the endurance of the would-be biographer.

Endurance is especially required for a multivolume biography, but we felt that we could not do Cornwallis justice in a single work. His career, his interests, and his importance were too great, and he influenced too profoundly too many important events. That decision forced us to consider where we ought to break his career, and we decided that his service in America provided a logical, coherent part of his life that could readily be encompassed in one book. He fought in several major engagements of the American Revolution; he managed the entire southern campaign; his operations helped determine the course of the war; and his surrender at Yorktown for all practical purposes marked the end of that war and the end of his concerns with America. Had any detailed study of his career in America previously appeared, we might have passed briefly over this phase of his life and included some of his later work in the first volume. But no detailed examination of Cornwallis in America exists.

To compile this study we called upon the resources of many archives, public and private, in Great Britain and in the United States. We should first like to thank the officials of the Public Record Office, where we did the bulk of our research, for their help with our work. The trustees of the British Museum kindly permitted us to search through several manuscripts pertinent to our study. The National Register of Archives extended the use of facilities which in turn enabled us to seek out several other archives. The West Suffolk Record Office at Bury St. Edmunds houses the Grafton Papers, which included several valuable letters of General O'Hara. We are particularly indebted to Mr. M. P. Statham, the county archivist, who extended us his help and courtesy. Through the kindness of the Department of Manuscripts at the University of Nottingham and the trustees of the Newcastle estates we examined the Newcastle Papers. The

Portland Papers, also at Nottingham, proved helpful as well. The central library at Sheffield allowed us full access to the Rockingham Papers. The East Riding County Record Office in Beverly, Yorkshire, contained a few letters in the Hotham Papers bearing on the early career of Cornwallis, and the archivist, Mr. Norman Higson, graciously consented to open the office especially for us when our schedule did not permit us to use its facilities during its normal hours of operation. Viscount Elveden generously permitted us to search portions of the Iveagh Papers at Elveden Hall in Suffolk. There we found valuable information about the extent and value of the Cornwallis lands. The historical records of Hoare's Bank at 37 Fleet Street, London, provided us with further information on the Cornwallis finances, and the gracious and invaluable assistance of the archivist, Mr. Winder, saved us much time in searching these records. The staff of the library of the University of London as well as the staff of the history department library at University College extended every help and consideration. The Institute of Historical Research, as always, made available both an invaluable store of published primary sources and many hours of stimulating conversation over tea. Fiennes Cornwallis not only encouraged us in our work but also provided interesting family information. A research grant from the United States–United Kingdom Educational Commission (Fulbright) made possible in 1965–1966 a year of study in Great Britain.

We are also indebted to institutions and people in the United States who aided us in our research. At the William L. Clements Library in Ann Arbor, Michigan, we met with unfailing courtesy and cooperation. We wish especially to thank William Ewing and the library's director, Howard Peckham. The University of Michigan Library, furthermore, extended to us the use of their facilities during the hours when the Clements was closed. Thanks are due also to the staffs of the Sterling Memorial Library, the Beinecke Library at Yale, and of the rare book collection in the Frost Library at Amherst College. We are especially appreciative of the efforts of Mr. Harlan Hubbard of the Library of the University of Massachusetts for his patient work on our behalf. A grant from the research council of the University of Massachusetts helped finance our travel through the area in which Cornwallis campaigned. We owe thanks to the many people, especially in South Carolina, who helped us in our inquiries.

Contents

PART IV *THE DISASTROUS DRIVE NORTH*
The Carolinas

PART V *THE WAR ENDS*
The Frustrated Commander

Cornwallis

THE

American Adventure

PROLOGUE

Yorktown

FIRING had ceased. During the unaccustomed silence men on
both sides still waited anxiously to learn what would come
of the negotiations that had occupied the night. On the previous
day Cornwallis had sent Major Alexander Ross (his aide-de-
camp and closest friend) and Colonel Thomas Dundas to discuss
terms of surrender with the allied commissioners, the Viscomte
de Noailles and Colonel John Laurens. The "solemn stillness"
that prevailed during these parleys seemed unnatural after
many weeks' subjection to the cacophony of war. To ease ten-
sion each side had serenaded the other. The British had
mounted their Highland pipers on the parapets and the band of
the French Deux-Ponts Regiment had reciprocated. The morning of October 19, 1781, dawned beautiful and unusually warm,
revealing the panorama of Yorktown. Men from the British,
French, and American armies lined the works that had been sav-
aged by three weeks of pounding. The two redoubts wrested
from the British five days earlier, now manned by French and
Americans, reminded the redcoats of their untenable position.
"Secretary" Nelson's ravaged house, "with one of the corners
broke off, and many large holes thro' the roof and walls, part of

which seem'd tottering," [1] testified that even the British commanding general, who had used the dwelling as a headquarters,
had found no haven from the heavy bombardment.[2] The York
River floated no British battleships. The shattered and sickly
British army of six thousand men, of whom only two-thirds were
now fit for duty,[3] could not be convoyed to safety, for a French
naval force under the Comte de Grasse bottled up the Chesapeake. Except by a major successful naval battle Cornwallis'
men could not receive succor from General Sir Henry Clinton
in New York. Water, so often before a highway to conquest and
glory for the British, now entrapped them.

In the forenoon, both sides at last signed the articles of capitulation. Charles, second Earl Cornwallis, lieutenant general and
commander of the British forces in the southern part of America, surrendered to an overwhelming force of American and
French regulars. The most active and aggressive general that
the British had sent to America now tasted the bitterness of defeat.

In this instance, the victor made the defeat a mortification:
George Washington refused to grant his fallen foe the honors of
war. Instead of allowing the British forces to march out with
their flags unfurled, their drums rattling, and their band playing a tune of the conqueror, the American commander demanded that they should "march out with colors cased and
drums beating a British or a German march." Washington was
retaliating for the shame inflicted upon American forces by Sir
Henry Clinton more than a year before, when at Charleston the
honors of war had been denied to the five thousand troops of
General Benjamin Lincoln. During the progress of the negotiations outside Yorktown, Major Ross had protested to Colonel
Laurens that Cornwallis had not been responsible for Clinton's
ungraciousness. Laurens had remained firm: "It is not the individual that is here considered. It is the nation. This remains an
article, or I cease to be a commissioner." [4]

Accordingly at two o'clock, in the heat of the day, the redcoats filed out and marched along the Hampton Road with colors furled, drums beating, and fifes tootling a tune that some thought peculiarly appropriate — "The World Turned Upside Down." The French lined one side of the road, looking fresh and trim in their smart coats and new black gaiters donned especially for the occasion. On the other side of the road the Americans in their heterogeneous garments presented a shabbier appearance but watched with no less satisfaction as the defeated foe trooped by.

Cornwallis did not ride at the head of the columns of the vanquished. Illness — perhaps a recurrence of the fever he had contracted in North Carolina — kept him, in these final moments, from leading out the soldiers who loved him so much. Instead Brigadier General Charles O'Hara, the rugged Irishman who had suffered with the Earl through the disastrous Carolina campaign, carried out the ceremonies. O'Hara tried to present his sword to the Comte de Rochambeau, the French commander, but the Comte Mathieu Dumas directed the brigadier instead to General Washington. Washington, anticipating O'Hara, said, "Never from such a good hand!" The American commander in chief could accept no sword save from his British counterpart.[5] Washington accordingly directed O'Hara's action to his own second, Lincoln. Then the redcoats piled their arms in the middle of a circle formed by the French hussars. The ceremonies were over.

For the Earl Cornwallis it was an end and a beginning.

PART I

Before the War

CHAPTER 1

A Suffolk Family

Horatio Nelson, high on his column at Trafalgar Square, seems to peer over the Admiralty Arch past the Mall at the government buildings which march down Whitehall. Behind his back stands the National Gallery, and behind the latter, apparently an afterthought, lies the National Portrait Gallery. There, in a high square room, whose walls are crowded with naval heroes (and Nelson's Lady Hamilton), the first Marquis Cornwallis is one of the few army figures so commemorated. Flanked by other colonial administrators — Hastings, Clive, Coote, Raffles, Impey, Rawdon — Cornwallis faces Burgoyne, Munro, and Elliott.

Gainsborough, who flattered less than Reynolds, painted Cornwallis in 1783. The portrait shows a man neither handsome nor in the first flush of youth. Underlying the repose of the face and the sadness of the eyes is an impression of strength. The eyes are shadowed (the heavy-lidded look is partly the result of an eye injury in his youth), the nose large. The lower half of the face is broad, giving it a nearly rectangular look, and there is the hint of a double chin. Indeed, just four years later Cornwallis referred to himself as "rather corpulent," [1] although a portrait drawn in Madras in 1792 shows him not much heavier than he was in the Gainsborough of nine years before. In the later picture, the eyes have extra crinkles at the corners, the face has been tanned by the fierce Indian sun, and the subject looks twenty years older.

Charles Cornwallis, first Marquis and second Earl Cornwallis, was born on December 31, 1738. It was the last day of the last year of England's longest period of peace during the century. Throughout the remainder of the eighteenth century England was at war more often than not. To many young men, a military career seemed natural and desirable. Cornwallis made such a choice and died a commanding general on October 5, 1805, just two weeks before Admiral Lord Nelson's death at Trafalgar. During the sixty-seven years of his life Cornwallis served his country in three continents, on fields of battle, amidst the intrigues of diplomacy and commercial enterprise, and as supreme governor over alien peoples. He knew the heat of the malaria-ridden swamps of the Carolinas and Virginia, the incredible green of an Irish spring, the winter drabness of Amiens, and the sweltering banks of the Hugli River at Calcutta. He was a man who dearly loved his family and his estates in Suffolk. Yet he denied himself the felicity of life at home, serving his country abroad for approximately twenty years and allowing himself the luxury of seeing his beloved son and heir, Lord Brome, for but twelve years during his lifetime. Although a staunch defender of the Church of England, he nonetheless pleaded eloquently for the emancipation of the Catholics in Ireland. Although a soldier engaged in a bloody occupation during a brutal century, he prized honor and good faith above all else and invariably practiced a notable humanity. Thoroughly, even conventionally, English himself, he sometimes displayed an uncanny knack of seeing other people clearly. He was, in the most complete sense, a member of the ruling class of eighteenth-century Britain. Indeed, his attributes made him almost an ideal aristocrat — a personification as it were of most of the virtues that presumably suffused the ruling class both as a group and as individuals.

It was a class that, over a period of centuries, had produced a remarkable assortment of people. As different from one another as the individuals in any other class, they yet shared certain common traits — or if not traits, then at least ideals, which the whole weight of aristocratic society contrived to perpetuate and reinforce by means of its common education. For generation after generation the same schools (or private tutors) taught the same things to the young men who were predestined by right of birth to rule the nation. What education and rearing began, church and government continued. All taught Duty and Honor.

Although often ignored by individual peers, these twin concepts yet constituted a living code for the aristocracy as a group. That only a few exceptional men, like Cornwallis, could actually live up to it did not make the code itself less alive. It exercised a powerful influence over men's minds, even if not over their actions. The first Marquis' sister Charlotte Madan demonstrated the force of these ideals when she earnestly said of her son, "his honor is much dearer to me than his life." [2] The first Marquis himself, but recently returned from seven gruelling years in India, instantly relinquished the comfort of his newly remodeled Culford manor when king and country called upon him to serve on the Continent. "My most earnest endeavours," he said, "shall be constantly exerted to promote the public interests." [3]

In the eighteenth century few avenues lay open to a member of the ruling class who wished to promote the "public interest." For aristocrats and gentry, honorable service could be found only in the army, navy, church, government, or legal profession. True, no other occupations carried the possibility for fame and fortune (or their pale cousins, eminence and a competency). Yet the possibility of future reward did not make less credible the aristocrat's wish to fulfill in these careers the ideals he had learned. Indeed, the members of the ruling class, could they be brought to speak about anything so obvious as their place in their country's society and government, would have said that they were the government and so were bound to do their duty and that since they were the society, they of course had fame and fortune. To be sure, heroism and other extraordinary services should have exceptional rewards, but for most members of the ruling class, neither fame nor fortune was expected to come as a reward. Rather, these blessings were the natural perquisites of the natural ruling class. They did not rule because they had earned the right. They ruled because they were born to do so and, therefore, were better at it than anyone else. As they held the reins of government, so they had money and social position: not because they had proved their superior merit, but because they were born to wealth and position and so were peculiarly entitled to it.

Wealth and position! Cornwallis claimed both as his birthright, although the latter had a firmer foundation than the former. The Cornwallises had acquired more than local preeminence in Suffolk: they had held national prominence for four centuries. The family's origin lies in obscurity in Saxon or early Norman England, but the name itself, together with the presence of Cornish choughs on the coat of arms, suggest that it had roots in Cornwall. A distant ancestor of the Barons Cornwallis must have broken his ties with that rocky, heathy land and trekked across the length of England to seek a new life. In the reign of Edward III, one Thomas Cornwallis gained some prominence as sheriff of London, and sometime before his death in 1384 he established his estates at Brome in Suffolk. From him the family takes its lineage. The Cornwallises achieved yet greater reknown two centuries later when Sir Thomas Cornwallis, eldest son to Sir John Cornwallis (who had been steward of the household to Prince Edward, later King Edward VI), proffered his services to Queen Mary. By his readiness to switch his religious allegiance to suit the new monarch, Sir Thomas managed to establish the family yet more firmly in Suffolk. He built a manor, Brome Hall.

Although two hundred years later the first Marquis emerged as a man of moderation and common sense, the other descendants of Sir Thomas were not invariably so endowed: the family had a wild streak which showed itself at regular intervals. One Cornwallis in each generation either stirred up political controversy, had scandalous marital difficulties, provoked interfamily quarrels, or instigated feuds with other families. Indeed, turmoil of one sort or another constantly bedeviled the builder and first inhabitant of Brome Hall. Good luck, not good sense, enabled the line to continue.

Born in 1519 and knighted in 1548, Sir Thomas rose high in his sovereign's service. He fought rebellion in Norfolk in 1549, became sheriff of Norfolk and Suffolk in 1553, and in the same year was appointed a commissioner to treat with Scotland. After various other assignments for Queen Mary, he became treasurer of Calais in 1554. Through her own ineptness Mary lost to France this last outpost of English empire on the European continent, thereby writing the final chapter in the Hundred Years' War. But suspicious minds thought something worse than military blundering accounted for the loss of Calais. A ditty soon became popular that ran: "Who built Brome Hall? Sir Thomas Cornwallis. How did he build it? By selling of Calais." [4]

The name of Brome became so strongly associated with the family that, when (in the eighteenth century) one of the Barons Cornwallis was advanced two steps in the peerage, he took as new titles Viscount Brome and Earl Cornwallis. The advancement also meant that thenceforward the eldest son of each successive Earl Cornwallis was given the courtesy title of Viscount

Brome until his succession to the earldom. Yet by the eighteenth century, despite its strong associations with the family, Brome Hall was better suited to a country gentleman with refined tastes than to a peer of the realm. Although its "pleasant village" lay in a "picturesque parish of fertile and well-wooded land," Brome's sparse acreage and small manor house did not measure up to what eighteenth-century British society expected of its nobility. While the first Marquis inherited both the title and manor of Brome from the line of Sir Thomas, he preferred to live on an estate that came into the family through Sir Thomas' daughter-in-law.

Jane Meautys (or Metwas) married twice. Her union with Sir Thomas' son William produced Frederick, the first Baron Cornwallis from whom the first Marquis descended. William died, however, while Jane was still a young woman, and she remarried. Her second husband, Nathaniel Bacon, was the seventh son of Sir Nicholas Bacon, the lord keeper of the great seal during Queen Elizabeth's reign. Nathaniel inherited Culford and lands around it to the value of about £1000 per annum. The estate should have gone to his issue instead of to the Cornwallis family, but the offspring of the Bacon marriage never managed to perpetuate the line. Two girls died in infancy, and the one son, Nicholas, died a year after his mother. With Nathaniel Bacon's line extinct, the estate went in 1660 to Jane's surviving son Frederick.[5]

Frederick's new inheritance cannot have been so impressive as Brome, for although Culford was larger, it was much less elegant. Built roughly in the shape of an inverted U, it had a quadrangle "so small" that it was "often damp and dark." A terrace in the front prevented carriages from depositing arriving guests close to the porch. The house had a large plain hall, which, together with a small, "useless" adjoining room, occupied the entire south front of the building. To enter the drawing room from the hall one had to climb five or six steps to the great staircase and walk through a "dark and narrow passage." The dining room next door had a low ceiling and three "awkward" windows, two of which faced west ("the worst aspect for an eating room"). The bedchambers were lacking in grace and insufficient in number. The upper story needed repairs. Indeed, by the time of the first Marquis the only part of the interior at once structurally sound and aesthetically pleasing was the grand staircase. The back stairs were "bad indeed," while the "damp and dark" quadrangle, really an open court in the middle of the house, let in the weather and rendered the entire house "cold and damp." [6] Nevertheless, Culford was the first Marquis' home for fifty years before he undertook alterations in the late 1780's and early 1790's. Then he not only remodeled the house but also hired Humphrey Repton to lay out beautiful grounds. When the work was completed the Cornwallises at last had a residence appropriate to the family's distinguished station in society and long service to government.

The imposing monument — proud clarion of success — did not take shape until Cornwallis had acquired ample funds to pay the heavy costs of alterations. The family fortune had never been of the first rank. Most of his forebears had not had enough money to remodel Culford. The few who might have accumulated adequate funds lacked either the time or the temperament for so large an undertaking.

Frederick Cornwallis, who would later become the first Baron Cornwallis, valiantly served his sovereign during the civil wars and then took refuge on the Continent. He returned with the new king, Charles II, upon his accession in 1660, and for his loyalty was rewarded. Frederick became treasurer of the household and a privy councillor in 1660. In the same year he inherited Culford owing to his mother's union with the Bacons. In 1661 the King created him Baron Cornwallis. He had less than a year to enjoy his barony, however, for he died suddenly of apoplexy at the age of fifty-one.

Frederick's son and heir — Charles, second Baron Cornwallis — did not acquire any great fortune before his death at the age of forty-one. While the third Baron lived to be only a year older than his father, he had a far more colorful career. Although he might have had ample means, he did not have the inclination to improve Culford. The restive disposition and unstable temperament that cropped up periodically in members of the family were full-blown in the third Baron. "He was a young spendthrift, was very extravagant, loved gaming, lost as much as anyone would trust him, but was not quite so ready at paying." In 1676, before his twenty-first birthday, he was tried by his peers for manslaughter. The Lords found him not guilty by a vote of twenty-one to five. Nonetheless, he got drunk while in the company of a Mr. Gerard and seems to have been present when Gerard killed a boy for a supposed insult. Despite his irregular behavior, the third Baron rose high in his sovereign's service, holding a variety of offices at one time or another: lord lieutenant of Suffolk, high steward of Ipswich, a privy councillor, and first lord of the admiralty. Whether or not he would have settled down in old age must remain unknown since he died in 1698 at the age of forty-two.

His son, the fourth Baron, led a more regular life, but he, too, died in middle age. He was joint postmaster general from 1715 to 1721 and paymaster general of the forces from 1721 until his death a year later. Had he held the latter office for any considerable length of time and had he utilized it as did most of its holders, he might have made himself and his heirs very rich. Parliament gave the paymaster general all the army's funds in a lump sum. The paymaster could then invest the money at interest as if it were his own, until he received orders to issue specific payments. In the eighteenth century Henry Fox (later Lord Holland) built up his family's wealth with the money he made from this office. But the fourth Baron, "a gentleman of sweet disposition," was not a speculator. Even had he been so inclined, he would have had little time to play with the army's money before he died of a stomach "gout" at the age of forty-seven.

His eldest son, the fifth Baron, lived into his sixties and married well. He enriched the family heritage by adding to it the titles of Viscount Brome and Earl Cornwallis. Yet he never possessed the high office, with attendent income, that would have allowed him to leave his heirs a fortune. He was a loyal but plodding servant of the crown, and none of his various positions — groom of the bedchamber, chief justice in Eyre south of the Trent, constable of the Tower, lord lieutenant of the Tower hamlets, member of the privy council — was in the first rank of government. However, he did marry Elizabeth, the daughter of Lord Townshend and the niece of Sir Robert Walpole; a match that probably helped obtain his advance in the peerage. Also, as might be expected of a man connected with Walpole, he kept a firm grip on the family borough of Eye: the Cornwallises could always send a member to Parliament.[7] Furthermore, one of his younger brothers, Frederick (who also married a Townshend girl), rose to the highest rank in the church, for he became Archbishop of Canterbury in 1768. But the restoration of Culford still awaited an heir who would combine longevity, ambition, and wealth.

That heir was Charles, Lord Brome, the eldest son of the first Earl Cornwallis. At the age of twenty-three he succeeded his father as the second Earl. Thirty years later, in recognition of his services to the crown, he would be created the first Marquis Cornwallis. With glory came affluence.

Glory and affluence, however, lay far in the future for the young Earl who returned from the field of battle to take his seat in the House of Lords. He inherited a distinguished name and a peerage but only a modest fortune. His family had served the crown long and faithfully but not spectacularly. Although most of his forebears had been men of sound disposition and good sense, some few had been possessed of a wild and unpredictable nature. By right of birth he belonged to a select group that numbered just over two hundred — the peers of the realm.[8] His birthright also included a special claim to the offices and rewards of his country. To take up that claim meant accepting responsibilities and meeting challenges.

CHAPTER 2

A "Very Military" Young Man

THE ARISTOCRACY of nobility and gentry exercised unchallenged rule over British society and government in the eighteenth century. Many factors contributed to their ascendancy, but among the most important were their education, their courage, and their sheer physical toughness. In an age when the majority of Englishmen were illiterate, a knowledge of reading and writing and languages distinguished the gentleman from the masses. In a brutal age full of rioting and robbery, the aristocrat's skill at fighting and riding won him a respect which mere inheritance could not have commanded. He had to be equally at ease in polite society and in the Hogarthian world of street brawls and squalor. Refined though his taste might become, he rarely forgot the Spartan lessons of his early life, which prepared him for the world outside the drawing room.

The upbringing of the young Lord Brome typified the rugged training received by the aristocracy. He learned to ride almost as soon as he walked, and when old enough he joyously rode in the daredevil pursuit of the fox. Early in life he learned to shoot, for grouse and pheasants abounded in the fields and woods around Culford. He developed strength and endurance even while growing up in surroundings more gracious than most Englishmen would ever dream of. But Brome's youthful training, like that of many of his fellows, included attendance at a school of harder knocks than the chase. Eton was not for weaklings.

Lord Brome had iron in his character (more than his father had, if one may judge from the first Earl's surviving letters). Eton even more than Culford forged that iron. It is not known precisely when young Lord Brome left his family home for the most famous of England's public schools, but by December of 1753 he was in the sixth form. He stayed at Eton for at least one year, perhaps two.

The parapets of Windsor Castle overlook the playing fields of Eton, whose history has long been intertwined with the history of kings. Founded by Henry VI in 1440, the school opened its first classes in 1442. From its beginning Eton was a private corporation, composed of a provost and fellows and financed by the income from lands given to it. Rents still supported it handsomely in Lord Brome's time, even though Henry VIII had earlier cheated it out of some property. Eton's original purpose had been chiefly to train clerics from among the poor children who lived in the vicinity of the town, but with the passage of time the school lost its clerical flavor. Although it continued to educate some poor and middle-class children, by the early seventeenth century Eton had become a fashionable school for the aristocracy. By the eighteenth century it trained statesmen and men of letters: its illustrious alumni included Pitt, Walpole, Gray, Cornwallis, and Conway.

Not all of the alumni who became statesmen, soldiers, and men of letters had belonged to the ruling class at the time of their matriculation. By virtue of an Eton education, however, they might hope to join it.

Latin was the most important subject in the curriculum and had been so from the beginning. For the first century or so it had been a useful language to know, since the church and various businesses employed it. But the utilitarian value of Latin declined greatly after Henry VIII broke with Rome. Yet even after the Henrician Reformation, Latin continued to be taught as a discipline, and its continued dominance in the curriculum served as a means of maintaining class distinctions. As a scholar recently said:

> In an age when only a minority of the population was to receive any education at all, an easy way of drawing a clear line of demarcation between those who were and those who were not educated was to have all such education as was to carry with it any social prestige in education in Latin and to make Latin an essential qualification for all the most desirable jobs in the land, whether the knowledge of it was in reality of any value for the performance of those jobs or not.[1]

Eton fostered class distinctions in ways other than through its curriculum. The entire structure and policy of the school reminded the boys every day of social divisions. Although any Eton alumnus was far superior to the ordinary masses, some Eton students were socially superior to others. A wide gulf separated the aristocracy from the lower ranks. For example, sons of the nobility usually (and sons of the gentry often) brought their own private tutors with them to the school. The aristocracy ate and lodged in the town, not on the campus. Young Lord Brome was listed as a sixth form oppidan (that is, a student lodging and eating outside the school) in December of 1753.[2] Peers "occupied the stalls in Chapel." On Saint Andrew's, Saint Patrick's, Saint David's, and Saint George's days respectively the Scots, Irish, Welsh, and English noblemen of the highest rank presented the headmaster with a badge. Other noblemen also dined with him on these days.[3] Furthermore, by the eighteenth century the nobility and gentry were unquestionably of higher social standing than the persons who taught

them. Since the days of Charles II the scholastic profession had
begun to decline. The assistant masters, who bore much of the
drudgery, were clearly regarded as inferior beings. Not only did
they have to buy their posts, but also, since the nobility and gentry brought along their own tutors, they ended by teaching only
the poor (and socially inferior). The headmaster, who came to
be as important as the provost in determining educational policy, often met open defiance of his orders from the nobility. Indeed, the aristocrat, receiving instruction from "a master whom
he did not consider a gentleman," knowing that his success in a
future career would not "in any way" depend upon his school
record, needed little inducement to flout discipline and challenge authority.[4] It is not surprising that rebellions erupted at
Eton several times during the course of the eighteenth century.

Had they exerted their authority, the headmasters might have
prevented some of the turbulence. But they allowed precedents
to grow up that needlessly emphasized the division between noblemen and commoners. Martin Whish, who had attended both
Eton and King's College, Cambridge (founded at the same time
as Eton and with special provisions for receiving Etonians),
commented on a practice which might have been customary in
Brome's student days. In a letter to the second Duke of Newcastle in 1768 Whish observed that the oppidans of the sixth
form had been made "prepositors" (prefects with authority
to discipline junior students). As such they had for "several
years" exercised almost dictatorial power over the younger
boys at the school and had defied the assistant masters who
tried to restrain them. On one occasion some disputes arose
between the assistant masters and the prepositors "concerning
the extent and limits of this privilege." The assistant masters
complained to the headmaster that two of the prepositors had
gone outside the school boundaries. The master, who wished
for no trouble, now had the difficult task of keeping the troublesome young sprigs of nobility under school authority (else all

would be anarchy), while at the same time allowing them enough latitude to prevent rebellion save from the most unreasonable. Accordingly the headmaster replied that:

> the prepositors certainly had from him leave exceeding the common bounds, & therefore were not to be deemed culpable *merely* for appearing beyond them: but, if they should be met by any assistant at a time or place, where their presence should be judged by that assistant improper or unnecessary, that they should return from thence, agreably to that subordination which in all cases requires from an inferior officer a compliance with the order of a superior.

At the time the two prepositors accepted this ruling.

The next day showed a change of attitude: "on farther consideration" the prepositors as a group — most of them, of course, were of the nobility — had decided that they were superior to the assistant masters rather than the other way round. Their appraisal of the situation was almost immediately put to the test, for on the same day an assistant complained of a prepositor's "offensive" behavior. When the master proceeded to punish the boy, "the other prepositors presented themselves to him & said that as their privileges were infringed they would resign their office." The master accepted their resignations but naturally tried to discover the reason for them. The prepositors gave as answer that: "acting under him they would be subject to him, & not to his assistants." If the master had delegated them power and privileges, "they were themselves, & not the assistants to be the judges of the reasonableness *where* it should be used." The issue remained at deadlock, the boys persisting in their claims and the master refusing to acknowledge their pretensions. The following day they again approached him in a group and stated that they would not speak (i.e., declaim) in school. When the master asserted that as sixth form boys they must speak when he required it, they replied that all the sixth form oppidans would instead combine and leave school. They then withdrew "in a turbulent manner," and by averring that all the prepositors had been expelled, they induced "the greater part of the oppidans of the 5th form & many of the 4th" to follow them. First they went to the playing fields, where they read to all those assembled the paper of combination drawn up by the prepositors. Next they went to Maidenhead Bridge and spent the night at "the great inn there." Assistants tried without avail to get them to return. Finally tiring of their game, they asked the master for a general pardon. Although he refused, most of them eventually drifted back to school. Such was the low state of discipline and the limited power of headmaster and assistants over the oppidans.[5] If at Culford young Lord Brome had realized how much better off he was than most Englishmen, at Eton he must have learned that he had a natural right to leadership and social predominance.

The school taught the sanctity of ranks, but it also taught that within each rank the strongest and the bravest survived. Etonians were never "coddled." Punishments were corporal, sports often brutal, fights frequent and occasionally fatal. Classical education at Eton had been utterly dehumanized and had been reduced to grammar and parsing. Woe to the boy who missed his assignment, for the rod awaited him. The lucky student who escaped a beating within the classroom was unlikely to avoid one outside it. Sooner or later he would fight with one of his classmates or take a thrashing from one of the older boys. When the headmaster Henry Bland (1719 to 1728) set up a system of declamations, he intended for students to present opposite sides of an argument. But in typical Eton fashion two senior collegers translated their words into deeds: one of them knocked the other's head against the chapel wall.[6] In 1730 a student named Edward Cockburn died after one of his schoolmates stabbed him with a penknife.

Although sports did attain some refinement during the century, many of them remained savage. A favorite pastime for the students was to roam about town in groups and beat up the burgesses. Not until a few years before Brome went there had the school finally outlawed another student "game": formerly it had been the custom to turn a ram loose in the schoolyard so that the young scholars could have the pleasure of beating it to death. Once a ram had escaped from the yard into town, but the boys had chased it and fortunately succeeded in hamstringing it so that it could not elude them while they clubbed it to death. Perhaps when he participated in this butchery the Duke of Cumberland (son of George II) was preparing for Culloden.[7] Even the less brutal sports could be dangerous. Cricket, football, and hockey were popular, but each had its hazards. Indeed, Brome was disfigured for life during a hockey game when Shute Barrington, who later became Bishop of Durham, accidentally struck him in the eye. As a result of the injury, Brome permanently wore a quizzical, cockeyed expression.

Most of the boys survived Eton, and they emerged tough enough to face the world. George III, who had a particular fondness for the institution, once asked the mythologist Jacob Bryant what he had been famous for at Eton. Everyone expected Bryant, a frail-looking man, to assert that he had been known for his Latin exercises. Astonishingly, Bryant responded: "Cudgelling, Sir: I was most famous for that." And indeed he was, for at one time he had knocked the future general Henry Seymour Conway sharply on the head.[8] No matter what his future occupation, an Eton alumnus had learned how to administer a beating and how to take one. Brome, like Bryant and the others, accepted the knocks as part of the game. Physical hardships strengthened, rather than weakened, respect and affection for the alma mater. Even later in life, when he was no longer Lord Brome, Cornwallis maintained his ties with his former school. In 1790 he was elected a member of the newly formed Eton Club in Calcutta. Naturally he sent his son to

Eton and followed with interest the young man's progress
through the forms.[9] When he returned to England after his
governor generalship of India he often visited his son at school.
Eton left its stamp on him in many ways.[10] Perhaps his attendance there explains at least in part why he was made of sterner
stuff than his father.

Brome's character, molded at home and school, was fired on
European battlegrounds. After Eton, he could have gone, like
so many of his fellows, to Oxford or Cambridge and could
have followed that by the customary grand tour of the Continent. Brome, however, wanted something different. He was, as
his father said, a "very military" young man, and he viewed a
European tour as a chance to further his plans for becoming a
professional soldier.[11] It is not clear when the thirst for military
glory seized young Lord Brome. Perhaps as a boy at Culford he
listened spellbound to his uncle, General Edward Cornwallis,
tell exciting tales of campaigns in faraway lands. Brome's wish
did not go long ungranted: on December 8, 1756, just a few
weeks before his eighteenth birthday, he received a commission
in the 1st, or Grenadier, Guards. Presumably his father purchased the ensigncy for him, for that was the usual beginning for
officers in the "professional" British army.

Had Brome followed the example of most of his colleagues, he
would have made no exertions to acquire professional knowledge and skill but would have relied instead upon chance to
teach him what he needed to know of his trade. With the
proper outlay of money and passage of years, he could still have
risen to the rank of general. He might have done so without
ever having seen a day of combat although his military career
embraced the period of the Seven Years' War, the War for
American Independence, the French Revolutionary and Napo-
leonic Wars.

Brome, however, was not like most of his peers. He was eager to go to war and to reap the glory supposed to accompany war. Many of the nobility looked forward to battle for its own sake, but few had any patience for the formal military schooling that might enable them, even while they lacked experience of war, to lead their men into action intelligently. Brome did have the patience. Before going to the battlefield he wanted to learn something about his profession in the schoolroom. In order to get that instruction, he had to go abroad. Although Woolwich Academy in England turned out engineer and artillery officers, no college yet existed in the country to train infantry and cavalry officers. Sandhurst, which would fill this need, would not be founded until three years before Cornwallis' death. Neither Brome nor his fellows, of course, would consider serving in the artillery or engineers. These were clearly "inferior" branches of the army, offering, at best, limited opportunity for promotion to the highest rank and command of armies in the field. But Brome wanted to learn his trade, and this desire turned his grand tour into something different from the usual affair.

Through his father's influence with the Duke of Cumberland he secured the King's permission to travel abroad in 1757.[12] Brome left England accompanied by his tutor-companion, Captain de Roguin, a veteran of the War of the Austrian Succession. The two traveled for a few months and then settled at Turin so that Brome could attend the military academy there, which was considered one of the best in Europe. After a formal audience with the King of Sardinia and the royal family, and a private audience (as the son of a peer) with the King, the eager student enrolled formally. His course of studies was varied, and not exclusively military: it included ballroom dancing from seven until eight, lessons in German from eight until nine, breakfast from nine until eleven, and instruction under the master at arms from eleven until noon. At a quarter past twelve he dined with the governor and lieutenant governor of the academy (old acquaintances of de Roguin from the war). At three he re-

sumed his studies and for two hours applied himself to mathe-
matics and fortifications. At five he received more dancing lessons, made some visits, went to the opera, and then supped.
Brome followed this routine five days a week. On the other two
days, Thursday and Sunday, he attended the King of Sardinia's
court.[13]

He continued this regimen for only a few months, but even a
week would have given him better preparation than most of his
fellow officers had for active military service. When Brome left
Turin he visited several German courts where the talk was all of
war and military matters. The long-anticipated conflict between British and French arms had already begun. In North
America, in Europe, in India, on the high seas — wherever the
two nations had contact, they fought. In Europe each collected
allies. Eventually Brome arrived at Geneva where he learned
that his own guards regiment was on the march — it had been
ordered to join an Anglo-German army collecting under Prince
Ferdinand of Brunswick for the defense of Hanover, Prussia,
and Prussia's allies against a threatened invasion by French and
Austrian forces.[14] How the eager young man burned to join his
regiment! The siren song of military glory wafted to his ears,
and he chafed at his inaction.

The movements of Brome's regiment were decided by one
man in London. As a leader of the parliamentary opposition,
William Pitt had constantly disparaged Hanover. Time and
again the House of Commons had heard him argue against British involvement in European struggles on behalf of King
George II's German territory. As war minister, however, he
changed his tune. Now he had decided that the French empire
in North America could be brought to an end by a British
victory in Europe. He eventually committed twenty-five thousand British troops to the defense not only of Prussia, Britain's
ally, but also of Hanover, the little principality he had so deni-
grated in the past. The Great Commoner hoped that France

would pound herself to pieces against these and allied troops and that in the process she would lose her colonial empire to England. The strategy paid off, since France lost Canada, but the struggle required Britain to send more soldiers to the Continent than at any time since Marlborough's day.

Brome wanted to be among those soldiers. He determined to join the army in Germany no matter what the obstacles. If he could not catch up with his regiment, he would serve in any honorable capacity. As he wrote to his friend, Thomas Townshend, several weeks after the event:

> I there [in Geneva] first heard of the expedition; and when I saw that the Guards were ordered, immediately ordered the horses, d——d Switzerland for having no posts through it, and made the best of my way to the Isle of Wight. At Cologne I found I was too late. Only imagine having set out without leave, come two hundred leagues, and my regiment gone without me! I wrote immediately to my father, and represented all this in the strongest light, and told him that, if he did not find out some service for me, I could never expect any promotion as long as I stayed in the army. The express orders of the King, and, as I then thought, Prince Ferdinand's resolution not to take any (volunteers), gave me but little encouragement. I resolved however to try, and was received in the kindest manner.[15]

Indeed, the King's orders, as explained to him by his father, could have given him no encouragement. Brome had joined Ferdinand's army without consulting English authority. He had then asked his father to secure the King's approval for what he had done and royal permission for him to remain with Ferdinand. The first Earl Cornwallis had in turn asked Newcastle to intercede with the King, for his son's heart, he said, was "very much set upon this matter." The Earl's apologetic letter to the Duke portrayed an anxious father unable to control a determined son.[16] But Newcastle's response, the gist of which Cornwallis almost certainly relayed to his son, showed that Brome would come near disobeying royal command if he stayed with Ferdinand as a volunteer. Newcastle reported that already the King had "absolutely refused the Duke of Richmond and my Lord Down leave to go volunteers to Prince Ferdinand's army: And his majesty has declared he will not give leave to anybody." Furthermore, Newcastle continued, "the only way for Lord Brome to remain with Prince Ferdinand would be to take no notice of his being there, and then perhaps no notice may be taken of it." [17] Apparently Cornwallis "took no notice" and let the matter drop. Undaunted, Brome remained with the Prince.

His determination soon had its rewards. "I had been here about six weeks as a volunteer," he wrote to Thomas Townshend, "when the English joined us, and have since that been appointed aide-de-camp to your friend Granby." [18]

That appointment was made on August 6, 1758.[19] The Marquis of Granby was then lieutenant general in the British forces, and after Lord George Germain disgraced himself at the battle of Minden, Granby became their commanding general. For Brome the summer of 1758 was the beginning of almost continuous service throughout the war in Germany, broken only by trips home during the winter lulls in battle. Service brought him swift promotion. A year later, on August 5, 1759, he became a captain in the 85th foot. On September 21, he added yet another office to those he already held: he became aide-de-camp to Granby in the latter's additional capacity as lieutenant general of the ordnance.[20] Although service for three years in the field as a member of Granby's staff exposed Brome to the hazards of war, it never gave him the training so invaluable for a professional soldier — direct command over troops in tactical operations. But on May 1, 1761, he achieved the rank of lieutenant colonel of the 12th foot.[21] During the year following his promotion he served with distinction as a regimental commander, especially at Kirch Donkern and Grebenstein.[22]

His campaigning ended in the summer of 1762, for in July he learned from the Duke of Newcastle that his father had died.[23] Thus he returned to England, not as Brome, but as the second Earl Cornwallis. In November he took his seat in the House of Lords.

He had had his baptism of fire and served his apprenticeship. Eton had made the boy a man, and the Seven Years' War had made the man a soldier. Already, before his twenty-fourth birthday, he had developed qualities of self-reliance, determination, physical endurance, moral and physical courage — resources he would need when he went to America. But that lay in the future. Now he must turn from the affairs of war to the numerous and difficult affairs of peacetime.

CHAPTER 3

Family and Politics

FOR THE FIRST two years after he returned from the Continent, the new Earl Cornwallis engaged himself to attend several balls and masquerades, entertained often at Culford, and joyfully abandoned himself to his favorite sport, fox hunting.[1] Although he retained his love of the chase all his life, he soon lost whatever love he may have had for the other diversions. The adult Cornwallis, while possessed of a wry sense of humor and a great humanity, never engaged in the excessive drinking, reckless gambling, and continual round of parties which consumed so many of his compeers. A dignified and sober man, he attended occasions of state and the balls and private parties which duty or friendship demanded. But he grew to prefer above all else that which he seldom had: the domestic tranquillity of Culford.

Even had he been left to himself and given a free choice, the second Earl might soon have come to prefer life in the country to the gaieties of London. But he was not left to himself: immediately upon succeeding to the peerage he had thrust upon him the burden of taking care of his relatives. For him, the transition from military to domestic concerns was instant. During the years between 1762 and the outbreak of the American Revolution, duty to his position demanded that he concentrate his attention on his family's interests. Possibly the duty was at first grudgingly performed. If so, no record remains of that unwillingness. The surviving records show that when he left England to fight in America, Cornwallis had a profound attachment to family and estate matters, deriving from them more pleasure and satisfaction than from all the other enticements so freely available to a man of his station in the eighteenth century.

Both the family and the estate badly needed attention in 1762. Thanks in part to the efforts of his father, the second Earl himself was by then well launched in a career and assured of a steady income from the family property. His brothers and sisters, however, had yet to be taken care of. Cornwallis, as the new head of the family, became responsible for providing for them, although he had few material resources for that purpose. Indeed, it is ironic that Charles had at an early age chosen the army for a career: it was probably the most costly profession in which he could have engaged, requiring a great deal of money and promising little reward above the chance for glory. But by the standards of the aristocracy into which he was born, Cornwallis did not inherit a fortune.

Grouse and pheasant thrived around Culford. They gave Cornwallis pleasure but no money. Nor did the land attached to the manor yield high dividends. At a rough estimate the second Earl received in income only about £3500 a year when he succeeded his father. The money came from rents (usually promptly paid) from his lands at Culford, Brome, Eye (the family borough where he held about 730 acres), other manors and advowsons in Suffolk, and a few more in Norfolk.[2] Cornwallis also owned part of an island somewhere in North America, but there is no evidence that it produced a substantial revenue.[3] He apparently had inherited no investments in stock. Indeed it would have been surprising if his father could have saved enough money to invest anything in securities. Yet, despite these slim resources, the second Earl had to maintain an estate, keep a town house in London,[4] and live in the affluent style that society expected of him.

Under such circumstances, Charles had to provide as quickly as possible for his brothers and sisters; he simply could not long afford to support them from the meager rents he received. The brothers needed positions suitable to their birth and of adequate income. The sisters needed good marriages. Charles set to work at once.

James, born in 1742, demanded first consideration as the elder of Charles' two younger brothers and as the next in line to the peerage.[5] He chose to enter the church, as had his uncle before him. Indeed, when the second Earl helped his brother toward a church living he was following a family tradition. In the 1740's the first Earl Cornwallis had solicited his cousin, the Duke of Newcastle, to do something for his brother Frederick. It was apparently the Duke who secured the Earl's brother a see in 1750. Then in 1768 Frederick Cornwallis, Bishop of Lichfield and Coventry, was "translated to Lambeth" — he was made Archbishop of Canterbury.[6] Newcastle also helped the next generation along: he launched the second Earl's brother on an ecclesiastical career by obtaining for him a fellowship at Merton College, Oxford.[7] After Oxford, James could expect to advance to a bishopric, as had his uncle. Thus his future was secured.

James became Bishop of Lichfield and Coventry, but he did not advance further. He was a respected though not particularly distinguished churchman. He deserves a closer look, however, for he later would prove of great help to Charles. Portly like his brother, with a large double chin and a broad, heavy face, James looked aloof and conscious of the dignity of ecclesiastical office. His countenance showed little trace of piety, and his letters are preponderantly secular. Indeed, it was not fashionable to be deeply religious. Like many other eighteenth-century ecclesiastics, he played the game, constantly seeking higher positions, not for the spiritual benefits he might thereby bring his flock, but for the greater emoluments and prestige that might become his. In 1787 and 1788, for example, because his elder brother had gone to Bengal and left the affairs of the family to him, he felt that the prime minister, William Pitt, owed him something:

> In consequence of Lord Cornwallis's residence in India [he wrote] "for the public service," at the request of his majesty, and "conferring a particular favor upon you," as you yourself were pleased to express it, I am involved in an infinite deal of plague and trouble with his money affairs, his estate, his borough, and his family, and also in no inconsiderable expence.
>
> Lord Cornwallis, aware of this, told me upon his leaving England with a great degree of satisfaction, that the King as well as you had promised him a very early promotion for me. The bishoprics of Durham and London, the Deanery of St. Paul's and the Deanery of Windsor have been vacant since his departure. And a residentiaryship of St. Paul's, which was holden by the late Bp. of Durham, with the see of Lichfield is now vacant. The intention of this letter is to request this preferment of you.[8]

For the next four years he plagued Pitt for church office of one sort or another — St. Paul's, Durham, Winchester, Worcester.

Although he was a secular bishop and may not have taken his spiritual duties very seriously, James was hard-working and conscientious in matters that affected him deeply. The reverence that he never gave religion, he freely gave to the family. In his letter to Pitt he had not exaggerated the difficulties he faced in handling his absent brother's affairs. Yet he handled that business well and faithfully. He undertook nearly sole responsibility for the restoration of Culford in the 1780's and 1790's. The results testified to his industry. Ironically, he could not then know that he would outlive both his elder brother and his elder brother's only son — that Culford would one day be his.

Charles' next brother, William, was two years younger than James. He achieved greater renown than James and, indeed, almost rivalled his oldest brother in fame. William chose the navy for a career and eventually became one of Britain's more famous admirals. He participated in the events that led to Nelson's defeat of Villeneuve at Trafalgar. William, who was his mother's favorite, resembled the second Earl in appearance. He was corpulent and even slightly cockeyed. But his face wore a dreaming expression his older brothers' never had. Perhaps it was this wistful look together with his dependent position as the youngest son which especially endeared him to the dowager Countess Cornwallis.

William entered the navy at the age of eleven. In 1761, when he was seventeen years old, and while his oldest brother was still fighting in Germany, he attained the rank of lieutenant. But in the following year two important events occurred: William's father (friend of the first Duke of Newcastle) died, and Newcastle was forced to resign his office as first lord of the treasury. These events might have spelled disaster for William's career. Like so many other young naval officers who lacked powerful patrons, he might have seen no more service during the next dozen or so years. For in peacetime the majority of the naval ships were laid up "in ordinary," so there were not enough places for all the officers. The unlucky ones languished on shore on "half pay." Obviously they had no chance of promotion either. Under these circumstances it was fortunate for William that his mother Elizabeth, now the dowager Countess Cornwallis, and his brother Charles, now the second Earl, could turn their attention to his affairs. They could do so because James had by then secured his fellowship to Merton and was no longer a financial burden on the family. Although laboring under the "heavy affliction" of her husband's death, Elizabeth was not too grief-stricken to think of her youngest son's future. She urged upon Lord Halifax, the new first lord of the admiralty, Lieutenant Cornwallis' qualifications for command of a sloop going to the West Indies. The appointment was a necessary step toward the captaincy that she desperately hoped William could secure before the war ended. She eventually got him the command. This gave him a temporary rank of "commander," properly known as lieutenant and commander. The next step up would be a captaincy. A captain had "post rank," giving him a permanent and unalterable position in the seniority lists which governed further promotion. Once peace came, there could be no prospect of any lieutenant "making post." During the next year the dowager Countess moved heaven and earth to bring her son the coveted promotion to post rank. Toward this end she importuned both Admiral Burnaby, who had command in the West Indies, and Lord Halifax.[9] Perhaps her sense of urgency was heightened by the knowledge that her deceased husband had settled only £100 per year on the young lieutenant. So small an income could scarcely have met William's ordinary expenses.[10]

The dowager's efforts on behalf of her favorite did not at first meet with success. The year 1764, however, looked more promising. Although William's ship was almost wrecked, he and his crew saved it and brought it into Jamaica. At this point his brother Charles also took a hand, declaring that he would "omit no possible means" to secure post rank for his brother. He would gladly supply pocket money if William needed it. Moreover, if additional sums would help his brother gain a captaincy ("for I have heard there are sometimes bargains of that sort"), the Earl said he would "answer any draft that you may find it necessary to draw a month after sight." [11] Despite all efforts by his family, yet another year passed before William got his promotion. Then it was not money but the Cornwallis name and political connections that finally prevailed. William became a

captain in 1765 — the same year in which the Rockingham
"whig" group, to whom the second Earl had attached himself,
returned to office. Now at last the youngest male member of the
family had an assured career and could support himself.

The Earl's sisters presented him with a different set of problems. For them, advantageous or at least suitable marriages
were needed. Since they did not have enormous dowries, they
could not expect to achieve brilliant matches. In fact, their portions were relatively small so some effort would probably be required to secure them husbands appropriate to their stations.

Gay and charming Mary — called Molly by her family — in
1769 wed a man of middle-class fortune. Many daughters in ti-
tled but less than affluent families made similar matches. Her
husband, Samuel Whitbread, became one of England's most famous and prosperous brewers. Unfortunately, Molly did not
live long enough to enjoy that wealth, for she died in childbed
in December, 1770.[12]

Another sister, Charlotte, brought heartaches to her family,
for first she did not wed at all, and then at the age of twenty-nine
she wed the wrong man. Naturally her parents had wished her
to make a suitable marriage, preferably to someone of wealth.
But she disappointed both these hopes. She met and fell in love
with a Dr. Spencer Madan. Eventually he would become
Bishop of Peterborough, but that dignified status lay far in the
future. Charlotte's mother and father understandably deemed
the match unsuitable, for although Madan's education at West-
minster and Cambridge had given him some social pretensions,
he had no money to maintain them, much less those of an earl's
daughter. As a result of this parental disapproval, the two lovers
promised neither to meet nor to hold any correspondence — a
promise they kept (according to Charlotte) until an accidental
meeting occurred. Then the lovesick girl, who had gone to keep
house for her uncle, found life intolerable. She complained to

her father that her position made her wretched, and she begged him to reconsider his unfavorable disposition toward Madan. According to Charlotte's account, the first Earl wished to extricate her from her painful position. So he proposed that she "marry without his knowledge." This she would not do, regarding it as an insupportable reflection upon her own and Dr. Madan's character. At last her father consented. Only two months after that accidental meeting Lady Charlotte and Dr. Madan were married. The Countess Cornwallis, however, never approved of the match. Her mother's continued hostility moved Charlotte to complain bitterly to her eldest brother. Nor would she cease her defensive attitude toward her husband's station in life: his family and connections, she insisted, were good enough for the alliance to bring no disgrace even on the "highest nobility." Charlotte may have found happiness in her love match, but she certainly cost her family severe trials. She pestered the second Earl with problems concerning her children and, with a profusion of epistolary tears, avowed that he was her only friend in the world, a man with all the virtues of the saints. "Your noble, generous, disinterested, affectionate disposition, I think can scarce be *equal'd*, I am sure not *exceeded*. . . . I never met with a character that appear'd to me so completely amiable . . . ," and so on.[13] Cornwallis, a matter-of-fact man of calm reserve, must have writhed inwardly at these effusions of sentiment.

Nonetheless he did what he could for his sister. Duty demanded it. Just before the American war, he and James worked out an agreement to help the Madans financially. In November of 1760 Cornwallis had become lieutenant of the Tower, and in 1771 he was appointed constable of the Tower and lord lieutenant of the Tower hamlets.[14] Through the influence of either Charles or his father (who had also been constable of the Tower) James had secured a sinecure, the office of gentleman porter at the Tower.[15] In February of 1773 James and Charles

struck upon a means of giving financial assistance to their sister.
James would resign the "job," worth around £200 per annum.
In his turn, Charles would make a settlement giving James'
wife £100 a year during her lifetime. Then Spencer Madan
would take over James' sinecure, reimbursing Charles the sum
of £100 a year for so long as he (Madan) retained the position.
These arrangements could only be made while Cornwallis was
constable of the Tower, for the gift of the sinecure was a perqui-
site of that office. The Earl and his brother thought "the present opportunity not to be lost. It will be a great thing for young
Madan." [16] That was not the last time Cornwallis helped Charlotte. While serving in India as commander in chief, he appointed her son, Captain Charles Madan of the 76th regiment,
as his aide-de-camp.[17]

Another relative who caused the second Earl concern was one
of the younger generation. The family's wayward streak revealed itself fully in Horace, a son of James. While in Ireland as
lord lieutenant, Cornwallis had to deal with the vagaries of his
nephew. Horace had told his father that he wanted to wed a
Dublin girl, but he promised not to marry her without the
Bishop's consent. Lord Cornwallis, however, discovered that
Horace planned to run off with the young lady and carry her to
Scotland. He at once took steps to prevent this scandal, but had
to keep his nephew "close prisoner" until he could send him
back to the Bishop "under the care of two messengers." "He is a
weak, idle Boy," Cornwallis observed, "and will always I am
afraid be a trifling character." [18]

Even while managing his relations' affairs as the new head of
the family, Cornwallis found time to woo and wed his own
bride.[19] His courtship, however, followed a more conventional
pattern than his nephew Horace's. Sometime in the 1760's —
possibly earlier — he met the young woman who in 1768 became his countess. Perhaps it was one of his army friends who

presented him to Jemima Tullekin (or Tullekins) Jones. She was the daughter of Colonel James Jones of the 3d regiment of foot guards, a professional soldier who had served with the same unit for at least twenty years.[20] Although the full colonelcy of a regiment was a great honor (and one rarely attained by persons who lacked the highest connections), his rank did not elevate plain Colonel Jones to a position of social equality with Earl Cornwallis. Moreover, while members of the aristocracy often married into the middle class in order to restore a dwindling fortune, Miss Jones could not have been wealthy. Her father died within a few years of the outbreak of the Seven Years' War. When his house and goods went up for auction in 1758 the total amount realized — on furniture, plate, china, library, clothing, firearms, paintings, and other household items — came to only £2805 9s 6d.[21] As this was a far from princely sum, Charles cannot have married Jemima for her money. The only conclusion left is that he married her for love. Indeed, the years they had together were extraordinarily happy ones. Jemima was utterly devoted to her husband and to every principle in which he believed. At one time she remarked to her brother-in-law William: "Don't laugh at my being political. I assure you I do not think a female *ought* to talk politics, but when it comes to husband, friends, &c., one must feel, and it will out." [22] The Earl returned her devotion.

She was certainly attractive. Reynolds' portrait of her, painted in 1771, shows an elegant woman with long limbs and an impossibly long neck. Yet despite the predictable flattery of the great portrait artist, she appears not so much a great beauty as a strikingly handsome woman. With her brown hair piled loosely — and despite what we know of Reynolds, it is tempting to say "naturally" — on top of her head, a few stray wisps nestling on her neck, a well-formed face with firm chin, gently arched eyebrows, large eyes, straight nose, shapely lips — she looks every inch a countess.[23] Charles thought so highly of her that one of the reasons he retired from active politics in 1768 was to devote more time to her and to the family they hoped to raise.[24]

That family was not destined to be a large one. Jemima bore one son, Charles, and one daughter, Mary. The children brought their parents yet more closely together. Over the years they came to love, trust, and depend on one another far more than did many of their contemporaries whose marriages had been arranged. In fact, observers reported that Jemima died from a broken heart because of her husband's long absences during the American War. "The separation proved too much for her weak nerves to bear; she literally fell a prey to love, sunk beneath the weight of her grief, and died; thus affording a most singular instance of conjugal affection." [25] Her death, in turn, so affected the second Earl that it may have altered the course of history; for after his second trip home in 1778 Cornwallis had resolved not to return to the war in America. He felt that he could no longer endure being perpetual second-in-command, and he had tired of carrying on a war he believed wrong in principle and bungled in execution. But the death of his wife in 1779 caused him such grief that he wished at any cost to get away from England. He could find nothing to live for save the army. He wrote to his brother that the loss of his wife had "effectually destroyed all my hopes of happiness in this world. I will not dwell on this wretched subject, the thoughts of which harrow up my soul." [26] So he returned to the war in America, serving continuously, and finally leading his little army into the trap at Yorktown.

The province of Virginia was separated by many miles and many years from Cornwallis' happy, peaceful days in the 1760's and 1770's. Yet British colonial policy had already embarked upon that fateful voyage which would drift ever more off course until it met its violent end on the shoals of stubborn American resistance. Although Cornwallis was not politically active to the point of seeking office, he foresaw the disaster that must come if the ministers continued on their erratic course and tried to steer them back into safer waters.

He voted with the Rockingham "whigs" against the Stamp Act in 1765. This parliamentary faction proclaimed that it alone carried on the whig tradition of guarding the country against undue monarchical influence, encouraging the merchant classes, and supporting the aspirations of protestant dissenters. Cornwallis did not follow the Rockinghamites blindly, however. Indeed, he soon showed his political independence. When in 1766 the British Parliament voted to repeal the Stamp Act, that retreat was associated with the Declaratory Act, a bill which proudly asserted Britain's right to legislate for the colonies "in all cases whatsoever." Lord Cornwallis was one of the tiny minority of five peers who voted against the Declaratory Act.[27] During the recurring crises that followed, he sympathized with colonial grievances.

Although these grievances did not cause great turmoil before 1765, they had their beginnings with the Proclamation of 1763, which restricted settlement beyond the Appalachians and called for a revised imperial system. In the very year in which, by the Peace of Paris, Britain had supposedly ensured her continued enjoyment of empire, she began to fumble it away. That year was also the prelude to a long period of domestic turmoil, stirred up by the excesses of John Wilkes. From this turmoil individual Englishmen had, by the time of the American Revolution, gained liberties they had never enjoyed before. Wilkes, a member of Parliament and a colorful rogue, had attacked the government in successive issues of a newspaper, the *North Briton*. In Number 45 he went too far. Acting under a general warrant, which practically gave the secretary of state a free hand to seize a person and his goods, agents of the government apprehended Wilkes and confiscated his papers. Parliament eventually expelled Wilkes and outlawed him. He fled to France, returned to England a few years later, and stood for Parliament again. Although he outpolled his opposition the House of Commons refused to seat him, and Wilkes ended up in prison for a short while. But he had stirred up a hornets' nest. Not only the London populace but also powerful noblemen (Earl Temple, for instance) supported him. The outcome was momentous. Wilkes had raised the question of freedom of the press, and several judicial decisions in the British courts arising out of the *North Briton* affair substantially affirmed, indeed really established, freedom of the press. Furthermore, Parliament outlawed general warrants. Many observers linked Wilkes and America, equating the Englishman's struggle for freedom at home with the American's struggle for freedom in the colonies.[28]

Cornwallis apparently viewed developments in this light, although he left few letters belonging to this period, and contemporaries commented but little on his affairs. The Earl had firm moral convictions: absolute loyalty to friends; duty to king and country before gratification of private desires; the sanctity of class divisions, balanced by the necessity of *noblesse oblige;* support of the established Church of England, with complete toleration of dissenters. These convictions were conventional enough. Cornwallis was different only in his always adhering to them in his actions. Nor would these convictions necessarily have put the Earl in any particular political faction. The Rockingham whigs claimed more vociferously than other groups, however, that they were fighting for the decencies in which Cornwallis believed. Thus the Earl, originally attracted to them through his attachment to Newcastle, could for a while support them in good conscience. In the same way he could in good conscience lead troops against the Americans whose cause he had championed in the House of Lords. Throughout his life he was loyal to his own moral principles rather than to any particular faction or party. Parties often change their principles and platforms to gain votes and political power. Many people do the same. A man like Cornwallis could not.

Although he would probably have gravitated to the Rockinghamites in the 1760's because of their position on certain issues, his friendship with Newcastle put him in their camp from the beginning. During the critical period of the Seven Years' War, the chief political figures (including Newcastle) had managed to cooperate in government. By the time of George III's accession in 1760, however, England was clearly out of danger and headed for victory. The politicians fell apart again into their more natural state of various factions constantly realigning themselves in order to find the magic combination of alliances that would gain them power.[29] Newcastle, who in 1762 resigned from the ministry in which he had been first lord of the treasury and "prime minister," allied himself with the Rockinghamites. Together they and their followers comprised one of these factions. They claimed that they alone carried on the old whig tradition. Cornwallis' deep loyalty to Newcastle put him in this faction. The Duke had always helped his family. Should he not help the Duke in return?

Newcastle thought so, for in 1763 he asked Cornwallis to politick for the whig cause in Scotland. The Duke also wanted Cornwallis to sound out an influential Scots nobleman on the prospects of a "formed opposition" to the administration. The nobleman concerned — Lord Kinnoul — had formerly been a political ally of Newcastle's and had received secret service money (a political slush fund) while the Duke headed the treasury.[30] Some caution was needed in approaching the subject, however, for the idea of a formed opposition was abhorrent to most Englishmen: in the days before a two-party system became the usual political way of life, a coalition to oppose the ministry seemed to smell of disloyalty to the King. The second Earl, therefore, was to assure Kinnoul that the politicians opposed to the ministry were all in agreement: "there is the most thorough

union amongst us all, my lord Temple & Mr. Pitt included
& . . . it is impossible for anybody, on any consideration, to
separate one man from us." [31] Although the opposition was not
in fact so thoroughly united, Newcastle may have believed it
was. At any rate, Newcastle's errand gave Cornwallis his first
venture into politics. The results were not impressive. Kinnoul, although "he disapproved very much of the present administration," was determined to retire from public life rather
than engage in an active opposition. The Earl's failure to move
Kinnoul from his "passive nonsense" did not put an end to his
own political activities. As he said at the time: "If the generality
of the people of Great Britain were of his [Kinnoul's] way of
thinking it was totally impossible that the constitution of this
country could last six months, & that in my opinion as he
thought the ministry bad, it was his duty to do all in his power
to demolish it." [32]

Cornwallis did not demolish the ministry, but his efforts
against it introduced him into strange company that shook the
government to its roots. When he returned from Scotland in
September,[33] he took up with John Wilkes. George Grenville,
first lord of the treasury and "prime minister," learned from
government spies that Wilkes and Cornwallis had met for a
stroll one day in autumn.[34] Two companions more thoroughly
mismatched could scarcely be imagined. John Wilkes — licen-
tious, leering, a member of the Hell-Fire Club — made up his
mind to go as far as possible in attacking the government while
advancing his own interests. So it came about that he walked
the London streets with the second Earl Cornwallis, a sober and
dignified man, a staunch supporter of society and the established
order. But politics breeds strange bedfellows, and that tête-à-
tête with Wilkes was a measure of the Earl's support for his
party's views.

His support brought him material reward (although such
considerations had never motivated his politics) when the Rock-

inghamites came to power in 1765. In that year he was made both aide-de-camp to the King and a lord of the bedchamber. He soon relinquished the second honor as being incompatible with the first, but in return asked for the colonelcy of a regiment. In March of the following year he obtained his desire. As colonel of the 33d foot he now, in a sense, "owned" a regiment. It would accompany him to North America.[35] Soon afterwards he voted with the Rockinghamites to repeal the Stamp Act and to outlaw general warrants.[36] Despite the offices they had helped him obtain, however, he did not follow them into opposition when the Rockingham ministry broke up in August of 1766. He had already voted against them in his opposition to the Declaratory Act earlier in the year.

Through the mediation of his friend Lord Shelburne (who had also opposed the Declaratory Act), he turned to the Chatham administration. Cornwallis was not thereby inconsistent in his politics, for Rockingham's faction did not oppose Chatham's principles and indeed had tried to bring him into their ministry. The gouty and volatile Lord Chatham — previously the "Great Commoner," William Pitt — was regarded by many Englishmen as a friend to their liberty and by most Americans as a champion of their cause. Friendship and principles thus coincided to prompt Cornwallis to leave the Rockinghamites and to accept from the Duke of Grafton, first lord of the treasury in Chatham's administration, the office of chief justice in Eyre south of the Trent in December, 1766.[37]

The new ministry — which included Charles Townshend — turned out to be anything but friendly to American liberties. When Shelburne resigned in 1768 Cornwallis withdrew his support from the ministry. But he had never been very active in politics for either the Rockingham or the Chatham administrations. He had never sought, nor apparently desired, high office. Furthermore, even had he wished for great power, he probably would not have politicked enough to attain it. Secret deals, judicious betrayals of confidence, securing support by means of bribery or intimidation — in short, all the dirty work required to keep a political group functioning — were activities totally alien to his nature. The honesty and openness which were two of his strongest characteristics did not make him a good politician.

Even though he formed no new political connections after 1768, he continued to receive favors from the government. In 1769 he gave up the office of chief justice in Eyre south of the Trent in order to obtain that of vice-treasurer of Ireland.[38] On November 21, 1770, he was made a privy councillor; and on January 10, 1771, constable of the Tower of London.[39] Why he continued in the King's grace despite his opposition to government policy is something of a mystery. The only explanation seems to be the obvious one that the King liked him better than other whigs. Probably George III liked Cornwallis for his domestic virtues. Charles was far more intelligent than his monarch, and, unlike the King, he usually had enough good sense to refrain from interfering in matters which he should leave alone. Apart from these important differences they were both sober, dignified, temperate, and devoted family men. That the King saw so few men of that type around his court must have made the second Earl yet more attractive to him.

After hostilities broke out in the colonies Lord Cornwallis was appointed a major general (September 29, 1775), and shortly thereafter a lieutenant general (January 1, 1776) of the army in North America. How many among either the British or the Americans appreciated the irony of his position? The aristocrat who at the dictates of his conscience had opposed the King's colonial policies was now compelled, by his duty to king and country, and by his military rank, to lead the King's troops in a fight to reestablish royal authority over the colonies.

PART II

The War Begins
The Frustrated General

CHAPTER 4

"Some Relief for the poor Foot-Soldier"

FOR THE NEXT six years that remarkable organization known as the British army demanded and received most of Cornwallis' attention. An organization of strange contrasts and contradictions, it exacted savage discipline from the enlisted men but indulgently permitted individualism, even eccentricity, in its officers. Most officers deemed their rankers little better than verminous beasts of burden, yet would go to inordinate lengths to preserve their lives. Although supposedly governed by a chain of command, the army abounded in confusing and overlapping jurisdictions. Composed almost entirely of professionals, it displayed remarkably amateurish qualities. Indeed, "the army, like the oligarchy that it mirrored, was still in the golden age of the amateur." [1] Yet, as it stepped smartly through its paces on the parade ground, drums beating and fifes shrilling, a British regiment of foot awed spectators whether in Boston or Bombay. It was a visible — and audible — symbol of imperial splendor and power. Few men saw, or tried to see, the imperfections behind the buttons, brass, and epaulets.

Not least among the imperfections were the men who wore the epaulets. Officers did not necessarily know their trade.

"The army had no Sandhurst, West Point, or St. Cyr; it consequently had no experts." [2] True, in the 1740's Woolwich Academy had begun turning out engineers and artillery officers with a technical education. High command, however, went to line officers — that is, officers of cavalry and infantry — and no English military school trained them. Money and influence secured a man's first commission and his subsequent promotions. Since the aristocracy and gentry had all the money and practically all the influence, they held almost all of the commands.

But they had to pay for them and pay dearly. The price of commissions was a staggering one, and the rules regulating their sale and exchange varied from year to year according to the wishes of the King.[3] During the Revolutionary War the lowest rank in the most ordinary service — an ensign in a marching regiment of foot — cost £400, more money than many of the poorer gentry made in five years and more than the lower classes might earn in a lifetime. By way of comparison, a man could keep himself, his family, and a pair of servants comfortably on £40 per year. In the elite foot guards the price of an ensigncy climbed to £900, but in the "aristocratic" cavalry, a cornetcy (the equivalent of an ensigncy in the infantry) demanded the huge outlay of £1600.

Normally, an officer joined a regiment and worked his way up through it; he might, however, get higher rank in another regiment if a vacancy occurred. In any event, higher ranks, whether obtained as commissions or as promotions, cost more than an ensigncy or cornetcy. A lieutenant colonel, who commanded a regiment in the field, paid £3500 for the rank in the infantry, £5200 in the cavalry, and £6700 in the foot guards, the last sum being nearly equal to the combined annual salaries of the first lords of the treasury and the admiralty.[4]

In exceptional cases a lowly ranker of extraordinary merit might become an officer without purchase, but the service begrudged him the appointment and hedged him in. Regulations forbade him to sell it except under extraordinary circumstances: "upon the grounds of *long service* (twenty years), *wounds*, or *entire* loss of health and inability for further duty." Even then the impecunious officer had to plead his case specially before the King.[5] Furthermore, an officer without independent income was unlikely to save any in the British army. His pay scarcely enabled him to support himself in the style expected of "an officer and gentleman." A lieutenant colonel in the infantry — a regimental commander in charge of five hundred men — made £2 2s daily. The elite guards gave him £3 9s daily. Ensigns made only shillings.[6] The salary for one of the higher officers may sound generous indeed, until it is remembered that he had to supply his own uniforms, food, wine, servants, and string of horses. Only a provident man could make do without incurring debt unless he had an independent income.

The King's regulations somewhat mitigated a few of the inequities in the system. For example, an officer had to serve time in grade before he could purchase into the next rank. Also, the rules encouraged promotion by seniority within a given regiment, provided, of course, that the senior officer eligible for the vacancy had the money to buy his way up. But the system often belied the spirit of these rules and sometimes produced pitiful incidents. One man spent forty-two years as a cornet. He had borrowed money to purchase his commission in the dragoons in 1723. Time had given him seniority and the opportunity for promotion, but he had never scraped together the cash to repay his initial debt, much less to buy a higher rank. The year 1765 saw him a debt-ridden old man, retired on half pay, his commission sold, looking forlornly for some employment to keep him alive.[7] He had owed his very seniority to lack of money.

Thus promotion went to the wealthy, and the wealthy scampered to the top when very young. Cornwallis, a lieutenant colonel at twenty-three, reached the rank of lieutenant general at age thirty-eight. In America he commanded older men, such

as his good friend William Phillips, an artillery general who
had served the army longer than he. But Sir Henry Clinton —
whose commission as lieutenant general preceded Cornwallis'
by a mere four months[8] — was only eight years older than
Cornwallis, and he was commander in chief in America for most
of the war. Clinton's first cousin was the second Duke of Newcastle. Howe, Clinton's predecessor, was only a year older than
Sir Henry, but he had a peer for a brother.

The reasoning behind this system lay rooted in England's
past. One hundred and twenty years before, Oliver Cromwell
had clamped England under a military dictatorship. The people "were ruled by Army officers who were professional soldiers,
and who, though admittedly the finest soldiers in the world,
usually had no stake in the country, and often were military ad-
venturers." [9] When the Restoration came the country determined never to repeat the experience, determined that "never
again should the Army be in the hands of men likely to bring
about a military revolution and impose a military dictatorship." [10] From the reign of Charles II on, both king and Parliament insisted that the army be "drawn from that social class the
members of which are more likely to lose than to gain by Military Aggression." The purchase system guaranteed to the "Civil
Community" their "good behaviour." [11]

If its officers skimmed the top of British society, the army's
soldiers dredged the bottom. The outcasts of British humanity
filled the enlisted ranks, impoverished young men, poachers in
the rural districts, thieves in the towns, and "silly lads befooled
by the glamor of the scarlet coat." [12] The additional companies
from each regiment assigned to recruiting haunted the taverns
and the jails. Often they would enter the grogshop, liquor the
prospective "volunteer" into a stupor, and slip him the "King's
shilling" or bounty for enlistment. The befuddled local would
awaken the next morning with a thudding head and an uncer-

tain future in His Majesty's land force. True, before the American Revolution the army required its volunteers to sign an oath. But the oath merely called upon the individual to affirm that he was a Protestant, that he had no rupture, "nor was ever troubled by fits." [13]

Hogarth knew his country and its army and portrayed both vividly. His engraving needle captured the essence of recruiting in Plate 2 of "England." Gathered outside the Duke of Cumberland Pub is a motley array of people. A grenadier lies languidly against a drum, playing on a fife. Above him a woman sprawls across a trestle table next to a boisterous-looking civilian with hat raised to cheer on a soldier's artistry. The redcoat has scribbled on the wall a caricature of the King of France, gallows in hand, ready to hang all Englishmen. A fellow soldier and a half-drunken woman have also encouraged the "artist." The soldiers apparently hope to entice the civilian into joining the army for a patriotic crusade against the French. To one side a recruiting officer crudely measures a lad's height by levelling his stick across the boy's head to a notched halberd. The officer refuses to notice that the prospective recruit stands on tiptoe and has the look of an imbecile about him. Two soldiers in their cups, one in the act of downing a draught, stand next to the officer and the boy. Soldiers parade in the background and a Union Jack flies above the whole scene. The observer concludes that the jovial man and the imbecile boy, their patriotism aroused, their wits befuddled by nature or drink and by dreams of glory, will soon find themselves soldiers of the King.

When the stream of "volunteers," such as those pictured by Hogarth, ran dry, Parliament authorized the army to impress able-bodied men not lawfully employed, disorderly persons, smugglers, men in debtors' prisons and in jails. Both felons and debtors could secure their freedom by serving His Majesty. But the American Revolution made such extraordinary demands on British manpower that Parliament went even further. It allowed Roman Catholics into the ranks,[14] and at the same time tried to attract better men than the debtors, felons, and yokels that the army had hitherto relied upon. It exempted men who would serve the army during the Revolution from further service with any British forces — army, navy, or militia — and allowed them to set up a trade anywhere upon discharge.[15] The army also relaxed its already loose physical standards and took in sixteen-year-old boys and fifty-year-old men who could stand five feet three inches tall.[16] Even then the British army never found enough soldiers to fight the American war, and the King had to depend upon his Hessian allies and loyalist volunteers.

How could the army shape its raw material — the yokels, debtors, felons, boys, middle-aged men — into a disciplined military unit? How could it utilize illiterate, surly, and uncooperative men? Drill sergeants and army rules supplied the means. Recruits had instilled into them blind obedience that would respond automatically to orders whether in the heat of battle or on the parade ground. Men had to load and fire their weapons, form ranks, move into line or column, and march always with precisely measured movements and instantly upon the words of command. Failure to obey orders exactly resulted in savage punishments, which sometimes proved fatal. Breach of discipline could bring down as many as one thousand lashes on the bare back of the offender.[17]

Nonetheless, soldiers often found it tempting to break discipline. So many regulations hemmed them in. They had to pipe-clay their belts, clean their equipment, and brush their uniforms endlessly in the constant expectation of a searching inspection. They had to parade into enemy fire with fixed bayonets and sixty pound packs on their backs. They often could not leave their camps to visit neighboring towns (and their grogshops) in peace or war. They were forbidden to gamble. Despite terribly meager rations, they were not supposed to forage upon their own. In fact, under the King's regulations they had legally available to them few of those amusements that make life bearable in modern western armies. So they flouted the regulations, gambled when they could, and deserted in droves.

The British army presented strange contradictions. Officers disciplined infantrymen savagely for not following the proper drill in an army where no proper infantry drill existed. The regiment, the basic tactical unit of the British army,[18] maneuvered according to the wishes of the regimental commander. As early as 1718 general officers had represented to the King that with each regiment performing its own evolutions to its own commands, it was difficult to exercise the army in units larger than the battalion or in detachments combining parts of different battalions. His Majesty in turn ordered his board of general officers to "draw up a methodical exercise to be practiced throughout all his forces." [19] They never did it. They continued rather to expect robot performances from their men while they themselves remained rugged individualists. The Hanoverian monarchs, who loved the army much as boys love toy soldiers, tried to create that uniformity which the generals would not. They periodically issued regulations which they ordered all regiments to obey. Yet no standard drill existed during the American Revolution, nor indeed until 1792.[20] The grim, determined lines of redcoats who charged the Americans at Long Island and Brandywine were better disciplined than their foes, but their formations were scarcely so uniform as they must have appeared to a foe almost totally lacking in training.

Lack of a standard infantry drill typified an army that defied standardization. Even the uniforms varied from regiment to regiment. An army clothing board supposedly prescribed the patterns for each branch of the service: infantry, cavalry, and artillery.[21] All British infantrymen wore the famous red coat, together with a white waistcoat, white breeches, and gaiters which reached to the breeches just above the knees. Each foot soldier also wore a pouch for ammunition on one side and a cartridge box on the other, and he strapped to his back a haversack stuffed with extra clothes, provisions, canteens, and tools needed in camp.[22] The King allowed the different regiments to wear different colors for the facings on their coats but demanded uniformity in all else. Lapels should be the same size, waistcoats and gaiters should be buttoned as tightly as possible, collars should be stiff (one can imagine the effect at Monmouth when the temperature climbed into the nineties). Certainly the redcoat army conformed closely enough to these requirements to impress the rag, tag, and bobtail of homespun-clad Americans, at least during the first few years of the war. But to anyone who had the oppportunity to examine the regiments closely, differences in attire became immediately apparent. For the colonels were responsible for uniforming their regiments, and they outfitted them according to their purses and their whims. An impecunious or greedy colonel might profit by skimping on his men's uniforms, for he could keep any surplus from the "off-reckoning" which the army allowed him for clothing his unit.[23] A wealthy and ostentatious colonel might give his men finer and fancier clothes than other colonels could afford so that his regiment could outshine the others on the parade ground. Colonels would change the size of lapels or the cut of the coats as the mood suited them. The King constantly complained, but to no avail.[24] For so long as the army took its officers from the aristocracy, it had to tolerate aristocratic eccentricity and waywardness.[25]

Waywardness even extended to the army's "system" of supplying provisions, stores, equipment, transport, and pay. Part of the deduction from the soldier's pittance of eight pence a day supposedly paid for his food — theoretically a balanced diet of bread, beef, peas, rum, and occasionally cheese and butter. But during the Revolution the infantry rarely ate the standard fare. They scratched what they could from the American countryside

— without much success save in South Carolina — and depended on the mother country for most of their food, provisions, stores, and equipment. Contractors brought the food over in victualling ships, and the portion of it that an enlisted man received depended upon the officers in his regiment. Hungry or greedy officers might appropriate the choicest foods for themselves. Good officers might distribute the rations equitably. But even with the most honest officers, the rations they distributed often bore no relation to the food a soldier was supposed to eat. Surveyors appointed to examine the cargo of one victualler which landed at New York reported the cargo to be "very old Bread, Weavile Eaten, full of Maggots, Mouldy, musty, and rotten and entirely unfit to men to eat." [26] Soldiers did not live on such garbage, but they could never be certain of a proper meal from one day to the next while they served in America.

Nor did the army give them certainty about other provisions. The regimental colonel supplied his men with most of the tools — axes, shovels, kettles, knapsacks, haversacks — necessary for an encampment. But he usually had to depend upon the ordnance department, at least during the first campaign, for tents, tent-poles, and blankets.[27] Unfortunately, the ordnance department was notoriously unreliable. Furthermore, even after filling its immediate needs, a regiment had no guarantee it could hold on to its equipment once it took the field. The transportation of army goods came under the supervision of the quartermaster general's department. Unfortunately, the service often proved undependable. Responsibility for the hiring of transport wagons rested with agents of the quartermaster general. Often, however, the agents themselves owned the wagons which they rented to themselves in the name of the army. A disjointed system resulted — good wagons, bad wagons, useless wagons, and no wagons.[28]

Even the enlisted man's pay, supposed to be standard throughout the British army, varied from regiment to regiment.

Each redcoat in the British army was entitled to eight pence a day. Rarely did he see the money. Funds voted by Parliament to pay the soldiers went to the paymaster general of the forces. From him the sums went to agents of the established regiments holding the colonel's power of attorney. Each agent in turn issued the money to the regimental paymaster, an officer appointed by the colonel to perform that function in addition to his regular duties. Paymasters paid the company captains, who then paid their men. In this long process — rendered doubly difficult by a confused acccounting system — each man took his cut. The paymaster general even kept large balances in his hands with which he speculated to the detriment of the public but to the enrichment of his family.[29] Noncommissioned officers sometimes appropriated the privates' pay if they thought they could get away with it. When Roger Lamb joined the 9th regiment of foot in Dublin as a private, he discovered that the sergeant in charge of recruits squandered all their money in a public house. The recruits, unaware of their rights, did nothing about it.[30]

But even when the commissioned and noncommissioned officers distributed the money properly, the enlisted man still never received his full eight pence. The army deducted from it remorselessly for defraying the cost of food, uniforms, medicines, repair of arms, and the cost of transportation aboard ship; for helping support the affluent paymaster general; and for helping to maintain Chelsea Hospital (a home for old soldiers).[31] Dead men and fictitious men swelled the muster rolls, and they had the same allowance as real soldiers. The army allowed regiments to carry a certain number of fictitious names on their rolls for whom they legally received money. But this money went for regimental expenses. It never went to the enlisted men. Officers of some regiments, in order to enrich themselves, also illegally added hosts of nonexistent men to their roles (sometimes using the names of children of officers or N.C.O.'s) or kept alive through bookkeeping men whom American bullets had long since killed. The army paid the company captain for the men he had on his muster lists, and it was in his interest to keep as many men there as he could.[32]

Thus a British army on the march, unlike that pictured by many Americans, was not always a neatly dressed, smartly stepping, well-supplied group of emotionless officers and men. Rather it presented a scene of chaos. Men stepped to the same cadence but wheeled and formed column and line on different commands. They marched with uniforms on their backs generally alike but different in detail. Wagons of all sorts — big, small, old, new — creaked along piled with baggage and forage. Behind the army trailed hordes of women, screeching and cursing.

Indeed, perhaps nothing better shows the chaotic nature of the British army than its inability to do without camp followers. Perhaps as many as two thousand women followed Burgoyne's army down to Saratoga. Some, but by no means all, of them appeared regularly on the regimental lists as wives of officers and enlisted men and often served as washerwomen for the units. Burgoyne allowed a limited number of them to draw provisions,[33] but they slowed down the unfortunate Gentleman Johnny's "dash" to Albany. Howe might have preferred not to take women with him when he evacuated Boston, yet he rationed them out six to a regiment and let them embark.[34] As befitted a general who, after he took command of the American armies, spent most of the war in New York with his mistress, Sir Henry Clinton allowed women and children to attach themselves to his army. Cornwallis' own 33d carried seventy-six women and forty-two children on its rolls shortly before it embarked in 1779 for the siege of Charleston.[35]

If the British army in America lacked that uniformity so often attributed to it, it merely reflected the organization that had sent it there. Army administration in England was a maze of conflicting jurisdiction, ambiguous offices and duties, and confused chain of command.

The King headed the army. Politicians by the time of the American Revolution had taken over much of the running of his government (although he appointed the politicians), but the monarch still jealousy guarded his army prerogatives. The army was the one part of British administration that had attracted all the Hanoverians, and they concerned themselves energetically with its appointments, procedures, and organization. George III, no less than George I, "continued the Government and Command of the Army in his own hands." [36] The King's regulations were often made by the King himself. In a sense he even bypassed Parliament, for his rules governed courts-martial. The principle established by the Glorious Revolution of 1688 that the King cannot be a judge in his own cause was "entirely ignored in the case of Military Tribunals." [37]

As captain general of the forces, the monarch could appoint a commander in chief to help him. He seldom did so during the eighteenth century because Parliament thought the office put too much power in the hands of a man not hedged in, like the King, by constitutional checks.[38] From 1770 until 1778 the King had not appointed a commander in chief of the armed forces. Not until France entered the war did Lord Amherst take that position. Great as his powers were, however, he shared them with the secretary of state. The secretary determined the size of the forces, their employment, and the appointments of qualified officers.[39] During the Revolution the American secretary of state, Lord George Germain, could to a large extent direct strategy simply because he had the power to determine where forces should be employed. Of course he had to work with the Cabinet, and much of his planning depended upon the cooperation of the navy, headed by the first lord of the admiralty, who could and did thwart his designs from time to time.[40]

Below the King, the commander in chief, and the secretary of state stood the secretary at war. His office exemplified the confused and overlapping jurisdiction of army administration. The secretary at war dwelt in a twilight kingdom, so ill-defined that no one, perhaps not even he himself, knew exactly what his duties were. "There was perhaps no office ever created," the military historian Clode noted in the nineteenth century, "the powers of which were, at its establishment, so undefined, as that of the Secretary at War. In the course of time, and in the progress of events, certain duties became definitely assigned to the office; but even in the discharge of these the Secretary at War held an ambiguous place of responsibility: neither a Military Officer — though the commander-in-chief claimed his allegiance as such, nor a responsible Minister — though the House of Commons strove to fix upon him that character." [41] Usually he was not a military man, and he did not sit in the Cabinet. Originally his duty consisted merely of sending the estimates for the army to Parliament.[42] But during the century preceding the American Revolution he took on other powers and duties. He sent out the regulations for buying and selling commissions; ordered the army to help other services, such as the customs, when he deemed it necessary; gave warrants on the paymaster general for army supplies; appointed chaplains and all other civil officers under the military establishment, as well as the deputy judge advocate, the deputy commissary general, and six deputy commissaries. While no one filled the office of commander in chief, he took upon himself most of the duties of that office, becoming the most powerful figure in the army next to the King. The secretary at war controlled the army's patronage, granted or rejected leaves of absence, and even selected which regiments should go to a particular theater of operations.[43]

Yet it was typical of army administration in particular, and of British governmental amateurism in general, that despite his heavy duties, the secretary at war had only a minuscule staff.

Some of the mistakes of the British army in the American Revolution can be more readily understood if it is kept in mind that the man who ran it — from Calcutta to New York, from St. Lucia to Sandwich — kept an office staff of twenty-one clerks and a few messengers.[44]

Although the secretary at war and his small staff ran most of the army, they did not run all of it. The war office had no control over two of the army's most important elements: the artillery and the engineers. The board of ordnance, under the master general of the ordnance, commanded them.[45] During the Revolution the ordnance board dispatched units of the Royal Regiment of Artillery to accompany armies in the field [46] and dispatched engineers to help the armies build bridges and conduct sieges. To confound and confuse jurisdictional lines, the ordnance board dispatched to the American theater all artillery, engineering, and ordnance stores in its own vessels, while first the treasury and then, after 1779, the navy board hired transports for sending army victuals.[47]

Neither the ordnance board nor the war office controlled the medical service. A physician general, surgeon general, and an inspector of regimental infirmaries supposedly ran this department, assisted by an army medical board. But, as in much of the rest of army administration, duties overlapped and lines of responsibility remained unclear.[48] In the end, the regimental colonel did as he wished. He usually appointed a surgeon and a surgeon's mate to his regiment at his own discretion without regard to their medical qualifications.[49]

Thus the British army, from commander in chief to company captain, had an organization distinguished by its confusion at home and overseas. Actual operations reflected this confusion during the Revolution. At the top, the generals in America always bickered among themselves. The commander in chief in America fought with his second in command — Howe with Clinton, Clinton with Cornwallis. Transportation by land proved slow and cumbersome — Clinton evacuated Philadelphia with a baggage train twelve miles long. But transportation by sea always involved endless negotiation and debate with the navy. Even the weapons were unreliable. The Brown Bess, standard firearm of the British soldier, was a clumsy smoothbore flintlock. Nearly five feet long with barrel and stock, it had no accuracy (not even a rear sight), had no range (its one-ounce ball often traveled only 125 yards before falling to the ground), and was often as dangerous to the man behind it as the man in front of it. In dry weather if a soldier tried to fire the Brown Bess into the wind, the back fire or flare from the touch hole could sear his face. Wet weather soaked all the powder in the priming pan and rendered the weapon useless. Army officials, from the King down, had witnessed an actual demonstration of the superiority of a weapon developed by Major Patrick Ferguson. Ferguson's rifle (now a collector's item since only about two hundred were made) was a breech-loading rifle impervious to the weather. The King and the army, however, preferred to retain the tried and untrue Brown Bess. In America it proved as worthless for individual skirmishing as for fighting in open ranks. It served admirably, however, as a stick to hold the bayonet. In that capacity it terrorized Americans, who were always impressed by the appearance opposite them of massed ranks loading and firing a simultaneous but unaimed volley on the words of command and then charging toward them with fixed bayonets and a loud "hurrah." [50]

That loud "hurrah" and the bayonet charge — the visible result of stern discipline — more than anything else accounted for the successes the British had in the American Revolution. Although Britain lost the war, the British regulars (not the Hessians or loyalists) won every major tactical engagement they fought, with the single exception of Cowpens (where command was in the hands not of an infantry officer but of a cavalry officer, Tarleton).

The British army was indeed chaotic. Its operations were poorly planned. Its generals, Cornwallis included, often blundered incredibly. But the army still had a little more than the Americans had of that all-important disciplined organization, the result of long experience in warfare. Officers quarreled among themselves, but they held more authority over their men than their American counterparts. Even after disciplined training and combat experience, the veteran Pennsylvania line mutinied in January of 1781. No regular British unit ever did. British maneuver was better than American maneuver.[51] British organization, muddled as it was, still supplied an army across three thousand miles of ocean in the age of sail. And within the regiment itself, where it mattered the most, discipline was absolute. One regiment might maneuver to commands different from another, but within that regiment obedience to command was total and unquestioning. It was the sort of obedience that held battalions stock-still under a withering fire, the sort of discipline that sent men charging against overwhelming odds.

In the end, therefore, the aristocracy relied upon the steadfastness of the very men it despised so much. Ignorant and ill-mannered — ex-jailbirds or debtors or country bumpkins — the enlisted men of the regular British army were the most truly reliable element in it. The army might lack medical services, transports, and decent provisions. Its officers might bicker and blunder. Yet the enlisted man always seemed to rise above all difficulties and perform herculean tasks. Time and again British officers pulled themselves out of a hopeless situation by means of a desperate bayonet charge against the foe. No matter if the officers knew no maneuvers, had no tactical sense, could not form column nor wheel into line, they still could order their troops forward, their gleaming steel presented to the enemy's gaze, their ranks advancing as one man. The generals knew this strength and stressed the bayonet charge. Burgoyne once ordered his officers "to inculcate in the men's minds a Reliance upon the Bayonet. Men of half their bodily strength, and even Cowards may be their match in firing; but the onset of Bayo-nets in the hands of the Valiant is irresistible." [52] The British were indeed valiant, a fact that Americans may lose sight of when considering the War for Independence. Washington suffered at Valley Forge, but so did Cornwallis in the chase through North Carolina. It required courage for an untrained militia to hold off British regulars at Bunker (Breed's) Hill, but it required just as much courage for those regulars to storm the hill. In the eighteenth century few men fought so well as, and none fought better than, the British redcoat.

Yet the men of the British army were much like soldiers in any armies of any time. Their foibles, their prejudices, their humor reflected their experiences in the army and made them eminently human. To Americans who faced them in the field they may have looked like armed robots, much as the Guards on parade in front of Buckingham Palace appear to tourists who gawk at them today. To their own officers they were instru-ments to be used. To themselves, however, they were men — men who often took pride in being soldiers.

For many of them, the army offered a second chance in life. Private in a marching regiment was better than felon in a jail. The country bumpkin had no future, whereas the soldier might. Soldiers felt that society looked down on them because it did not understand them. But it had also looked down on them when they had been civilians because it had not understood them then either. In the army, at least, if they obeyed orders and kept faith with their fellows, they could receive recognition and promotion, if not understanding, from their aristocratic officers. "The private soldier's and non-commissioned officer's good name and moral character," Sergeant Lamb once said, "are most precious to him, they constitute his best property, they often, it is notorious, recommend him to that honourable pre-

ferment and rank in the army, which the sons of the nobility
and gentry purchase with money; and thus station and fortune
in the service are sometimes obtained by humble meritorious
men, who otherwise must have forever remain'd in poverty." [53]
Lamb, a Dubliner who had run away from home at age seventeen to join the 9th regiment of foot, rejected the all-too-perva-
sive civilian notion of soldiers as rowdy wastrels. Perhaps many
had been before they joined and perhaps some still were, but the
army made new men of most of them:

> Honor & Virtue are names which some of my readers may con-
> sider too high for a private or non-commissioned officer, but it will
> be granted by individuals acquainted with the laudable economy
> which maintains and organizes his majesty's forces, that it is very
> properly attempted to inspire the soldiery through all the grada-
> tions of the army with an ardent spirit of propriety and self-
> estimation.[54]

"Propriety and self-estimation." The army required Lamb
and many like him to earn these qualities in a rugged and demanding, yet honest and honorable, life. The men who survived that life and retired from the army, Lamb felt, were better
men than they had been when they joined it.

Survival was not easy. For those new soldiers who entered the
army during the American Revolution it was but a matter of
time before they had to face up to themselves and their fellows,
perhaps for the first time in their lives. The army was an instrument of war, and war came to many men shortly after they
stepped ashore from the crowded transports that had carried
them across three thousand miles of ocean to the hostile shores
of North America. The redcoats may have gone into battle with
better discipline than the Americans, but at the beginning of
the Revolution perhaps the majority of them, like the majority
of Americans, had never heard a shot fired in anger. They felt
what every man has felt going into his first fight: fear. Recruits

became veterans only after they had tasted that fear. Combat-hardened men in the ranks helped them through the ordeal, but each soldier had to fight the empty feeling in his stomach, had to force his rubbery legs to move him forward, and had to steady his shaking hands when he heard the order to "charge bayonet."

This being the first skirmish I ever was engaged in [Roger Lamb said], it really appeared to me to be a very serious matter, especially when the bullets came whistling by our ears. In order to encourage the young soldiers amongst us, some of the veterans who had been well used to this kind of work, said, "there is no danger if you hear the sound of the bullet, which is fired against you, you are safe, and after the first charge all your fears will be done away." These remarks I found to be perfectly true many a time afterwards.[55]

In the army, death came in many forms and not always in a fierce engagement. The veteran who surmounted his fear of battle never overcame his fear of the hospital. For an eighteenth-century redcoat there were very few "million dollar" wounds. A wound meant at worst a horribly painful death. At best it usually brought a permanent, crippling disability, loss of sight or limb. Regiments never mustered enough surgeons to tend the wounded nor enough medical supplies for them. The soldier unfortunate enough to become ill on board the crowded transport that brought him to the New World had a foretaste of what would be in store for him if he stopped a rebel bullet. Only the desperately ill dared report to the badly lit, unclean, stinking area of the ship that passed for a hospital.[56] The badly wounded had no choice. A man felled in combat had to take what the doctors gave him, on or off the battlefield. It was often so little that the pathetic aftermath of battle shook men who had remained unmoved during it. Wounded were frequently left to die when the surgeons thought they had no hope of recovery. Sometimes those men with a chance to live had to be left be-

hind so they would not slow down a fast-moving army (Cornwallis left some of his wounded in a makeshift "hospital" near
Guilford Courthouse). Always help was too slow in coming to
the disabled men, groaning where they fell on bloody fields from
Long Island to Guilford Courthouse. The horrible panorama
that opened before Captain Thomas Anbury after a hotly contested fight moved him to write of those who had been
wounded:

> The one were all past all pain, the other in the most excruciating
> torments, sending forth dreadful groans. They had remained out
> all night, and from the loss of blood and want of nourishment,
> were upon the point of expiring with faintness: some of them
> begged they might lie and die, others again were insensible, some
> upon the least movement were put in the most horrid tortures,
> and all had a mile to be conveyed to the hospitals.[57]

A mile to the hospitals was a long walk, but what awaited the
wounded there? Sometimes the field hospital gave no more protection than the open ground. Baroness von Riedesel, who followed her husband down to Saratoga from Canada, recorded
that as one soldier lay on a table waiting for the surgeon to hack
off one of his legs, a cannon ball whistled in and took off the
other one.[58] Even if the soldier found himself in a hospital that
sheltered him from the weather and enemy bullets, he still faced
an ordeal. He would be crowded in with his fellows, stretched
out on a wooden bench that served for a bed, with a pallet often
empty of straw,[59] and thus he would wait for the surgeon. It
could not have been a pleasant wait, nor could the surgeon's
appearance have reassured him. Many of the army's doctors and
most of their assistants were untrained. As a rule, they also
lacked adequate medicine and depended perforce upon the saw
and home remedies. One physician poured a bottle of Rhenish
wine down the gullet of a soldier whose tongue had been grazed
and whose cheeks had been pierced by a bullet. The doctor

hoped the "acid would cleanse his wounds." [60] Yet that doctor's remedy was more sensible than many of those prescribed by his fellow physicians. Most of them lacked even an elemental idea of "cleansing" or cleanliness. "One of the unfortunate things we had to bear," Madame Riedesel noted, "was the odor which came from the wounds as they began to fester." [61] Indeed, the air must have been foul, not only from festering wounds but also from festering sores. For doctors crowded into the same "hospital" both the wounded and the diseased — men suffering from gunshots and men suffering from smallpox, dysentery, and malaria.

Despite his suffering and his privations, the British soldier managed to retain a sense of humor throughout the disasters of war. Crude, unsophisticated, and almost always related to the elemental conditions under which he lived, this sense of humor enabled him to bear the disasters. Officers who scarcely noticed many other human characteristics in their men, often noticed that sense of humor which bubbled to the surface under the most dreadful circumstances.

Dreadful, indeed, were the conditions aboard the transports that brought the army to America. The sick were herded together with the well aboard the ships so that if any man had an infectious disease it spread. Usually the ships lacked medicines, and sometimes livestock was packed into them along with the men.[62] Yet a captain aboard the fleet sailing to relieve Quebec heard one of his men make light of matters:

> One of my recruits coming upon deck, not observing anyone there, and the sea so tremendous, immediately went below, and cried out to his companions, "Oh! by my soul, honeys, the sea is very dreadful, and we are all sure to be drowned, for the ship's a sinking. However, I have this consolation, that if she goes to the bottom, the Captain must be accountable for us when we get to Quebec." [63]

Modern infantry vary the same joke to their means of transportation. Some of them have asked, when issued parachutes before boarding an airplane, what will happen if the plane gets into trouble, they have to bail out, and their parachutes do not open. The invariable response has been: "The parachute riggers are responsible, so after you hit the ground keep your parachute, take it to the riggers, and demand a new one."

Army humor — like much of army life — seems to be universal and timeless, but the British soldier faced one ordeal that his modern counterpart does not: terrible corporal punishment. Yet the redcoat seemed to take even the stripes on his back as a part of army life which, since he could not escape them, he would take with a grin. At one court martial a ranker who had no defense to offer for the charges against him said: "Oh! and plaise your Honours, I have nothing to say, but to save your Honours and the Court any further trouble, you may set me down two hundred [lashes], I'm sure your Honours will think that enough." [64]

Soldiers took their whippings and laughed at them. But it was a mistake to think, as some officers did, that lashes on the bare back were the only way to secure discipline from uneducated men. Rankers worked better for officers who, like Cornwallis, used the lash sparingly. Sergeant Lamb revealed more good sense than some of his superiors when he discussed corporal punishment. "Soldiers deserve to be treated at all events as human beings," he said, "and not beaten like beasts of burden; for cruelty is not the best means of producing improvement of manners. No doubt the lash cannot always be withheld, but the severe exercise or application of it to the back will seldom eradicate the inveterate vices of the mind depraved." Officers who avoided severity "as much as possible" were the best loved and best obeyed. [65]

For soldiers whose code it was to laugh at two hundred lashes, the prospect of such punishment would not likely deter them from forbidden amusements. When they had the opportunity they indulged themselves in the few pleasures their life allowed: shirking work whenever possible, picking up souvenirs wherever they could, chasing women, drinking whatever liquor they could find, singing, and complaining endlessly.

The British regular considered it his duty to face the enemy's fire but not to work at menial tasks assigned by his officers merely to keep him from mischief when he was not in combat. He avoided work when he could. "The Chief Engineer," so reads a set of General Orders in Rhode Island in 1777, "is to supply a sufficient number of Tools, that the want of them may not any more be given by the Men, for an Excuse for the little work they sometimes do." [66] But the chief engineer may have been chary of issuing tools, for no souvenir was beneath the attention of the enlisted man. Indeed, General Howe on one occasion had to order all entrenching tools issued by his engineer's department to be returned, "as it is apprehended the Soldiers may have lost or embezzled some of the tools." [67] Howe once discovered that his regulars had even run off with some fire buckets. [68]

"It is notorious," Sergeant Lamb noted, "that soldiers in most quarters, can without difficulty find wives." [69] The British redcoats, like many soldiers before and since, engaged in a never-ending pursuit of women. But the British army in the eighteenth century eased the difficulties of the chase by allowing the enlisted men's "wives" to campaign with their men. Every army carried camp followers along with it, and the women helped make the soldier's hard life bearable. Yet the women also had to endure that life, with the result that the woman camp follower in the eighteenth century was as hard as the soldier whose camp she followed. She did the washing, the cooking, and the mending. She sometimes had to fight and tend the wounded. Subject to military law, she also faced the lash if she violated that law.[70] "Women who follow a camp," one of Burgoyne's officers observed, "are of such a masculine nature, they are able to bear all hardships." [71]

Many are the instances of their courage and fortitude. One woman had a baby in an open baggage cart during a heavy blizzard. One fetched water for wounded soldiers from a creek constantly exposed to a heavy American fire. But perhaps the most determined wife in the British army was the pregnant girl who tramped the American wilderness all alone in search of her husband. Evidently left behind when Burgoyne's army advanced down from Canada, she set off after her sergeant despite her pregnancy. She stopped at a Quaker house in the forest to have her baby. Next morning she gathered up her newborn child and marched on to Ticonderoga where she was reunited with her husband.[72]

The British soldier took hard liquor as well as hard women along on his campaigns. Officers considered rum not a luxury but a necessity for their troops and bent their efforts to have an adequate supply at all times. But the soldier, seldom content with his regular rations, haunted the dramshops and bootleggers from Boston to Charleston. Before the army evacuated Boston, soldiers there received a constant inexpensive supply from the townspeople. The Bostonians hoped to get them drunk and entice them into deserting.[73] Howe tried to restrict the sale of alcoholic beverages to licensed retailers.[74] Still the liquor trade went on to the end of the war.

If soldiers occcasionally sought oblivion in drink, they expected not oblivion but fortitude and solace in their music. The army marched to music, deployed into battle formation to music, and sometimes attacked the enemy to music. If no fifers could be found, drums had to serve. The Scots, of course, kept their bagpipers playing even in the midst of battle. Many an American waiting to be attacked heard the sound of a drum in the misty dawn, the squeal of fifes, the eerie wail of the pipes, and then saw the grim lines of scarlet-coated men emerging from the mist and heading straight toward him with naked steel. Often, until he received training equal to that of the British, he ran. The untrained militiaman who stood firm possessed an unusual courage.

Redcoats liked music for other than purely martial purposes. Songs such as "The Girl I Left Behind Me" and "On the Banks of the Dee" revived old memories as they sat around their campfires. When they were in a less mellow mood, other songs could give them a chance to taunt their enemies when they could not reach them with musket ball or bayonet. It is possible that the British regulars marched to Lexington and Concord singing a parody on "Yankee Doodle."

> Yankee Doodle came to town
> For to buy a firelock:
> We will tar and feather him
> And so we will John Hancock [75]

The rankers never caught Hancock, and they had little to sing about after Lexington and Concord, but they indulged themselves in that luxury seemingly natural to all armies at all times, grousing and complaining. The officers, too, indulged in the sport. They groused about their allies: Hessians were "more infamous and cruel than any . . . a dirty, cowardly set of contemptible miscreants." [76] Indians were "more like infernals, than of the human kind." [77] They groused about their enemies, civilians and military. American civilians were stupid. One family in Massachusetts supposedly thought England was a "fine town" not far from Jerusalem.[78] American soldiers were cruel and merciless. Better to die in battle than fall into their hands.[79] They groused about their own government and its politicians who talked endlessly over their fine port and good cigars about how the war should be won while the soldiers themselves sweated, starved, and died. "This expedition appears to have been planned by those, who sitting in their closets, with a map before them, ridiculously expect the movements of an army to keep pace with their rapid ideas, not only directing general operations but particular movements of a campaign." "The war might have ended long before now, if it was not for the great men who want only to fill their purses." [80]

Grousing, drinking, womanizing, singing — the British soldiers in North America campaigned bravely up and down a long seacoast. That they lost the war was not for their want of mettle as soldiers. They ran from the Americans in only one important pitched battle, at Cowpens, and only there because their leader let them down, not because they lost courage or stamina. Soldiers from the lowest ranker to the highest general always grumble about politicians. In the American Revolution, however, their complaints were too often justified. But the generals also let their soldiers down and often matched the politicians in blundering stupidity.

Cornwallis was one of those generals, and he must share the blame for the British defeat. The disaster at Yorktown was not entirely of his own making, but his generalship certainly contributed to it. Yet one could never have convinced his men of the fact. They loved him. He was a popular general and deservedly so. His soldiers were prepared to blame the navy, the politicians, or Sir Henry Clinton for Yorktown but not Lieutenant General Earl Cornwallis. He was "a favorite not only with his own but with this [Clinton's] army." "In truth there is no saying what is not to be expected from troops under the command of a general they adore, of whose ability they have the highest opinion, and in whom they have been accustomed to place the fullest confidence." [81]

The troops gave him that "fullest confidence" because they knew he devoted himself far more to the army, and especially to the welfare of his men, than did most generals. "I have many friends in the American army [i.e., the British army in America]," he once said, "I love that army, and flatter myself that I am not quite indifferent to them." [82] He showed that love in many ways. First of all, he took more pains to become a profes-sional than did many of his colleagues. He hoped to learn his trade well, and from the time he began his military schooling in Turin until the time he left for his final long voyage to India, he never stopped applying himself to problems of military ad-ministration, tactics, and strategy. He was not strikingly origi-nal, as his thoughts on the military reveal. "Cavalry acts chiefly upon the nerves & if once it loses its terror it loses its greatest force [a lesson for Tarleton at Cowpens]." "Great care should be taken by all officers . . . not to make ministers too sanguine. And you know they are apt to lay too much stress on those kind of professions." Detaching too greatly from a large army risked being "beat in detail." [83] These are sufficiently conventional maxims. The Earl was a little unusual, however, and somewhat ahead of his time, in that he proposed actual maneuvers, or "war games," to keep armies constantly prepared for combat when not fighting. But the maneuvers he planned, he wished executed in the stiff and formal manner so characteristic of the eighteenth century. "In all marching, whether in column or line, it is abso-lutely necessary that the officer who is posted on the flank to which the troops are ordered to dress, should observe a steady & uniform pace, & that he should march perfectly straight. . . . In marching in column it is of the greatest consequence that the distances between the divisions should be observed with pre-cision & that the pivot files should cover exactly." [84] Despite his conventional notions, in America he showed more dash and daring than the other senior officers. When he went to India he displayed masterful strategy and tactics.

Secondly, in army administration he displayed more origi-nality and made a more lasting impression than in either strategy or tactics. He knew the chaotic system as well as any man: he had had to live with it all through the war. While not a

utopian reformer, he thought substantial changes in that system
would benefit the army and the public purse. During the time
he served in America under men who cared little or nothing
about improving the service, he stored up a number of ideas
about bettering the army administration. From the time he
took command in the South — where he tried to improve the
supply system and eliminate abuses in the quartermaster general's department — almost until the day he died, he concentrated on putting those ideas into effect. No detail was too
small, no task was too large, to escape his attention. He agitated
for the maintenance of full-strength regiments instead of the pit-
ifully reduced ones he had served with in America. He pushed
for a system of commands and maneuvers standard for the entire
army. He pleaded for better opportunities for the army's only
trained officers, the artillerymen and engineers.[85] His governor
generalship of India eventually would enable him to apply his
ideas to the British Empire. His tenure as master general of the
ordnance would permit him to unsnarl some of the administrative knots at home and to render more efficient the most often
condemned department in the military structure. The army
unquestionably benefitted from his serious attention.

But why did Cornwallis bother to give the service so much
serious attention? He was not by nature a meddler or a busy-
body who could not let well enough alone. Nor did he think
that by parading his interest in reform he could bring greater
attention on himself and promote his military and political career. Indeed, it is doubtful if he thought consciously of himself
as a reformer: he was certainly satisfied with the class structure
of the army and of society in general. Secure in his place in that
society and in his profession, he cared nothing for personal ag-
grandizement nor even for all the mystery and ceremony that
surrounded a commanding general. "No man despises the
pompous etiquette of command more than I do," he once told a
subordinate.[86] Yet he did become a reformer both of the eti-

quette and of the army. Several reasons accounted for his interest, yet underneath them all lay a genuine and enlightened concern for that lowly creature, the British private soldier. As a general in America he displayed a grasp of strategy inferior to that of Clinton and others. As a man he displayed, far more than Clinton and others, qualities of honesty, justice, endurance, tolerance, humanity, and eagerness to better the life of those under him. Those qualities made him a better man than Sir Henry Clinton and, to some degree, a better soldier. He could not plan as well as his superior, but whatever he planned he could carry through better than Sir Henry because he had a stronger will to do so and troops far more eager to follow him.

Perhaps he first thought of enlisted men as human beings when he secured the colonelcy of the 33d and had thrust upon him the sole responsibility for an entire regiment — its food, its clothes, and its general well-being. Shortly after that time his feeling for them became apparent. In 1767 he pleaded with Clinton (with whom he was then on excellent terms) to show compassion toward a soldier who had deserted:

> The bearer James Wilson deserted from your regt. at Edinburgh in the year 1763. He had been many years in the regt., & had really merit as a soldier & a tailor. I did endeavour, in consequence of his long services & former good character, with the consent of the regt. to find him out & give him his discharge, but he kept out of the way till now. I believe both Picton & Campbell will tell you that he is a proper object of compassion.[87]

Cornwallis combined a concern for discipline and justice with his compassion. He had endless sympathy for a hard-working and honest soldier (a trait which many of his fellow officers lacked) but no sympathy for the shirker. He knew an army only survived as long as it was disciplined. He never used the lash to break a man's body or spirit, but he never hesitated to use it to instill discipline.[88] Accordingly, by the time of the Revolution he had one of the finest regiments of foot in the British army, headed by a lieutenant colonel whom the enlisted men admired and whom even the Americans, in the course of the war, came to respect. The 33d regiment in 1775 was, according to Sergeant Roger Lamb who observed it daily, "in a high state of appointment, and exceedingly well disciplined, by that able disciplinarian, Colonel Webster. . . . I never witnessed any regiment that excelled it in discipline and military experience." [89]

The Earl's sense of discipline, justice, and compassion made him, more than Howe or Clinton, a *part* of the British army in America. He did not consider himself above it. If it prospered, he prospered. If it failed, he failed. He could never maintain that detachment from it that many of his fellows could. He could not write plays, as Burgoyne did, nor organize the festive revelries that entertained Howe in Philadelphia nor spend idle hours with a mistress as Clinton did in New York. He lived and marched and suffered with the army. He campaigned through the Carolinas on the same simple food as his men. Like them he went for a period with barely enough clothes to cover his body. Like them at one point he sickened and almost died. He never asked of his soldiers anything he was not prepared to do himself, from facing enemy bullets to facing starvation. Later, in India, he wholeheartedly supported the adjutant general's efforts to force the government to serve the infantry three "ample" meals a day, affording "some relief for the poor foot-soldier." [90] Indeed, although he was by no means wealthy, the Earl even donated to his troops the entire £42,000 in prize money which his victory over Tippoo brought him.[91] He had no prizes to give his troops in America save his own devotion. But they were aware of that devotion and of his unremitting efforts on their behalf. No wonder they wept openly and bitterly at Yorktown.

CHAPTER 5

Never in Command: 1776 to 1779

WHEN THE AMERICAN COLONIES rebelled against the authority of their mother country, Cornwallis volunteered his services. On November 26, 1775, he approached Lord George Germain through a friend and asked if he might accompany the expedition preparing to embark from Ireland for the Cape Fear River. He would serve even though he knew a general senior to himself had been assigned to take over command of the forces after they arrived on the American coast. Duty demanded that he help suppress the rebellion, just as conscience had prompted him to support the colonists until they had resorted to arms. Germain told the King of Cornwallis' "handsome offer" on the same day it was made. George III not only complimented, with many "obliging and gracious" remarks, the Earl's conduct but also allowed him to take his own 33d regiment overseas, instead of the previously scheduled 53d, and promised him Canadian service at the end of the expedition. This last favor was important to Cornwallis, for in Howe's army he would have been "last in command," whereas in Canada he would be senior to all generals save the commander himself, Guy Carleton.[1]

So Major General Earl Cornwallis packed his bags in December and hastened to Cork where seven regiments of infantry awaited his orders. By now the youthful dreams of military glory must have undergone a change. The father of two children, responsible for an estate that needed attention, thirty-eight years old, in love with his wife, his family, and his lands, he went to America from a sense of obligation to king and country.

He certainly cannot have thought highly of his prospects for a command. Even if he should get to Canada, he would be junior to Carleton, and if he should join Howe's army, both Howe and Henry Clinton would be senior to him. On the other hand, time and fortunes of war might raise him to the top. Certainly the King and Germain appreciated his action. His handsome offer to serve, even in a subordinate capacity, had impressed both men favorably. The American secretary at once cultivated a cordial relationship with the Earl that continued throughout the war. Accustomed to finicky and complaining generals, Germain liked a man willing to do his duty and take orders. Since he had been cashiered from the army for failing to charge at Minden and had been taunted ever since for his conduct, Lord George found especially gratifying the service of this particular officer whose military conduct and honor had never been impugned. All during the war he corresponded in private with Cornwallis. He offered him leave to continue with the army or come home whenever he wished. He even encouraged him, at the expense of Clinton, to proceed with his southern ventures in 1781. Indeed, at only one point did the American secretary's feelings cool toward Cornwallis, and then only temporarily, during the parliamentary inquiry into Howe's conduct in 1779. At that time Germain believed that the Earl did not sufficiently condemn Howe's handling of American operations.[2]

So Cornwallis could count upon ministerial favor throughout the war. The first instance of that favor showed itself in his orders. He was to command the expedition until it arrived at the Cape Fear River. There he was to put himself under the senior general present. But should none senior to himself arrive, he would have command and the responsibility for carrying out the instructions Germain had sent with him.[3] So difficult were transportation and communication in America that any number of things might prevent a superior's getting to the Cape Fear ahead of the Earl.[4]

Command for Cornwallis was not yet to be. Howe had already detached a senior general, Henry Clinton, who had in fact arrived in North Carolina well ahead of the Earl. Cornwallis had known beforehand, of course, that Clinton might be waiting to take command, but so far as he was then concerned Howe could not have made a better choice. A friend of both Cornwallis and Clinton, Brigadier General William Phillips, reported the Earl as "very happy to think he shall serve under an old friend and a man he has so good an opinion of." [5] Neither Phillips nor Clinton nor Cornwallis could foresee that the campaign would end in a fiasco, bringing neither glory nor honor to the generals involved and that the stress of war in America would reduce the cordiality between Cornwallis and Clinton to a mutual dislike.

The expedition augured ill from the beginning. Supposed to sail in December of 1775, it did not get under way until February. One delay after another frustrated its timely departure. "The transports had drawn too much water for effective loading, and their masters had crammed them so full of supplies to sell on their own in America that the cavalry horses could not be reached at feeding time." December 1, the originally established departure date, "arrived with no detailed instructions issued to the commanders, the naval convoy force not ready, the transports not finally fitted, the ordnance stores still to load, and the composition of the force not finally decided." [6] Finally on February 12 the convoy of forty-four vessels sailed. On the first day out nine ships vanished, blown back to England. Three weeks later only fourteen remained, six of them transports. The

Earl, trying to get off a letter to Germain in his pitching fifty-gun ship *Bristol* (which would lose her main and mizzen masts to rebel batteries in Charleston), complained of the "almost always contrary" wind and the "constant and most violent gales." [7] By the middle of April miles of ocean still separated Cornwallis from his destination, and he began to find his passage "very tedious." [8]

The first transport managed to drift into the Cape Fear River in the middle of April, but Cornwallis did not reach his rendezvous until May 3. There as a fitting sequel to an unpleasant voyage, he faced an unpleasant situation. The loyalists had risen prematurely and had been soundly trounced at Moore's Creek Bridge while Cornwallis was tossing and rolling in the middle of the Atlantic. After their defeat they had scattered to the backcountry, rendering futile the entire purpose of the expedition which was to help them reestablish royal government. Clinton had sailed from Boston in January and had arrived in March. There he had sat day after day searching the horizon fruitlessly for the Earl and the fleet, commanded by Commodore Peter Parker. As weeks turned into months Clinton's forces deteriorated. They lacked beef and salt. Although they managed to capture some molasses from a passing French schooner, they subsisted mostly on a meager allowance of fish, oysters, and cabbage, all cadged or pilfered from the surrounding country. Only the stale biscuits they consumed with their meals had come with them.

Thus when the Earl reached the coast of North Carolina he brought an army weakened by a difficult three months' ocean voyage to reinforce another, half-starved by its attempts to live off the countryside. The purpose of their joining, to aid the loyalists, had already been defeated. Indeed, on his first trip to the Carolinas, Cornwallis saw only a coastline, a few islands, and an action of no consequence. After he arrived he led a retaliatory raid against rebels harassing British small boats. He took a

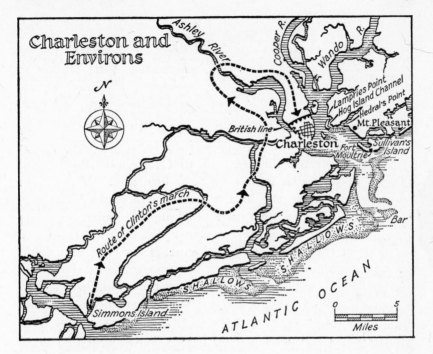

detachment ashore, marched against some inadequate entrenchments to which the rebels had retreated, carried the trenches,
took some artillery and cattle, and rowed back to the fleet "without having been scarcely missed," as Clinton put it.[9]

After this skirmish, which salvaged nothing but British egos,
the land and sea commanders still had to reach a decision. Although Clinton consulted Cornwallis,[10] the latter shared very little in the final plans of Clinton and Parker. It was just as well,
for those plans proved as senseless as many of the others the British formulated during the course of the war. Clinton and Parker decided to attack Charleston.

Not that the scheme entirely lacked logic. After Moore's
Creek Bridge, Clinton rightly refused to move into the interior.

He also disregarded the absurd orders of Germain to reestablish tranquillity in four provinces quickly and then rejoin Howe, preferably in the early spring. Howe, late in May, sent a communication encouraging an attack on Charleston. The idea appealed to Clinton primarily because he had already thought of it before receiving Howe's letter. It also appealed to Parker after he learned from some junior officers who had scouted the city's fortifications that only a small fort on Sullivan's Island, Fort Moultrie, protected the entrance to Charleston. Parker and Clinton thought that if they took the fort, they could prevent rebels from closing the harbor with fortifications. The city would then be "ripe for future plucking." [11] Apparently they never considered, nor is there evidence that Cornwallis pointed out to them, the pitfalls in their scheme. They knew they could not take Charleston, because they had no siege guns. Even had they taken Sullivan's Island, the garrison they could have spared to defend it, after their departure, would have been too small for the task. Finally, even if the small garrison somehow managed to hold on, it could scarcely have served as a rallying point to inspire loyalists.

Poor as was the planning, the execution was worse. At the end of May, Cornwallis, Clinton, and the fleet sailed off to Charleston on their madcap venture. They anchored in the lower harbor in early June and then considered their next move. Fort Moultrie commanded the passage between the lower and upper harbors. Charleston lay on the latter. If Clinton and Cornwallis could land on Sullivan's Island and assault the fort from the rear, in conjunction with a naval bombardment in front, they could undoubtedly reduce the American strongpoint. Warships might then sweep through the channel and lay the city at the mercy of British naval guns.

First, however, the British army had to land on Sullivan's Island. Clinton chose to disembark his forces on Long Island, above Sullivan's Island and separated from it by a narrow channel. He seemed to have excellent reasons for his choice. The milder surf of Long Island would render disembarkation easier than at Sullivan's Island, and no enemy would oppose the landing. He then thought to march straight over to Fort Moultrie. The water separating the two islands, he was told, reached a depth of but eighteen inches. Only after he had landed all his troops and artillery did Clinton discover that the channel dividing Sullivan's and Long Islands measured seven feet deep instead of eighteen inches. He had no boats to bring his army across — they could scarcely wade — and before he procured any, the Americans brought up artillery to harass him. So the British sat down and, like Mr. Micawber, waited for something to turn up. Cornwallis reconnoitered the position and found no solution to their difficulties.[12] Clinton concocted and abandoned one scheme after another. Commodore Parker offered no suggestions, but he finally decided to act on his own. Determined to salvage the navy's honor, he could think of no better way than by bombarding the fort. On June 28 he moved into position and opened fire. As might be expected, the Americans hurt him badly with their big guns and suffered little damage themselves. The army then packed itself up in its transports and sailed for New York. The navy followed.[13] Cornwallis' first venture in America under Clinton ended in failure.

Although he said little about it and apparently remained on good terms with his superior for three more years, the Earl could not have been impressed by Clinton's abilities as a leader. Nor did Americans ever allow him to forget the mortification of Charleston: they taunted the British in song, ballad, and newsprint.

Some good did come of Charleston, though: the bungling there had made it impossible for him to get to Canada in time to work with Carleton.[14] In June, Howe had dispatched the 47th regiment to Canada, in place of the Earl and the 33d.[15] The British commander intended to use the 33d for his operations in

New York when they arrived. Had Cornwallis not got bogged
down at Charleston, he might have gone to Canada; instead of
marching into Philadelphia in triumph in 1777, he might have
surrendered in humiliation at Saratoga.

On August 1 he and Clinton sailed into New York. The
"very fine apppearance" of their ships and the reinforcement of
troops which they brought to Howe — "an agreeable circum-
stance" — enabled the American commander to plan his operations. On the very day of their arrival in New York, Cornwallis
sailed over to Admiral Howe's flagship to participate in those
plans.[16]

General William Howe (in October of 1776 he became Sir
William, K.B.) and his brother Admiral Richard, Lord Howe,
the British naval commander in America, had been building up
their forces during the summer of 1776. General Howe had
sailed into New York from Nova Scotia in July and disembarked
his army at Staten Island. Cornwallis and Clinton joined him in
August, and shortly after their arrival, eighty-four hundred Hessians and twenty-six hundred British soldiers came from England to reinforce him. When Parker and the rest of his fleet
dribbled in, the Howe brothers could muster thirty-two thousand troops, over four hundred transports, ten ships of the line,
twenty frigates, ten thousand seamen, and twelve hundred guns.
They had the largest force "that the mother country had ever
sent overseas." [17]

General Washington — Clinton always called him Mr. Washington — had split his forces in the face of this British threat.
He had posted about six thousand men, two thirds of them militia, on Long Island, where he did not think General Howe
would land. But these forces comprised only one fourth of his
army. The other three fourths he had left on Manhattan.
When the British surprised Washington by attacking Long Is-

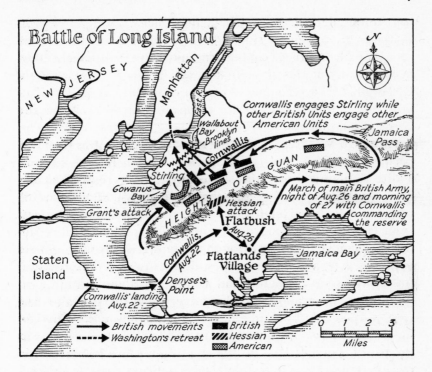

Battle of Long Island

Cornwallis engages Stirling while other British Units engage other American Units

March of main British Army, night of Aug.26 and morning of 27 with Cornwallis commanding the reserve

→ British movements
----→ Washington's retreat
■ British
/// Hessian
▨ American

land, Cornwallis was with them. For perhaps the only time in his entire military career, the odds favored him overwhelmingly. The British mustered seven times the number of the Americans, "in military efficiency, man for man, one might say fifteen times their number." [18]

At eight o'clock on the morning of August 22, Cornwallis and Clinton sailed with an advance guard of about four thousand men to a landing at Denyse Point on Long Island. The rest of the army followed that day and the next. The Earl took the reserve — ten battalions of light infantry and a corps of Hessian grenadiers — to Flatbush, where he camped. The next day he found himself skirmishing with the Americans, whose cause he had so long defended in Parliament. They exchanged shots in Flatbush Pass. Neither side did much damage, but the Americans gained "courage, confidence, and service," qualities they needed badly at this stage in the war.[19] On the twenty-sixth, Cornwallis left a regiment of regulars and the Hessians at Flatbush and moved the rest of his troops to Flatlands Village, the British headquarters.

Although Washington did not suspect it, Howe was now preparing to outflank him. The American lines at Brooklyn ran in a direction roughly northeast-southwest, their right flank anchored at Gowanus Bay and their left at Wallabout Bay. A range of hills, the Heights of Guan, ran slightly north of east from Gowanus out toward the end of Long Island. Howe intended to move his army through the most easterly of the passes over these hills and then turn west directly toward the American fortifications. Washington had strung out about twenty-eight hundred men, or about half his force, along the passes for the very purpose of thwarting such a British advance. Unfortunately for the American general, he had left the most easterly of the passes, Jamaica Pass, to the care of only five young militia officers. Howe chose to march through Jamaica Pass.

To divert attention from his flanking movement, the British commander placed about five thousand men under Major General James Grant on his left at Gowanus Bay with orders to demonstrate there against the American lines. He left the Hessians at Flatlands and, with the bulk of his forces, moved on the evening of the twenty-sixth toward Jamaica Pass. Cornwallis commanded the reserve, and Clinton the van, which easily captured the five American militia officers before they could warn the American army. By morning Howe had completed his maneuver and turned west. Now the Americans faced disaster. Grant opened his attack on their right, the Hessians attacked their center, and Clinton and Cornwallis swept down behind them. Washington's stunned men reeled from the triple assault and stumbled back to their lines. General "Lord" Stirling did try to hold his 950 Marylanders steadfast against Grant's five thousand, but just then the 71st regiment and a battalion of grenadiers, led by Cornwallis, thundered down on him. Stirling turned and led part of his force — the rest having been ordered to retreat across Gowanus Creek into the American lines — directly against Cornwallis. The Earl now tasted his first real fighting in America, fighting as bitter as any he had experienced on the European continent. In the contest he learned to respect the fury of Americans fully aroused and truly desperate. Five times Stirling led 250 Marylanders against the British infantry and two field pieces. Five times the British repulsed him. The Marylanders tried yet a sixth time when Cornwallis, now reinforced, broke them and hurled them back, scattering them to the American lines. Howe's victory was complete.

Yet the British commander could have had more than a victory. He could have taken the entire American army on Long Island. His men longed to charge directly into the enemy lines and demolish them. Instead, Howe decided to settle himself into a regular siege of the Brooklyn fortifications. He issued repeated orders to his troops to cease their assault. In the opinion of most British observers, the Americans were so demoralized that the British could easily have forced the Brooklyn lines. But the British commander's decision to conduct a regular siege gave Washington a breather and a second chance, which he took. On the night of August 29 he slipped his forces out of Long Island during a thick fog and landed them on Manhattan. The next morning the British discovered they were beseiging empty works.[20]

Howe's refusal to let the redcoats press home the attack tormented several officers at the time. Clinton was one of them, although he never said anything in public against Howe. Neither did Cornwallis, whatever he may have thought. In 1779 Parliament inquired into the conduct of the war. In early May it summoned Cornwallis, who was in England at the time, to testify. Several times members pressed him to say whether he thought the Brooklyn lines could have been carried by an immediate assault. One zealous inquirer asked him whether he realized that men from his own 33d had had to be called back from trying to carry the works themselves. Each time the Earl offered no opinion, maintaining that he had been too much engaged to the south of the lines to gain a clear impression of whether or not an immediate assault would have taken them. "I never did hear it suggested by anyone," he said, "that those lines could have been carried by assault." [21] He never revealed what he actually thought of Howe's conduct on that day. Unlike Clinton, Howe had at least led the British to victory. Nevertheless, Cornwallis' second American campaign, like his first, failed to bring a decisive victory to British arms.

During the rest of the New York campaign the Earl played a minor role. He crossed with the army to New York and advanced with it to White Plains, where Howe achieved nothing against Washington and where Clinton, fed up with his superior, exploded his dissatisfaction into Cornwallis' ear. The British army moved south and gobbled up Fort Washington, a large American post with two thousand men on the northwestern tip of Manhattan. Across the river stood a second stronghold, Fort Lee, garrisoned with four thousand men, under the command of Nathanael Greene. Howe thought it could also be taken, so on November 18, he sent off a force of forty-five hundred men under Cornwallis. They crossed the Hudson to the Jersey shore about eight miles above Fort Lee and moved south. Once again, however, the Americans wriggled eellike from the British grasp, for a deserter warned Greene of Cornwallis' approach. Even so, the latter captured from his future Carolina antagonist huge quantities of stores, guns, and tents which the Americans left behind in their flight.[22]

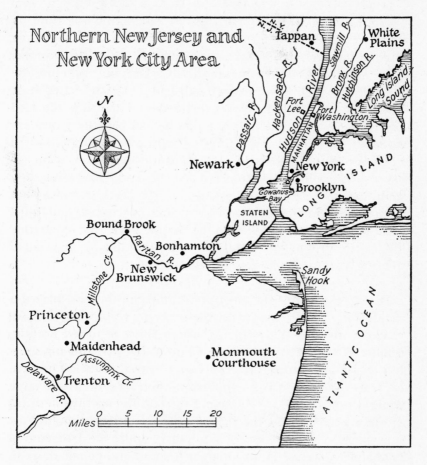

Northern New Jersey and New York City Area

That flight now gave the Earl his first chance to act independently and to catch the army which Howe had failed to trap. On November 10, Washington had moved with ten thousand men from his untenable position at White Plains leaving General Lee with five thousand to cover New England. The garrison that escaped from Fort Lee joined Washington's forces, now hurrying south across New Jersey. Howe entrusted Cornwallis

with the pursuit of the Americans. The Earl tore out after his
quarry on November 25, after he had been reinforced with nine
battalions. Could he now succeed where Clinton had bungled
and Howe had faltered? Could he catch and destroy an American army? He had already seen his superiors fail. Would he
profit from the example of their mistakes?

Cornwallis stuck to the heels of his adversary. On November
28, his van marched into Newark as Washington's rear guard
scrambled out. Pressing on, he made a desperate attempt to
catch Washington on December 1, marching his men twenty
miles over very bad roads, only to reach New Brunswick and
discover his elusive quarry gone. Cornwallis now stopped. His
men were worn out and hungry. They had been so intent upon
pursuit that they had not even taken the time to bake their flour
into bread. Even had they been able to march farther that day,
the artillery and baggage horses would have been too fatigued to
move. Furthermore, the Americans had torn down the only
bridge over the Raritan. Cornwallis did have orders from Howe
to relinquish the pursuit at New Brunswick, but they were not
so binding as to preclude his seizing a victory if he thought one
possible. As he said later: "I could not have pursued the enemy
from Brunswick with any prospect of material advantage, or
without greatly distressing the troops under my command. . . .
But had I seen that I could have struck a material stroke by
moving forward, I certainly should have taken it upon me to
have done it." [23]

Critics of Cornwallis — some of his contemporaries as well as
some later historians — speculated that had he pushed a little
harder, he could have caught Washington. True, he could not
have crossed the Raritan over the broken bridge, but he might
have forded the river in one of several places. Washington's
army was tired, poorly equipped, and not really prepared for a
fight. It had only a small detachment of light dragoons to protect the American flank and impede the British advance. Most

of those dragoons were middle-aged and were lacking in discipline, decent weapons — some carried fowling pieces — and even the remotest idea of an ordered march.[24] On the other hand, the Earl's defenders also believed that he could have caught Washington, but they blamed Howe's orders for his halt. Sir William himself seemed to admit responsibility when he wrote to Germain on December 20 that "Lord Cornwallis had orders not to advance beyond Brunswick, which occasioned him to discontinue the pursuit." [25] One defender maintained: "Had the noble general been left to act at his own discretion, if we may form a conjecture from that activity and good sense which distinguish his usual conduct, he could have pursued the weakened and alarmed enemy to the Delaware over which, without falling into his hands, they never could have passed." [26] Yet the Earl's "usual conduct" with a semi-independent command seldom included paying attention to the orders of his superiors if he thought he could gain a military advantage by disregarding them. He displayed no penchant for following Clinton's orders in the South, and as he said later, he would not have obeyed Howe at New Brunswick had he seriously believed he could have caught Washington. Revolutionary ardor often drew an exaggerated picture of Washington's army as weak, ill-equipped, and ill-fed but armed with a righteous cause which in the end enabled it to overcome the haughty, well-equipped, and well-disciplined British. But the British could also get tired and hungry, as men do, and there seems little reason to doubt that on the banks of the Raritan the Earl's army was too exhausted for further effort. He who doubts the reasonableness of that explanation can make the trial for himself: let him eat nothing but flour for three days, strap a sixty-pound pack to his back, and march twenty miles in the rain on muddy, unsurfaced roads. If he then deems himself prepared to wade across a river and fight a battle, his doubts are justified.

Although Cornwallis could not rush across the Raritan to

grab Washington, he might still have helped take the American before he crossed the Delaware. Howe caught up with his subordinate on December 6, and on the next day, with Howe now in command, they resumed the pursuit. Despite this delay of a week, the British could still have netted Washington, for they arrived at Princeton around four in the afternoon of the seventh, barely an hour after Washington's rear guard had left. Howe camped his troops in the college buildings, allowed them a good night's sleep, and waited until nine o'clock the next morning before resuming his march. Cornwallis again led the van and "marched slowly and cautiously, with flankers thrown out on both sides to scour the woodland and look out for ambushes. The broken-down bridges and other obstacles also delayed him." [27] Consequently Sir William's forces arrived at Trenton at two in the afternoon, just as the last of Washington's army put off for the Pennsylvania shore in the only available boats, "as if," Commissary Stedman commented, "he [Howe] had calculated, it is observed, with great accuracy, the exact time necessary for his enemy to make his escape." [28]

Why delay after New Brunswick? Why dally once the army had rested and been reinforced? The chief responsibility, of course, rested with Howe, who took charge when he joined the army on December 6. Thereafter, Cornwallis could no longer act independently. Yet could he not have pushed his chief? The hitherto-dashing Earl, who had swept in behind the enemy on Long Island and chased them relentlessly through most of New Jersey, had apparently metamorphosed into a model of caution. Just as Howe had missed his opportunity at Long Island, so Cornwallis missed his opportunity after New Brunswick. It is a story that repeats itself over and over during the American Revolution, no matter who is leading the British — Gage, Howe, Clinton, or Cornwallis. Victory is within reach. The enemy is nearly trapped. One more push will destroy him. Yet the moment is lost, and the war churns on and on.

Although he did not necessarily have the best opportunities to catch his foe, Cornwallis probably had more chances than most of the British generals. Yet he never bagged him. Occasionally, as in New Jersey and later in the Carolinas, he stretched his supplies and men to the limit and then could not move them further without rest. Yet at other times, he seemed to be in the grip of the same strange lethargy that so often overcame British generals in America. When that lethargy came upon him it might cost him dearly, as it did the month following New Brunswick.

Once Howe had watched Washington cross the Delaware safely, he decided to end the campaign for the year. His general orders for December 14, 1776, stipulated that Cornwallis' pursuit had closed the campaign "much to the honor of his lordship and the Officers and Soldiers under his command." Troops would now march to winter quarters.[29]

Cornwallis applied for leave to go home. He had reached New York when Washington gave Howe a sort of reverse Christmas present by defeating the Hessians at Trenton. Sir William recalled the Earl and once again sent him to catch the daring American. Cornwallis wasted no time. On New Year's Day, 1777, he rode fifty miles from New York to Princeton, arriving in the college town toward evening. There he hurriedly rounded up the British forces — about eight thousand regulars and a large artillery park — and prepared to march toward Trenton. He took little thought for his own comfort. Indeed, he scarcely rested before he put his army in motion. He left a rear guard of about twelve hundred men under Colonel Charles Mawhood at Princeton and moved out before daylight on January 2. At Maidenhead he left another force of about fifteen hundred men under General Alexander Leslie and proceeded with the remainder, about five thousand men, directly toward Trenton. Washington, who had crossed and recrossed the Delaware since his victory over the Hessians, awaited the Earl with five thousand men. At the same time his advance guard disputed with deadly long-rifle fire every inch of the British advance along the Princeton-Trenton road, now a quagmire from the heavy rains of the night before. "The men sank halfway to their knees; the guns continually threatened to bog down. . . . At every turn of the road, from every flanking thicket and ravine, the bullets whistled. Frequently the march had to be halted until troops of the advance guard could be deployed to clarify the situation, and when they had done so, the opposition simply melted away and had to be dealt with afresh at the next natural obstacle." [30] In the face of such opposition from both nature and the Americans, Cornwallis took the entire day of January 2 to go from Princeton to Trenton, a distance of only ten miles. During this slow march Washington formed his line on a ridge across from Trenton along the south bank of the Assanpink Creek. Cornwallis' forces did not reach the town until around five o'clock. In the winter twilight advance elements tried and failed to get across the creek to Washington, who drove back one British column at the lower fords and thrice repulsed, with heavy losses to the British, a second column that tried to cross a bridge over the creek. As darkness fell the Earl rode up with the main body of the army and called a council of war. Sir William Erskine, the quartermaster general, urged him to attack. Others pointed out that the Americans were trapped, having left their boats above Trenton, and could be dealt with in the morning. Regardless of his own fatigue, Cornwallis might have attacked if his men had been fresh. But they had tramped and fought in the mud all day. Although Washington's right flank lay exposed, the British general would have had to send his men over unknown terrain on soggy ground in the dark in order to attack it. The other alternative, a frontal assault with tired troops across a swollen stream in darkness, seemed suicidal. Cornwallis did not like night fighting anyway. So he decided to "bag the fox" the next morning.[31]

The decision to wait was probably wise. Cornwallis' subsequent action was not. He should at least have anticipated that Washington might try to slip out of the trap, might even try a flanking movement against the Princeton detachment. "His reconnaissance should have been so complete that he could have made an atttack when the American army commenced its movement." [32] Instead he bivouacked his men in the hills north of the village. While the British warmed themselves around their campfires or loitered through the Trenton streets, Washington planned his escape. He lighted up his campfires brightly and left four hundred men to tend them and to keep up regular patrols and challenges. Then he muffled his artillery wheels in heavy cloth. In absolute silence his army crept out and around the right flank of the unsuspecting British. Cornwallis awoke at Trenton, as Howe had awakened at Long Island, to find his enemy gone.

What followed wrecked the British plans for the winter of 1776 to 1777. Washington marched to Princeton, smashed against Colonel Mawhood's brigade there, and sent it reeling. The American would probably have liked to continue on to New Brunswick to capture the British war chest. Cornwallis, however, quickly recovered from his surprise and sent his troops hotfooting toward the town. Washington, who declined any open engagement, led his exhausted men into the protective hills and woods around Morristown for winter quarters. The Earl did not dare pursue there, so he stopped at New Brunswick. Shocked at the turn of events, Howe evacuated all New Jersey save the line along the Raritan from New Brunswick to Perth Amboy.

Almost five years after this British debacle, at a dinner following an even drearier event for the British, the surrender at Yorktown, Cornwallis reputedly rose gallantly and addressed Washington in response to a toast. "When the illustrious part that your Excellency has borne in this long and arduous contest be-

comes a matter of history," he said, "fame will gather your
brightest laurels rather from the banks of the Delaware than
from those of the Chesapeake." [33] Unquestionably, Washington
had campaigned brilliantly and the Earl's tribute did him no
more than justice. The whole affair of Trenton and Princeton,
on the other hand, showed Cornwallis at his worst. Perhaps he
was not guilty, as Clinton later said, "of the most consumate ignorance I ever heard of [in] any officer above a corporal." [34]
But that Washington upset all British plans for holding New
Jersey owed to the Earl's negligence at Trenton. A tiger at
Long Island, a greyhound in pursuit of Washington across New
Jersey, he became a turtle south of New Brunswick. After the
Princeton fiasco he recovered his initiative and dash to act
again as an active and relentless foe of the Americans. Yet, in
the Carolinas, when he had another semi-independent command, he displayed the same curiously contradictory qualities
— extraordinary energy, superb leadership, and brilliant tactics, coupled soon before or after with foolish blunders, and an
amazing insensitivity to those critical moments, great and small,
which demand immediate and decisive action. In hot pursuit of
the foe, none excelled him. When engaged in actual fighting, he
was an inferno of energy, initiative, command, and immediate
decision. Indeed, he was never dull on the battlefield, and he
was often brilliant. But in a prolonged endeavor, it almost
seemed sometimes as though he lacked mental staying power, a
form of patience — it was as if he grew bored or inattentive.
Perhaps it was merely that he needed the stimulation of action
and that during the routine part of soldiering, he did not truly
engage his mind. Certainly he seemed sometimes to take too
long to arrive at decisions. Maybe students of history use too
much hindsight and too little insight. Nevertheless, it remains
true that in America, Cornwallis always operated at his best
under pressure. Of course, this is not to say that, in a long campaign, he lacked will or determination. Far from it. His march

through the Carolinas showed his great will power and English bulldog persistence. But he displayed his verve only in fits and starts. Not until a decade later, in India, did he seem willing and able to devote his entire attention and all of his soldierly mind to the full planning, down to details, of a long campaign. And in India he won.

At Trenton, Cornwallis lost the only opportunity he ever had to catch Washington and to smash the American Revolution. The winter and spring of 1777, by contrast, offered him nothing but skirmishing against small bodies along the Raritan line. He commanded the garrison at New Brunswick and became increasingly annoyed with American raids on his outposts, especially on the one manned by the 71st regiment and his own 33d at Bonhamton. In retaliation he led a detachment out of New Brunswick to attack an American advanced post at Bound Brook about ten miles away. There he routed the twelve hundred troops of the American general (whose name, confusingly enough, was Clinton) and took some artillery and about one hundred prisoners.[35] In June, as Howe tried several maneuvers to bring Washington into battle, Cornwallis very nearly cut off a part of the American army under Stirling, inflicting upon it one hundred casualties and taking seventy prisoners.[36]

A lack of forage in the late-coming spring of 1777, however, seriously hampered British maneuvering.[37] When he failed to draw Washington into an open fight, Howe shifted the war away from New Jersey. In New York, after debating with his generals as to the next course of action, he chose one of utter folly. He decided to capture Philadelphia. In order to deceive Washington as to his intention, he would go as far as possible toward the city by sail. He figured that "Gentleman Johnny" Burgoyne, who would march down from Canada toward Albany that same summer, could take care of himself. Sir William did, however, leave Clinton (now Sir Henry, K.B.) with seven thousand men,

mostly provincials, to hold Manhatttan and to create a diversion
for Burgoyne if necessary. The entire plan — Howe to Philadelphia by sea, Burgoyne to Albany by land, and Clinton in between with a motley provincial force — had little to recommend
it. Indeed, "the planning of the campaign of 1777," Clinton's
biographer asserts, "was the worst that the British perpetrated
throughout the war. Their strategy in the Yorktown campaign,
four years later, was even more disastrous in its outcome but far
more defensible in its design. The strategy of 1777 can scarcely
be defended at all." [38]

Yet Cornwallis defended it at the time. Sir Henry Clinton
objected to it, and so, too, did Sir William Erskine, the quartermaster general. According to Clinton, when Erskine pressed
Howe to march north in support of Burgoyne, Cornwallis
quipped: "Faugh, faugh! Wooly [Erskine's nickname] only
wants a junction with Burgoyne that he may crack a bottle with
his friend Phillips." [39] Wooly may only have wanted a bottle
with Phillips, but the Earl would have done better to favor the
drinking bout rather than the Philadelphia venture. For the
move assumed that Washington would fight for the city, which
he did, but which Howe had no rational reason for assuming at
the time. The venture also assumed that Burgoyne would have
no trouble, an opinion firmly held by Burgoyne himself until
disaster overtook him. Finally, it assumed that Burgoyne at Albany and Howe at Philadelphia would somehow end the Revolution. Yet, as events showed, the taking of Philadelphia
scarcely affected the war, save to make the American army
stronger and better disciplined in the winter of Valley Forge.
Americans in 1777 did not accord their "capital" the same importance that the British attached to London or the French to
Paris. What could the holding of Philadelphia promise for the
recovery of New Jersey or New England? Burgoyne at Albany
supposedly would affect New England, but how? For between
Albany and Clinton's forces at Manhattan lay a vast country

through which the middle provinces could communicate with New England. Indeed, what Howe's plan effected was to leave Washington's army intact, New England still connected with the other provinces, the British army in three separate places — Philadelphia, Albany, and Manhattan — and the Americans free to carry on the war.

Had he been in overall command would Cornwallis have recommended the journey to Philadelphia? Of course, one cannot answer with certainty. As a commander he liked to move around, but he usually found more sensible objectives to move after than the one presented by Philadelphia in 1777. Every march in the south, even the march to Yorktown showed more sensible purpose than the Philadelphia campaign. But he held no command in 1777, and he may have urged Howe to that folly simply because he chafed at the thought of inaction in New York. Unlike his colleagues, he kept no mistresses to help him while away the tedious hours and days of idleness. The pleasures of a city did not suit him. Simple in his tastes, faithful to his wife, uninterested in gambling or theatricals, he wanted action in the field. He probably foresaw little action in cruising up the Hudson to meet Burgoyne.

After dawdling around Manhattan for half the summer, Howe finally embarked his army in late July. The fleet took a month to sail from New York to Head of Elk and did not land there until the "distressingly hot, close morning" of August 25. Later, under Clinton, the same army took a mere two weeks to march overland from Philadelphia to New York, even though it was encumbered by a baggage train twelve miles long and even though it paused to fight a battle along the way.[40] Washington, at first baffled by the disappearance of the British army, eventually discovered its movements and marched south to dispute its advance up to Philadelphia. Howe cautiously felt his way toward the city, slaughtering cattle, burning houses, and living well. His slow movement enabled the American commander to post eleven thousand men on the east side of Brandywine Creek directly in the path of the oncoming redcoats. What followed almost repeated Long Island. Again Cornwallis flanked the Americans.

Washington had strung his army along the Brandywine in three divisions. Greene at his center and the Pennsylvania militia on his left prepared to defend Chadd's Ford, where he thought the British would try to cross. He posted Sullivan on his right, upstream from Chadd's Ford, in anticipation of a possible flanking movement.

But he had not placed Sullivan far enough upstream. The British skirted the Americans anyway. Howe split his forces on the morning of September 11. He sent about half his troops under General Knyphausen directly to Chadd's Ford to create a diversion. Knyphausen's demonstration there, he hoped, would deceive the Americans into believing that he intended to attack across the ford with his whole army. But he and Cornwallis took the other part of his forces far to the north. Cornwallis would cross the creek to the north and sweep down on the rear of the American right flank. The maneuver fooled Washington completely. Indeed, even after he learned of Cornwallis' movements he refused to believe, until too late to avert defeat, that Howe had split his forces.

About four o'clock on the morning of September 11, Howe and Cornwallis led seven thousand men out of Kennett Square and marched almost due north. They crossed the Brandywine at Jeffry's Ford and, by early afternoon, emerged from the woods on Osborne's Hill above the American right. They surprised their enemies so completely that they had time to form two lines and a reserve. When Sullivan became aware of his danger he hastily tried to mass his divisions at right angles to his former position along the creek in order to face the attack. As he struggled to form his line on a hill opposite the redcoats, Cornwallis loosed his artillery. The British front line — guards on the right, grenadiers in the center, light infantry and Anspach and

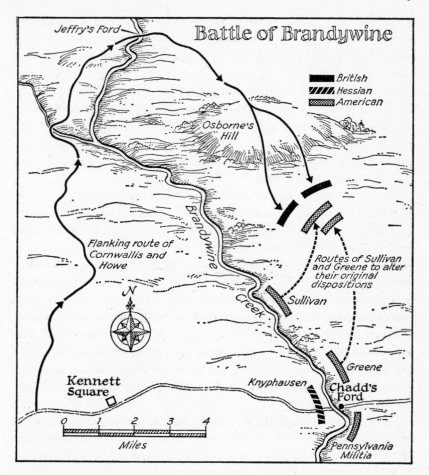

Hessian Jagers on the left — watched the cannonade. Although anxious to charge, they stood fast. The sight inspired awe and terror. Joseph Townsend, a Quaker youth of twenty, said the British arms and bayonets "shone bright as silver" in the glaring sun. Cornwallis and Howe sat erectly astride their horses, splendid figures in red coats, gold lace, and gold epaulets.[41]

At around four o'clock that afternoon the British soldiers

finally received the order to charge. The two generals watched
as the panoramic splendor opened before them. Despite the
death and mutilation that ensued, there was a strange beauty
about a British army in attack. It was a set-piece engagement
that Cornwallis relished. A band struck up the lively "British
Grenadiers," [42] and the "exactly formed columns marched down
the long slope of Osborne's Hill and across the vale. There was
no irregularity, no hurry. They came on with the arrogant assurance that marked the disciplined troops of that period of formal dress-parade warfare." [43] The Americans reeled back from
the charge. Soon Sullivan's entire corps gave way, save only
some isolated units which managed to fight the British "muzzle
to muzzle" for nearly an hour. Only the appearance of Greene
spared them annihilation. He brought up two brigades and deployed them effectively enough to allow Sullivan's broken men
to melt through them, re-form, and retreat in an orderly
fashion.

Knyphausen, however, had not been idle. He had opened a
terrific bombardment against the Americans at Chadd's Ford at
ten o'clock that morning. When Washington had to weaken the
forces facing the German in order to support Sullivan, Knyphausen's corps had attacked across the Brandywine and hurled
the Americans back. Washington's army had been hit in front,
flank, and rear. It might have been destroyed had not darkness
closed the action.[44]

Cornwallis entered Philadelphia in conquering triumph. He
did not remain in the city long enough, however, to savor the
fruits of victory. Although he was not with the forces that
fought Washington at Germantown, he did have a skirmish with
the Americans soon afterward along the Delaware. In mid-
November he occupied one of their forts on the river that Howe
needed in order to protect his supply route to Philadelphia.[45]
In early December he led the van of the army in another of Sir
William's attempts to draw Washington into a general engagement. Washington declined the offer, although some hotly con-

tested small fights took place. On December 11, Cornwallis once again skirmished with Americans when he led out a foraging expedition.[46] But winter now settled upon the armies, and the Earl foresaw little prospect for action until the spring. He therefore asked Howe for that leave to go home which had been postponed nearly a year before because of the affair at Trenton. Howe, of course, granted the request.

He left for England with Howe's dispatches on December 13 and arrived home about mid-January, 1778. Cornwallis devoted most of the next three months to personal affairs — his wife, family, and estates. He also took the trouble to visit the families of his fellow officers, Grey and Clinton.[47] Public business, of course, demanded some of his time: he informed the government of the war's progress and voted on the side of government in critical debates in the Lords.[48] But he had never been a parliamentary orator, so he attended Parliament infrequently. On the other hand, he did find time to dabble in another portion of public business, one requiring no oratory — administration. Eventually the subject of his dabbling became his occupation in India, at the ordnance, and in Ireland.

The Tower hamlets, of which he was lord lieutenant and *custos rotulorum,* scarcely demanded the concentration that he later accorded to the affairs of India. But they offered him his first opportunity to improve administration in an organization for which he held sole responsibility. He never regarded his office as a sinecure. When he actually began examining conditions in the hamlets, he decided to institute changes. He held responsibility for the administration of justice in his "liberty" (as it was called) and for trials and imprisonments. He discovered, however, that neither the courthouse nor the jail was in decent repair. Indeed, his bailiff, Richard Ruston, reported to him that if nothing were done to repair the decay, "all prisoners committed to the present prison will escape, and there will not be any court house for the justices to hold their session, or for

the court of pleas, or court leet to sit in, or any place of confinement for felons, and other persons committing misdemeanors as
aforesaid, nor any place for debtors." Since hitherto he had
been fighting in America, this was the first opportunity he had
had to oversee the administration personally. When a grand
jury supported the bailiff's report, Cornwallis determined to improve matters. First, he personally investigated conditions and
found them as bad as represented. Then, on March 10, he urged
the treasury to undertake the necessary repairs. After its usual
diddling, the treasury authorized the board of works to go ahead
with the necessary reconstruction in early August. By that time,
of course, the Earl was back in America and the bailiff was probably reduced to a mass of nerves, fearing prisoner escapes daily.
The repairs at any rate now bore a promise of completion.[49]

Cornwallis also undertook another needed reform in the
spring of 1778. His position as constable of the Tower entitled
him to a house in that grim fortress, a house in which he never
resided. He naturally preferred the comforts of a large apart-
ment or house for his visits to London. He took his duties as
constable seriously, however, so he looked at his house during a
visit to the Tower. He found it in total disrepair, a situation
which he deemed both wasteful and unnecessary. The structure
occupied an area that could more properly be used as dwellings
for men who did have to live at the Tower. He therefore recommended to the treasury either that his house be torn down and
two new ones raised in its stead for the deputy lieutenant and
major of the Tower or, if that were too expensive, that it be
restored and converted into two separate residences for them.
Again he got results. The treasury referred his memorial to the
board of works on June 23, the board made recommendations
on June 26, and repairs began toward the end of July.[50]

Cornwallis did not remain to see the results of his administrative efforts. He hoped to leave for America in early spring, and

the sailing of North's peace commissioners presented the opportunity. Ignoring their grumbles and growls, he forced them to
make room for him on their ship, the *Trident*. They sailed
from England on April 21. Cornwallis enjoyed this voyage to
North America much more than his earlier stormy trip from
Cork. Although he and his suite (in New York he had seventeen servants, but probably not all of them came with him in the
Trident) took up some of the space that Lord Carlisle, one of
the members of the peace commission, would have preferred for
his own purposes, the Earl and his fellow peers soon became
good friends. Perhaps they enlivened their long passage with
rounds of whist, Cornwallis' favorite card game. Certainly they
dined together, a practice they continued in New York during
the coming summer.[51]

On June 3, Cornwallis reached the Delaware, and a few days
later he came up to Philadelphia.[52] He arrived just in time to
fight his last major battle in the northern part of America. To
be sure, he was still a subordinate in the bloody affair at Monmouth Courthouse, but his status had changed during his stay in
England. On October 22 of the previous year, shortly before
Cornwallis had left America, Howe had sent in his resignation.
Germain had received it in December and presented it to the
Cabinet for consideration. For two months the Cabinet mulled
over its course of action. Once it even offered the American
command to Lord Amherst, who wisely declined it. Finally the
ministers decided upon the only logical course. They accepted
Howe's resignation in early February and promoted his second,
Sir Henry Clinton, to the command.[53] Cornwallis, in turn, automatically became second in command. Shortly before he left
England Germain tendered him a dormant commission bestow-
ing upon him the rank of general in America only.[54] The government customarily bestowed such commissions on the American seconds — Clinton had held one under Howe — in order to
insure that British instead of German generals would assume

control in America should anything happen to the commander in chief. This precaution, however sensible, scarcely fostered good relations between the American commander in chief and his second. For the subordinate always knew that only one man stood between him and supreme command. Even if the men were friends, the dormant commission tended to draw them apart.

Clinton and Cornwallis were still friends, but already the war had strained their relations. The first rift had opened between them after White Plains when Cornwallis had revealed to Howe a derogatory comment that Clinton had made about the commander in chief. They had apparently smoothed over their disagreement since then, and in March Cornwallis had written a warm letter to his new commander. "I must sincerely hope to find the war over," Cornwallis said, "but should that not be the case, I will do all in my power to contribute to your ease in a situation which I fear you will not find a bed of Roses. That health, happiness & success may attend you is the sincere wish of your very faithful servant and friend." [55] Yet Clinton only half believed these professions. He convinced himself that Cornwallis only went home in the first place in order to "plan a command for himself similar to Burgoyne's, with a commission of genl. or at least Lt. g." [56] Nor did Cornwallis himself, once he got to Philadelphia, do everything he could to contribute to Sir Henry's ease. Almost as soon as he landed he requested to be relieved of command and to be allowed to return to England.[57]

Personal considerations alone, however, did not motivate him. The ministry had altered its entire scheme of operations. With France's entry into the war, it had determined to switch the major effort away from the Continent to the Caribbean, where the navy could defend the British sugar islands and possibly help capture some of the French ones. Clinton received orders to chop his army to bits, sending five thousand men to St. Lucia and three thousand to the Floridas. The remainder of

Clinton's force would have to act defensively. The Cabinet ordered Sir Henry to evacuate Philadelphia and to retreat all the way to Nova Scotia, if necessary. Clinton never had to go that far, but he was preparing to fall back upon New York when Cornwallis arrived. The Earl seethed at the Cabinet's decision, which he gave as his reason for requesting to resign: he did not choose, he said, to serve in a theater where "no offensive operations can be undertaken." [58] The King, however, refused to accept the resignation, for he did not wish to dispense with the services of one of his favorite noblemen. [59]

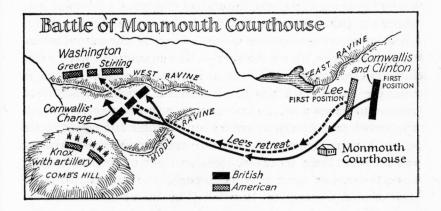

Ironically, less than two weeks after he tried to quit Clinton's army because he thought it would not fight again, Cornwallis found himself in one of the hottest actions he ever fought in America. Clinton undertook "no offensive measures" for another year and a half. But his defensive maneuver of evacuating Philadelphia and returning to New York brought on the battle of Monmouth Courthouse.

Shortly before noon on June 18 Sir Henry began his lumbering march overland from Philadelphia toward New York. His army of ten thousand stretched out for twelve miles along its route of march, encumbered by "provision train, baggage, army wagons, numerous private carriages, a large number of bat-horses, bakeries, laundries and blacksmiths' shops on wheels, large hospital supplies, boats, bridges, magazines — withal a crowd of female camp followers and 'every kind of useless stuff.' " [60] Washington with thirteen thousand men followed the clumsy British train through New Jersey.[61] When it turned east on the road toward Sandy Hook, instead of north toward the Raritan, the American general apparently decided against a major action. Still, he did not want his enemy to depart totally unscathed. The opportunity he sought was not long in coming. When he discovered that Clinton had divided his forces in half in the vicinity of Monmouth Courthouse — one division under Knyphausen in the advance with the baggage, the second under Cornwallis bringing up the rear — he determined to fall upon Clinton's rear guard. He felt that if he could attack the British rear, the baggage train would hinder the front division from coming to its support. So on June 28, a day of scorching heat, the British and American armies fought their last major battle in the North. General Charles Lee commanded the American van of about four thousand. Within sight of the Monmouth Courthouse, Lee came into contact with the rear of two thou-sand under Cornwallis, supported by about four thousand under Clinton himself. Both British and American forces im-mediately found themselves in difficulties for both were sepa-rated from their main bodies. Lee, however, was in particular trouble, since he had only made contact after marching eastward over three ravines (named West, Middle, and East) "that cut through the sandy pine barrens at right angles to his line of march." Lee, who might have had an opportunity to cut off some detachments of the rear guard, lost his opportunity. Then Clinton and Cornwallis with their six thousand men threw him back over the rough terrain with such effect that Lee's men "ran grave danger of being cut to pieces." Clinton, of course, had to punish his opponent in a hurry. For the farther the American general retreated westward, the closer he came to the main army under Washington, while the farther Clinton and Cornwallis pursued him, the more they separated themselves from the first division under Knyphausen.

The British redcoats, clad in wool uniforms quite unsuitable for the ninety-six degree temperature (in the shade), pushed home their attack with sixty-pound packs on their backs. Many of them fell from heat exhaustion, but their officers drove them on relentlessly. Lee drew back in disorder and confusion through the East and Middle ravines. But by the time he reached West Ravine, the complexion of battle had changed. Washington had now come up with his main force, which he deployed on the west side of West Ravine. Lee's troops found safety when they melted into the American line. A fierce artillery duel now followed for an hour. Clinton, aware of his changed circumstances, decided to feel out the American line and advanced some light infantry and Highland foot against the American left, commanded by Stirling. The Yankees mowed them down. Clinton then tried the American right under Greene. Determined to break through Greene, Sir Henry entrusted Cornwallis to lead the assault with some of the best units of the British army — two regiments of light infantry, a battalion of grenadiers, and a battalion of guards.

It was almost a suicide mission. The Americans had erected an artillery battery on Comb's Hill on the left flank of the British. General Knox, the most brilliant artilleryman in either army, took personal charge of it. The Earl knew his precarious position, yet he led his men forward. As the redcoats charged, an enfilading fire from the American cannon mowed his men down like falling dominos: "one round shot struck the muskets from the hands of an entire platoon." Still he urged his soldiers on against Greene with fixed bayonets and a steady line. The Americans — undoubtedly to his surprise — stood rocklike and poured volley after volley into his superb infantry. These were no longer the rag, tag, and bobtail he had mauled at Brandywine: since then the American Continentals had been disciplined by Steuben and Valley Forge. Cornwallis could not carry the enemy line. Indeed, it scattered and broke his corps. Finally he had to order some of the finest troops of the British army to retreat. He left the field to the Americans.

When a charge on Washington's center also failed, Clinton withdrew his entire army to a sound position behind Middle Ravine. The battle, which had used up most of the day, ended about six o'clock. Washington dared not assault Clinton, who by now was partially entrenched. Anyway, both armies were too tired to do much more. Sunstroke, thirst, and exhaustion had taken nearly as heavy a toll as musket and cannon shot. Clinton rested his men until midnight. Then he resumed his march toward Sandy Hook. Washington let him go.[62]

All in all, Monmouth Courthouse was a standoff. First the Americans retreated. Then the British retreated. Then both sides stood still and stopped fighting. Cornwallis, however, may not have regarded the battle as a draw. In his first venture under Clinton's direct command he had seen no major action at all — indeed, had seen an entire British army retreat from an insignificant fort without firing a shot. In his second action under Clintons's direct command he saw his troops decimated and forced to retreat. He may not have loved Howe, but Howe had always led him to victory. Clinton had never done so. Furthermore, Clinton did not even think well of the counterattack: although he commended Cornwallis for his "zealous services" at Monmouth,[63] in retrospect the commander considered as an error, resulting from either the zealousness of the British light infantry or a misunderstanding of orders, all the British advances after Washington had formed the American army's main line.[64] True, Sir Henry had not done badly, but he had not won. He lacked the dash and vibrant personality that had attached men to Sir William Howe even during his foolish ventures. Clinton was a better general than Howe. But to Cornwallis, in 1778, he had proven himself neither a better general nor a better man.

At Monmouth Courthouse Cornwallis fought his last major engagement under another officer's leadership. No doubt already disgruntled at the outcome, as the summer passed and no possibilities opened for the action he craved, he developed an aversion to further service in America. He could do nothing but sit in New York with Clinton's army. Only once, in the fall, did he have a chance for action, and then it was action not to his liking. He commanded an operation designed to entrap a regiment of Continental horse and a body of American militia, but which instead ended in a bayonet massacre of the Continental dragoons while they slept.[65]

Small actions against helpless men, however, scarcely satisfied the Earl's conception of honor or his thirst for action in the open field. He had not joined the army to sit around New York City or to send out redcoats to bayonet Americans in their sleep. When he made up his mind to go home and resign his commission is not known. Possibly it was word of his wife's illness that brought him to the decision. Clinton could hardly refuse his subordinate's application for leave. Germain had in the previous spring ordered Sir Henry to grant Cornwallis permission to return in case the peace commissioners had managed to arrange a cessation of hostilities.[66] Hostilities still continued, but Clinton planned no offensive operations. In any case winter would soon hinder movement. Furthermore, Sir Henry considered heavy reinforcements for his army imperative, and toyed with the idea of resigning if the ministry did not send them out to him.[67] Cornwallis agreed on the need for more troops. Clinton believed that if the Earl went home he could, with his rank, his friendships (even with the King), and his influence, persuade the government to ship over the desired reinforcements. The two men had patched up past differences and again seemed on the best of terms. "You may depend on my taking care of your letters," Cornwallis told Sir Henry the day before he sailed, "& seeing your children, & obeying your commands in every respect." On November 27, 1778, Cornwallis left Sandy Hook, again in company with the peace commissioners who had failed in their mission. After a short passage they dropped anchor at Plymouth on December 19.[68]

His wife's illness prevented Cornwallis from pleading determinedly for Clinton's reinforcements. He arrived in London on the twenty-third and discussed Clinton's situation with Sir Henry's cousin, the second Duke of Newcastle. But he talked neither to Germain nor to the King, except to resign his position in the American army. The monarch now accepted the resignation he had refused before.[69] Cornwallis then hurried up to Suffolk to the bedside of his ailing wife.

He spent perhaps the bleakest Christmas of his life in the lovely, rolling countryside he loved so much. He found his lady in "a very weak state indeed," [70] and nothing he did seemed to help her. He stayed by her side all through January and into February, refusing to leave his country home either for business or for the relaxations of society.[71] Toward the end of January, for the only time in his life, he became frantic with anxiety. "The very ill state of health in which I found Lady Cornwallis," he wrote Clinton, "has render'd me incapable of any attention but to her, & the thoughts of her danger is forever present in my mind." [72] Still the Countess weakened. On February 14, 1779, she died.[73]

Her death was the greatest emotional experience in Charles' life. Always outwardly calm, whether in the society of friends or the heat of battle, he nonetheless broke down when his wife died. Everyone noticed his "greatest distress." For a while he would neither see nor talk to anyone.[74] Even in letters he could not control his emotions. Normally cool in conversation, he believed that good taste forbade sentimentality and metaphor in letters. But even so long as eight months after Lady Cornwallis' death, his deep feeling for her overcame his natural reserve. In correspondence with his brother he admitted that Jemima's passing had "effectually destroyed all my hopes of happiness in this world." The mere thought of her, he said, was enough to "harrow up" his soul.[75]

Everything he loved became repugnant to him. His young family, his beautiful country, his ancestral home — all served to remind him of his wife. He had to get away. Only the army promised him a change of scenery and a chance to work himself out of his sorrow. It could not console him for his loss nor make him forget his wife, but it might tear him away from obsession with her memory. It might give him new life and new action.

By early April in 1779 he had made up his mind to return to the service, and even to America, if the King and Clinton would have him. He poured out a portion of his feelings to Clinton in a letter on April 4. He did not wish to command in America, he told Sir Henry, and he hesitated to return lest Clinton should resign, which would force that responsibility upon him. Yet he wished to be back in the fight for empire. If Clinton planned any operations in the South, or against the French islands, he would "with great pleasure come out & meet you; This country has now no charms for me, & I am perfectly indifferent as to what part of the world I may go." [76] But the Earl's desire to return to service soon overrode his hesitations about supreme command. By April 9, he had determined to come back to America regardless of what happened as a result.[77] The King willingly accepted his offer. Thus by early May he again prepared to embark. "I am now returning to America," he wrote his brother William, "not with views of conquest and ambition, nothing brilliant can be expected in that quarter; but I find this country quite unsupportable to me. I must shift the scene; I have many friends in the American army; I love that army, and flatter myself that I am not quite indifferent to them." [78]

In May only one item of business separated him from that army — the parliamentary inquiry into the conduct of General Howe. He did not testify gladly, but his new resolve to overcome his grief showed itself during his appearance before the House of Commons. He marched in with confidence. He even sat for two or three minutes with his hat on, as if defying the world. Before the proceedings started he told members firmly that under no circumstances would he answer questions of opinion (a position to which he adhered) and that Howe "deserved greatly of his country," which he had served "with fidelity, assiduity, and with great ability." Charles Cornwallis had now recovered his strength, his resolve, his personality, and his dedication to the army. No civilians would hang the general who had led that army to victory after victory in America.[79]

As soon as the Commons finished with his testimony he sailed for America, where he arrived on July 21. Horace Walpole, the prolific writer and gossip, commented acidly at the time Cornwallis departed: "I remember when I was a boy hearing that it had been a great joke in Queen Anne's war that Lord Peterborough was galloping about in Spain inquiring for his army — Lord Cornwallis will have none to hunt for." [80] In the end, however, Walpole proved a poor prophet. The most exciting part of Cornwallis' life in the New World lay ahead of him. Not only would he find the army that Walpole believed ephemeral, but he would also command a large portion of it.

PART III

The General Gets a Command

Success in South Carolina

CHAPTER 6

A Taste of Independence
Autumn, 1779, to Summer, 1780

CLINTON SEEMED TO WELCOME the return of his chief subordinate. "I must beg leave to express how happy I am made by the return of Lord Cornwallis to this country," he wrote to Germain. "His lordship's indefatigable Zeal, his knowledge of the Country, his professional Ability, and the high estimation in which he is held by this Army, must naturally give me the warmest confidence of efficacious support from him in every undertaking which opportunity may prompt, and our circumstances allow." [1] Clinton's pleasure, however, was destined to be short-lived. Almost immediately after he wrote to Germain, the previously strained friendship between Clinton and Cornwallis began to dissolve. It needed only a push for the two men to grow so distant that neither one would speak to the other save when protocol demanded it.

Given Clinton's personality — a personality so different from Cornwallis' — the break was perhaps inevitable in any event. Clinton was a complex of contradictions, and he rarely showed his best side to the world. As a general he was perhaps the soundest planner in the American war, whether designing single battles, campaigns, or grand strategy. Yet as a commander he rarely showed a single-minded devotion to carrying out his plans, so obviously correct to him when as a subordinate he did not hold responsibility for their execution. He feared responsibility yet, despite his protestations to the contrary, enjoyed being the supreme commander, a post for which he was temperamentally unfit. He invariably understood opposition to his ideas to mean disloyalty to him personally and, as a consequence, lost as friends most of his colleagues in America. And while he hated opposition of any sort, he did not have the strength of will to stop it. He was afraid to face and argue with people who disagreed with him and to give them a precise and clear statement of his wishes. Instead he would resort to letter writing, in which he so contradicted himself that his subordinates often could not understand what he wanted. So they would simply come to dislike and disregard him and go their own way.

Since Clinton allowed them to do so, his own plans often would not be carried out. When they failed, however, Sir Henry would never take the blame for failure. Somebody else was always at fault. He would concoct orders from superiors telling him not to do this or that if, as a result of his own inaction, an operation failed. Also, of course, he believed his subordinates always crossed him. For wrongs real or imagined, he had a memory like an elephant and wrote down most of what he remembered. Thus he would gather information on individuals, noting their foibles, their casual conversations, their tone of voice, even their facial expressions. Later if these men opposed some plan of his, he would turn their opposition, based upon his minute observations, into a conspiracy against him. Then he would make up imaginary conversations in which he faced them with their treachery and forced them to admit it and to apologize to him humbly. As a result, few people liked or trusted Sir Henry Clinton. He had many strengths, but he simply could not get along with people, especially when he was in a position of authority.

Even if Cornwallis had arrived in New York as a complete stranger to Clinton, their respective situations probably would have turned them eventually into enemies. Clinton's disapproval of Howe's generalship and his itching to replace him had brought about a coolness between those two long before Howe's resignation. Only the unusual subordinate does not envy his superior.

But the difficult relationship between Clinton and Cornwallis was aggravated by a history of past disagreements. Perhaps the first one came with Cornwallis' disillusionment over Charleston. He certainly cannot have been satisfied with Clinton's leadership there, although he probably kept his opinions to himself. Bad feeling flared into the open, however, after Howe withdrew before Washington at White Plains. Clinton commanded the rear guard moving to Dobb's Ferry. He decided to alter its route of march from that originally stipulated, only to be confronted by a message from Sir William bidding him to do as he was told. Furious, Clinton shouted to Cornwallis: "I cannot bear to serve under him, and had rather command three companies by myself than hold my post [as] I have done last campaign in his army."[2] Although Clinton did not discover it until nearly a year later, Cornwallis carried this remark to Howe. The Earl must have been highly displeased with Clinton's conduct, for "tattling" was an act totally uncharacteristic of him. Even as a youth of twenty-five, he had written of one Charles Hope that "although he abandoned his friends so shamefully last winter in Parliament, [he] cannot I think be villain enough to read my letter."[3] Now the Earl came close to doing that which he condemned in others. The spoken word had not quite the sanctity of the written word, but it still could reveal a man's innermost feelings. He may not have read Clinton's letters, but he carried Clinton's words to a man the general obviously had never intended them to reach. Cornwallis had a nice sense of honor, especially where his friends were involved. Yet he tattled. Was he motivated by loyalty to Howe or military ethics

(Clinton had skated very near both disobedience and defiance)? Or did he merely feel that after his fiasco at Charleston, Clinton had no business criticizing Howe, who had led the British to one victory after another?

To outward appearances Clinton and Cornwallis continued friends after White Plains. But neither of them forgot their differences, which came to the surface again in July of 1777. In that month Clinton tried to dissuade his chief from his foolish plan to go by sea to Pennsylvania. He did not succeed. Indeed, his words had no more effect than rain drops falling in the sea. By then Clinton and Howe had become totally alienated. In the course of their argument they dredged up, as people will, their differences of the past two years. Inevitably the White Plains incident entered into their conversation. During an interview on July 6, Howe accused his subordinate of "criticizing his chief's operations to other officers." Clinton stiffened. Howe's enmity he had expected but not treachery from a friend. Clinton's anger did not help him present his case to Sir William. It served, however, to reopen old sores. Shortly after the July 6 interview, Sir Henry upbraided the Earl for his betrayal of a confidence. Cornwallis, according to Clinton, "made a very awkward apology." [4] It may indeed have been awkward. Cornwallis knew he had been wrong to bear tales, but Clinton's reminding him of it now, a year after the event, scarcely warmed his feelings toward Sir Henry.

Once again they patched up their differences. Howe went off with Cornwallis to Philadelphia. Clinton stayed in New York. Time and distance may have healed the old wounds, but the scars remained, and in bad weather they throbbed. Cornwallis looked in on Clinton's family while on leave in England in 1778. The two exchanged cordial letters. Of course, neither man forgot. Clinton (who readily convinced himself of conspiracies where none existed) believed Cornwallis schemed for an independent command when he was home in 1778. When they

met again in Philadelphia in June of that same year, Clinton
had command of an army under orders not to take the offensive.
Although the two men greeted each other warmly, Cornwallis
almost immediately requested to resign. The battle at Monmouth Courthouse followed, providing him another sample of
Clinton's leadership against Americans. Again he must have
been dissatisfied. Not only had Sir Henry failed to win, but also
he had contrived — so it may have seemed to Cornwallis — to
humiliate his second in the face of the enemy.

Again they glossed over their disputes and continued ami-
cably until Cornwallis went home in late 1778 and resigned.
Had his wife survived, the two men might eventually have
buried their past differences and remained friends to the end of
their lives. But Jemima's death brought the Earl back to the
army and renewed his close contact with Clinton. Future events
would take him and his superior further and further apart.

When Cornwallis sailed into New York Harbor in July, 1779,
he did not bring with him the large reinforcements that Clinton
had hoped he would. Almost at once, the disgruntled Sir
Henry turned in his resignation: since the government had not
sent him the reinforcements he had requested, he felt compelled
to turn the command over to someone else.[5] Yet he naturally
could not leave until he knew whether the ministry had accepted or rejected his request. Thus for a long while, neither
Clinton nor Cornwallis knew from one day to the next who
would command on the morrow. All during that fall and into
the winter, both men served together in New York, waiting for
the ministry's response. Even with nothing else between them,
they might, under these circumstances, have come to dislike
each other intensely. There were, however, other things between them. Inevitably, each man brooded over the wrongs he
thought the other had done him. Neither was guiltless, but each
may have believed himself so. Even if one admitted to himself

that he had wronged the other, that self-knowledge did not lay the groundwork for a better relationship. No wonder tongues wagged in New York! Gossip had it, before the end of 1779, that Cornwallis had "no sincere regard for his chief." [6]

Only separation — by distance and by an independent command — could have restored the Earl's "sincere regard." The last chance for such a happy event came in September when the governor of Jamaica appealed to Sir Henry for reinforcements against an expected French attack. Clinton, reluctant to spare troops from a projected invasion of the South, nonetheless allowed Cornwallis and Marriot Arbuthnot, the admiral commanding at New York, to persuade him to support the governor's request. The Earl, naturally enough, "was very anxious for the measure and with a commendable zeal offered himself to conduct it." [7] So, Sir Henry, "entirely ignorant of the state of the island of Jamaica, its force, or G[overnor] Dalling's projects defensive," in late September sent Cornwallis off to the Caribbean with four thousand troops. The convoy barely cleared Sandy Hook before it turned back. On the third day out it chanced upon a ship with news that the French admiral D'Estaing was making for North America, not Jamaica. The British convoy, of course, immediately put about for New York. Grumbling at his misfortune and tormented by rheumatism, Cornwallis almost refused to believe this new intelligence that forced him back into Clinton's army. His chances for an independent command seemed to have slipped by.[8]

Neither general liked the return to their previous situation. Of the two, Cornwallis was probably the unhappier, for he wanted action. He would have preferred action of any sort to idling in New York with a man whom he did not trust. On the other hand, although Clinton never seemed to mind sitting around with an army — he did it for most of the time he held supreme command — he cannot have been happy with his eager, impatient, and unfriendly subordinate always watching him. If they could not get away from each other, they both needed some diversion.

A campaign to the south at last offered that diversion. The British had first opened a successful offensive there in 1778 with an expedition to Georgia supported by troops from St. Augustine, Florida. By the middle of February, 1778, they had taken both Savannah and Augusta. Redcoats even threatened Charleston in May, but they had to retreat to defend Savannah in September. The same D'Estaing who had forced the abandonment of the Jamaica expedition joined with Americans to besiege Savannah from the middle of September to the middle of October. But the British repulsed a premature American assault so decisively that the Franco-American force abandoned the siege. Georgia remained under the Union Jack.

When he learned of D'Estaing's repulse, Clinton considered the time opportune to put Georgia's neighboring provinces under the same flag. Lord George Germain agreed, for he had long hoped to strike a deathblow to the American cause in the South. Royal officials there had also pressed for an offensive. Now, with Georgia secure and the Jamaican expedition defunct, the time seemed to be ripe for the move south. Clinton had enough troops to hold New York while he took six thousand men south to besiege Charleston and to garrison the interior. He also had the promise of naval support from Arbuthnot's fleet. So in December he began embarking. Cornwallis, anxious to fight again, greeted the expedition with enthusiasm.[9]

The elements may have dampened his enthusiasm somewhat, for again they challenged him, just as they had in 1776. Wind, waves, and ice hindered the embarkation of the Earl's own 33d regiment. On December 10, boats full of troops put out toward the ships, only to be forced back.[10] Finally, after a prolonged struggle, they got the transports loaded. On the day after Christmas they put to sea in company with Arbuthnot's warships. The voyage turned into a frightful ordeal. Ice in New York harbor destroyed seven transports at the very beginning. The mountainous seas which hit the rest as soon as they left sheltered waters inflicted severe damage. Heavy winds blew one transport clear across the ocean and fetched it up at St. Ives, Cornwall. The fleet took over a month to reach the shelter of the Tybee River, near Savannah. During the long voyage men lost their baggage, horses died, and clothing was ripped to shreds. Cornwallis endured the trip better than Clinton, who was a terrible sailor, but both men must have suffered. The voyage certainly cannot have improved their dispositions toward each other.

At the Tybee River, Sir Henry and the Earl laid their plans for the siege of Charleston. Clinton of necessity consulted his second closely on all matters. Orders might come from the ministry any day accepting Sir Henry's resignation and appointing the Earl his successor. If operations bogged down after Sir Henry relinquished command, Clinton figured his second could not blame him for the trouble if both men had agreed previously on the campaign's broad outlines. They did in fact agree. For Charleston and its garrison lay temptingly vulnerable to a classical siege. If General Lincoln, the American commander, determined to defend the city at all costs, he would doom his army of five thousand men.[11] Charleston sat at the end of a neck of land between the Ashley (on the west) and Cooper (on the east) Rivers. If the British could manage to establish themselves on both rivers and across the back of the neck, the defenders could not escape. Only an overwhelmingly powerful fleet or army could save them, and no such succor appeared likely.

Clinton set to work and with "supreme competence" carried out the siege. He secured guns and gunners from the fleet. He "requested artillery and stores from St. Augustine, the West Indies, and the Bahamas." He sent to New York for reinforcements and he ordered most of the forces in Georgia to come to his aid.[12] Naval support proved a thornier problem for him, since he was not on the best of terms with Arbuthnot. Yet the army needed the navy. Without having command of the waterways, the army could not cross the Ashley River on the east of the city, build up its siege lines along the neck, and extend itself across the Cooper to cut off the Americans.

Both geography and the city put some obstacles in the way of that command. A bar outside the harbor effectually blocked the entrance for all vessels save small ones. Arbuthnot eventually left his ships of the line outside the bar. He did not even try to bring his frigates over until he had lightened them by removing their guns and provisions. Finally on March 20, both frigates and small craft passed safely over. Once across the bar, however, Fort Moultrie on Sullivan's Island still challenged the navy. It dominated the narrow channel which led to the upper harbor of the city itself, and it had repulsed Parker four years earlier. Yet Arbuthnot managed to run his ships past the guns with relatively little trouble and to anchor safely in the upper harbor in early April.

During Arbuthnot's maneuvering, Clinton established his siege lines. He landed his main body at Simmons (Seabrook) Island on February 14 and moved them up the North Edisto inlet toward the city. After Arbuthnot passed his ships over the bar on March 20, the army used his smaller craft to ferry itself across the Ashley. On April 1, Clinton broke ground for the siege works. Two days later he completed the first, two-mile-long parallel. When Arbuthnot's squadron a week later ran past the guns of Fort Moultrie and anchored before the city, Charleston's fate was nearly decided. Only the Cooper offered a means of entrance or exit from the city. Arbuthnot refused to send ships up the river so on April 12 Clinton sent Lieutenant Colonel Webster, of Cornwallis' own 33d, with fifteen hundred men to secure the Cooper's upper reaches. Soon, however, Webster was destined to turn the command of that force over to Cornwallis.

The Earl's position in the army had changed abruptly on

March 19 when the long-awaited letter from Germain arrived.
It shattered whatever hopes Cornwallis may have nourished for
becoming commander in chief. The ministry was "too well satisfied" with Sir Henry's achievements to let him resign, even
though it praised Cornwallis' abilities. Once he learned the
ministerial decision, Clinton's second altered his entire attitude.
Sir Henry had hitherto consulted him during every stage of the
siege. Now Cornwallis requested that he be consulted no more.
"The Earl," the historian William Willcox notes, "was in a
difficult position. He was trying to evade a responsibility that
belonged by rights, not to a subordinate, but to the commander
in chief. He had been willing to assume some of that responsibility when he had expected the command, just as he had been
willing to draw the courtiers away from headquarters. Now he
had to retreat." [13] Cornwallis would play second fiddle to Clinton's tune no longer. He had patiently supported his superior
when each mail brought the possibility of his succession. Patience vanished with the lost hope.

So the Earl requested a separate command and withdrew completely from the commander in chief. Clinton boiled over. At
first he contemplated forcing his second back into the old relationship by demanding his formal advice in council. Then he
called the Earl to an interview at the beginning of the siege,
raked up old scores, and discovered new ones. He insinuated
that the differences between the two men had resulted in the
junior officers' aligning themselves on the side of Cornwallis
against their commander in chief. One junior had even said
"with a sneer," Sir Henry fumed, that if Clinton wanted to resign all he had to do was ask the King once more. Cornwallis
denied that anyone close to him had ever said anything about
Clinton's command "with a sneer." Indeed, he asserted that he
had only returned to America to support Clinton, not to take his
job, and that he had told the King so. But he also counterattacked with a new issue. He reprobated his chief for his failure

to enforce the ministerial order that officers with commissions in both provincial and regular regiments should resign either the one or the other. This negligence, the Earl charged, had antagonized the officers of the army, and he himself sympathized with their grievance. Clinton, who had long ago promised to end the dual commissions, lamely assured his subordinate that he had only received official instructions on the matter the day before their interview. He could not resist adding that Cornwallis should not encourage complaint, "calculated only to make me enemies in the army." In the end, neither man received satisfaction. Cornwallis still did not have an independent command. Clinton still believed that the Earl's "unmilitary" conduct was undermining the commander's position.

Sir Henry grew nearly frantic when he discovered that Cornwallis maintained reasonably cordial relations with Admiral Arbuthnot, whom he had grown to dislike and distrust exceedingly. To be sure, the admiral has been described as "imperceptive and vacillating." Clinton, however, took him for a sinister villain plotting behind his back. Sir Henry soon convinced himself that both the army and the navy hated him. He could do nothing about the navy, for Arbuthnot was his equal rather than his subordinate. But he could send Cornwallis away.

Clinton consulted with his aide-de-camp, Major John André, as to how and where to send the Earl. André advised Sir Henry to detach Cornwallis with a command separate from the main army. Webster's corps suited that purpose. When reinforcements arrived from New York, Clinton hastened Cornwallis on the way with nineteen hundred men. On the night of April 23, Sir Henry called in the Earl for last-minute instructions. Cornwallis' mission was to "seize the Rebel Communication." [14] The next day he crossed the river and took up his headquarters at St. Thomas' Church. [15]

Cornwallis new duties took him away from the siege of Charleston, and he never returned to the city until after it had fallen. He did not direct the British bombardment. He did not witness a moment of eighteenth-century gallantry when on May 5 Clinton allowed some American ladies to enter the town to take leave of their sons. He did not hear, save from a distance, the terrific bombardment of May 9 and 10, which broke the American will to resist, nor did he watch the ceremonies of Lincoln's surrender on the twelfth. And yet, while he missed the main events of the siege, he ensured its success by slamming shut the only door — across the Cooper — by which the Americans might have escaped.[16]

Two strong points in particular engrossed his attention. The first one the Americans had erected at Lampries Point (spelled in different ways) at the termination of the Cooper and Wando Rivers opposite the northern part of Charleston. It commanded the entrance to the river by the Hog Island channel. The second strong point at Mount Pleasant on Hedral's Point (also spelled in different ways) below Fort Moultrie lay within easy artillery range of Arbuthnot's ships. Within a short time, Americans placed an 18-pounder on Mount Pleasant and fired on the British squadron. The Admiral, of course, feared they meant to erect a complete battery against his fleet. He wanted the army to clear the strong points before his ships entered the Cooper, but Clinton insisted that the army could not secure the posts until the navy controlled the river. By late April matters had reached an impasse.

Cornwallis helped remove the difficulty. First he led a force against Mount Pleasant in the early morning of April 26. The Americans scuttled away, and he captured the worrisome eighteen-pounder without firing a shot. Lampries remained. That afternoon Cornwallis reconnoitered the position and discussed with Arbuthnot, who had rowed ashore, how best to take it. The Earl did not want to bring his forces together for an assault, because "my remaining here so long," he explained to the Admiral, "would probably defeat the intent of my passing the Cooper River." On the contrary, he thought he should scatter his forces to cover the various escape routes. Yet only a large body of men could carry the post, especially since the American armed shipping on the Cooper River would fire into any storming party. Lampries had to be taken, for it opened the door "to the only complete investiture of Charleston on this side the Cooper." Perhaps as a favor to Cornwallis Arbuthnot finally decided to risk part of his own forces in an assault. On the night of April 27, the Admiral landed a detachment of five hundred marines and sailors who took the post without opposition, capturing three 18-pounders and two 4-pounders. Cornwallis then sent Major Patrick Ferguson, of the 71st regiment, to take possession.[17] The Earl had sealed off the last escape route. A despairing rebel wrote his wife on April 30: "Our communication is entirely cut off from the country (excepting by small boat at great risque) by Lord Cornwallis, who occupies every landing-place from Haddrill's Point, a considerable way up the river, with two thousand five hundred men." [18]

Cornwallis had disposed his troops well and ensured the fall of Charleston, but he himself had seen virtually no action at all. His subordinate, Lieutenant Colonel Banastre Tarleton of the British Legion had already routed the enemy once: he had fallen upon Brigadier General Isaac Huger's cavalry at Monck's Corner before Cornwallis had come to the command.[19] Then on May 2, Ferguson stormed and carried a small redoubt on a bridge that led from Mount Pleasant to Sullivan's Island.[20] On May 6, Tarleton again drew blood. As Cornwallis pushed inland he detached the Legion commander against Colonel William Washington, who was attempting to cross the Santee at Lenud's Ferry. Tarleton cut his force to ribbons.[21] But Cornwallis shared these victories from a distance. He was never at the scene of action, danger, or glory. As the siege progressed and the Americans weakened, he grew restive. Rumor reached him that Clinton planned an assault, and in his eagerness to partici-

pate the Earl momentarily forgot the past troubles that lay between himself and his superior. He pleaded to return and join
any storming party Sir Henry intended to push forward. "I
shall take it as a favour," he said, "if you will let me be of the
party. I can be with you in eight hours from your sending to
me. I should be happy to attend my old friends, the grenadiers
and light infantry. . . ." [22] But Clinton never needed to storm,
for Lincoln surrendered on May 12. At last Sir Henry had won
a victory, but Cornwallis was too far away to share in the triumph.

While the Earl moved toward Camden to continue his task of
securing the interior, Clinton remained in Charleston to organize the conquest. He detached forces to different parts of the
backcountry to help in the task of pacification. He created a
board of police for the city. He formed loyalists into militia regiments and entrusted their supervision to Ferguson, whom he
appointed inspector of militia. Furthermore, in order to bring
the rebels back to their allegiance — he and Arbuthnot, after
all, were commissioners for restoring peace — Clinton issued a
series of proclamations which culminated in one of June 3.
Both Ferguson's appointment and the June 3 proclamation
later brought incalculable trouble to the Earl, and rendered
doubly difficult his task of restoring the Carolinas to royal government. Sir Henry undoubtedly did not intend such a result,
but he failed to recognize the magnitude of the problem, and he
was in a hurry to get back to New York. "I am clear in opinion," he wrote his friend Phillips, "that the Carolinas have been
conquered in Charleston." [23] They had not been conquered
there, as the Earl soon discovered. Clinton's measures had not
even simplified the job of conquest.

That job remained for Cornwallis, who requested to stay and
command the southern forces after Clinton left for New York.
Sir Henry readily granted the request. Cornwallis, as the senior
officer next to the commander in chief, deserved the command.

Furthermore, the two men did not enjoy each other's company. "Whenever he [Cornwallis] is with me," Clinton told a friend, "there are symptoms I do not like." [24] Clinton boarded the *Romulus* in early June, anxious to be off for the North where he planned a surprise for the Americans in New Jersey. Just before he sailed, Cornwallis sent him a going-away present, news of another Tarleton victory. Cornwallis had detached the Legion commander against a regiment of 350 Continentals under Colonel Abraham Buford. Buford had started out to help relieve Charleston and had marched to within forty miles of the city before it fell. When news reached him of the surrender, he hastily turned around and quick-stepped north. Tarleton rode one hundred five miles in fifty-four hours, caught the Virginians at the Waxhaws and badly trounced them. He killed, wounded, or captured 316 men. Clinton received the casualty accounts on June 5.[25] Three days later he sailed, leaving the fate of British arms in the South to his second. Charles, Earl Cornwallis, after four hard years of campaigning directly under someone else's orders, now at last was to enjoy a taste of independence.

He applied himself to his tasks immediately. They would not prove easy. He needed to reestablish government, organize militia, deal with the disaffected, post military garrisons into the interior, supply his army, prepare it for a possible American counterattack from the north, and keep in touch with the British forces in Georgia and Florida. He did not succeed universally in all these endeavors, but he created imaginative and basically sound arrangements in one summer of work at Charleston. Had not the incursions of American regulars induced him to move north, South Carolina might have remained British for many years.

The week before his departure, Clinton had hastily drafted instructions, supplemented by a memorandum which prescribed the Earl's powers and responsibilities. Cornwallis could post his forces where he deemed necessary and could act offensively or defensively. He could manage all stores and provisions, but it should be done with the "utmost economy." He could give any orders he chose to the British troops in Georgia and the two Floridas, but he should forward to Clinton copies of such orders as well as messages from army commanders outside of South Carolina. His warrant constituted sufficient authority for the paymaster general to issue money. He had the power to hold general courts martial and to confirm all sentences, save capital ones and those that reduced commissioned officers in grade. He might even confirm these sentences in "very singular circumstances." He could also embody militia and organize captures. Save that he should communicate from time to time with Clinton, Cornwallis had virtually independent powers.

Yet despite the wide latitude and the discretion they allowed, these orders helped account for Yorktown. Nearly half of them concerned operations in the Chesapeake Bay area. Clinton had planned a campaign there before the threat of the French forced his return to New York. Sir Henry did not relinquish the Chesapeake plan just because he would not be there to conduct it personally. He instructed the Earl to move north and "recover" North Carolina after he had pacified its southern neighbor. Then, after leaving sufficient garrisons to hold both provinces, he should move into Virginia. "I should wish you," Sir Henry said, "to assist in operations which will certainly be carried on in Chesapeake as soon as we are relieved from our apprehension of a superior fleet and the season will admit. . . ." Sir Henry thought that happy event might take place in September or early October. A three-thousand-man army "would be quite sufficient" for Virginia if the Earl had first settled the backcountry. Their numbers in any event could be augmented from New York.[26]

The burden of the instructions was clear, if not the means of implementing them. Cornwallis should pacify South and North Carolina, maintain order in Georgia and the Floridas, and then move north and take Virginia. Yet Clinton scarcely left his subordinate sufficient troops for such a large purpose. Sir Henry liked to juggle figures to suit his opinions. When he wrote his memoirs after the war he attributed to the Earl fantastic numbers of soldiers. He asserted in one instance that he left Cornwallis with 6000 men at Charleston in June. Somehow by October, without any reinforcements, these grew to 11,306 effec- tives. In itself "effective" is misleading. For the only troops that counted were those present and fit for duty. "Effectives," however, included the sick and wounded, men in England re- cruiting, and men prisoners of the rebels. Clinton did send 1900 men to the Carolinas in November, but he would have to have sent several thousand men to the Earl for his arithmetic to make sense. He never sent the men. Furthermore, his initial figure of 6000 with Cornwallis at Charleston is suspect. Sir Henry stated that he sailed to Charleston with 7500 men and took back about 4500. That would have left the Earl 3000 troops to pacify North and South Carolina and to march into Virginia. But his forces were larger than that, since detach- ments from New York reinforced Clinton during the siege. In June, after Sir Henry left, the Earl had with him in South Caro- lina six understrength British regiments of infantry: the 7th, 23d, his own 33d, the 63d, 64th, and the two-battalion 71st. He had no regular cavalry save for sixty men of the 17th Dragoons. The higher ground of South Carolina offered some of the finest cavalry country in the world, yet Clinton took most of the regu- lar cavalry back to New York with him. In addition to the British troops Cornwallis commanded two German infantry regi- ments, the Huyne and Ditfurth. He also had six provincial regi- ments, special units created by the British during the war, whose training and discipline copied that of regular regiments but whose officers (with a few exceptions) and enlisted men were

Americans. The status of provincial regiments, neither regulars nor militia, created confusion and quarreling between the ministry and interested Americans.[27] Those provincials under the Earl in South Carolina included the British Legion, the Volunteers of Ireland (both created by Clinton in 1778), the New York Volunteers, the Prince of Wales American Regiment, the South Carolina Royalists, and the North Carolina Volunteers. He also had around a hundred artillerymen. Altogether the British, German, and provincial troops amounted to about four thousand present and fit for duty. In addition, Cornwallis could count upon some of the Georgia troops to help him in the border areas of South Carolina, especially around the Ninety-Six district. Georgia now had no British regulars, but it did have two German infantry regiments, a small detachment of German artillery, and four provincial regiments, including the two-battalion DeLancey's. All told, Georgia would afford about 1250 men present and fit for duty. The thousand men in East and West Florida could be of no use at all to any campaign in the Carolinas. Assuming the best possible situation for the British — that the fall of Charleston had so demoralized the rebels that the British needed only token forces to control the interior — Cornwallis still could not spare more than three thousand men for an offensive in North Carolina, unless he got reinforcements. Again assuming the best possible situation for the British — that in North Carolina they met no resistance and therefore sustained no casualties — Cornwallis still would have to garrison the province, which might require two thousand men. That would leave him with a thousand for Virginia, a ridiculous number to pacify one of the most actively rebellious provinces in North America. From the very beginning Clinton, who complained constantly that the ministry never sufficiently heeded his request for troops, left his subordinate with a piddling number of soldiers to achieve a monumental task. Cornwallis must have begun to feel especially bitter as his campaigns progressed. For while he moved and fought and worked, reinforced only once from New York with 1900 men, Clinton loitered in the city with the main units of the British army.[28]

Fighting and moving characterized Cornwallis' southern operations, but only after a period of initial quiet. First he needed to plan his campaign and consolidate his position. To that end, he returned in late June to Charleston and settled down for a summer of administration. The problems of supply to, and communication with, the interior garrisons first demanded his attention. Necessarily he kept a core of regulars at Charleston and a core of regulars with his second, Lord Rawdon, at Camden. But he had to find the proper troops and commanders for the smaller posts. Lieutenant Colonel Nesbit Balfour of the regular army went to Ninety-Six, but was replaced in July by Lieutenant Colonel John Harris Cruger of the provincials. Balfour then returned to Charleston to replace General James Pattison who went home because of illness. Cornwallis sent other detachments to Hanging Rock, Rocky Mount, the Cheraws, and Georgetown. He also sent the inspector of militia, Patrick Ferguson, to the Ninety-Six district to organize militia and range across the backcountry. The Earl rapidly and effectively completed these arrangements within one month of taking command.[29]

Garrisoning these posts was easier than communicating with them and supplying them. Much of the interior of South Carolina (contrary to popular belief) was not swampy but was fairly negotiable — the land being slightly rolling and covered by widely spaced tall pines and sparse underbrush. Nevertheless, Cornwallis had to struggle to keep open his communications. Clinton had taken the cavalry and its horses back to New York. The Earl had to find a substitute, and eventually he tapped the services of the British Legion cavalry. The many work details required of it weakened the Legion as a fighting force. "This service," its commander lamented, "injured them infinitely more than all the preceding moves and actions of the campaign, and though hitherto successful against their enemies in the field, they were nearly destroyed in detail by patroles and detachments required of them during the intense heat of the season." [30] Yet thanks to Clinton, Cornwallis had no choice. Either he used the Legion or he lost contact with his army. Lone couriers could not be useful, for they rarely escaped rebel militia.

Once Tarleton's dragoons arrived from a garrison with information of its needs, Cornwallis had to try to fill those needs. Although he attempted to feed his army off the land, and perhaps succeeded better than Clinton or Howe ever did, he still had to supply it with arms, ammunition, uniforms, camp equipment, and other necessaries. These goods came from Britain to Charleston, usually by way of New York. But Clinton in New York often proved dilatory in shipping them. Supply vessels did not call at Charleston frequently. Even when they did, they often failed to reach the harbor safely. On August 10, Cornwallis wrote to Arbuthnot that rebel privateers were "constantly off the bar & taking vessels in our sight." [31] But since British frigates could not pass the bar to scare the Americans away, the privateers continued to harass British shipping. Cornwallis' victories on land in no way daunted the privateers at sea, and even after the American rout at Camden, the rebels continued to stop the supply vessels. "I fear," Balfour lamented in September, "nothing concerning South Carolina is thought of, by land or water." A week later a ship did arrive with stores and men, but the transport sent to bring them in was "taken just off the bar by two twenty gun ships." [32] The Earl's troubles in South Carolina began, just as they did at Yorktown, at the water's edge.

Even for cargoes that escaped both the Americans and the sea, however, the trouble was but half over. The supplies still had to move inland from Charleston. Several factors combined to defy Cornwallis' efforts to transport goods into the interior: bad roads, heavy rains, and scarcity of wagons. Roads that cut the Carolina red clay, such as those around Ninety-Six, became impassible bogs in rainy weather. The summer of 1780 saw little but rainy weather. If the Earl attempted to use the streams instead of the roads, he ran into equal difficulties. Rains swelled and clogged the rivers so that boats found navigation on them extremely hazardous. Cornwallis struggled against the elements all during August, hoping for better weather the next month, only to be lashed by a hurricane in early September.[33] He tried to repair the weather-beaten roads for the wagons that had to roll across them to the interior posts.[34] But he also had to find wagons. Clinton had taken all the army's wagons back to New York with him, leaving the Earl to fend for himself.[35] Cornwallis initially kept his supplies moving by running a shuttle service. The commander at Ninety-Six, for instance, immediately sent back the wagons which had brought him provisions, placing them aboard flatboats for the return to Charleston. There Cornwallis filled them quickly and sent them back upriver to the garrison.[36] Such expedients served well enough temporarily, because the forces occupying Charleston and the interior posts had captured quantities of provisions from the Americans. At Ninety-Six, for example, the British had captured a small cannon, 638 stands of arms, powder, cartridges, bullets, shot, flints, bayonets, miners' tools, and other stores.[37] When the Earl occupied Camden he managed to find engineers' tools, if no arms and ammunition.[38] Tarleton, furthermore, overcame part of his deficit in horses by appropriating for his Legion the best mounts he could find in South Carolina.[39] Temporary shifts and expedients served for the summer when the British could live off their captures. They would soon need some better system, however, for as captured supplies dwindled, their own needs increased.

Even more than military stores, the troops needed clothing and food. Cornwallis captured some hats and green cloth in Camden in June, but usually he could not rely upon taking

American clothing. Rather he had to depend upon New York. Precious little of that item came from New York in the summer, but some would have to be sent as the season progressed. Then, of course, when the uniforms arrived, the British would need enough wagons and boats for a transport service. The troops could not campaign naked and shivering in the Carolina winter.

Nor could they campaign on empty stomachs. The necessity of procuring food led Cornwallis into a new set of administrative problems. He could not depend upon rations from New York. He had to live off the countryside in South Carolina. This necessity in turn meant that he not only had to secure wagons to haul food to the army but also had to find victuals without leaving the countryside a desert. His needs were not acute at first, for the British captured large supplies that could sustain them for a few months.[40] But he had to think in longer terms. He had to take from the country and, at the same time, keep the country productive.

One way to achieve his purpose was to buy supplies from the loyalists and pay handsomely. Clinton, unfortunately, deprived Cornwallis of this easy and relatively painless way to secure food. He kept the Earl chronically short of hard money, and devices like bills of exchange or signing of warrants that promised future payment, though used extensively, could not substitute for ready cash in the minds of the loyalists.[41] They rarely exchanged their produce willingly for promises, especially since many of them felt they had to store up any surplus against the periodic depredations of the patriots. For the British simply to grab loyalist stores would defeat their whole purpose in the South; they could never return the province to George III if they antagonized the only loyal citizens.

If the Earl could not afford to pay loyalists for their goods, he certainly could not afford to pay rebels. Thus from the very beginning of his command, he depended upon confiscation of rebel property to supply his men. He systematized the practice, however, to insure a steady flow. He strictly forbade looting, which brought nothing to the army and only hardened resistance. As a result his redcoats lived well enough when they were not on the move. He suffered desperate shortages occasionally but always managed to pull through.

Cornwallis entrusted the confiscation and distribution of supplies to two officers and their assistants, the commissary of captures and the commissioner of sequestered estates.[42] For the former he chose Charles Stedman, a conscientious and zealous man. Stedman, a Pennsylvania loyalist, had lost his estates, had been imprisoned five times, and had once been tried for his life by the rebels. His previous administrative experience included work as a deputy commissary of prisoners in Pennsylvania and, since February of 1780, as a deputy commissary of captures.[43] Stedman remained forever grateful. Not only did he serve his chief well and loyally, but also he later honored Cornwallis' character and generalship in one of the few contemporary "British" accounts of the American Revolution.

Stedman received orders to move with the army and to use his assistants to garner spirits and provisions. He should search out mills and discover their capacity for grinding grain for the army. Whatever he found he should guard carefully — especially from the thieving wagoners of the quartermaster general's department. The commissary would have to account for and issue any and all captured goods when called upon by the commanding general. He should also handle provisions such as wheat, indigo, or oats that were delivered voluntarily to the army by loyalists and issue receipts which promised payment at a fixed rate.[44] Stedman ran into a few snags. Sometimes unit commanders on detached service denied his assistants control of captured provisions.[45] Sometimes he could not get the Negroes on the plantations of "bad men" [46] to help him load or ship produce because "upon the approach of any detachment of the King's troops [they] thought themselves absolved from all respect to their American masters, and entirely released from servitude: Influenced by this idea, they quitted the plantations, and followed the army. . . ." [47] One regular complained that Stedman's assistants paid too much to the loyalists for provisions around Ninety-Six and believed he could secure them for much less.[48] But despite occasional complaints and setbacks the commissary of captures organized his system sufficiently well to feed Cornwallis' army for most of its time in South Carolina. As Tarleton said: "The officers and men of the different regiments and corps were supplied by the flour and cattle, whilst the horses were foraged by the produce of the country. An expenditure of the provisions brought across the Atlantic was unknown except in Charleston and Savannah." [49] North Carolina would prove a challenge to the commissary's ingenuity, but the trek to that province lay months in the future.

To supplement the work of the commissary of captures, Cornwallis created a new office, the commissioner of sequestered estates.[50] While the commissary of captures moved with the army and picked up goods along the way, busying himself only with the army's immediate needs rather than with the continuous productivity of plantations, the commissioner of sequestered estates had more permanent concerns. Cornwallis intended for the commissioner to work the confiscated rebel plantations for the lasting benefit of the army. Those plantations could furnish his forces with a permanent supply of horses, food, and other provisions, and the sale of any surplus from plantation production might even bring the army the cash it so often needed. The Earl explained these aims in the document he issued to John Cruden on September 16 as his first commissioner of sequestered estates. Upon receipt of a warrant from the commandant in South Carolina or the commandant at Charleston, Cruden could seize real and personal property of every kind: movables, lands, cattle, horses, household goods, even Negroes. Those plantations in healthy cultivation he should retain and improve for the "public interest," to feed and fatten horses and cattle and to grow crops which could be sold for the army's benefit. Other real and personal property he could sell at public auction after due notice (twenty-one days) in the newspapers. Cornwallis put checks on Cruden, however, to safeguard the army and the public. The commissioner had to inventory the seized property in the presence of loyal militia officers in the country or of freeholders in a town. As a further check, he had to present his accounts to the board of police in Charleston twice a year in January and July.[51] Furthermore, Cornwallis never intended that Cruden should have the power to starve the wives and families even of the most notorious rebels. The commissioner had to pay a fourth part of the annual produce of any plantation for the support of the wife and children of the former owner, or a sixth part to a childless wife.[52]

The office worked well enough at first, especially after Cornwallis broadcast an official proclamation which stated the nature of Cruden's job, revoked the arbitrary powers of seizure hitherto given to militia officers and required them to account to Cruden, and called upon civil and military officers to help the commissioner.[53] But for various reasons Cruden never fulfilled the Earl's expectations. Indeed, he ran into debt and finally proved a burden instead of a help during the harsh winter at Winnsboro. That Cruden's duties often overlapped those of the commissary of captures[54] and that rebel raids often destroyed what Cruden had built up accounted in part for the eventual failure of the scheme.

Although the supply of the army demanded Cornwallis' first attention at Charleston in June and July, other matters also occupied him. Of primary importance was the reestablishment of some sort of civilian participation in the government. Ultimate authority had to rest with the army for the present. But the Earl knew that the army could serve only to restore order, not to run the government indefinitely. Subjects, accustomed to civilian authority, could not willingly give their allegiance and their loyalty to muskets and bayonets. Cornwallis had even requested power as a commissioner to restore civil government upon his own discretion, but this request had been denied.[55] Nonetheless, he did what he could in the face of heavy obstacles.

One of these obstacles concerned the proper maintenance of records. When he took command at Charleston, Cornwallis discovered that the "records and other public papers" of South Carolina had been "taken down from the places where they used to be deposited and promiscuously thrown into casks and boxes." If someone did not take care of them immediately they faced destruction. Of course the "revenue of the Crown as well as all the private property in the country and the interest of many British subjects" would be "much prejudiced" by loss of the records.[56] But to straighten them out would require a degree of skill in administration as well as a legal knowledge that many loyalists, if Josiah Martin is a fair example, lacked. Martin, the governor of North Carolina before hostilities, had hoped to return with the British in triumph to his colony at the head of a regiment of North Carolina Highlanders. He revealed his administrative skill in a letter to Cornwallis toward the end of July when he forwarded a proclamation for approval.

In proof of my readiness to obey your lordship's commands upon all occasions, I had the honor to send you, last night, a very clumsy specimen of my unskillfulness in law instruments, in form & shape of a proclamation. I am very sensible that it proclaims my shame as a civil engineer, who ought to be better versed on such legal knowledge. Your lordship knows, however, that provincial governors have not been always chosen in our country for the fitness and competence of their talents, and therefore will not be surprised to find me as ignorant as many of my brethren in office, or more so.[57]

Martin's modesty did him credit. But his lack of skill, if typical of the loyalists found in Charleston, scarcely helped in sorting out public records. And it would not take many loyalists so diffident and meek as Martin in positions of high civil authority to dampen enthusiasm for a return to civil government.

Nonetheless, Cornwallis tried to encourage a return to more normal civilian life. He enlarged the powers of the board of police that Clinton had created in order to give civilians some authority in running Charleston. He also opened up the city's trade with the interior "by allowing merchants to convey to Charleston a variety of manufactures which had been long wanted throughout all the southern provinces, and permitting them to receive payment in the produce of the country." [58] He returned to the jurisdiction of ordinary courts questions of wills, estates, and inheritance "in the manner heretofore accustomed." [59] He permitted officers in the interior to use their discretion with regard to reintroducing civilians into positions of authority. At least one of them appointed the former justices of the peace to their old positions to help reestablish "writ authority." [60] The Earl even set up a newspaper to counteract rebel propaganda and to proclaim the virtues of the return of South Carolina to His Majesty's authority.[61]

Despite these "virtues" and despite Cornwallis' strenuous efforts to reinstitute civil authority in so far as he could, success eluded him. Perhaps no one could have succeeded. Cornwallis and his men could win battles, but they were not equipped to win hearts and minds. Since, of course, the whole purpose of the British army in America since 1775 had been to stamp out rebellion and win hearts and minds, and since that had not been accomplished in the previous five years, one cannot blame the Earl too harshly for failure in the summer of 1780. Certainly he did not fail for want of effort. He started doubly handicapped, as a general whose purpose was war and as the successor of Clinton whose efforts toward peacemaking through proclamation had provoked rather than pacified discontented individuals.

Cornwallis first had to deal with the openly disaffected whose persons had already been secured by British arms. These people fell into two categories, American prisoners of war and civilians. Charleston alone in July contained over fifteen hundred American Continental prisoners. Cornwallis had to figure out what to do with them. He sent officers on parole to the islands around Charleston. Some of the men he managed to exchange.[62] But he still had to imprison the rest — he could not allow an enemy army to roam free — and the only quarters he found were the prison ships in Charleston.[63] Conditions there soon degenerated into a living hell for the Americans. The mortality became "truly shocking," and according to one observer, "the rebell prisoners die faster, even, then they used to desert." [64] Perhaps eight hundred of them died in thirteen months.[65] The fault was not entirely or perhaps even primarily the Earl's, for he lacked adequate medicines and surgeons' mates even for his own troops, who died during the summer months almost as rapidly. But it would have been hard to convince a man suffering away his life in a hulk that the return of the King's government was good for South Carolina.[66]

Cornwallis did, however, win a few of the Continentals over to the British side, if only because they wished to escape the prison ships. Germain later suggested to the Earl, with Clinton's approval, that American prisoners might be induced into enlisting in the British army for service in the West Indies. The scheme offered advantages to both Americans and British. The Americans could exchange their dreary prison for a British uniform and the outdoors. They would also serve in a theater where they would not have to fight their own countrymen. The British would not need to maintain them as prisoners but could use them as veterans to augment their thinly scattered forces in the western hemisphere. The plan, finally worked out after Cornwallis left Charleston, succeeded in taking over five hundred prisoners out of the hulks and transferring them to British service.[67]

American civilians presented a different problem. A Continental soldier wore a uniform, subjected himself to military discipline, and agreed to serve for a fixed term. He fought openly and took his licks as part of the game. But American civilians refused to abide by such rules. Friendly one minute, they turned up in arms the next. As militiamen they were not very effective against regulars in open battle, but they disrupted communications, harassed supply trains, raided loyalist plantations, and picked off foraging parties. Cornwallis had a tremendously difficult task in trying to separate the loyal from the disloyal civilians and in attempting to disband all rebel militia. The most open and avowed civilian enemies of British rule (including a few women) he shoved into the provost, a dungeon constructed in the cellars of the old exchange along the eastern sea wall of the city. But he could not imprison all the enemies to British rule; indeed, he could not get many more than fifty into the provost.[68] Many civilians Clinton had put on their paroles not to oppose the British, and some he had exiled to the islands off Charleston. Cornwallis soon discovered the unsatisfactory nature of these arrangements. The "principal & most violent inhabitants" held "constant meetings in town & carried on correspondence with the country to keep up the flame of rebellion." They spread "false reports throughout the whole province to encourage the disaffected & intimidate others." [69] Beyond Charleston, of course, were thousands like them, organizing into militia bands, terrorizing loyalists, and harassing his regulars. Despite strenuous efforts and despite his other administrative achievements in his busy summer at Charleston, Cornwallis never solved the one problem he needed to solve above all others. He never found out how to return civilians to their former allegiance nor how, if that were not possible, to restrain them from fighting his army. Indeed, that summer he came to the conclusion that he could never restore civilian authority unless he won another victory in the field against an American army. Perhaps if he smashed the Americans decisively in open combat they would see the folly of their ways. He needed "something decisive," [70] and events of early August presented him with the opportunity for it. On August 9, word reached him from Lord Rawdon at Camden that General Horatio Gates was marching down from the North to dispute British possession of the South. It was welcome news. So Cornwallis put aside at Charleston the problem of civilian allegiance hoping that he might solve in the battlefield the problem that defied him in his city offices.

Probably he did not regret the prospect of leaving Charleston. To be sure, it was a beautiful city, with its magnificent houses, well-kept gardens, and intricately worked iron gates. Certainly, too, the heat would be no less oppressive outside the city. Indeed, it might be worse, since in the evening, at least, residents of Charleston could hope for a tempering sea breeze. But the Earl was not a man to rest easily in a lovely city; it was his nature to hanker for action. If, at this point, he thought about his months in Charleston, he had cause to be reasonably satisfied with his administration. He had at least restored a semblance of order. He had garrisoned the interior strongly and arranged to supply it. He had restored a measure of trade. He had reinstituted civilian authority as far as he could. He had not brought all civilians back to their allegiance, but he had begun this most difficult task. Now, however, it was time for the Earl to leave the city. The opportunity he had long sought now hastened toward him. Soon he might be able to distinguish himself in battle as an independent commander. He might even recover the South for the British Empire. Battle would decide, and he relished battle.[71]

CHAPTER 7

Camden: "A Severe Satire upon Saratoga"

I N AUTUMN of 1780 General Horatio Gates had a high reputation which, his detractors felt, far exceeded his capacity. That Gates had served in the British army as an officer, they could point out, did not guarantee his ability. Charles Lee had served the same army and he had, according to George Washington, disgraced himself at Monmouth. Born in England in 1728 of humble origins (his father has been described variously as a revenue officer, an army officer, a clergyman, and a greengrocer), Gates had climbed the ranks to major. Then further promotion seemed to elude him. He had served under Prince Ferdinand of Brunswick in Europe and on the American continent and in the West Indies during the Seven Years' War. After a tour of duty in Ireland from 1768 to 1769 he had retired on half pay and sailed back to America. In 1772 he had settled in the Shenandoah Valley. But the Revolution interrupted his peaceful life as a Virginia squire. When the United States organized its army, Congress made Gates adjutant. From that position his driving ambition and astute political sense led him to one important command after another.

Perhaps Gates' appearance and personality had also helped

him make his way to the top. A fatherly looking man, he bore an aspect at once dignified and lugubrious. His eyes slanted downward at the outside corners, giving him a rather hangdog look. A large, hooked nose on a long, thin face completed the features of a countenance at once interesting and hard to read.

For behind the jovial appearance lay an ambitious schemer. In 1776, Gates managed to supersede Sullivan in command of the American troops in Canada. Shortly afterward, he undertook to repeat the same performance with General Schuyler, who thought himself safely in command of the northern army gathered to face Burgoyne. Gates slyly encouraged certain rumors then circulating — rumors reflecting on Schuyler's character, competence, and even loyalty. New Englanders in Congress took up Gates' cause because he had championed their rights to disputed territory with New York. During the winter of 1776 to 1777 the vacillating Congress fiddled with the idea of ousting Schuyler and at last, after reversing itself a few times, in August appointed Gates to replace him. Congress apparently ignored Gates' slothfulness in doing nothing, in the early summer of 1777, to strengthen Fort Ticonderoga against Burgoyne's advance while Schuyler had been busy defending himself to Congress. Indeed, Gates had not even been able to get adequate food supplies up to the fort. Nonetheless, he took up his new command of the northern army on August 19. By that time Schuyler had already completed the organization that would have given any "discreet commander"[1] a victory over the impetuous Burgoyne. The Saratoga campaign followed in which Benedict Arnold distinguished himself far more than Gates. But the commanding general, rather than the brilliant Arnold, reaped the laurels of Burgoyne's defeat and surrender — the greatest victory American arms had yet achieved in the war. Now in 1780 Congress chose this man to command the American army marching into South Carolina. Perhaps he could revive the failing American cause in that province.[2]

On August 9, 1780, Cornwallis at Charleston received a dispatch from Lord Rawdon at Camden advising of Gates' approach from the north.[3] Here was good news: it was the chance the Earl had been waiting for, the opportunity to win a victory on his own. Preliminary reports, however, did not encourage him to believe the victory would be easy, for they put his adversary's strength at five thousand men, exclusive of militia. Still, as Cornwallis knew, one could always expect initial reports to exaggerate the enemy's strength. He would have to look the situation over himself. On August 10 he hastened toward his rendezvous with battle. He was glad to exchange the flat, swampy, terrain of Charleston for the gently rolling land of tall pines which he now entered, for such ground held promise of easier movement for both his cavalry and infantry.

Arriving at Camden the night of August 13, Cornwallis took up his headquarters in the three-storied, wide-verandaed house of Joseph Kershaw, a prominent merchant and patriot, "a very violent man . . . said to have persecuted the loyalists." [4] The Earl, as might be expected of a commanding general and an aristocrat, customarily took the best houses for his headquarters, and Kershaw's residence was one of Camden's finest. Commandeering it gave Cornwallis the additional pleasure of punishing a rebel, and although he allowed Kershaw's wife and children to occupy an upper room for a while, he shipped the unfortunate merchant off to Bermuda.[5]

On the following day, August 14, Cornwallis walked out into the spacious, poplar-covered grounds and proceeded to inspect his forces and assess his situation.[6] One question overrode all others: whether to fight or retreat to Charleston. He had to decide in a hurry, for while he foresaw "no difficulty in making good" his retreat to Charleston with the troops able to march, he would have to leave immediately if that was his intention. Sumter, in his rear to the west of the Wateree River, was growing in strength. Indeed, even as Cornwallis pondered his course of action, Sumter was laying plans to gobble up an escort bringing clothes and ammunition to Camden and to capture the British redoubt guarding the ferry over the Wateree.[7]

For several reasons, however, the Earl soon decided against retreat. If he withdrew now, he would lose all the considerable gains, both material and psychological, that he had made so far. British arms at last ruled that portion of the province that had hitherto been so troublesome. Now a victory over Gates might crush the spirit even of a Sumter or a Marion.

Another consideration was that the British army needed thriving communities like Camden to serve as symbols of royal authority. The town, only recently emerged from Indian wars and frontier turbulence, presented a bustling appearance. Settled by Scots-Irish Presbyterians and Irish Quakers, it now boasted neatly apportioned lots and streets laid out around a town square, with a special plot reserved for a fair. Meeting houses for Quakers and for Presbyterians, with no Church for the Anglicans, not only showed the town's religious preferences but also helped account for its energy. Industries prospered. Camden boasted numerous mills (several of them Kershaw's) for both grain and logs, breweries, and a pottery. Handicraftsmen made farm tools which they traded to farmers from the Waxhaws in exchange for their locally distilled whiskey. A courthouse, built nine years earlier to serve the entire surrounding district, symbolized law and order. As Cornwallis thought more and more about his situation, he determined that that courthouse would henceforward have to administer British law and order. He would have to fight Gates, no matter what the odds. He could never win the war unless he could convince the farmers, millers, sawyers, distillers, artisans — in short, the Americans — in places like Camden that the British intended to stay. He could not convince them by retreating to Charleston.[8]

In addition, Camden offered him solid material support. The town and the surrounding countryside could provide indigo, tea, flour, Indian corn, rum, bacon, hams, butter, tobacco, cattle, sheep, axes, hats, and green cloth — in short whatever the British forces needed.[9] The town also offered some human resources. Although overwhelmingly patriot in sentiment, Camden also counted among its outlying residents substantial merchants like Henry Rugeley — whose mills lay ten miles to the north — who were loyal to the crown, who helped Cornwallis keep order, who raised loyalist militia, and who could eventually prepare the way for the desired return to civilian government. Thus to abandon Camden meant to abandon both supplies and loyalists.

Furthermore, Cornwallis had to consider the eight hundred regulars and provincials sick in hospitals in Camden. He could not afford to lose so many fighting men. Yet he could not carry them down the road to Charleston.[10] The British general emphatically decided that he could not afford to retreat. "I must have not only left near 800 sick and a great quantity of stores at this place," he later told Germain, "but I clearly saw the loss of the whole province except Charlestown, and of all Georgia except Savannah, as immediate consequences, besides forfeiting all pretensions to future confidence from our friends in this part of America." [11] Camden's very name symbolized defiance to British authority, for in 1768 it had changed its name from Pine Tree Hill to Camden in honor of one of the peers who had voted against the Stamp Act. Cornwallis, too, had voted against the act but not against monarchy. He would fight to return royal power to this South Carolinian community from which it had been so long absent.

But could Cornwallis afford to stay and fight? That depended partly upon the forces arranged against him. He had to find out more about them, and on August 14 and 15 he "adopted the most likely measures" to do so.[12] He even slipped a spy into Gates' headquarters at Rugeley's Mills. The tory pretended to be a Marylander sympathetic to the patriot cause and happy to see the Marylanders with Gates. "So Plausible was his manner" that the sentries led him right to Gates' headquarters. There he offered to spy on Cornwallis, all the while noting the state of the American army. He fooled the American commander completely, and after a long conversation Gates "dismissed him, with many promises, if he would faithfully observe his engagements." [13]

On the fifteenth Cornwallis hustled Tarleton and the Legion off to gather more information. In the evening the Legion's advance guard managed to snare three American soldiers. They told their captors that Gates planned to march toward Camden immediately. Tarleton galloped back to the Earl with the prisoners bouncing along mounted behind his dragoons. Cornwallis interrogated the Americans personally, deemed their story "credible," and found it "confirmed all the other intelligence of the day." [14]

At the end of that day the Earl had all the information he seemed likely to get. All the pieces fitted together. "Seeing little to lose by a defeat, and much to gain by a victory," he later told Germain, "I resolved to take the first good opportunity to attack the rebel army." [15] Though the fate of British arms in the South now rested upon him, Cornwallis did not seem overly worried. He was heading for the sort of fight he liked — a straightforward, honest battle against a foe in the open field, at the head of the finest infantry in the world.

According to his most recent information, the enemy would outnumber him. His intelligence credited the Americans with 5000 men, exclusive of the 1200 or 1500 Virginia militia whom he (correctly) expected to join Gates before the battle. Cornwallis, on the other hand, mustered only 2043 men fit for duty. Of these, 382 were militia — always unreliable. He counted upon his 844 provincials to be steady enough when fighting alongside regulars. But he relied the most upon his 817 regulars of the 23d regiment, his own 33d, and the two-battalion 71st.

Altogether he commanded only a small force, but as he noted, the troops present and fit for duty were "perfectly good."

The same could not be said for the army of Horatio Gates. He had a nucleus of good troops, the Delaware and Maryland Continentals, but they numbered only 1400 infantry. He lacked regular cavalry. The British redcoats and provincials thus outnumbered the American regulars. The victor of Saratoga, however, mustered, in addition to his Continentals, large numbers of militia in whom he trusted too much and with whom he was very popular. The North Carolina militia of Richard Caswell and the Virginia militia of Edward Stevens brought Gates' total force close to the 5000 that Cornwallis estimated. Yet militia came and went as the mood suited them so that not even the American commander knew his exact troop strength. When on the day before the battle Gates asserted that he had 7000 men, he astounded Otho Williams, his adjutant general. Williams asked general officers to return an exact muster. When they complied the adjutant discovered the army totalled only 3052 men. Although surprised at the difference between his estimates and the facts, Gates still reasoned that "there are enough for our purpose." [16]

Cornwallis later wrote to Germain that Gates' army was "well-appointed." If he believed that, the spy he slipped into American headquarters at Rugeley's Mills lied to him. Even the best troops opposed to the Earl, the Maryland and Delaware Continentals, were in poor physical health.

Poor health was to be expected after the summer that these men had lived through. Washington had decided to send them south to meet the British challenge in the Carolinas, and they had been on the march since June. Under the command of "Baron" Johann DeKalb, they left their base in Petersburgh, Virginia, and started toward North Carolina. They endured many hardships and DeKalb himself made heavy weather of the march: "lack of food, limited transportation, long stretches of barren and unsettled country, the pestilential voraciousness of insects, violence of thunderstorms, the indifference of the inhabitants to the Revolutionary cause, all these things were strange to DeKalb." Indeed, the Baron at one point feared a lack of provisions might force him back. He wrote to a friend that Europeans could form no idea of real warfare because they had never fought in America and could not "know what it is to contend against obstacles." [17]

By July 24, when Gates caught up with them, the men were near Hillsboro, North Carolina. Gates (who had received the command in June but had been too busy with correspondence and conferences to join his men before now) chose to ignore his soldiers' weakened condition. Taking over from DeKalb, he ordered a parade for the twenty-fifth and then at once began to move his troops further south. He now thought only of marching as fast as possible and coming to grips with his enemy. He hoped he might fall upon Rawdon at Camden before the British called in their scattered forces. His haste proved his undoing. He should have allowed some rest to his exhausted army and should not have tried to clip days off his march by taking the direct route to Camden. This route led him through a country short of supplies, unlike the more westerly direction DeKalb had planned. Adjutant Williams' remonstrances about Gates' line of march — "barren, abounding in sandy plains, intersected by swamps, sparsely inhabited, and capable of furnishing but little provisions and forage" [18] — fell on deaf ears.

The suffering of the troops increased steadily as they progressed, confounding Gates' hopes for swift movement. The American commander crawled rather than galloped from Hillsboro to Rugeley's Mills. It took him two weeks to cover the one hundred twenty miles. During that time his men nearly starved. The present year's unripe corn, "unfit for use," had to supplement last year's "nearly expended" crop. Officers, lacking flour, used hair powder to thicken their soup. Soldiers butchered whatever lean cattle they found and boiled the stringy beef together with the green corn. They substituted green peaches for bread. They also lacked rum, considered so necessary for an eighteenth-century army.[19]

North Carolina militia, who scoured the countryside around this sick army and thereby increased its supply difficulties, did not join Gates until August 7. Stevens' Virginia militia dragged their heels even more, arriving a week later (although other Virginia militia had been with Gates since Hillsboro). This "grand army" assembled on August 15 at Rugeley's Mills to receive its battle orders. Gates, as yet unaware (the tory spy had ensured it) that Cornwallis had assumed personal command, thought Camden his for the taking. Deceived as to his own strength, deceived as to the enemy's strength, in command of an army debilitated by a painful journey and a miserable diet, he issued marching orders for ten o'clock that night. The general determined to feed his men before they left and issued a "hasty meal of quick-baked bread and fresh beef, with a dessert of molasses, mixed with mush or dumplings." This generous banquet "operated so cathartically, as to disorder very many of the men who were breaking ranks all night, and were certainly much debilitated before the action commenced in the morning." [20]

Curiously enough, at precisely the same hour Gates left Rugeley's Mills, Cornwallis slipped out of Camden. He, too, hoped to surprise his enemy, whom he knew to be "badly posted." He marched along the road toward Rugeley's Mills. Flat at first, the road dipped down sharply to cross Saunders Creek, then climbed up again. Suddenly he heard firing. His advance guard of twenty Legion cavalry and twenty mounted infantry had stumbled into Gates' advance guard. Now the two commanders discovered for the first time that their main armies faced each other. They reacted very differently. Cornwallis, pleased to have encountered his foe even if he had not surprised him, immediately halted his men and formed them into a line stretching across both sides of the road. He did not attack: his stakes were too high to risk in a night action, which was a type of encounter always "particularly liable" to "uncertainty and confusion." Furthermore, the ground here favored the British. Gum swamps lay on their right and left, making it impossible for the Americans to outflank them. "Confiding in the discipline and courage of his Majesty's troops," the Earl eagerly awaited the morning.

In Gates' headquarters all was confusion. The American general had thought to surprise a thin force at Camden and had instead run into an army. Furthermore, a British prisoner had just astonished him with the news that the army numbered three thousand men led in person by Lord Cornwallis. Gates fell completely apart. He called in his general officers and pleaded for advice. Although the way for retreat still lay open, General Stevens exclaimed: "Gentlemen, is it not too late *now* to do anything but fight?" Nobody else offered any advice. Officers returned to their commands.

During the early morning hours of August 16, both sides prepared themselves for battle. The day broke hot and hazy. Through the early morning mist Cornwallis observed his enemy facing him in line stretching across the road at about two hundred fifty yards distance. He had but a brief time to take in the American dispositions before firing erupted — the tall, widely spaced pines, leafless to the height of forty or fifty feet, offered few impediments to vision. Soon, however, the smoke of battle would obscure everything, hugging the ground, enveloping the forces, and choking the combatants, for not a breath of air stirred that morning. The Earl quickly noticed the weakness of his adversary's force at its left and center. The Virginia and North Carolina militia under Stevens and Caswell respectively formed this part of the American line. Opposite them Corn-

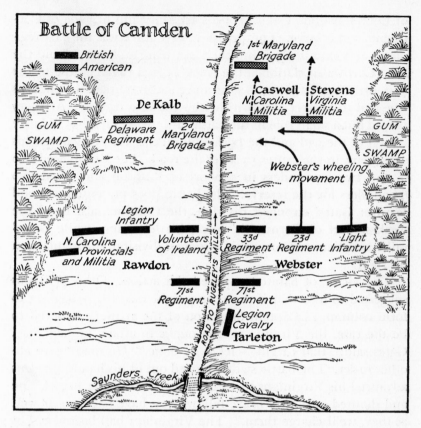

Battle of Camden

British
American

De Kalb

1st Maryland Brigade

Caswell
N. Carolina Militia

Stevens
Virginia Militia

Delaware Regiment

2d Maryland Brigade

Webster's wheeling movement

GUM SWAMP

GUM SWAMP

Legion Infantry

N. Carolina Provincials and Militia

Rawdon

Volunteers of Ireland

33d Regiment

23d Regiment

Light Infantry

Webster

71st Regiment

71st Regiment

Legion Cavalry
Tarleton

ROAD TO RUGELEY'S MILLS

Saunders Creek

wallis had posted, from his right on the gum swamp to his center at the Camden Road, a small group of light infantry, then
the 23d, and finally the 33d regiment, all under Lieutenant
Colonel Webster. The enemy's right appeared more formidable,
for there Gates had put his Continentals — the 2d Maryland
brigade and the Delaware regiment, both under DeKalb. Facing
them, from the road to the gum swamp on his left, Cornwallis
placed the Volunteers of Ireland, the Legion infantry, and some
North Carolina provincials and militia, all under the command

of Lord Rawdon. Gates kept his 1st Maryland brigade of Continentals in reserve. The British reserve force was the 71st regiment, one battalion behind the right wing and one behind the left. Cornwallis stationed the crack Legion cavalry close to the 71st, ordering Tarleton to seize any chance to break the enemy's line and to protect any British who got into trouble. Artillery played but a small role in the battle, although grapeshot did take its toll of the 33d and the Irish Volunteers. Gates anchored his small park in the center to cover the road. The Earl placed two 6- and two 3-pounders in support of Rawdon and saved two 6-pounders for the reserve. The battle lines presented one odd feature: Gates' strongest division, the Continentals, faced the weakest part of Cornwallis' force, his left wing, while Gates' militia challenged Cornwallis' strongest division, the regulars on his right.

The victor of Saratoga opened the action. Otho Williams suggested to him that if the enemy right was still struggling to form column, as Captain Singleton of the artillery believed to be the case, the Virginia militia ought to attack immediately. Gates said: "that's right — let it be done." He never gave another order. The battle swiftly moved out of his hands. Stevens advanced his Virginians to within fifty paces of the British line and shouted out: "My brave fellows, you have bayonets as well as they, we'll charge them." The Virginians had bayonets, but they did not know how to use them, as the redcoats soon demonstrated. The Virginian charge resembled more a Donnybrook Fair than a battle tactic, and Cornwallis mistook it for a last-minute attempt by Gates to alter the disposition of his left flank. Thinking to catch Gates as Gates had thought to catch him, the Earl rode quickly over to Webster and told him to attack the milling masses in his front. At the same time Cornwallis sent an aide-de-camp flying along the line and across the road with orders for Rawdon to open fire. Rawdon immediately loosed a tremendous volley. Gates replied, and firing became general. Sergeant Roger Lamb, carrying the colors of the 23d near the middle of the right wing, noticed Webster, "cool, determined, vigilant, and active," leading him and his comrades straight toward the ragged enemy. Then the Sergeant lost sight of Webster, the Americans, and even some of his own comrades. Smoke "occasioned such thick darkness, that it was difficult to see the effect of fire on either side." The Virginians did not care about the effect of fire, in fact did not bother to fire. They suddenly discovered Webster's force upon them, and seized with panic, they threw down their loaded muskets and ran as fast as they could toward the swamps and safety. An officer with a hotter head than Webster — Tarleton, for instance — might have pursued the Virginians, thus hazarding the outcome of the contest. Instead, Webster assured victory by letting them run. He wheeled his light infantry and the 23d to his left, hitting the flank of the North Carolina militia, who were then engaged with the 33d. The North Carolinians fled pell-mell after their comrades toward the swamps. Only a few of them under General Gregory checked the British momentarily. They held their ground as long as they had cartridges to fire. Gregory himself suffered two bayonet wounds. His men, attacked in front by the 33d and in the flank by the 23d, soon gave way.

Now only DeKalb's Continentals stood between Cornwallis and triumph. Their actions gained more honor for the American cause than had the deeds of Gates and all his militia on that hot morning. DeKalb with the 2d Maryland brigade and the Delaware regiment not only repulsed Rawdon twice but also counterattacked with bayonet and threatened to break him. For half an hour the situation was doubtful. But Cornwallis saw the trouble and rode to meet it. His sheer will power and determination saved the British left. A captain of the Volunteers, who had lost more than half his company and who had seen two thirds of a neighboring company cut down by "hoorid showers of grape" from Gates' artillery and by the determined attack of the Continentals, took heart from his commander's example.

The Earl had ridden over to the Volunteers as soon as Webster's attack had succeeded. Now, "with great coolness, in the midst of a heavier fire than the oldest soldier remembers," he called out: "Volunteers of Ireland, you are fine fellows! Charge the rascals. By heaven you behave nobly!" His words and his example inspired the captain and the regiment, who at that time "wanted something to encourage" them. The Volunteers held.[21] DeKalb was now doomed, despite the desperate attempt made by the 1st Maryland brigade (the reserve) to save him. Momentarily shaken by the militia fleeing back through their ranks, the Marylanders recovered and struggled along the east side of the road to link up with their comrades. They never joined. Smoke obscured their vision and the redcoats soon fell upon them. When Webster finished with Gregory, two thirds of the American forces had fled. Now Cornwallis could concentrate his entire army on the Continentals. He enveloped them in an overwhelming fire. Tarleton's cavalry fell upon their flank while British infantry charged down upon them from all directions with fixed bayonets. "Rout and slaughter" followed. Hit on both flanks and in front, cut to shreds by musket ball and bayonet, they turned and ran. Nearly alone, DeKalb stood his ground. He refused to flee, refused even to believe the day was lost, and stuck it out to the end. British fire knocked his horse from under him. He struggled up and flailed about him with his sword. Stabbed again and again he still fought on. He fell only after eight bayonet thrusts and three musket balls had pierced his body. His splendid troops had done their best, but they lost all hope when their leader fell. Only a hundred of them escaped with any semblance of order by wading through the gum swamps on their right. In less than an hour Earl Cornwallis had shattered the only American army in the South. He had gained the most crushing victory that British arms ever achieved over the Americans in the Revolutionary War. No fortifications saved the rebels, as at Long Island. No Greene came up to cover their retreat, as at Brandywine. Cornwallis had totally destroyed Gates' American army as an effective fighting force.

Roger Lamb at this moment felt even more satisfaction than did his commander in chief. For Lamb had been a part of the British army defeated at Saratoga by the same Horatio Gates who even now was riding away as fast as his horse could carry him. To Lamb revenge was sweet. The Earl, however, mingled sorrow with exaltation. Happy with his victory, he regretted its price. He rode down the line with his aides inspecting his own dead and wounded, "brave men" whose behavior "was beyond all praise." When he spied the gravely wounded DeKalb, he drew rein immediately and said: "I am sorry sir, to see you, not sorry that you are vanquished, but sorry to see you so badly wounded." The brave Baron did not long survive the battle. He died on the nineteenth from his wounds. He may have had only a shaky claim to a title in the European hereditary aristocracy, but at Camden his nobility of spirit won his case in the court of history.

After the battle the country to north and south presented a scene of chaos. Militia scurried northward. Gates did too. So swift was his flight that in three days he reached Hillsboro, one hundred thirty miles from Camden. Continentals likewise scattered, and barely seven hundred managed to muster in Hillsboro ten days after the battle. The wounded could not run. Tarleton never gave the slow men a chance to escape. The road north to Rugeley's Mills bore witness to the devastation of war and to the Legion's ruthlessness. The sight appalled Charles Stedman:

> The road for some miles [he remarked] was strewed with the wounded and killed, who had been overtaken by the legion in their pursuit. The number of dead horses, broken waggons, and baggage, scattered on the road, formed a perfect scene of horror and confusion: arms, knapsacks and accoutrements found were innumerable: such was the terror and dismay of the Americans.[22]

Nor was the scene any brighter for the Americans to the south of the battlefield. As long as she lived, Mary Kershaw, seven-year-old daughter of the exiled patriot, never forgot the day and night of August 16, 1780. From her room in her father's house, then the British headquarters, she looked out in the afternoon and watched the exhausted American prisoners driven into the backyard like sheep. The British brought in barrels of water to assuage the prisoners' thirst in the stifling heat, and passed it out to them in tin cups. Then the wounded from both sides poured into her house. She did not sleep that night, for the distress of the men kept her awake. Their groans reverberated throughout the house to the crazy accompaniment of an American fiddler who tried with lively tunes to cheer up his comrades.

When the Earl examined the results of his victory, they both astonished and pleased him. He had captured all the American artillery (seven brass cannons), almost 150 baggage wagons, most of the baggage, camp equipage, military stores, 20 ammunition wagons, colors, and even most of the muskets the militiamen had tossed aside in their haste to escape. He had killed between 800 and 900 men in the battle and taken a thousand prisoners.

To complete the victory he sent Tarleton off after Sumter. On the eighteenth the active Legion commander caught the American partisan lolling at Fishing Creek and "totally destroyed or dispersed his detachment." He killed 150 men on the spot and took 2 brass cannons, 44 wagons, and 300 prisoners. For Cornwallis, it was a fitting end to the Camden campaign.

Jubilation filled the British camp. Rawdon, highly pleased with his Irish Volunteers, ordered a silver medal struck off. He presented it to several of his men who had distinguished themselves in the action. Cornwallis' aide-de-camp, Captain Alexander Ross, hastened with the glad tidings to Charleston, embarked on August 30 for England, and arrived there on October 9. He immediately took the news to the capital, and

Captain Ross became Major Ross. For two weeks London society talked of nothing but the victory and doted on the martial virtues of Earl Cornwallis.[23] The Earl himself was not displeased, but he knew the realities of his situation, as London society never could. The best he could hope from the victory was that "the internal commotions and insurrections in the province will now subside."[24]

PART IV

The Disastrous Drive North

The Carolinas

CHAPTER 8

The Loyalist Militia
"A Useless, Disorderly, Destructive Banditti"

ALTHOUGH CORNWALLIS had routed Gates at Camden and confidently expected to do the same to any army the Americans dared send against him in the future, ultimate British victory in the Carolinas did not depend upon the cool steadfastness of the British redcoat. Rather it rested precariously upon the whims, the courage, the initiative, and the dedication of the southerners themselves to the British cause. In the South, more than in any other part of the continent, the American Revolution took on the nature of a civil war. In the struggle which had gone on intermittently since 1776, each side — patriot and loyalist — had mastered the deceit and sudden violence so necessary to a successful, protracted, partisan struggle. Each side had learned to hide and snipe, to hit and run, in the hopes of eventual victory. But until the British army came permanently to Charleston and from there penetrated into the interior, the advantage had lain with the whig patriots. Loyalists — "tories" as their enemies called them — had risen prematurely in 1776 and been defeated at Moore's Creek Bridge. Now Cornwallis faced the formidable task of mustering enough well-armed loyalists to overcome the disaffected. He still hoped the victory over Gates would render the task easy. Easy or not, it had to be done. Without loyalist support he could expect no permanent victory. Doomed to a never-ending guerrilla warfare against a foe more adept than British redcoats at bushwhacking, the Earl from time to time detached units in vain pursuit of an enemy who avoided pitched battle but ceaselessly delighted in ambushing, sniping, and other forms of harassment.

This harassment had needled Cornwallis ever since he had taken command from Clinton in June. From that time until he abandoned the Carolinas to pursue a will-o'-the-wisp into Virginia, he heard daily how the patriots deceived, tricked, plundered, and killed loyalists. Rebel methods varied but the end stayed constant: to turn loyalists from their allegiance or, at the very least, to stop them from aiding the British. They did not flinch from using any means they thought would prove effective. Knowing that tall tales often convinced the credulous or intimidated the weak, the patriots became masters of propaganda. For example, a group of them told the loyalist David George that they planned to kidnap the wives and children of all tories.[1] On the day Cornwallis took command, Lieutenant Colonel George Turnbull of the New York Volunteers wrote to tell him about a rumor spreading over the countryside: the British, it was said, seized all young Carolinians and sent them "to the prince of Hesse." "It is inconceivable," Turnbull concluded, "the damage such a report has done." [2] The patriots did not rely solely upon words. They also employed mild pressure, persecution, terrorization, and killing — not necessarily in that order. Often they terrorized and killed first.

"The violence and the passions of these people," wrote Brigadier General Charles O'Hara, after his introduction to campaigning in the Carolinas, "are beyond every curb of religion, & Humanity, they are unbounded & every hour exhibits dreadful wanton mischiefs, murders, & violences of every kind, unheard of before. We find the country in great measure abandoned, &

the few who venture to remain at home in hourly expectation of being murdered, or stripped of all their property." [3] Barely two months after he took command, Cornwallis informed Clinton that "the whole country" between the Peedee and the Santee was "in an absolute state of rebellion, every friend of government has been carried off, and his plantation destroyed." [4] This state of affairs never improved during the entire period of British occupation.[5] Cornwallis tried in a variety of ways to end active disloyalty and to promote loyalty, but he did not succeed.

He failed for several reasons. Probably the chief reason was distaste for the matter, which admitted of no soldierly approach. It never depended upon the outcome of an honest battle between opposing armies. Cornwallis possessed a soldier's conception of honor and straight dealing. He enjoyed fighting openly against a declared and courageous foe. By the same token he abhorred cruelty, deceit, and dishonesty. Here, however, he found himself in a situation where the last three qualities counted the most in winning the war. American armies granted him few pitched battles because he was too good at them. Only once did they challenge him to a knockdown fight in South Carolina, and then they bruised themselves badly. After that they carefully avoided him for seven months and then only fought him in North Carolina with an advantage in numbers and on ground of their own choosing.

If he could not win the South on the battlefield, Cornwallis had to win it by other means, and these he neither liked nor believed in. His two forays to the north, in 1780 and 1781, showed the extent of that disbelief. Underneath all his thoughts on how to pacify the country lay his conviction that nothing but the promise of American armies flooding down from the north kept alive the spirit of rebellion. Nothing but the army in North Carolina sustained the rebellion in South Carolina. In turn, he believed that nothing but Virginia's harboring of

American armies kept North Carolina aflame. So in the end he marched to Virginia.

But rebel leaders like Sumter and Marion needed no American armies to fire their spirits. Their supporters steadily increased during 1780 and 1781. "The British occupation," one observer remarks, "aroused the patriotism of many who had previously been indifferent. And it was precisely this situation that the British did not understand. . . . To thousands of South Carolinians, the Revolution became an active issue for the first time in 1780. Now forced to choose between their revolutionary government, which had made few demands, and the British, who neither restored order nor protected peaceful citizens and who governed by martial law, these inhabitants chose to oppose their new oppressors." [6] Before he left for North Carolina, Cornwallis had bitter experience of the uncertain nature of loyalist support. He never quite understood how to render that support certain so that he could safely leave the country in the hands of loyal citizens. He never quite understood that to quell revolutionaries — men fired with dedication to an ideal above themselves — he had to be as ruthless as they; that he had to use terror, oppression, confiscation, and brutality on a grand scale; that to eliminate the revolution he had to eliminate revolutionaries, not just beat their armies in the field. Even if he had understood it, he could not have won, for he would have resigned his commission rather than use such methods. Had he been brutal or terrifying, which might possibly have held South Carolina for Britain, he would not have been Charles, Earl Cornwallis.

Those Americans, civilian and military, who encountered the Earl directly, knew his humane nature. Personal appeals from distressed civilians rarely failed to move him. A Mr. Keaty Simons, for example, petitioned him to exercise his "well-known humanity." Simons said that smallpox had broken out among the people on his plantation and that he expected it to spread like wildfire since only one person there had immunity from a previous bout with the dread disease. Figuring that perhaps four fifths of his plantation's inhabitants, including his wife, were doomed, Simons asked for release from militia duty in order to attend his family. A harder man than the Earl, needing as he did every able-bodied man for service, might have turned a deaf ear to such pleas (Tarleton would have paid scant attention to Simons). But the Earl granted his request.[7] He believed that enemies also deserved humane treatment, as his two antagonists in the Carolinas, Gates and Greene, both knew. Once the rout and slaughter of Camden ended, Cornwallis exerted himself to tend the American wounded as well as his own. He even allowed American physicians to come into his army to look after their own wounded. "I am to thank your Lordship," Gates later wrote, "for the Attention, and Tenderness with which Capt. Hamilton assures me, the Wounded, and Prisoners have been treated at Camden." [8] Although in such desperate circumstances after Guilford Courthouse that he could scarcely care for his own wounded, Cornwallis still attempted everything in his power for those of Greene's army who had fallen into his hands. Greene felt "much obliged to you for the attention you have paid the unfortunate wounded of my army." [9]

Although by the time of Guilford he had learned that kindness won few adherents to George III, Cornwallis never stooped to meanness. He had come to realize that terror was perhaps the only effective weapon, so he threatened the rebels with death and destruction. But against every threat worked his natural humanity. In the final analysis, because he rarely carried out his threats, they stimulated opposition rather than fear, boldness rather than retreat, disorder rather than order. And as opposition grew, loyalist support necessarily diminished. Fearless in battle, magnanimous in victory, honest and humane, a gentleman in the truest sense — Cornwallis had no place in a civil war.

The month after Camden he revealed that he knew what had to be done to win that war. He knew but subconsciously refused to believe what his rational mind told him. "I am clearly of opinion," he informed Lieutenant Colonel John Harris Cruger, the commander of the 1st battalion of DeLancey's provincial corps, "that in a civil war there is no admitting of neutral characters, & that those who are not clearly with us, must be so far considered against us, as to be disarmed, and every measure taken to prevent their being able to do mischief." [10] An acute observation but one which the Earl never allowed himself or his subordinates to implement. Almost every threat of destruction allowed the Americans a way to escape his wrath. Furthermore, he restricted, when he could, the terroristic activities of his less scrupulous subordinates. The result was an ambivalent policy.

His own treatment of rebels, for instance, showed this ambivalence. In a proclamation of September 15, he noted that rebel militia had taken one John Hutchison from his plantation and that they now threatened to hang the poor man. If they carried out the execution, Cornwallis would "instantly cause two of the most violent persons of your party who are now in our custody to be hanged." Should the rebels inflict "any other corporal punishment" on Hutchison, the British would "severely retaliate on two of your friends." The threats were real enough, but the rebels gauged the Earl's true inclinations when he promised to exchange a man "of nearly the same station of life" if they released Hutchison. He wanted clemency, not "examples." [11] His conduct immediately after Camden revealed his character yet more clearly than this incident. The British captured, in arms against them, three men who had previously taken the oath to preserve peace. The punishment for such treachery was the gallows. The redcoats prepared to hang them, but at the last moment Cornwallis "benevolently interposed and pardoned them." Sergeant Lamb, the recorder of this incident, states that the three rebels were so overjoyed at their reprieve that they prayed for the prosperity of King George and Lord Cornwallis and promised to fight for the British.[12] Perhaps they did, but was this effect what Cornwallis really wished? If he had pardoned his own soldiers under sentence of death in a harshly disciplined army, he might have impressed his men wonderfully (as he did later in India). What, however, must loyalists think if they saw men who had plundered them go scot-free? What, for that matter, must rebels think? Both might well grow convinced that no matter how grossly a man betrayed his sworn word, the British would not punish him severely.

The ruthlessness he would not permit himself, Cornwallis also refused to his subordinates. While he admitted to Cruger that a civil war allowed of no neutrality, he ordered Cruger to disarm rebels "guilty of no new offences" by the "gentlest methods which the nature of that business will admit of." [13] Cruger, a loyalist himself, knew "that business" admitted of no gentle methods. Lieutenant Colonel George Turnbull certainly did not use them when he destroyed an iron works in the vicinity of Rocky Mount, and Cornwallis even allowed him to let loyalist militia "do what they please with the plantations abandoned by the rebels." Yet the Earl "strictly" forbade and promised he would "severely punish any act of cruelty" to the families of rebels.[14] Modern "civilization" has taught that threatening a man's family often secures his submission. Tarleton, Cornwallis' most flamboyant and most ruthless subordinate, was not above such measures. Tarleton frequently was able to inflict cruelties forbidden other British officers because the Earl often detached him and his Legion for missions some distance away from the main army. Then, too, Tarleton usually won impressive victories (at least before Cowpens), and success speaks loudly. Yet the Legion commander felt his general's frosty gaze whenever Cornwallis learned of irregularities committed by the dragoon. "I am sorry," Tarleton once said, "your lordship has cause to complain of the plundering of the legion." [15] Sorry he may well have been, for a gentle reprimand from Cornwallis had the effect of a stern dressing down from another officer. The extent of the Earl's feelings about anything that smacked of cruelty can be gauged by his "severe, though gentle," reproach to Tarleton: "There spoke the sabre." [16] Unlike some commanders, Cornwallis never blustered. Quiet and resolute, he kept an even temper in public, and he disliked rebuking his subordinates in public or private. If they had let him down, he preferred to recall them to their sense of duty, to ask them to try harder next time, rather than to admonish them for past mistakes or failures. Subordinates respected him for this characteristic, but they also felt keenly his mild reproach. Years later in India, a young lieutenant colonel almost wept after an interview with him: "Never shall I forget it the longest day I live . . . to be told by Lord Cornwallis — my commander in chief — that I had not acted like a gentleman was too severe." [17] Tarleton was not given to tears, but the meaning of his commander's reprimand cannot have escaped even his insensitivity. He was aware that he ranked among Cornwallis' favorites and that Cornwallis knew he usually won his battles. Yet even he could not escape censure where brutal treatment of Americans, civilian or military, was involved.

Earl Cornwallis never allowed cruelty or wanton brutality, if he could prevent it. That he nonetheless acquired a reputation for cruelty in the South is ironic. It seriously hampered his efforts to gain loyalist support and to maintain order. That reputation was partly the fault of his subordinates, partly his own fault, and partly the fault of the patriots.

In an area as vast as South Carolina, with communications precarious and distances great, he naturally could not keep tight control over the actions of his subordinates. Whenever he detached a unit here or there to fight a battle or to pacify an area, he had to relinquish full command over affairs, leaving the battle or the pacification to the senior officer of that detachment.

He might order the strictest adherence to the rules of war and to common decency, but once the unit departed, he lost control of events. He might enjoin Tarleton to mercy, but Tarleton could forget the injunction when he took the field independently. Thus it had been at the Waxhaws. When the Legion commander routed Buford at the end of May, 1780, according to the American accounts, he butchered the defeated enemy after it had surrendered. "The demand for quarters, seldom refused to a vanquished foe, was at once found to be in vain," a survivor reported, for "not a man was spared, and it was the concurrent testimony of all the survivors that for fifteen minutes after, every man was prostrated. They went over the ground, plunging their bayonets into everyone that exhibited signs of life and, in some instances, where several had fallen over the others, those monsters were seen to throw off on the point of the bayonet the uppermost, to come at those underneath. . . ." It was "a scene of indiscriminate carnage, never surpassed by the ruthless atrocities of the most barbarous savages." [18] Tarleton, of course, told the Earl a different story. He had summoned the enemy to surrender. They had refused. He had attacked.[19] Obviously Cornwallis had to give public support to his subordinate's version and had to regard most of the American accounts as fabrications. If he did not back up his best officers openly, he could not keep a fighting army. So he dealt with Tarleton, publicly congratulating him while privately cautioning him to a humane course of action.[20] Perhaps that was the Earl's mistake. If he had allowed Tarleton to ravage at will he might have terrorized South Carolina into submission. Cornwallis might not have held the province for long by this method, but it was his only chance to hold it at all.

Tarleton deserved his reputation. Many other subordinates of Cornwallis did not. Yet rebel propaganda often painted them all black so as to stir followers to greater efforts and to gain the support of waverers. The very fact that British officers did their jobs — which sometimes involved going after partisans — was grist enough for the propaganda mill. Colonel Cruger from his base at Ninety-Six "scoured" the country.[21] Major Weymss of the 63d regiment took a detachment to the Cheraw Hill area and "burnt and laid waste about 50 houses and plantations, mostly belonging to people who have either broke their paroles or oath of allegiance, & are now in arms against us." He reported that he captured twenty prisoners, "one of whom, a notorious villain I mean to hang tomorrow." [22] But according to the Americans the "notorious villain" had "neither taken parole as a prisoner, nor protection as a British subject," and they said Weymss eventually hanged him because he refused "to transport some British officers over a ferry" and started "shooting at them across a river." [23] Such incidents in a bloody civil war naturally gave rise to rumors and tales of atrocity which the patriots spread, one imagines, almost gleefully.

British words, however, perhaps even more than British deeds, allowed whigs to picture them and their leader as unfeeling monsters and, as a result, to win adherents to the patriot side. Cornwallis and most of his regular officers were unwilling to abandon themselves to an orgy of plundering, but in order to hearten loyalists and scare rebels, they wrote of plans to destroy the enemy ruthlessly. Patriots often intercepted these communications which, if fiercely worded, they broadcast unaltered. If messages needed textual changes in order to make the British appear in a terrible light, the patriots did not hesitate to make the changes. In either event, captured British letters served the rebel cause well and increased the Earl's difficulties.

Two such rebel interceptions troubled Cornwallis during the summer of 1780. In July, apparently in a fanciful mood, Lord Rawdon composed out of whole cloth a letter in the form of orders which he sent to a colonel of loyalist militia, Henry Rugeley. The orders, which promised horrible treatment to rebels, Rugeley read to all the militia companies under his command. But Rawdon had designed the commands only "to act upon the fears and prejudices of the vulgar." He had connived with Rugeley and other militia officers to make them up in the first place. They threatened whipping, imprisonment, or deportation to the West Indies for all people in Rugeley's area who helped deserters, either actively — by sheltering, guiding, or giving them horses — or passively — by failing to help capture them. They further promised ten guineas a head for dead deserters from Rawdon's regiment, the Volunteers of Ireland, but only five guineas for live ones. Of course, Rawdon knew he could not reward Americans for killing soldiers nor arbitrarily ship people off to the West Indies. He intended his bluff to frighten. Perhaps he did scare a few men, but in the long run the orders hurt his cause more than they helped it.[24]

So it was with one of Cornwallis' letters. Rawdon intended his communication to Rugeley for public consumption. Cornwallis did not intend for his letter of August 18 to Colonel Cruger at Ninety-Six to reach enemy hands. Yet the rebels captured it. As the Earl originally wrote it, his letter gave Cruger news of his Camden victory and informed him of the operations of other portions of his army. It also prescribed a course of action — harsh but not unjust — for Cruger to take toward the rebels:

> I have given orders that all the inhabitants of this province, who had *submitted,* and who have taken part in this revolt, should be punished with the greatest rigour, that they should be imprisoned, and their whole property taken from them or destroyed; I have likewise directed that compensation should be made out of their effects to the persons who have been *plundered* and oppressed by them. I have ordered in the most positive manner, that every militia man who had borne arms with us and had afterwards joined the enemy should be immediately hanged. I have now, Sir, only to desire that you will take the most *vigorous* measures to *extinguish the rebellion* in the district in which you command, and that you will obey in the strictest manner the directions I have given in this letter, relative to the treatment of the country.[25]

When the whigs looked at this missive they thought it too mild in tone. So they proceeded to alter it. The intended recipient became Nesbitt Balfour, a regular officer (Cruger was a provincial officer), presumably because patriots thought it would be more effective to make a regular officer merciless. After all, the whigs already knew that provincials (the most offensive of the tories) needed no prodding to brutality. Next, words of the text were altered here and there so that the message breathed wanton oppression. They took the harshest-sounding parts, which were incidental to news of the Camden victory, out of context. The finished production magnified an almost casual letter of Cornwallis into an important, considered, methodical statement of British policy:

> I have given Orders that all the Inhabitants of this Province who have subscribed, and have taken Part in this Revolt, should be punished with the greatest Rigour, and also those who will not turn out, that they may be imprisoned, and their whole Property taken from them or destroyed. I have likewise ordered that Compensation should be made out of their Effects, to the Persons who have been injured and oppressed by them. I have ordered in the most positive Manner that every Militia Man, who has borne Arms with us and afterwards joined the Enemy shall be immediately hanged. I desire you will take the most rigorous Measures to punish the Rebels in the District in which you Command, and that you will obey in the strictest Manner the Directions I have given in this Letter relative to the Inhabitants of this Country.[26]

After they finished their alterations and spread their creation about the countryside, patriots lifted their cause from local to continental proportions by forwarding to George Washington the altered text of the Cornwallis letter and Rawdon's "commands" to Rugeley. The American commander, in turn, engaged in an acrimonious debate with Clinton over atrocities. "Humanity revolts" at the policies of the two British officers,

Washington said. Clinton defended his juniors and blamed the rebels for their cruelty and deceit.[27] The entire business served the rebel cause well and Cornwallis ill. Not only did he acquire a local reputation for cruelty, which helped to turn neutrals against him and to harden the convinced rebels into more determined resistance, but he also acquired continental infamy. Thus the whigs almost immediately rendered his task of pacification extremely difficult.

If Cornwallis hurt rather than helped himself when he tried to scare the rebels with words, could he win loyalist support and patriot submission in other ways? Could he enlist enough active, energetic men into a loyalist militia to enable them to stop the rebels themselves? At first he thought he could. In July he told Lieutenant Colonel Allured Clarke that the British would likely have a militia "of at least 8000 men within a month, from which all rebels are excluded." [28] Lieutenant Colonel Nesbitt Balfour, to whom Cornwallis entrusted the administrative control of Charleston, was equally optimistic. "From every appearance," Balfour said, "I am almost certain of no resistance from the back country." [29] Unfortunately for the British, these hopes rapidly proved unfounded. Summer enthusiasm gave way to autumn despair.

The fault for failure lay as much with the British as with the loyalists themselves. During their years of fighting in the North, the British had paid scant attention to the loyalists and included them only incidentally in their planning. Then, for the Carolina campaign, they suddenly relied on loyalist energies to recover the South. After allowing their friends to vegetate for five years they actually believed that somehow, as soon as they themselves put in an appearance, masses of loyal subjects would rally to their cause. They thought they had the support of the majority of the population. But most people in the Carolinas (like most people anytime and anywhere) simply wanted to be left alone.[30] The ones who really wanted to take part were active rebels, and Cornwallis would not play the role of butcher to stop them.

Thus, as commander in the South, Cornwallis faced the problem posed by the long-standing errors of British policy in general. More specifically, he also had to overcome the problem posed by the errors of his immediate predecessor. Sir Henry Clinton had made two very bad decisions relative to the loyalists before he turned the command over to his subordinate. The first lay in his issuing contradictory proclamations that intended to conciliate but served to intimidate. The second lay in his appointing Patrick Ferguson as inspector of loyalist militia and in giving him a virtually free hand. These two follies, as much as anything else, lost the British the Carolinas.

On June 1, Clinton and Arbuthnot, both commissioners for restoring peace, issued a proclamation designed to restore South Carolina to order. This proclamation concerned two groups of people: prisoners on parole who had been captured either at Charleston or at the interior posts and persons who had participated actively in rebellion. It promised all of them — save those who had shed the blood of their fellow citizens — a full pardon and British protection if they would return to their allegiance. Once they took the oath, the British guaranteed them all the "rights and immunities" they had formerly possessed under British rule and promised exemption from taxation save by their own legislature. A sensible and humane move, it would have been a fitting prelude to Cornwallis' occupation of the interior. But Clinton reversed all the good effects when he took it upon himself on June 3 to issue his own proclamation, which "reawakened the spirit of revolt in South Carolina and marked a sharp change in the southern attitude." [31] The new proclamation released all prisoners from parole as of June 20 and restored to them all the "rights and duties of citizens." [32] But it further stipulated that all men who after their release failed to take an oath of allegiance and failed to support the British actively would be treated as rebels. Clinton had thought to "divide the sheep from the goats," but instead he herded them all together. The damage was inconceivable. Rebels who had gone on parole and retired quietly to their homes, content to sit out the war, were now forced either to become actively loyal subjects or to be treated as rebels. Since their sympathies lay with the patriots, most of them chose once again to support rebellion. Many hitherto-loyal subjects deserted the royal cause because they figured that the proclamation allowed "notorious firebrands" to retain all the privileges of British subjects by a "mere gesture" of allegiance. All their past suffering seemed to count for nothing. The British appeared intent on rewarding the bad instead of the good. Convinced rebels with few scruples about violating their oaths swore allegiance to the crown and immediately went over to the rebels. Rawdon, at Camden in July, summed up the mischief Clinton's proclamation had done. He wrote Cornwallis that although the majority of inhabitants in his area had been "ill disposed" toward the British, previously they had not actually resorted to arms against them. But the proclamation now freed men from the paroles he had imposed upon them with the result that "nine out of ten of them are now embodied on the part of the rebels. . . . The greater part of the Waxhaw people have joined the rebels. The rest live under the enemy's protections." [33]

Thus Sir Henry laid the ground for the "second rebellion" in South Carolina before he left. He did so without consulting Cornwallis and, indeed, without even telling him about the proclamation after he had issued it.[34] Cornwallis did not discover what Clinton had done until he returned to Charleston in June. Then he wrote to Arbuthnot: "I hope you will not be offended when I assure you that the Proclamation of the Commissioners of the 1st, and that of the General of the 3rd, did not at all contribute to the success of my operations." [35]

The Earl strove mightily to rectify Clinton's error. Within a week of taking over from Clinton on June 10, Cornwallis arbitrarily revoked Sir Henry's decision and exerted himself to secure the disaffected on their paroles as prisoners of war.[36] Some of the worst men he shipped from Charleston to Saint Augustine. Washington considered that this measure violated the capitulation, but Cornwallis claimed justification. The men he exiled had propagated lies, threatened the loyal, intimidated "our friends," and corresponded with the enemy. As he saw it, he had but two choices: to confine them closely, perhaps in the provost, or to ship them out of the colony. He chose the latter course as the more humane.[37] So Cornwallis locked one of the stable doors in July and August. The horse had been stolen in June.

He failed to close, much less lock, the door on Clinton's second error — the appointment of Ferguson as inspector of militia. Sir Henry had given the major primary responsibility for organizing and leading loyalist militia. Ferguson did not lack ability. Indeed he was brilliant. He was also erratic, unstable, and overconfident. From the outset, Cornwallis distrusted Ferguson, but he could find no sufficiently weighty reason for dismissing him from a post to which the commander in chief had personally appointed him. Had Ferguson been a little less cocky and confident, he might have mustered enough loyalists to hold their own against the patriots.

Unfortunately for the British neither Ferguson nor the other British officers had very firm material with which to work. Militia, whether patriot or loyal, rarely proved a reliable instrument of war even under the best of circumstances. Despite the legends that have grown up about them, patriot militiamen were not good soldiers. They almost never shook regulars in pitched battle. They could not keep a formation. They seldom mustered their promised number at the beginning of a campaign, and those who did come would not stay to the end. When seriously threatened, they usually ran. Because in the South most of them had horses, they usually escaped capture by regular infantry trying to follow up a victory.[38] Under peculiar circumstances, as at King's Mountain, or when properly led, as by Morgan at Cowpens, militia might prove effective. Most of the time, however, they could not be trusted, which Gates learned to his sorrow at Camden.

Bad as the patriot militia was, for two basic reasons the loyalist militia was even worse. In the first place, they simply lacked the patriots' enthusiasm. Even Ferguson, usually overconfident in his loyalists, admitted that the rebel militia was "more warlike" than his.[39] Men who prefer the status quo to any change are usually less dynamic than revolutionaries. Even though they may be dissatisfied with many aspects of their world, defenders of the existing order would usually rather continue with the government and society they know than gamble everything on the uncertainties of a new order. Revolutionaries are prepared to risk all to win all. With exceptions for special circumstances,[40] it was thus in the American Revolution. Many were loyalists because they did not wish to have their way of life disturbed. Such men, when untrained, make poor soldiers. Training them required time, money, and good leadership. The British could give time, money, and leadership to the training of a limited number of provincial regiments. For the most part, however, they had to turn to loyalist militia groups. Perhaps because they were less dynamic than the rebels, these groups furnished few able leaders. Herein lies the second basic reason for the failure of loyalist militia: unlike the patriots, the loyalists could seldom bring up competent leaders from their own ranks. They did not have a Sumter or a Marion. Lieutenant Colonel George Turnbull, himself a provincial officer, noted that: "Our officers of militia in genl. are not near so active as the rebels, and great numbers of their privates are ready to turn against us when an opportunity offers." [41] "I am clearly of opinion," Balfour told Rawdon, "that if an officer and an active one, is not at the head of militia, nothing can be expected from them." British regular officers could lead militia competently, "but no militia officer unassisted, ever will." [42]

The coming months afforded Cornwallis ample opportunity to witness the truth of his subordinates' observations on the inferiority of loyalist leadership. As early as June 7, Balfour stated that although he had used his "best endeavours to find out proper people for militia officers," he had been unable to find "a single man of any property or consequence that has not been in the rebel service." [43] When at length the British did find such men, they often proved unsatisfactory. Lieutenant Colonel Thomas Browne of Georgia was as much a fire-eater as any of the rebels. The whigs had tarred and feathered him for his political opinions, and he never forgave them. Eager to raise and lead militia against the patriots, he cared little for the nicer rules of human decency. He mercilessly burned, plundered, and looted the whigs around Augusta. To his credit as a soldier, he later gallantly defended the city from American attack in the spring of 1781.[44] But Browne and his colleague, Major James Wright Jr. (presumably the son of the royal governor of Georgia), gave more trouble than help to Cornwallis. Both of them volunteered to raise militia for service on the Georgia–South Carolina frontier. By their methods they probably alienated more loyalists than they brought into the militia. First they raided the prison ships in Savannah for men. Next, when the hulks yielded a paltry return, Wright sent a recruiting party to Charleston to enlist American prisoners of war from the barracks there. Even then, however, Browne and Wright had not filled their units. So they beat the countryside, practicing "all the tricks of recruiting to the great terror & disgust of the inhabitants." When Cornwallis learned of their activities he ordered them out of South Carolina and refused to let them serve in that province again.[45]

Other loyalist leaders, as enthusiastic as Browne but more scrupulous, sometimes showed equally bad judgment. Even before Clinton left Charleston, Cornwallis had warned the North Carolina loyalists that it would be "prudent for them to remain quiet" until a force of British regulars could bring them "effectual support." Disregarding this advice, Lieutenant Colonel John Moore called out a large group of his followers. On June 20, they assembled at Ramsour's Mills in Tryon County, North Carolina, where the rebels attacked and routed them. In his own defense, Moore asserted that he mustered but eight hundred men to oppose a thousand rebels, including two hundred Continentals. But Lord Rawdon, to whom Moore eventually fled at Camden, sifted over the facts and arrived at a different conclusion. He estimated that the whigs numbered only three hundred and that the disaster occurred because the loyalist leaders, instead of preparing themselves for an attack, had wasted precious minutes in council arguing over the leadership at the very moment when the patriots fell upon them.[46] Cornwallis regarded the incident as yet another example of the "imprudence and folly" [47] of loyalist leaders.

Probably at no time before King's Mountain did their "imprudence and folly" harm him more than it did just after the battle of Camden. His rout of Gates there had encouraged him to expect renewed loyalist activity. Indeed, while Gates hotfooted it toward Hillsboro, the loyalists "disarmed several of the enemy's stragglers" near the Peedee River. "But the leading persons of the loyalists," Cornwallis learned, "were so undecided in their councils that they lost the critical time of availing themselves of our success, and even suffered General Gates to pass to Hillsborough with a guard of six men only." [48]

Although loyalist leaders recruited unwisely, rose inopportunely, and acted indecisively, Cornwallis still had to use them. He finally set to work with the material he had. Some loyalists went into provincial regiments, where they proved far more use-

ful than in the militia. Both the North and South Carolina regiments of provincials served well and faithfully. Lieutenant
Colonel Alexander Innes, of the South Carolina loyalists, was
the inspector general of provincials. He compared the quality
of provincials to that of militia: "I look upon it that every man
intitled to serve in a provincial corps during the war is a usefull
soldier gain'd to the King's Service and I am well convinced the
Militia on their present plan will ever prove a useless, disorderly,
destructive banditti." Innes concluded that "it may seem extraordinary that the same people of which the Militia are composed
shou'd be such different men in a regular provincial corps," but
different and better they were.[49]

Provincial regiments, however, were necessarily limited in
number. The British government helped support them and,
with its finances stretched to the limit, could establish only a few
such regiments. Indeed, the status of even those few often remained confused. The ministry never worked out systemati-
cally the answers to such questions as pay, rank, amount and
type of British supplies, or status of the provincials in relation to
the regulars.[50] The provincial regiments also remained few in
number because of a feature that made them solid but unattrac-
tive: they demanded long-term service, often for the duration of
the war and, if necessary, outside the province. Most enlisted
men did not want to leave their homes for long periods or be
subject to the harsh discipline of the regulars. In raising his
provincial regiment Innes found it "absolutely impossible to
prevail on them [loyalists] to serve from home with any chear-
fulness." [51] Officers often felt the same way. Barely two weeks
after Cornwallis took command from Clinton, Lieutenant
Colonel George Turnbull, who led the New York Volunteers in
South Carolina in 1780, threatened to leave the service altogether. Turnbull believed that New York men ought to serve
in New York. "There is surely," he said, "a duty which a man
owes his family and if I see no relief after settling the peace and

quiet of this province I shall be drove to the disagreeable necessity to quit the service entirely." [52] In face of such strong feelings, even among the best provincials, the government could recruit only enough regiments to give thin support to British regular units. For the rest, it had to rely upon militia to return peace to South Carolina.[53]

Before he left for New York, Clinton made provision for loyalist militia and, unlike his course with the peace proclamation, informed Cornwallis of what he had done. "I have allowed Major Ferguson to take charge of the militia under the title of Inspector of Militia Corps and to propose regulations for them." [54] Clinton gave Ferguson his commission on May 22[55] and wrote out brief and uncomplicated instructions for him (an unusual feat for Clinton). The inspector was to round up young unmarried men from Georgia and the Carolinas, form them into companies of fifty to a hundred men each and, when sufficient in numbers, into battalions of six to twelve companies each. Service would be for a precise period. Ferguson should not scare potential militiamen away by pressuring them to enter the regular army.

Despite the inferior quality of loyalist militia, Cornwallis enjoyed a certain limited success with it. He never achieved absolute order anywhere, but loyalists held patriots to a stalemate on the Georgia–South Carolina border until the time that Cornwallis left the Carolinas for Virginia. In particular, the militia around the British base at Ninety-Six showed more spunk than other loyalists. On the other hand, from the day he took over until the day he left, Cornwallis never could maintain order on the North Carolina border or, indeed, in much of the eastern and northern parts of that province. From the mouth of the Santee north to Cowpens, the British incessantly faced violent opposition. Not even the presence of a large British army in their vicinity encouraged loyalists to muster with sufficient numbers and energy to stop rebellion there.

Cornwallis could achieve limited success on the Georgia–South Carolina frontier for two reasons. In the first place, Georgia was Britain's "most royal" province. Its zeal infected its South Carolina neighbor. Patrick Ferguson considered the border loyalists of the highest quality. "The militia of 96 that have been admitted to bear arms," Ferguson commented, "are certainly loyal, almost to a man." [56] Captain Abraham DePeyster, his second, echoed these sentiments. He noticed at the battle of King's Mountain that after other militia had fled, the men from Ninety-Six still held.[57]

They held, not only because they believed more deeply in their cause than did many of their colleagues, but also because they had known security in their area. That they had a haven to which they could retreat if the war went badly had encouraged them to dish out punishment as well as take it.[58]

A second reason for their limited success along the Georgia border was that the British established a strong fortification at Ninety-Six and sent able leaders to command it. These leaders rendered Ninety-Six impregnable. As the months rolled by, the post came to symbolize imperial steadfastness. It became the Gibraltar of South Carolina and even withstood the siege of a regular American army. Owing mostly to the efforts of its commander, Lieutenant Colonel John Harris Cruger, the fort never fell.[59]

While Ninety-Six held its own until the end, the northern border of South Carolina did not get the chance. Turbulence never subsided from the mouth of the Santee to the foothills of the Appalachians. Unlike the other border, in the North British victories affected rebel activity very little. Men such as Francis Marion, the "Swamp Fox," continually harried the redcoats, stirred up the countryside, and kept the flame of rebellion alive.[60] "Colonel Marion," Cornwallis said later, "had so wrought the minds of the people, partly by the terror of his threats and cruelty of his punishments, and partly by the promise of plunder, that there was scarcely an inhabitant between the Santee and the Peedee that was not in arms against us." [61]

Within a month of taking command Cornwallis had suffered his first reverse (apart from Moore's defeat) in this area. In early July the commander at Rocky Mount, Turnbull, detached Captain Christian Huck of the Legion to operate against some "violent rebels" thirty miles away. Although he left with only thirty or forty dragoons from that unit, twenty mounted men of the New York Volunteers, and about sixty militia, Huck succeeded in gathering loyalists along his route until his force numbered around four hundred. But Mary McClure, daughter of one of the patriot leaders, brought word to her father of Huck's march. So the patriots turned the tables on the tories. Huck made it easier for them because he foolishly "camped in an unguarded manner." At dawn on July 12, the patriots infiltrated his camp, positioned themselves between the bivouac and the picketed horses, and opened fire from behind fences. They "totally surprized and routed" Huck's command, killing him in the process. Of the original tory party, only about a dozen Legionnaires and a dozen militiamen managed to escape. [62]

The defeat of Huck emboldened partisan Thomas Sumter — whose militia had effected that defeat — to attack Turnbull himself at Rocky Mount. Sumter gathered about six hundred men and moved upon the small post — a fortified frame house cut with loopholes, situated in a clearing in the woods on the west bank of the Catawba. Before his attack, Sumter sent a man with a flag to demand the post. "Col. Turnbull sent word that he might come and take it." The patriot leader tried, but when an impetuous assault failed, he withdrew. [63] Undaunted, Sumter moved on to another encampment of the provincials at Hanging Rock, which he attacked in early August. He would probably have fared better there had not Lord Rawdon visited the post a week earlier and removed the commanding lieutenant colonel, whom he found drunk when he arrived on the night of July 29.[64] As it was, Sumter's men nearly routed the provincials and might have done so had they not occupied themselves with looting the commissary's stores and drinking themselves into a stupor with the liquor they discovered.[65]

No regular British units participated in small engagements of this sort, but patriot activity caused Cornwallis to fear for the regulars in the area. Major Archibald McArthur had taken the 71st regiment to Cheraw Hill on the Peedee, but the post had proved so unhealthy that nearly two thirds of the regiment became too sick to be listed as fit for duty. Fearing for the safety of this crack unit, Cornwallis ordered McArthur to fall back toward Camden. The major loaded about one hundred of his sick on boats and sent them downriver under the escort of Lieutenant Colonel Robert Mills of the Cheraw Hills Militia. But when a party of patriots surprised Mills at Mars Bluff, most of his own militia, "who had just before taken the oaths of allegiance," turned against him, joining the patriots in attack. They captured those who had not deserted and chased Mills and a few of his officers nearly to Georgetown.[66]

Cornwallis had hoped that his victory at Camden would discourage whig activity, for he had partly attributed such activity to the encouragement that Gates' army gave the rebels. But Camden had made no difference to the partisan warfare. So Cornwallis, who always believed that only the American regular armies kept the flame of rebellion burning, convinced himself that North Carolina had to be taken. It gave shelter to the shattered remnants of Gates' corps, and it offered a place for future armies to gather. "It may be doubted by some whether the invasion of North Carolina may be a prudent measure," he wrote Clinton even before Camden, "but I am convinced it is a necessary one, and that if we do not attack that province, we must give up both South Carolina and Georgia, and retire within the walls of Charleston." [67] Events after Camden strengthened him in his conviction. How could rebels continue active after such a crushing defeat to American arms, unless they obtained protection and encouragement from the province to the north? Cornwallis resolved to move north and open a new campaign.

CHAPTER 9

King's Mountain
The Riderless White Horse

> "Poetic fantasy might find a subject for meditation, in
> the fact that the device of the House of Hanover, the
> riderless white horse, should have been the emblem
> of victory to the rebel host on the well-contested field."
>
> James Ferguson, *Two Scottish Soldiers*, p. 101.

ALTHOUGH AFTER CAMDEN, Cornwallis had hoped to carry the
war quickly to North Carolina, the needs of his army delayed his progress. During August and early September of 1780
he busied himself with preparations, scraping together wagons
and provisions for the march, organizing the supply train, and
seeing to the myriad other details attendant upon moving an
army.

His activities in the South, sometimes criticized as hasty and
ill-considered, were actually undertaken slowly and deliberately
in the weeks after his Camden victory. By late August, he harbored few illusions about the capacity of North Carolina loyalists to act independently of a regular British army. "Our
friends," he told Clinton on August 20, "do not seem inclined to
rise until they see our army in motion." [1] But he hesitated to
put his army in motion unless Sir Henry sped the promised
force toward the Chesapeake so as to divert some of the American forces away from his own troops. If Clinton could not create

such a diversion, Cornwallis wanted reinforcements for his own command. Extensive rebel activity had occurred the previous summer on the same border toward which he planned to march. Now he was uneasily aware that he would be leading a very small army into what would probably prove a very tough campaign. To garrison Camden he would need to leave behind the New York Volunteers and Hamilton's North Carolina Provincials. There then would remain to him a mere twenty-two hundred men, fifteen hundred from the understrength 23d, 33d, and 71st regiments, together with seven hundred from the Legion, Volunteers of Ireland, and Bryan's North Carolinians.[2]

For three weeks before his departure Cornwallis struggled to ensure, insofar as he could, that every one of the twenty-two hundred would arrive in North Carolina healthy. At length, on September 8, he was ready, and on that day he marched toward Charlotte. His eventual goal was Hillsboro, where he hoped to form "a very large magazine for the winter, of flour and meal from the country, and of rum, salt, &c., from Cross Creek, which I understand to be about eighty miles carriage." At the same time he would "try to arrange the friends who are in our favor."[3]

The advance proved "anything but impetuous."[4] Illness dogged his army. Even Tarleton came down with a fever, and the Earl had to pause for two weeks at Waxhaws to allow the army to convalesce. There patriots gave him a sample of the trouble which the future promised. While the Legion — the most dreaded loyalist unit in British service — was camped on the right side of the Catawba River at Wahab's Plantation, almost within calling distance of a British army, a group of rebels under the command of Colonel William Davie skirmished with it.[5]

Not until September 25 did Cornwallis consider his men sufficiently recovered to resume their march. He now sent the Legion cavalry in advance to scout for the enemy and to serve as the eyes of the army. They were led by Major George Hanger, who had temporarily taken the place of the incapacitated Tarleton. As the British approached Charlotte on September 26, Cornwallis sent Hanger ahead with orders to advance cautiously and to look over the town. The Earl expected militia to dispute his approach.

Unfortunately for Cornwallis, caution formed no part of Hanger's character. Indeed, his whole reckless career summed up his impetuousity. The third son of Gabriel, Lord Coleraine, he grew up sampling the country women and avoiding study. His father eventually packed him off to Reading school in Berkshire. Here he so interrupted academic routine that the headmaster beat him regularly with a long rattan cane. His father then enrolled Hanger in other institutions and eventually sent him to Eton. There, one gathers, he learned more about the local women than he learned about Latin grammar. Eton bored Hanger. Like Cornwallis, he wanted a military career. Coleraine shipped his wayward boy off to Europe to study, but Hanger deserted the University of Göttingen for the army of Frederick the Great, where he learned cavalry tactics. When Hanger came back his father bought him an ensigncy in the 1st Foot Guards. The young ensign then proceeded to fritter away a fortune in England. He spent exorbitantly on clothes — "my morning vestments cost me near eighty pounds, and those for the ball above one hundred and eighty" — on fencing lessons, gambling, and "every pleasure in life which that age of pleasure, extravagance, and elegance, was calculated to afford." In 1776 his regiment, so he said, treated him "most unjustly" by promoting a junior over him. Hanger resigned his commission, and volunteered in the Hessian service then embarking for America. He secured a captaincy in the Jagers, mortgaged his estate of £13,000, left it in the hands of an agent, and sailed for the New World. He had scarcely begun service there when his agent died. The estate went up for public auction and sold for half its

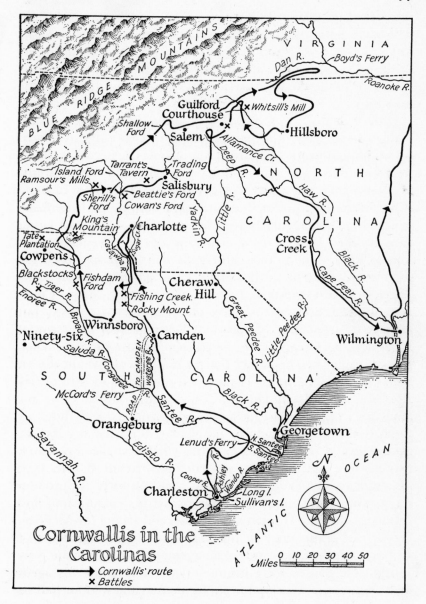

VIRGINIA

Boyd's Ferry

Dan R.

Roanoke R.

BLUE RIDGE MOUNTAINS

× Whitsill's Mill

Guilford
Courthouse

*Shallow
Ford*

Salem

•Hillsboro

Allamance Cr.

Deep R.

Tarrant's
Tavern ×

*Trading
Ford*

NORTH

Island Ford

Ramsour's Mills

× Salisbury

Haw R.

Sherill's
Ford ×

Beattie's Ford
Cowan's Ford

Yadkin R.

Little R.

CAROLINA

King's
Mountain

•Charlotte

Catawba R.

Sugar Cr.

Cross
Creek•

Tate×
Plantation

Black R.

Cowpens

Cape Fear R.

Blackstocks×
*Fishdam
Ford*

Broad R.

Tiger R.

Enoree R.

× Fishing Creek
× Rocky Mount

Cheraw•
Hill

Winnsboro

•Camden

Great Peedee R.

Little Peedee R.

•Ninety-Six

Saluda R.

Broad R.

Congaree R.

ROAD TO CAMDEN

Wateree R.

CAROLINA

Black R.

Wilmington

McCord's Ferry

Santee R.

SOUTH

Orangeburg

Edisto R.

Savannah R.

Lenud's Ferry

N. Santee
S. Santee

•Georgetown

Charleston•

Cooper R.

Ashley R.

Wando R.

Long I.
Sullivan's I.

N

OCEAN

ATLANTIC

Cornwallis in the
Carolinas

→ Cornwallis' route
× Battles

Miles 0 10 20 30 40 50

value. Now Hanger, a penniless Englishman in a German army, looked forward to an uncertain future. But Clinton noticed him and, upon Tarleton's request, eventually promoted him to major in the British Legion during the second Charleston campaign.[6] This impetuous wastrel now had the chance to grab some of Tarleton's glory for himself. He disregarded Cornwallis' orders and forgot his duty to the men marching behind him.

Throwing care to the wind, Hanger galloped his cavalry headlong into Charlotte, leaving his infantry — who ought to have searched out the area first — to walk in after him. This foolish maneuver perfectly suited Colonel Davie who, after his earlier skirmish with the Legion, had entered Charlotte on September 20 with one hundred fifty cavalry. Davie now prepared to receive his visitors.

Charlotte lay on ground slightly elevated above the surrounding country. The courthouse, a frame building raised on eight brick pillars ten feet high, dominated the town's center. A wall of rock three and one-half feet high extended between the pillars and served the town as a market. The two main streets crossed at the courthouse. Davie used his ground to advantage. He drew up three lines of militia north of the courthouse straddling the north-south road and posted one troop of cavalry on each side of the courthouse along the east-west road. The troop to the west hid behind and in a log house, while the one to the east used a brick house to similar advantage. The patriot colonel put about twenty men behind McComb's house, south of the courthouse along the line of the British advance. His ambush was perfect. If he had had a large force, Davie might have hurt the British severely. As it was, even his one hundred fifty men did considerable damage.

Blithely indifferent to the elementary rules of caution, Hanger swept forward. As he approached McComb's house the twenty American militiamen opened fire. The major, instead of dismounting his cavalry and waiting for his infantry to come up, galloped straight for the courthouse. There he met a withering fire from the first rank of Davie's men behind the rock wall. Even this blast did not deter him nor prompt him to take stock of his situation. When the first rank of patriot militia wheeled outward toward the rear to allow the second rank to come up, Hanger mistook the movement for a retreat. He continued his rush toward the courthouse and galloped his Legion into the withering crossfire loosed by the troops hidden in the buildings to the east and west. This fire wounded him and broke his cavalry, which pelted back toward the Legion infantry just advancing into Charlotte. The foot soldiers stopped and deployed into skirmish line while the dragoons re-formed their ranks.

Cornwallis, at the head of the main body, heard the firing and immediately noticed the confusion in his front. He rode up to the Legion, took in the situation at a glance, and ordered them to advance. But Davie had shaken Hanger's men and they hesitated. The Earl, angry with them already, shamed them into action. "Legion," he shouted, "remember you have everything to lose, but nothing to gain." Under the lash of this sarcasm and encouraged by the presence of regular light infantry which had now come up close behind them, the Legion advanced. Cornwallis soon cleared the town. The whole action was, as Hanger later said, "a trifling insignificant skirmish." But it was prophetic of the Earl's luck in North Carolina, and it wrecked temporarily whatever plans he still held for moving on to Hillsboro.[7] His army, already weakened from sickness, had twice been challenged. On the second challenge it had been hurt unnecessarily because of Hanger's irresponsibility, and the wounded Hanger soon succumbed to a fever so that he could no longer serve actively. With Hanger disabled and Tarleton sick, Cornwallis could scarcely send the Legion forward again. So, deprived of scouts and with a weakened army, he decided to sit down at Charlotte to wait upon events.

Those events would be determined by another British major commanding Americans — Patrick Ferguson, Clinton's appointed inspector of militia. From the outset Cornwallis had planned to coordinate his own advance to Charlotte and his attempt to rally the North Carolina loyalists with Ferguson's movements in Tryon County. If Ferguson could succeed with his detachment, the Earl might yet move from Charlotte to the heart of North Carolina and win the province for George III.

Patrick Ferguson was one of the most colorful figures in the British army. Ebullient and complicated, he was both ahead of and behind his time. He invented a rifle which proved better than anything the British adopted for another century. His gallantry and chivalry recall the "perfect gentle knight" of Chaucer's England. A man of slight build and a "delicate constitution," [8] Ferguson nonetheless possessed a commanding appearance. He seemed to the observer proud, perhaps even arrogant. Yet the haughty look only mirrored an inward self-confidence. With square face, wide-set eyes, large nose, and firm chin, his handsome, heroic countenance ought to have rested on a large frame. For the face, not the body, showed the true man, who was known as Bulldog to his militia. Ferguson was brilliant in invention, perhaps the best marksman in the British army, contemptuous of danger, and a tiger in battle.

Only six years younger than his commander, Patrick, the second son of James Ferguson, was born on the family estate of Pitfours in 1744. His father, a lawyer, defended the Jacobites in 1745 and achieved sufficient eminence to become a lord commissioner of justiciary in Scotland. While the young Patrick never had the same privileges as Lord Brome — Scottish gentry was not English aristocracy — he nonetheless grew up in relatively comfortable circumstances. Like his future commander, he learned at an early age to shoot, ride, and hunt, and he determined to channel these talents into soldiering, a trade where they could be of the most use. Indeed, the sporting instincts he developed as a youth bore unforeseen results when years later they were translated to the military profession.

In 1777 Captain Ferguson lay in ambush with his riflemen on the battlefield of Brandywine. He suddenly noticed an American officer, "dressed in dark green or blue, mounted on a bay horse, with a remarkably large cocked hat," pass toward the British army within a hundred yards of Ferguson's right flank. The American was accompanied by a fellow officer of hussars. Ferguson immediately ordered three of his good shots to fire at them. He then retracted the command almost as soon as he had issued it, for the thought of shooting down two unsuspecting men "disgusted" him. The officers rode on out of sight but soon returned, having reconnoitered the field. The hussar this time did not come within rifle range, but the other officer again passed less than one hundred yards from the British captain. Ferguson walked out from cover, advanced toward the American, and yelled for him to stop. The rebel officer, after coolly inspecting his challenger, rode slowly on. Ferguson estimated that he could have "lodged a half a dozen balls in or about him before he was out of my reach." But his sporting blood boiled to the surface, overriding his military learning. "It was not pleasant," he said later, "to fire at the back of an unoffending individual, who was acquitting himself very coolly of his duty, so I let him alone." Shortly after this encounter Ferguson was severely wounded and carried to the rear. There he learned from fellow officers that the man he did not bring down could have been none other than George Washington.[9] If one of Ferguson's men, not raised in the same tradition, had had the same opportunity, how might the Revolution have gone? The death of the American commander in chief would have been a grave blow to patriot hopes. This same sporting instinct undoubtedly prompted Ferguson to shoot it out at King's Mountain. It would be a good fight at nearly even odds. Why continue to run like a rabbit toward Cornwallis at Charlotte?

Brandywine and King's Mountain lay in the distant future, however, when young Patrick, at age fourteen, joined the Royal

North British Dragoons (the Scots Greys). His father had purchased a cornetcy for him, and the boy entered upon active service in July of 1759. Like Cornwallis he served in Germany during the Seven Years' War. He showed his indifference to danger
— some would call it foolhardiness — during an engagement
in 1760 when he returned in the face of enemy cavalry to pick
up a pistol which had jostled from his holster into a ditch.

His connections might have helped Ferguson advance further
than he did during the war and the years of peace that followed.
For example, his uncle General Murray, who became governor
of Quebec, said in 1759: "I mean to push him [Patrick] in my
profession." But a severe illness struck Ferguson in 1762 and
kept him home until 1768. In that year his family purchased
him a captaincy in the 70th foot, and he sailed to the West Indies, where he helped put down a slave insurrection in Tobago.
But ill health dogged him again, and after a short visit to North
America he returned to Britain in 1774. There he devoted himself to an extensive study of military science and tactics and to
the development of his rifle.

Ferguson's impatience with the cautious counsels of his superiors, including those of Cornwallis, may have resulted at least
in part from the reception accorded his new weapon. He developed a rapid-firing, breech-loading rifle — better than anything
used by the British for the next hundred years. The firing tests
he conducted with it at Blackheath and Woolwich arsenals in
the summer of 1776 conclusively demonstrated its advantages.
Ferguson fired for four or five minutes, at the rate of four shots
a minute, at a target two hundred yards distant. In one minute
he managed to get off six shots. He also fired four shots a minute
while advancing at four miles per hour. In an impressive dis-
play of marksmanship, the captain, while lying on his back on
the ground, shot into a gusty wind and hit a target one hundred
yards distant. "His execution in firing," one awestruck com-
mentator remarked, "was such that it almost exceeded the

bounds of credibility." [10] Finally, Ferguson showed his rifle to be unaffected by wetting. He poured a cask of water into the pan and barrel of the piece after it had been loaded, so as to soak every grain of powder. In less than half a minute the weapon fired as well as ever. During this entire series of tests, Ferguson missed the target only three times. He later repeated his demonstration before the King at Windsor. When George III asked him how often he could load and fire in a minute, he replied, "Seven times." He added pleasantly, however, "that he could not undertake to knock down above five of his Majesty's enemies." [11] Yet the army did not adopt the weapon and only two hundred of the rifles were manufactured.

Ferguson went to America with the rank of captain but did not attain his majority until 1779, shortly before the expedition to Charleston. A brilliant man aware of his brilliance, the inventor of a superior rifle that the authorities ignored, he was by 1780 a mere major, although his seniority and birth might have entitled him to the command of a regiment. Under these circumstances, he was understandably a willful and impatient subordinate. In his eyes, his appointment in 1780 as inspector of militia now gave him a semi-independent command. Having secured the position at his own request, he intended to use it to prove himself to his superiors. The Scotsman had resolved to make up for the years of sickness and frustration by getting to the top in a hurry.

Some qualities worked in his favor. Haughty he might look, but he cultivated a familiarity with loyalists unusual among British officers, who tended to treat American civilians of whatever political persuasion with contempt. "He would sit down for hours," one historian noted, "and converse with the country people on the state of affairs and point out to them, from his view, the ruinous effects of the disloyalty of the ringleaders of the rebellion. . . . He was as indefatigable in training them to his way of thinking, as he was in instructing them in military exercises. This condescension on his part was regarded as wonderful in a King's officer and very naturally went far to secure the respect and obedience of all who came within the sphere of his almost magic influence." [12]

Ferguson was, furthermore, humane and chivalrous, merciful and gentlemanly, with a nice sense of duty and honor. "We came not," he said, "to make war on women and children, but to relieve their distress." A story is told that the major at one time took a detachment to the home of a noted whig, Captain Thomas Lytle. Mrs. Lytle, warned of his approach, donned her best finery to face up to the Britisher, easy in the knowledge that her absent husband was beyond his reach. When Ferguson rode up she greeted him courteously and invited him in. The major declined the invitation, asking instead after her husband. She replied that Captain Lytle was away with "others of his friends whom you call Rebels." "Well Madame," Ferguson is supposed to have replied, "I have discharged my duty; I felt anxious to save Captain Lytle, because I learn that he is both brave and honorable. If he persists in rebellion, and comes to harm his blood be upon his own head." Mrs. Lytle replied that her husband might fall in battle, but he would "never prove a traitor to his country." "Mrs. Lytle," Ferguson concluded, "I admire you as the handsomest woman I have seen in North Carolina — I even *half way* admire your zeal in a bad cause; but, take my word for it, the rebellion has had its day, and is now virtually put down. Give my kind regards to Captain Lytle, and tell him to come in. He will not be asked to compromise his honor; and his verbal pledge not again to take up arms against the King, is all that will be asked of him." "He then bowed to Mrs. Lytle," the story goes, "and led off his troops." [13] Yet another story has Ferguson punishing one of his own followers who had killed a chicken on the plantation where his troop was encamped. When the wife of the owner reported the theft to the major, he ordered the culprit punished and paid the lady for her loss.[14]

Such a man naturally attracted loyalist militia to his cause. Had prudence and discretion balanced his noble qualities, he might in the end have achieved what Cornwallis' army could not. But Ferguson was willful, impatient, and headstrong. He had been with Tarleton when he defeated Huger at Monck's Corner. After that affair, some of Tarleton's marauding dragoons burst into the house of Lady Colleton, wife of the plantation owner, Sir John Colleton. One dragoon wounded her with his sword and attempted to rape her, but her shrieks and struggles scared him away. More dragoons attacked two other ladies at the plantation. When Ferguson discovered the affair he wished instantly, despite military law and custom, to put the troopers to death. Lieutenant Colonel Webster finally had to step in, preventing the Scotsman's rough justice by requesting a court martial.[15]

The Earl appreciated his major's brilliance and zeal. Indeed, shortly after he took over from Clinton, Cornwallis adopted a cipher of Ferguson's invention in preference to his own.[16] On the other hand, Cornwallis knew the major's background, realized the quirks in his character, and feared that his subordinate would get either himself or the British army into trouble. Ferguson glowed with confidence in himself and his militia, but the Earl was more dubious. On July 3, he wrote to Balfour, then temporary commander of Ninety-Six, *"Entre nous* I am afraid of his [Ferguson's] getting to the frontier of N. Carolina & playing some cussed trick." [17] And yet, throughout 1780, Ferguson seemed to succeed in spite of his rashness. He spent the summer moving through South Carolina, scouring the country, and exacting submissions from whigs. Although patriots won some of their fights with tories that summer, they never could come to grips directly with Ferguson and defeat him. He, on the other hand, though arriving too late to prevent loyalist defeats in the backcountry, came in time to chase the patriots away from their

victories. During these exchanges he acquired an almost legend-
ary reputation, and whigs wished to "get" him more than any
other Britisher.[18] Thus it seemed natural to Cornwallis to call
upon Ferguson in his autumn drive to the north, and to coordinate the major's movements with his own when he marched toward Charlotte. So he dispatched the leader of partisans into
Tryon County, North Carolina. Ferguson would cover the left
flank of the Earl's march, organize the North Carolinians and, if
opportunity offered, try to defeat once and for all the pesky patriot militia. "Ferguson is to move into Tryon County with
some militia," Cornwallis wrote Clinton before he left Camden,
"whom he says he is sure he can depend upon for doing their
duty and fighting well." Despite Ferguson's fame in the backcountry, however, the Earl still harbored grave doubts about his
dashing subordinate, for he added: "But I am sorry to say that
his own experience, as well as that of every other officer is totally against him." [19]

Ferguson, of course, was anxious for his chance. Like Cornwallis, he saw the reduction of North Carolina as the key to the
pacification of its southern neighbor.[20]

In October the over-the-mountain men ("backwater plunderers," Ferguson once called them), aided by some South Carolinians, contested with him the settlement of the northwest corner
of South Carolina. They came from what is now eastern Tennessee, from western Virginia, and from the North Carolina
border. Molded by the American frontier, they had developed a
rugged independence and a fierce attachment to their lean
homesteads. Their leaders, although not backwoodsmen themselves, had the toughness to command them. Benjamin Cleveland, born in Bull Run, Virginia, and reputed to be at least the
equal, if not the better, of Daniel Boone as a hunter and Indian fighter, possessed a ruthlessness unknown to a sportsman
like Ferguson. James Williams — farmer, miller, merchant, and
delegate to the provincial congress of South Carolina — was a

veteran of several fights with tories. Joseph McDowell of the "gentry," born in Virginia, later moved to the wild Piedmont region of North Carolina. A convinced democrat, he would later oppose the ratification of the North Carolina constitution because it contained no Bill of Rights. When he became a member of Congress for the newly independent republic he condemned the Alien and Sedition Acts. The westerners of North Carolina idolized McDowell. Joseph Winston, whose family came from Yorkshire, at age seventeen joined a company of rangers to fight Indians. In the Revolution he fought in the backcountry of South Carolina and continued his fighting until after Guilford Courthouse. William Chronicle, from the south fork of the Catawba, "a young man of great promise," the "idol of his friends and soldiers," had fought through the skirmishes of 1780. To King's Mountain he would carry the gold ring of his fiancée. Edward Lacey, from Pennsylvania originally, had run away from home at age thirteen and joined the packhorse unit of Braddock's army. His father eventually found him, but he only returned home to run away again, this time to South Carolina, where he settled and married. He had led the detachment that defeated Huck and had served with Sumter at Rocky Mount, Hanging Rock, and Fishing Creek. James Hawthorne, born in Ireland, had migrated with his family to the frontiers of North Carolina, had learned the blacksmith's trade, and fought Indians. Like Lacey, he was a veteran of Sumter's activities. Isaac Shelby — a florid, portly, balding, droopy-eyed, yet determined-looking individual — had moved from his birthplace in Maryland to Virginia. Shelby fought Indians and British, explored the wilds of Kentucky, and later became the new state's first governor. "Nolichucky Jack" Sevier, the distinguished-looking Virginian, would become Tennessee's first governor. In fashionable dress his appearance resembled that of a French aristocrat. Sevier had founded New Market, Virginia, and had been a merchant, innkeeper, and farmer. He eventually moved to the frontier, where he was instrumental in forming the state of Tennessee and where his wife became known in song and story as Bonny Kate. Finally, there was the colorful William Campbell of Virginia, a man of commanding appearance and imposing figure, standing six and one-half feet tall. Campbell, whose wife was a sister of Patrick Henry, had raised the first militia company in southwestern Virginia to support the patriot cause. After King's Mountain he would take a small force of riflemen to the support of Greene at Guilford Courthouse.[21]

All these patriot leaders came to confront Ferguson at King's Mountain. They were not backwoodsmen, for they all had some sort of education and some claim to gentility. These social pretensions elevated them to command. But they stayed in command only because they also had initiative, courage, and sometimes as much rugged experience as their backwoods followers.

Ferguson moved north to Gilberton in early September and there camped his forces as a rallying point for the loyalists. He also dispatched messages warning patriot officers on the western waters of the Watauga, Nolichucky, and Holston that "if they did not desist from their opposition to the British arms, he would march his army over the mountains, hang their leaders, and lay their country waste with fire and sword." [22] Ferguson's threats, like those of Rawdon and Cornwallis earlier, did more harm than good. They prompted Shelby to meet with Sevier at Jonesboro and to call for volunteers: all men staunch enough to face the redcoat major should meet at Sycamore Shoals on the banks of the Watauga (near the present Elizabethton, Tennessee) by September 25. Many frontiersmen converged upon the rendezvous. Over a thousand strong, they arrived on horseback armed with long rifles. Lloyd Branson later limned in meticulous detail this gathering of the over-the-mountain men. Some men are drilling; others are loading or saddling their horses. The rest stand about singly or in groups. Their heterogenous clothes — buckskins, homedyed cloth, coonskin hats — are a far cry from British spit and polish. Yet boisterous or hushed, they all breathe an air of confident expectancy. They look unruly, but they do have a discipline. It comes from within and results from living in a harsh and hostile wilderness. When they clustered together for the Reverend Samuel Doak, they heard the biblical story about Gideon's people rising against the Midianites. Doak finished by admonishing the frontiersmen to take as their battle cry: "The sword of the Lord and of Gideon."

Now the hunt was on. The quarry sensed it. At Gilberton, Ferguson soon learned of the combination against him, which grew almost daily as patriots flocked to join the backwater army. Sensing danger, the major moved south on September 27. On the thirtieth, intelligence confirmed his fears, and he immediately realized the gravity of his situation. He had previously furloughed some of his followers. Now he issued hasty appeals for loyalists to join him. At the same time he sent messengers off to inform Cornwallis of his danger. He also dispatched a hurried call for help to Cruger, but Cruger had no men to spare. Then the Scotsman feinted in the direction of Ninety-Six, hoping to throw his pursuers off his trail. On the night of October 2, he crossed over the Broad River, and the next day he marched twenty miles eastward toward the Little Broad. That night he evidently decided to fight the patriots without awaiting reinforcements, for he wrote to Cornwallis that if enemy numbers were "within bounds," he would take strong ground and meet his pursuers head on.[23]

Ferguson tarried a few days at Tate's Plantation on Buffalo Creek, presumably waiting for intelligence of whig movements and for loyalists to swell his numbers. But on October 5, he informed Cornwallis that he intended to head straight for the British army at Charlotte. "I am on my march towards you," he said, "by a road leading from Cherokee Ford north of King Mountain." [24] The next day, after hurrying through rolling countryside, Ferguson at last drew rein and challenged his pursuers. He led his men to the top of a ridge known today as King's Mountain. The "mountain" was actually only a high point in a series of ridges, the sixteen-mile-long King's Mountain range, named after an early settler in the region. Impressive-looking from a distance, the high point had some distinct advantages. Although not so high as "The Pinnacle," a few miles to the east, it stood well above the surrounding countryside. While "The Pinnacle," with its nearly vertical barren rock sides would have made an American ascent in face of Ferguson's fire almost impossible, King's Mountain was steep enough to render the patriot task formidable. An abundance of springs gave the mountain one of its chief defensive advantages. Ferguson's men would have enough water to sustain them during an extended engagement. In fact, local tradition tells that both sides shared one of the springs during the battle.

But Ferguson also suffered from disadvantages. Although he held high ground, it was stony and bare. The tree line extended almost to the top, affording ample cover for an attacking force. Then, as now, the mountain was heavily wooded, deliciously cool, and lovely. Fierce fighting would raise sweat in the men despite coolness, and probably neither tory nor whig appreciated the beauty of his surroundings. The backwoodsmen could appreciate, though, the tall pines. The scrub evergreens and heavy underbrush that cover the mountain today formed no part of it in 1780. Instead, tall pines marched from its base nearly to its summit, and the ground, heavily carpeted with pine needles, sprouted scarcely enough undergrowth to impede an American charge toward the top. Even so, as one walks around the sides of the mountain and looks, so it seems, straight up, to where Ferguson and his men waited with rifle and muskets at the ready and bayonets fixed, the patriot feat seems incredible. To "face to the hill," as Major Chronicle exhorted his men, demanded courage and endurance of the highest sort.

Ferguson did not deign to erect fortifications.[25] On October 6, he arranged his force of about a hundred provincials and a thousand tory militia in a rough circle near the northeastern extremity of the ridge, with a picket line extended along the crest to the southwestern end. The major was in high spirits, exuding confidence and cockiness. Only the day before he had written Cornwallis that he deemed the enemy beneath contempt. Their leaders, he said, "are obliged to feed their followers with such storys, & so flatter them with accounts of our weakness & fear, that if necessary I should hope for success against them myself. . . . This is their last push in this quarter & they are extremely desolate and awed." On the sixth he wrote: "I arrived today at King mountain & have taken a post where I do not think I can be forced by a stronger enemy than that against us." [26] Ferguson had now taken the war in the Carolinas out of the hands of Lord Cornwallis. Only thirty-five miles from Charlotte, he could easily have reached the Earl with his swift-moving force in a matter of hours. But, said one rebel narrative, Ferguson declared "he was on King's Mountain, that he was king of that mountain, and God Almighty could not drive him from it." [27]

The patriots hurried after their quarry from Gilberton but temporarily lost his trail where he crossed the Broad. They too crossed the river and stopped at a ford on Green River on October 5. Perplexed about their adversary's movements, they might have missed him entirely had not a patriot spy slipped into Ferguson's camp at Tate's Plantation and fooled the major into believing he was a loyalist. He learned of Ferguson's intentions and reported them on October 5 to a group of South Carolina whig militia under Colonels Hill, Lacey, and Williams, camped at Flint Hill northwest of King's Mountain. After some bickering (Colonel Williams, whose interests lay at Ninety-Six, had attempted to divert the mountain men toward that post), Colonel William Lacey rode to the camp of the frontiersmen at Green River and told them of Ferguson's whereabouts. They

agreed to make a junction with the South Carolinians at Cowpens, and the two groups joined there on the evening of October
6. Another spy, a cripple by the name of Joseph Kerr, who had
been in Ferguson's camp six or seven miles from King's Mountain, brought to the assembled host the news that the major
planned to march to the mountain the next day and that he had
not over fifteen hundred men, an accurate account since Ferguson's force totalled about eleven hundred.

The over-the-mountain men and the South Carolinians now
formulated their battle plans. As an improvised group rather
than a regular army, they had no commander. They elected
Colonel William Campbell to the position. Then they chose
nine hundred of their number with the swiftest horses as an advance party to follow Ferguson, while a small group of un-
mounted men, whose number remains elusive, tagged along
behind them.[28] Their total number must have equalled or surpassed Ferguson's force as they started their pursuit.

David Vance, a youthful volunteer among them, described
the tense hours that followed. It soon started raining and Vance
began to worry. Following Ferguson's trail, yet not knowing his
exact location, the youth feared attack at any moment. When
Vance and his comrades came to Cherokee Ford on the Broad
River it was dark and the pilots lost their way. One Enoch Gilmer of Chronicle's command splashed ahead to see if Ferguson
knew their whereabouts and might attack them as they crossed.
Orders went out to keep weapons dry, and some men wrapped
their flintlocks in shirts or blankets or whatever cloth came to
hand. As time passed Vance fretted that Gilmer had blundered
into tories. Then he heard a voice singing "Barney Linn," "a
favorite black-guard song," and he knew all was well. Gilmer
had returned, the passage was clear, and they forded the river.[29]

In the morning they discovered Ferguson's location from two
captured tories. By noon even the weather favored them, for the
rain stopped, the air cleared, and a cool breeze freshened the

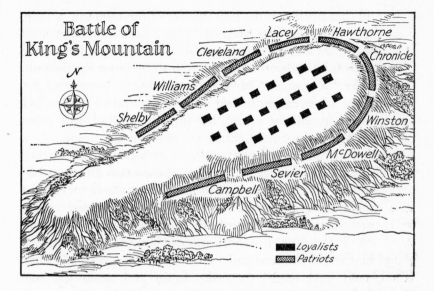

Battle of King's Mountain

Loyalists
Patriots

countryside. About three o'clock they arrived at King's Mountain and took up positions around its base. Chronicle stationed his unit at the eastern end. Campbell, McDowell, Winston, and Sevier took positions along the southern slope. Hawthorne, Lacey, Cleveland, Williams, and Shelby completed the encirclement from north to west. They dismounted, formed two lines, primed their weapons, and prepared to attack.

Ferguson with his one hundred provincials — men of King William's American Regiment, the Queen's Rangers, and New Jersey Volunteers — and one thousand militia prepared to receive them. A dashing figure, he wore a hunting shirt over his uniform, wielded a sword in his left hand, and slung a whistle about his neck to be used for rallying his men. He intended to use volley fire and bayonets to repulse his adversaries. Had he faced regulars with muskets instead of militia with rifles, he might have succceeded.

Fighting exploded when Shelby's men on the northwestern

slope and Campbell's on the southwestern raised the war whoop, fired their flintlocks, and charged. These forces took the most punishment, for Ferguson concentrated fire on them before the other patriots had advanced far enough to threaten the summit. One of the "backwater" boys, sixteen-year-old James Collins, told how he lay sweating in fear from the sound of the bullets. Yet however fearful the sound, the musket fire had little effect upon the whigs crouched behind big pines in the heavy forest. According to Collins the tory position on high ground worked to their own disadvantage: "Their great elevation above us had proved their ruin; they overshot us altogether, scarce touching a man except those on horseback." To be sure, massed volleys frightened a few of the greenhorns, for the bullets tore over them "like hail." But "the shock was quickly over." [30] Ferguson hoped that where muskets and a few of his own special rifles had failed, cold steel might succeed. Again and again his men charged downhill against the patriots, now coming up on all sides. In one of these attacks a provincial thrust his bayonet through the hand and into the thigh of patriot Robert Henry who had been in the act of hurriedly cocking his rifle. At the impact Henry involuntarily yanked the trigger. Both men fell together amidst the smoke and fire. A friend named Caldwell saw Henry and pulled the bayonet from his thigh. When it still clung to Henry's hand Caldwell kicked it out. The two men left the loyalist there, his blood spurting over the ground from the shot that had passed through his bladder and cut a main artery.[31]

Bayonet charges repulsed the attackers but could not stop the killing fire of long rifles. James Collins threw four or five balls into his mouth to prevent thirst and to speed reloading. Others did the same. The resulting fire was rapid and deadly: "Every rifle from below seemed to have the desired effect." [32] "I recollect I stood behind one tree," patriot Thomas Young (who had lost his shoes during the march) said of his part in the battle, "and fired until the bark was nearly all knocked off, and my eyes pretty well filled with it." [33] Ferguson's bayonet charges had pushed Campbell and Shelby back down the hill two or three times and checked other groups momentarily, but each charging loyalist presented a target for the long rifles. Ferguson's men fell in droves.

According to Captain Abraham DePeyster of King William's Regiment and Lieutenant Anthony Allaire of the Loyal American Volunteers, the North Carolina militia ran out of ammunition and began to give way. Ferguson noticed their dismay and tried to regroup his men for a charge through the rebel lines to escape the fire pouring in from all directions. But the militia panicked. They "got all in a crowd on the hill," even jumbling themselves among the hitherto-rocklike provincials, breaking their ranks. Out of ammunition, hot, tired, desolate — they were ready to quit.[34] Ferguson chose this moment for a final attempt to break out. Shouting "Huzza, brave boys, the day is our own," and cutting down with his sword two flags already raised in surrender, he rallied a few men and charged directly down the southeastern slope, hacking all around him with his sword. Before he advanced twenty yards, long-rifle balls knocked him from his magnificent white charger which plummeted riderless down the mountain. James Collins estimated that perhaps fifty rifles had been levelled at Ferguson at the same time. "Seven rifle balls had passed through his body, both his arms were broken and his hat and clothing were literally shot to pieces." [35] In order "to save the lives of some brave men still left," DePeyster surrendered.[36] The battle had consumed little more than an hour.

Today King's Mountain is a National Military Park. The land is set aside in commemoration of the courage and foolhardiness of those who once struggled there. The mountain lies wrapped in a lovely tranquillity. Nonetheless, so far from civilization is it that the battle readily recreates itself before the imagination. The sound of musketry and patriot cries drifts upward to the hilltop to mingle with the sound of surprised and desperate officers urging on their men to greater endeavor. The acrid puffs of gunsmoke that float across the wooded hillside are a reminder of our violent and hardwon heritage. Although cowards undoubtedly died there, a look at the mountain is enough to convince one that most of the dead were courageous. No coward charged up that hill, not even in the press of his comrades' fervor; no coward, having charged down that hill, retreated up it constantly exposed to the enemy's fire. The entire hillside, even the small streams of cool, fresh water, are testimonials to a great patriotic engagement, fiercely felt on each side and dearly paid for by each. It was an American battle — a small Gettysburg.

The hopes of Cornwallis in North Carolina had hinged upon the outcome of that battle, yet only one man in it was British. That man was the commander of the loyalists, Major Patrick Ferguson. He never again saw the hills of home. After the battle he was buried a short way down the southeastern slope. His grave is marked by a cairn in the style of a true Scottish warrior chieftain. Far from the highlands, however, the grave is not protected by clansmen and tradition. Ferguson, one knows, would have resented the intrusion of the curious and the lack of isolated grandeur: American children can now scramble in joyous abandon over the rocks of his cairn, innocently ignorant of courage, sacrifice, pride, and ambition. As a result, the monument is perhaps more touching to the sentiment. It is the grave of more than a courageous and brilliant British officer: it is the grave of the last British hope of subduing the United States.[37]

CHAPTER 10

Bitter Aftermath

THE VICTORS at King's Mountain could have afforded to be magnanimous. Unfortunately they were not. James Collins said after the battle that the situation of the tories "appeared to be really pitiable; the dead lay in heaps on all sides, while the groans of the wounded were heard in every direction." [1] Patriots did not trouble to remedy this "pitiable" situation. Some riflemen continued firing after the loyalists had surrendered, shouting "Tarleton's Quarter" in justification for slaughtering helpless men. Finding no place to hide, the tories stood "like a herd of deer in a corral" and went down. [2] When the butchery finally ended, the surviving prisoners faced further ordeals. According to DePeyster the patriots dumped the wounded loyalists at a site four miles from the battlefield and left them without clothes or blankets, attended only by an incompetent who had no medicines. The unwounded provincials lacked shoes and clothes, "and not a blanket amongst us all." The victors gave them none, nor would they let DePeyster know the state of the militia, the other part of his force. [3]

The day after the battle the patriots marched their prisoners away from Cornwallis toward Gilberton. For two days Ferguson's men tramped "without any kind of provisions." According to Lieutenant Allaire, Campbell ordered his men to shoot the prisoners in the event of a loyalist or British attack.[4] On the third day the victors divided up the loyalist baggage, although acccording to Allaire "they had promised on their word we should have it all." By October 13, the whig army and its prisoners had reached Bickerstaff's Plantation, about ten miles from Rutherfordton. There the whig leaders decided to hold a drumhead court which sentenced nine men to death, among them Colonel Ambrose Mills, neither a plunderer nor a murderer, as some of the condemned men were, but "always a fair and open enemy" to the patriots.[5] The whigs herded their prisoners to the foot of a giant oak which served as a gallows and there, on the night of October 14, forced them to watch the nine hangings in the gloomy light of pine torches.

The next day their captors awakened the prisoners at five o'clock and forced them to march thirty miles under strong guard, without food, over a road rendered nearly impassable by heavy rains. Some men, exhausted and weak from lack of food, slumped down into the road. The patriots trod over them or hacked at them. Even so, about a hundred tories managed to escape during the long tramp.[6] By October 24, the group arrived at Bethabara, about five miles from Salem. Here, at least, the provincial officers received adequate lodgings. Although the sympathies of the Moravian people of both Salem and Bethabara lay with the loyalists, a drunken patriot captain almost killed Lieutenant Allaire. The captain stormed into Allaire's room, raised his sword menacingly, and kicked the lieutenant right out of bed. On another occasion whigs knocked down and beat a surgeon, Dr. Johnson, for attempting to dress the wounds of one of the loyalists who had been cut down at King's Mountain. On yet another occasion a "backwater" boy tossed a knife at a loyalist provincial entering a room. Eventually the patriots eased the confinement of the provincials when Captain DePeyster gave his word for their good behavior. Three officers — Allaire, William

Stevenson, and John Taylor — then took the opportunity to escape.[7] Others also soon managed to get away. Indeed, after their initial fierceness with their prisoners, the whigs grew increasingly indifferent as to their fate. Of the six hundred or so men captured at King's Mountain, by November only one hundred thirty militia and provincials remained in patriot hands. These men were marched under strong guard and confined at Hillsboro.

Perhaps it was just as well for the rebels that so many of the persons escaped. Although Greene later mourned the loss of tory prisoners, who might have been exchanged for patriots, those loyalists who got away may actually have aided Greene's campaign more than did those who remained in confinement to be exchanged. Disheartened, dispirited, full of stories of rebel ferocity, the escapees cannot have returned home ready to inspire their neighbors to a renewal of efforts in behalf of King George. Rather they must have pleaded the uselessness of supporting the royal cause and dissuaded the more zealous from taking up arms.[8]

Accounts of King's Mountain, "largely colored and exaggerated by the fear-stricken Tories,"[9] soon reached Cornwallis' ears at Charlotte. He dispatched Tarleton, now recovered from his fever, to ascertain Ferguson's fate. During the Legion commander's absence, the Earl learned the bitter truth of the Scotsman's defeat. Perhaps the defeat alone would not have forced Cornwallis to change his plans for a campaign in North Carolina, but it coincided with other distressing events. Even before King's Mountain, the British position had begun to deteriorate. At the very time the mountain men were pursuing Ferguson, Cornwallis learned that all his efforts to raise militia in the Cheraw Hill area had failed. Lieutenant Colonel of Militia Robert Gray told him on September 30 that at least three fourths of the population opposed the British and that only a

force of regulars could keep a semblance of order in the Cheraws.[10] Major James Weymss of the 63d, in charge of recruiting
there, had said the same thing a week earlier in stronger terms:
"Every inhabitant has been or is concerned in Rebellion & most
of them very deeply. Wherever I have gone the houses were
deserted by the Men, even their Negroes & Effects were in
general carry'd away." [11] Weymss restated the bad news in a letter that must have reached Cornwallis at just about the time he
learned the outcome of King's Mountain. The Cheraw Hill
area, Weymss said, "cannot be kept by militia." Marion and
others were "burning houses, and distressing the well affected in
a most severe manner. Several people from that Country have
been with me to represent their distressed Situation. The highlanders in particular who are very numerous here, have been
treated with such Cruelty & Oppression as almost exceeds belief." [12] In addition, Marion forced the British to evacuate
Georgetown during this same period.[13]

Nor was news from the other end of the frontier any better.
Cruger wrote from Ninety-Six on October 13 (although the
message cannot have reached Cornwallis until after he left Charlotte) that he soon expected a siege from superior numbers.
The loyalist militia, he was sure, would dissolve in case of any
threat.[14] Cruger, of course, feared the victors of King's Mountain might attack him, a possibility of which Cornwallis was
aware before Cruger wrote. Even news from the main army's
rear sounded discouraging. The garrison at Camden had no
flour, and the story of the King's Mountain defeat had contributed to the disintegration of the militia in the area.[15]

Meanwhile, even the Earl himself had been encountering
difficulties. The presence of his army in Charlotte had failed to
encourage loyalists. Indeed, not only had they refused to join
him, but also they had refused even to bestir themselves to help
him in any way. They left the field entirely to the whigs, who
were "so inveterate" in their "rancour" that they frequently
murdered messengers with expresses for Cornwallis and fired on

British foraging parties.[16] Cornwallis decided, even before King's Mountain, that loyalists were "dastardly and pusillanimous." After it he concluded that "it is throwing away good Arms, or what is worse helping the Enemy, by giving them to the [loyalist] Militia." [17] Sickness added to his problems. Although the area around Charlotte provided ample supplies — Stedman said one mill alone furnished "28,000 weight" of flour, the well-cultivated farms furnished other food, and cattle for beef roamed in plenty — the heavy rains, exposure, and primitive medical facilities brought his troops down with fevers.[18] Cornwallis himself began feeling ill.

Total defeat at King's Mountain, bad news from Ninety-Six, from Georgetown, and from Camden, the utter despondency of the loyalists, illness, the impossibility now of achieving his mission in North Carolina — all these matters forced the Earl to abandon his campaign for 1780 and retreat to South Carolina. He recalled Tarleton and left Charlotte on October 14 for Winnsboro, South Carolina, midway between Ninety-Six and Camden and within striking distance of each. He had barely begun the march when fever, undoubtedly brought on by the cold he had caught on October 10, prostrated him.[19] This bout of illness would prove so severe that he would not even be able to hold a pen to write a letter until November 1.[20]

Rawdon now took command of the retreat, which turned into a ghastly march for all of them. The people who were well suffered terrible privations. It rained nearly every day, yet the army lacked tents for shelter. The roads soon became mires, in which men marched in water and mud over the tops of their shoes. For days the troops went without rum. Sometimes they had beef and no bread. At other times they had bread and no beef. For five days the army lived on Indian corn collected as it stood in the fields. Even then the pickings were so slim that five ears had to last two soldiers for twenty-four hours.[21] The water they drank was as thick as a puddle. Weakened by such a diet, they still had to push and shove the baggage and artillery wagons along. The horses were too exhausted to pull their loads by the time they got to Sugar Creek, one of the first of many streams that challenged the army. Militia served for draft animals and struggled through the icy water drawing their heavy loads.[22] All the while, rebels sniped and harassed the rear and flanks of the army.

But if the men who could walk suffered terribly, the sick men who jounced along in the wagons endured nightmares of agony. Major Hanger, wounded at Charlotte, fell an easy prey to the fever which prostrated him at the time that Tarleton recovered. When the army moved out from Charlotte, rough hands piled Hanger and five other officers suffering from the same illness — "yellow fever" Hanger called it — into wagons. The others died within the week and were buried along the route of march. Hanger himself barely survived. The rains had so swollen the innumerable streams (normally ankle-deep) which barred the army's way that water reached above the axles of the wagons. Many times water soaked the straw on which Hanger lay in his cart. The rough journey reduced the major to "something very like a skeleton." The bones of his back and hip even protruded through his skin, and he became so weak he could not turn himself over. Since the army had so little to eat he sustained himself on opium and port wine.[23] The Earl suffered similar privations, although fever never laid him so low as Hanger, and he recovered soon after the army reached Winnsboro on October 29. In a sense, the suffering of their leader and other officers heartened the army. Soldiers bore their hardships without a murmur. "Their attachment to their commander," Stedman observed, "supported them in the day of adversity; knowing as they did, that their officers; and even lords Cornwallis and Rawdon's fare was not better than their own." [24]

At Winnsboro, the consequences of Ferguson's defeat intruded themselves even more forcefully upon the Earl's atten-

tion, for nothing now went right for him, even in South Carolina. Between November 1 and the end of the year he saw every
element of his forces — regulars, provincials, and the only loyalist militia he had ever counted upon — beaten, not by American regulars, but by patriot militia.

First to fall were the "invincible" British regulars. In an
effort to retrieve the initiative, Cornwallis dispatched on horse-
back one hundred thirty-five regular infantry from the 63d and
about forty Legion cavalry under the command of Major James
Weymss to surprise General Thomas Sumter, who was operating
in the vicinity of Camden under orders from Gates. Weymss
eventually caught up with the "Gamecock" at Fishdam Ford on
the Broad River, where the British estimated that their enemy
bivouacked between four and nine hundred men. These were
long odds for Weymss' two hundred, but the British needed a
striking success if they hoped to recover their position, and
Weymss thirsted for a chance at the pesky partisan. He reached
the ford about one o'clock in the early morning hours of November 9. Sumter, sensing danger, had sensibly posted his men to
avoid just such a surprise as Weymss planned. Forgetting he was
an infantry officer, the 63d's leader galloped into the attack at
the head of dragoons. Sumter's pickets knocked him off his horse
with their first five shots. Cavalry nonetheless continued to
charge and drove Sumter's right wing toward the Broad River.
But the charge led Weymss' men into the rest of the Gamecock's
army, which, from its positions in swamps and hills to the front
and right of the British detachment, poured in a withering fire.
The 63d stopped, dismounted, and began to return fire. At this
point Lieutenant John Stark, who took command when Weymss
fell, decided to break off the action. He knew neither the
ground nor the enemy's strength, and he had not formulated a
tactical plan. He only knew that deadly rifle fire poured in on
his men, so he retreated. He left his disabled commander in a
cabin with other British wounded where Sumter, who had

barely escaped with his life by jumping a fence and running
through a briar patch, found them the next day. Cornwallis,
who learned on the tenth of this reverse, barely contained his
anger as the truth of the battle filtered in. He learned from the
sergeant major of the 63d — who had been left with a flag of
truce — that daylight had revealed a deserted field. The enemy
only ventured to the cabin two hours after dawn and picked up
Major Weymss and the other wounded. Had the inexperienced
Stark remained and fought it out, he might have brought a
badly needed victory to British arms.[25]

Tarleton had been trying vainly to catch the elusive Francis
Marion. Now it was up to him to stop the equally elusive
Sumter. The Legion tore off to avenge Weymss. Tarleton gathered up elements of the 63d regiment and the 71st at Brierly's
Ferry on the Broad to beef up his forces. Sumter also increased
his own numbers to around a thousand men when he added
some Georgians he had encountered. Tarleton probably hoped
to push the Gamecock toward Cruger's post at Ninety-Six and
crush him between the two British forces. Sumter, however, did
not wish to be pushed, and he drew up his militia at Blackstock's
Plantation on the steep hills above the Tiger River during the
afternoon of November 22. In his haste to catch Sumter, who
he feared would cross the Tiger before dark, Tarleton left behind the infantry of the 71st and the artillery, and hurried on
with his Legion and mounted infantry of the 63d. But when he
reached Blackstock's he hesitated to attack. Sumter had placed
his main force in thick woods on the hills above and to the left of
the road along which Tarleton advanced, and a group of riflemen in the plantation outbuildings to the right of the road.
Tarleton only had about three hundred men and no artillery to
face a thousand — odds which daunted even his foolhardy spirit.
Sumter, however, took the situation out of his hands. He advanced four hundred men against the 63d, who had dismounted,
on Tarleton's right. The regulars chased the militia back, but

back too far, for the 63d ran into a withering fire from men in the plantation buildings. At roughly the same time Sumter sent another group against the flank of the dragoons idly watching the action of the 63d. The Gamecock's men opened up on Tarleton's horsemen from seventy-five yards with buckshot. Twenty dragoons fell from their saddles. The Legion commander hastily decided a charge would save the 63d, and he led his riders forward to rescue the infantry. The dragoons managed to cover the withdrawal of the redcoat foot soldiers — a withdrawal that saved the day. During their retreat, a platoon of the 63d levelled their muskets at an American officer and fired. They wounded Thomas Sumter.

Tarleton withdrew to wait for his infantry and artillery in hopes of renewing the attack the next day, but Sumter's militia, disheartened by the fall of their chief, melted away during the night. The next day Tarleton lied to Cornwallis, claiming a victory where none existed. He excused his failure to pursue the "defeated" enemy by citing his lack of infantry (which must have struck Cornwallis as a curious device for falling upon a routed foe), the difficult nature of the ground, and the coming of nightfall. Lacking other information, Cornwallis had to believe Tarleton's claim to victory. Yet even this "victory" could not encourage the Earl. For Tarleton also wrote that Sumter had hurt him severely and that his numerous wounded inhibited the effectiveness of his force. The best he offered Cornwallis after the bout with Sumter was the information that he had promised three young men fifty guineas if they could find and "fix" the disabled Sumter.[26] Tarleton, in fact, had been defeated, and if the Earl did not realize it at the time, if indeed he could still sing his Legionnaire's praises to Clinton on December 3,[27] he found the "victory" had in no way recovered the ground lost at King's Mountain.

Blackstock's proved more than just a check to Tarleton. It brought a deep, personal loss to Cornwallis who had grown fond, perhaps overly fond, of his young aide-de-camp, Lieutenant John Money. He had come to treat the lieutenant as a father might treat his son rather than as a commanding general usually treated a subordinate.[28] Money went with the 63d to Blackstock's and never returned. He was wounded severely in the infantry charge against the plantation outbuildings. Tarleton barely managed to scoop him up and return him to the British lines. When Cornwallis heard what had happened he ordered his officers to take the strictest care of his aide and to report constantly on the state of his health. Despite their efforts, the young lieutenant died during the evening of December 1.[29]

Money's death plunged Cornwallis into a gloom not relieved by the bad news he received regarding Colonel Henry Rugeley. This militia colonel managed to fill the Earl's cup of bitterness to overflowing. Although by December Cornwallis had come to expect little from militia, he still at least hoped that when armed, entrenched, not outnumbered, and within ten miles of solid support from a regular army, they might hold their own. Rugeley proved they could not. He owned a mill about eight miles from Camden. Gates had camped there before his big defeat. The mill was on a creek, named Granny's Quarter (or Granny Quarter or Graney Quarter), noticeable, in a country of muddy-looking streams colored by red clay, for its delightfully clear, sparkling water. On a hill above the creek Rugeley had constructed a blockhouse of strong logs pierced with loopholes, with a platform inside for an "upper tier of musquetry." He had also thrown earth around the outside and surrounded his position with abatis. "In short, it was a Post that ought not to have been touched without cannon." Thus fortified, Rugeley dared the enemy, led by Colonel William Washington, to do its worst. The enemy did. Washington fashioned the likeness of a cannon from a tree trunk, "advanced suddenly" to the blockhouse, and demanded submission. Although aid was but a short distance away and Rugeley was in constant touch with Rawdon's forces at Camden, the loyalist colonel felt more discreet than valorous and surrendered without firing a shot.[30]

Rugeley's disgrace merely emphasized what Cornwallis had already openly acknowledged — the final defeat of his plans for 1780 — and this occurred despite the fact that Clinton had at last dispatched Major General Leslie toward the Cape Fear River for the diversion Cornwallis had requested. But on the day before Blackstock's, Cornwallis had admitted the insecurity of his position by sending for Leslie's force. He ordered the major general to Charleston, whence he could move up to join the Earl's forces.[31]

Although Cornwallis would bivouac at Winnsboro to husband the strength of his regulars and although Leslie's reinforcement would eventually reach him, never again in the Carolinas would he be so strong as before King's Mountain. Never again would the militia serve in such numbers and with the same degree of effectiveness as they had before Ferguson's costly engagement. After King's Mountain every element of Britain's forces — regulars, provincials, and militia — was beaten. Only the Earl's main army remained undefeated. It would indeed never be defeated in battle in the open field. But it was too small to restore the South to Britain. King's Mountain marked the beginning of the end of the British Empire in the South.

To what extent was Cornwallis to blame for this misfortune? As the commanding general in the South, he, of course, held ultimate responsibility. Clinton charged later that his subordinate's exercise of that responsibility led to disaster. Yet Sir Henry apparently failed to examine the facts. First of all, Clinton asserted that Cornwallis knew as early as September 6 that Ferguson was in trouble. Since the "backwater boys" did not even gather at Sycamore Shoals until September 25 in response to Ferguson's very success, Cornwallis must have been a prophet to realize the Scotsman's danger so early.

Sir Henry also averred that it was the Earl's "too great par-

tiality to detachment by which he was often liable to be beat in
detail, and to avoid little affronts he often risked great ones.
That he trusted the Militia by themselves without support, &
lost Ferguson . . . and as his Ldship risked him contrary to his
own experience, and that of the Army, he alone is answer-
able." [32] Once again, Clinton failed to examine all the evidence.
True, Ferguson's men were unsupported militia, but so were
the men who beat him. The very fact that no American army
was available in any numbers to oppose the Scotsman had enabled the Earl to send him off independently in the first place.
Indeed, in terms of regulars, Ferguson had the advantage at
King's Mountain with his one hundred provincials. The numbers engaged were roughly equal, and the Earl had every right
to expect that at roughly equal numbers a regular British army
major, supported by one hundred provincials and commanding
the best of the South Carolina militia, could beat any combination of patriot irregulars.

Furthermore, Sir Henry had his facts wrong. Ferguson first
told the Earl of his troubles on September 28. On September 30
and again on October 3, 5, and 6, Ferguson dispatched messages
to Cornwallis. The Earl received the letters of September 28
and 30 on October 5. He immediately ordered Ferguson to
march to Armer's Ford on the Catawba to the southeast of Charlotte, there to meet Major Archibald McArthur. At the same
time he ordered McArthur to take the 1st battalion of the 71st
regiment from the Waxhaws to reinforce Ferguson at the ford.
He further enjoined Ferguson not to fight but merely to gather
intelligence. The Scotsman had not received these instructions
on October 3 when he intimated to his commander that he intended to stand and fight. Cornwallis received this distressing
news on October 6 and again wrote his subordinate not to give
battle but to march where relief awaited him. That Ferguson
received Cornwallis' letter of the fifth and willfully chose to disregard the orders contained in it is suggested by his dispatch of

October 6 expressing the hope that His Lordship would not supersede him with a superior officer.[33] Ferguson must have referred to McArthur, whose commission as major predated his own by two years. But whether or not the Scotsman ever received any of Cornwallis' orders, the British commander acted as soon as he received information of his subordinate's difficulties.

Tarleton, in a vindictive mood after the war, published an account of the southern campaign which blamed Cornwallis for not sending the Legion to rescue Ferguson. But Tarleton's charge was false. An officer of the 71st, Roderick Mackenzie, expressly repudiated it in a publication attacking Tarleton.[34] Cornwallis also repudiated it in a private letter to his brother, the Bishop of Lichfield and Coventry. In this letter Cornwallis emphasized that he had ordered Ferguson not to engage (which contemporary evidence overwhelmingly supports) and that he *had* ordered, indeed entreated, Tarleton to march to Ferguson's relief. Tarleton, the Earl said, had "pleaded weakness from the remains of a fever [the one he had contracted during the march to Charlotte], and refused to make the attempt." [35] That Cornwallis may well have ordered Tarleton to march as soon as he felt able is attested by the Earl's letter to Ferguson of October 6. "Tarleton shall pass at some of the upper fords," it said, "and clear the country; for the present both he and his corps want a few days rest." [36]

Cornwallis erred in judgment several times during the Revolution but not in his arrangements for marching into North Carolina in 1780. Through no fault of his own, a man whom he had not appointed led a military force into an engagement that he had expressly ordered it to avoid. Now, back in South Carolina, the disastrous consequences of that battle weighed heavily on his shoulders. As Cornwallis settled down at Winnsboro, the Carolina winter promised to be bleaker than usual.

CHAPTER 11

Winter at Winnsboro

THE GHASTLY MARCH from Charlotte to Winnsboro was an omen, had Cornwallis but known it, of what lay in store for his army during the next months in the Carolinas. After his tactical losses in numerous small engagements, winter seemed to bring even more trouble and from all sides. The many logistical problems which, in the flush of victory, the Earl had tossed aside at Camden for his tramp north now came crowding back upon him at.Winnsboro. He hoped that the prolonged bivouac at Winnsboro would refresh his army, allow supplies to catch up with it, and enable his sick to convalesce. He also hoped to use the breathing spell to establish firmer communications and to improve his intelligence service. Instead, at Winnsboro his men barely survived, his sick increased, his communications worsened, and his hitherto-superb intelligence service collapsed. In 1781 he thought his troops sufficiently recovered to renew the offensive, but he did not conceive of the conditions they would face. The chase after Greene in February made the retreat from Charlotte the previous October seem like a Sunday hike. Had the Earl taken the lessons of Winnsboro to heart, Greene might not have been able to lead him a country dance.

Cornwallis encamped his troops at Winnsboro during November and December on a gently sloping plain above the town (now the present school grounds). For winter shelter, he had his men construct log houses cemented by mud — dwellings perhaps not dissimilar to those of Washington's men at Valley Forge. He himself lived at least part of the time in one of these cabins.[1] Pouring over his returns by candlelight, bemoaning his sick list, cursing his lack of intelligence, he had much to think about during that winter. The commander in chief of the South, reduced to living in a log cabin, discovered all too quickly that logistical problems defied easy solutions.

His most pressing need was wagons and horses. Even if the countryside had always supplied ample food (which it did not) and even if numerous British provision ships had reached Charleston bountifully laden with arms, ammunition, uniforms, and accoutrements (which they did not), he would still have needed wagons and horses, in vast numbers, to transport the goods to his army. During his entire period in South Carolina, Cornwallis never found enough of both items simultaneously. "We have plenty of waggons, but the situation of the horses & gear is wretched beyond description." "We are ordered to collect forage, corn and fuel. . . . Unless more carriadges can be got we shall be much distressed." "Upon the most acurate account I can get of our strength in waggons, I find it will be quite impracticable to go near supplying you with rum, salt, & carrying up the necessaries sent for." "Waggons were so scarce in these parts that the corn which was promised us, could not be brought to the mill." [2] So the complaints went from August of 1780 to January of 1781. On January 7, as he prepared to leave South Carolina, Cornwallis wrote: "By the great assiduity of Philips and his militia & the fortunate arrival of some country waggons, I am enabled to move tomorrow not without leaving a quantity of meal behind." [3] After a winter of trying to refit and refurbish his army with a permanent, efficient transportation service in anticipation of a long, hard campaign against a clever foe, only the opportune arrival of a few country wagons enabled him to open the offensive. Even then he could not carry enough food for his army.

His perennial shortages owed as much to Sir Henry Clinton and to the army system itself as to his own failings. When Sir Henry left for New York in June he took most of the wagons back with him.[4] Since the suppression of the mounted, swiftly moving, patriot guerrillas depended upon equal mobility in the British army, Clinton's selfish, or thoughtless, action hamstrung the Earl from the very start of his Carolina campaign. So did the army's administrative system. In all theaters of the war at this time, the quartermaster general's department held primary responsibility for furnishing the army with wagons. But such a service under his control, hiring wagons on long-term contracts — reasonable in theory — degenerated, in practice, into a profiteering racket. Primarily because of the venality of the quartermaster general's officers, the annual cost of the wagon service in America was outrageous, perhaps as high as £145,000. These officers had quickly discovered that they could make enormous profits by owning wagons and horses which they could in turn hire at exorbitant prices for the use of the army. No law specified which wagons or horses the quartermaster general must hire, so his deputies hired their own. "His Trust and Interest draw oppposite ways," as a parliamentary investigation later noted.[5]

In South Carolina the quartermaster general's men added some embellishments of their own. They, of course, continued to profit financially.[6] In addition, they often pressed wagons and horses needlessly, kept them from service at times when the Earl needed them most, and alienated the loyalists unnecessarily.[7] Such erratic behavior undoubtedly delayed the march to Charlotte. And, even if the department did find enough horses at the beginning of the return from Charlotte, it lost many on the march through the stupid ingratitude and haughtiness of its own officers. As Cornwallis lay ill, bumping along uncomfortably toward Winnsboro, only the exertions of loyalist militia kept the army wagons moving. The terrible trip frequently exhausted the wagon and artillery horses, and when they reached Sugar Creek the over-driven creatures could not pull their loads across the slippery clay bottom and up the nearly perpendicular banks. So the militia unhitched the horses from some of the wagons and got into the harnesses themselves. "In return for the exertions," Commissary Stedman observed, "the militia were maltreated, by abusive language, and even beaten by some officers in the quarter-master general's department." As a result, "several of them left the army next morning, forever, chusing to run the risque of meeting the resentment of their enemies rather than submit to the derision and abuse of those to whom they looked up as friends." [8] Of course they took their horses with them.

At Winnsboro the troublesome department continued its tricks, and Cornwallis tried — in vain — first to thwart it and then to bend it to his will. Finally, he resolved at least to deprive it of its profits and force it to a strict accounting. To do so, he attempted circumvention. "I hope," he told Balfour, "by getting rid of everybody belonging to the Qr. Mr. Genl's department, & by paying conductors, drivers &c their wages, instead of putting them into our own pockets, to procure a sufficient provision train to enable us to subsist." [9] In November, however, he returned management to the department when he appointed Major England, a subordinate whom he thought he could trust, as his deputy quartermaster general. "England has great merit," the Earl remarked, "& considering all the difficulties and hardships his waggons & horses are in wonderful good order. His thoughts are taken up with supplying the army, & not making money, which is the only object of all the departments." [10] But whether because England let him down or because England's men proved intractable, in December Cornwallis yet again found it necessary to deal severely with the quartermaster general's department. He directed "that the Quarter Master General should have no Property in either the Waggons or the Horses." He further issued a public proclamation on the twenty-third which demanded strict accounting:

> As I consider myself a Steward for the Public Money expended by the Troops under my Command, I think myself bound, by the Duty I owe my Country, to regulate the Charges to be made by the different Departments.
>
> The QuarterMaster General must absolutely be restricted from charging more for Waggons and Horses than he has actually paid, for which he must produce his Vouchers; and he is not to charge the hire of Horses and Waggons purchased; nor is he to purchase either Horses or Waggons but upon Government Account. If the Necessity of the Service should oblige him to hire Waggons and Horses in the Country, either to attend the Army, or to carry Supplies to the different Posts, he is to pay the Proprietors the full Price allowed by Government for the Hire of such Waggons, for which the Receipts of such Proprietors will be his Vouchers.[11]

Yet despite all these measures, Cornwallis never could bring the quartermaster's office to heel. In January of 1781 as he prepared to open his campaign against Greene, the quartermaster general's officers presented to him a final absurd effrontery. While the commissaries of the British general were provisioning some wagons against the anticipated demands of the coming months, Tarleton's quartermaster came upon them, interrupted their work, and took their wagons. "In vain the commissaries represented that they were the waggons of the army," the Earl later fumed to Tarleton, "employed by my order in the public service. He [Tarleton's quartermaster] swore he did not care, that he had Col. Tarleton's orders to press waggons & he would have them & appealed to the *ratio ultima* of the broad sword."

JEMIMA, COUNTESS CORNWALLIS

Mezzotint by James Watson,
after Sir Joshua Reynolds

Courtesy of the New-York Historical Society, New York

SIR HENRY CLINTON

Engraving by A. H. Ritchie

BANASTRE TARLETON

Portrait by Sir Joshua Reynolds

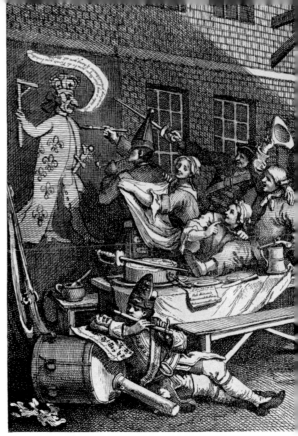

RECRUITING
IN THE
18th CENTURY

From England, *Plate II,*
designed and etched
by William Hogarth

YORKTOWN
IN THE
18th CENTURY

Sketch by a
British Naval Officer

GEORGE WASHINGTON

Portrait by James Peale

HORATIO GATES

Engraving by Tiebout,
after Gilbert Stuart

GATHERING OF THE MOUNTAIN MEN
AT SYCAMORE SHOALS

Painting by Lloyd Branson

Courtesy of the Tennessee State Museum.

NATHANAEL GREENE

Portrait by Charles Willson Peale

DANIEL MORGAN

Portrait by Charles Willson Peale

SURRENDER OF BRITISH STANDARDS AT YORKTOWN

Engraving from Pictorial Field-Book of the Revolution,
by B. J. Lossing

Cornwallis presumed that the quartermaster acted without Tarleton's knowledge, but he ordered the Legion commander to deal with the man "severely" or the "conducting this army through the country will be impracticable." The Earl later discovered that the Legion quartermaster had used the wagons to haul a "fork load of forage" to a plantation.[12]

Such incidents drove Cornwallis very nearly to despair, yet he could not prevent them. He as much as admitted defeat to Balfour: "I fear at last I shall be foiled," he wrote, "at least as far as the So. Carolina waggons. For unless I had a person I could depend on to purchase the Qr. Mr. Genl's waggons & horses & to take care of them afterwards, I fear he would take very effectual methods to prevent my economy being admired." [13]

So great was the Earl's dissatisfaction with the quartermaster general's department that he took his grievances to the chambers of Parliament after the war.[14] But part of his difficulties in organizing the transportation service owed neither to Sir Henry Clinton nor to the quartermaster general. They related, instead, to the larger problem of supply. Even had the quartermaster general's men been models of impeccable virtue, they still could not have furnished adequate transportation without first finding a sufficient supply of horses. South Carolina had no lack of these animals. Patriot militia were effective chiefly because they were always mounted. Yet although horses in plenty roamed the Carolina meadows, the British army rarely shared in the abundance. Its methods of procurement worked against its interest. Basically, of course, the army had two sources of supply: the loyalists and the patriots. From the one they should buy, from the other take. But they often took as much from their friends as they did from their enemies. Stedman described the South Carolina militia as "in general faithless, and altogether dissatisfied in the British service." He considered the quartermaster general and the cavalry mainly responsible, for these two units of the army constantly pressed loyalist horses. There was perhaps a reason for their actions: loyalist horses might be easier to come by than patriot ones. Loyalists might openly parade their possessions in the presence of redcoat regulars, while patriots hid theirs. His Majesty's army, however, could depend upon loyalist naïveté for only a brief period. Word soon spread, and the King's friends grew as wary as his enemies.

The British did institute a method of payment but one so inequitable that few men received full value for their goods. When the Carolinians learned that British "purchase" deprived them of their property as surely as British confiscation, they became increasingly loathe to sell. As Cornwallis' army took horses it gave most of the former owners certificates, evidence that their property now served King George and that they ought to be reimbursed. But reimbursement often depended upon contingencies. Desperate loyalists, in need of money, often sold these certificates at a tremendous discount to speculators. Only rarely did the army give receipts which guaranteed the owners payment upon presentation at Charleston. Receipts, however, listed only the property taken, not its value. A man would not often venture a trip to Charleston to recover the value of his property if the trip cost as much as the property taken and if that property consisted of horses which he would need for the journey in the first place. Furthermore, once in the city he had no guarantee that the British army would reimburse him to the full value of his loss.

The injustice of the system probably prompted men to hide their horses from the British army while it was at Winnsboro, for Cornwallis altered his methods after he left winter quarters. He anticipated, of course, that he would require more horses for his moving army than for his bivouacked one, and the old arrangement did not promise to answer his needs. So he ordered that in the future, receipts must specify not only the property taken but also its value. He thus bestowed upon the slip of paper a "negotiable authority." His subordinates continued to issue the old certificates to men of doubtful allegiance, but the Earl intended for the new receipts to go to the truly loyal in the hope that they would grow less reluctant to part with their property for the cause. Unfortunately, commissaries thwarted Cornwallis' purpose, for they rarely issued the receipts. Horses continued to be sorely needed.[15]

But even if the commissaries had found thousands of healthy steeds for the army, they would have solved only a part of the supply problems. Greater and more constant than his need for horses was his need for food. While he always seemed to find enough to satisfy his day-to-day needs, he could never store a bountiful surplus against contingencies. His army never actually starved to death in South Carolina, but it rarely knew whether to expect feast or famine from one day to the next. In a province that produced wheat, corn, and rice in quantities, Cornwallis subsisted only with difficulty.

But he did subsist. After he returned from Charlotte he sent Rawdon to command the forces at Camden, while he retained charge of the men at Winnsboro. Both parts of the army gathered food from the country between the two towns and south of them. Charles Stedman exerted himself mightily to collect provisions. He daily attended several mills, some of them six miles apart, and to keep them producing he used one hundred twenty Negroes, a sergeant of the 71st regiment, one cooper, and four overseers. By his own estimate, his efforts enabled the army to open its campaign in January of 1781 with "50,000 weight" of meal packed and ready for use.[16]

Stedman used methods far from gentle, and by stripping the countryside he alienated friends and hardened the resistance of foes. As a result, when Cornwallis went in pursuit of Greene, the troops he left to garrison South Carolina — who outnumbered the force he took with him — would face even greater

difficulty in finding victuals than when he had been at Winnsboro. The country would feed them less and less adequately.

Cornwallis was caught in a terrible dilemma during that
winter of 1780 to 1781. He had no wish to be ruthless at Winnsboro, yet he had to feed his army. Dr. David Ramsay, the patriot who in the 1780's wrote a history of the Revolution in
South Carolina, accused Stedman of seizing provisions from
helpless people and of cheating the British by charging the army
for what he had obtained by robbery. Although Stedman hotly
denied the accusation, and he seems to have been more honest
than many other men in similar positions of trust, he certainly
took unsparingly. The wife of Joseph Kershaw, the patriot
whom Cornwallis exiled to Bermuda, suffered for her husband's
convictions. Kershaw had owned most of the mills around Camden, and much of the grain that went to them grew on his plantations. Stedman exhausted mills and plantations alike to feed
the army. Although Mrs. Kershaw pleaded for some means of
subsistence, Stedman disregarded her pitiful condition. By permitting cavalry and artillery horses to roam in grain too unripe
for use, he dashed her hopes for future crops. He refused her
new supplies of sugar and salt when she ran out of these com-
modities. Although she had formerly reimbursed her help and
fed her Negroes from the cornmeal people paid her for the use
of her mills, the commissaries denied her this toll. Toward the
end of November her agent, Samuel Mathis, entreated Cornwallis for help. Mathis wrote one of Cornwallis' aides, Henry
Haldane, that "whatever his lordship is willing to grant will be
very thankfully receiv'd by Mrs. Kershaw." "We have no resources," Mathis concluded, "but in his lordship's bounty and
your goodness." [17] Other pleas similar in nature reached Cornwallis during his winter at Winnsboro. Eventually he tried to
combine duty with humanity. He did not stop the commissaries,
indeed he could not, but he strictly reminded Stedman that the
British did not make war on women and children. On the con-

trary, humanity commanded the British to support women and children of whatever political views. On December 15, he enjoined Stedman to "pay the most exact attention to leaving the proportion to the wives & children of the absentees whose estates are under sequestration." [18]

No matter how gently the Earl wished to treat suffering patriot families, he could not get away from the stubborn fact that his army had to eat. Had the British been able to gather supplies from the entire province instead of from just a small area and had the commissioner of sequestered estates been able to manage plantations and use them to grow foodstuffs for the British instead of taking from other people, the army would not have had to strip bare the surrounding countryside. Cornwallis would have marched after Greene with stronger, healthier troops, and he would have left Rawdon with a firm control of South Carolina.

In the previous autumn Cornwallis had formulated long-range plans to provide for such a happy state of affairs. He had appointed John Cruden commissioner of sequestered estates. But Cruden had discovered himself in difficulty from the first day in office. He had found the rebel plantations in his charge deserted, neglected, or ruined. Slaves, needed to harvest the crops, had disappeared or so lacked the necessities of life that they could not work. How could Cruden make the plantations pay? Only, he thought, by pouring money into them instead of taking it out. He needed food, clothes, tools, farm equipment, stock of every kind, draft horses, and money to pay for them. He needed to inoculate the plantation hands against smallpox which "raged in general over the country," and that, too, cost money. He required great numbers of overseers and an army of clerks to keep records. They, of course, wished to be paid for their labor. As a result not merely did Cruden prove unable to supply Camden, Winnsboro, Ninety-Six, or Charleston, he even proved unable to support his own department. He spent far more than he took in, with no appreciable results. The horses supposed to fatten on the rich plantations never fattened, and the crops supposed to feed them and the British army never felt the harvester's sickle. The £50,000 to £60,000 supposed to accrue from the sale of the plantations' produce — tobacco, rice, indigo, wheat, peas, cattle, sheep — never materialized to fill British coffers.

Of course Cornwallis had anticipated little from Cruden in 1780, but he hoped that in 1781 the commissioner might feed the men who garrisoned South Carolina. Unfortunately, the year 1781 brought even greater trouble to Cruden than 1780. When the Earl left South Carolina, according to the commissioner, he left the field to the rebels. The frontiers became scenes of "confusion, robbery, and murder." Whigs destroyed plantations which might otherwise have produced in 1781, murdered overseers, razed houses, and slaughtered horses, cattle, and sheep. In addition, despite his increasingly slim resources, Cruden had to feed and maintain an ever-growing number of loyalists who fled from their homes to the shelter of the British army at Charleston. When the police board in the city finally examined Cruden's accounts in September of 1781, they found that the commissioner had expended £16,432 while he had collected only £9578.[19] Cornwallis could not have foreseen the ultimate difficulties to which Cruden would be reduced, but he certainly knew, before he left South Carolina, that the army had not solved its food problems.

Nor had it solved other problems of supply. There remained the difficulty of finding enough uniforms, ammunition, camp equipage, and especially rum, considered so necessary for the troops in the eighteenth century. Cornwallis did capture considerable supplies of arms, ammunition, and accoutrements. He did not capture rum or uniforms, and as winter deepened at Winnsboro, his need for both became desperate. Rum and uni-

forms came from New York to Charleston. From there they had
to find their way into the interior. But the roads and waterways
proved unsafe, and Cornwallis' men dressed in rags for winter's
rains before a supply of uniforms managed to reach them.

At first Balfour tried to ship goods into the interior by wagon
trains along the roads. But the limited supply of draft horses
seriously handicapped this method of transportation. "It is impossible to send the whole way by land," Balfour wrote to Rawdon toward the end of October, "as it takes six weeks, and having only one sett of horses, they are totally knocked up by the
journey." [20] Rebel depredations, furthermore, rendered the
wagon route precarious. The "sending all the way to the army
from Monk's corner by land," Balfour concluded in early November, "is now absolutely impracticable." [21] The waterways
offered an alternative route since South Carolina boasts several
large rivers, navigable for considerable distances into the interior. The Santee presented the most direct route to Cornwallis'
forces, for it flowed from its headwaters in North Carolina
(where it was called the Catawba) past Camden (where it had
become the Wateree) down to the ocean between Charleston
and Georgetown. About thirty miles south of Camden the
Congaree River, which ran down from the interior west of
Winnsboro, emptied into the Santee. Near the forks of the two
streams, at McCord's Ferry, a good road went directly up to
Camden. If the redcoats could secure the Santee as far as
McCord's, Rawdon could send his wagons south to pick up army
supplies and then distribute them to his garrison at Camden and
to Cornwallis at Winnsboro.

Eventually Cornwallis and Balfour worked out this supply
route. But it required large detachments to secure the river. "I
cannot think," the Earl told Rawdon on November 10, "that
the large cargo of rum & salt can come safe by the mouth of
Santee. The navigation is very long, and cannot be protected by
my floating force." [22] But on the very day he talked of insuper-

able obstacles Cornwallis exerted himself to overcome them. He dispatched Tarleton with a roving force south of Camden to protect the Santee supply route "so very essential to our existence." [23] A garrison at Georgetown covered the mouth of the river. Balfour, anticipating his commander's needs, dispatched the 64th regiment from Charleston to Kingstree Bridge on the Black River, almost midway between the mouth of the Santee and its fork with the Congaree,[24] to protect interior navigation. When goods for the provincials and the regulars finally arrived at Charleston in November,[25] Balfour rounded up all the boats he could find, sent them to the mouth of the Santee, and thence upriver to McCord's.[26]

They reached the army just in time. By the end of November the lieutenant general himself lacked even a greatcoat — a bath rug served as substitute — and the entire 71st regiment was "really quite naked." [27] December 9, however, saw the end of their worries. "Our clothing is all come up on every man & plenty of rum," he told Balfour on that day. Presumably there arrived also the seven cases of wine — claret was his favorite — which the commander in the South had ordered from London to warm his vitals for the rest of the drizzly winter.[28]

Victory in battle, however, required more than a well-fed, well-clothed army, although both those factors would help immeasurably. Victory required more even than the courage, stamina, and discipline which the redcoats possessed in abundance. Often victory required knowledge of the enemy's movements and intentions. A very important key to Cornwallis' past successes had been his superb intelligence system. Tarleton had surprised his enemies almost every time, and the Earl had managed to slip a spy into Gates' headquarters before the battle of Camden. Now the British intelligence system fell down so badly as to be not only worthless but also comical. "Our friends hereabouts are so timid and so stupid that I can get no intelligence,"

Cornwallis complained to Tarleton in the middle of December. The remark summed up his own experience of that winter[29] and Lord Rawdon's as well. "All my accounts about Smallwood [General William Smallwood] agree with yours," the Earl told Rawdon in November, "but mine are: 'I went as far as Fishing Creek, & there Billy McDaniel's wife told me that she saw Dicky Thomson who said he saw young Tommy Rigdom that just came from camps &c &c.' No offer can prevail upon any man I can find to go & see . . . with his own eyes." [30] Rawdon might well have sympathized with his commander's plight, for he too had to depend upon gossip, rumor, and women's wiles for his "intelligence." In late November Rawdon reported to his chief: "About an hour ago two of my spies came in. They had not been to the enemy's camp, but sent a woman thither, who returned to them yesterday morning reporting that she had left Gates & Smallwood at six mile run on Monday night. I am disposed to credit this intelligence." [31] "An emissary, upon whom I place much dependence," he wrote the Earl in December, "has this morning returned from the neighborhood of six mile run. He is too well known to have ventured into the enemy's camp. But he sent his niece thither, and her report I now transmit to your lordship." [32] All through November and December Cornwallis and his second depended upon hearsay of a similar nature for their knowledge of the enemy. As the time approached to move out of winter quarters, the Earl continued to receive the same sort of intelligence. Typical of his sources of information was David George, whose judgment can be gauged by his calling a man a rebel because he had stolen some rum, brandy, and horses from him. George told the following tale a week before the British army marched: "My wife's sister last night came to my house out of strong rebel settlement up at Prince's fort. By her I have heard the design & intention of the rebels." Such information might have been reliable had the wife gathered it herself, but she had depended upon others for what she purveyed. "She understood," George continued, "from Captain Francis Prince's and Henry Prince's wives that they were awaiting for Colonel Morgan and Colonel Washington who was on their march to join them." [33]

Cornwallis did not require sophisticated intelligence during his inactivity in winter quarters. As the time approached to open a campaign in which he could anticipate major battles, however, intelligence became increasingly important. Yet he never seemed able to improve his service, despite all his efforts. He had ordered Leslie, who had landed in Charleston in December, to move his army into the interior and join his commander for the campaign in North Carolina. Yet inadequate intelligence would render the junction uncertain. When the time came, the Earl was unsure of where they should meet because he did not know the location of particular plantations and crossroads and could find no one who would point them out to him.[34] It is not surprising, therefore, that during most of his North Carolina offensive in the spring of 1781, Cornwallis would have to move blindly. How indeed could he have expected it to be otherwise? Since even while at Winnsboro he gathered no reliable information from the many loyalists living in that vicinity under the protection of the British army, how could he hope to do better farther north in a country of fewer loyalists and to whom he could offer no permanent protection?

Possibly he thought that if he could maintain his full complement of regulars, he could defy all his unsolved problems of logistics. Regulars had taken Charleston. Regulars had thrashed Gates. Regulars almost always beat militia in open battle, no matter what the odds. Loyalists took heart at the sight of a regiment of redcoats — determined, disciplined, invincible. If Earl Cornwallis intended to take and hold North Carolina in the face of all obstacles, he needed full-strength regular regiments.

But could he depend upon having them? Numerous engagements in South Carolina had thinned his ranks. Reinforcements, such as Leslie's, would make good some of the losses. In the Carolinas, however, sickness incapacitated as many men as bullets did, and it sometimes kept them away from the line longer. Sickness had attacked his army during the summer of 1780, and continued to shorten the muster rolls from then on. In July of 1780 Balfour at Ninety-Six worried that his command was "turning sickly fast." [35] Major Weymss reported from Georgetown in August that "within three days 6 men have died of putrid fevers. 4 Sergeants and 28 men are now ill." [36] When in August Cornwallis came to challenge Gates at Camden, illness kept eight hundred fifty-nine men, more than a battalion, from action. Later the situation worsened. Sickness delayed the march to Charlotte. "But we must get healthier," the Earl wrote to Balfour the week after he left Camden, "or there is no doing anything. I find the ague and fever all over this country, full as much as at Camden. They say go 40 or 50 miles farther & you will be healthy. It was the same language before we left Camden. There is no trusting such dangerous experiments." The entire 63d regiment fell so ill as to be "unfit for any active service." [37] Within another week the 71st was reduced to a similar state and Cornwallis had to bivouac for several days before continuing. He had one hundred twenty sick, their numbers increased daily, and he lacked sufficient wagons to transport them back to Camden.[38] He eventually resumed his march, but himself fell ill at Charlotte and had to suffer through the jolting wagon ride back to Winnsboro.

At Winnsboro he surely anticipated that illness might strike him again after he started moving north, even though the "sickly" seasons of summer and autumn had given way to winter. He knew also that battle would take its inevitable toll. Both wounded and sick were bound to increase greatly when he next took the field.

Sickness and wounds were, of course, the hazards of war. A general could not abandon his plans for a campaign because some men might become disabled. Cornwallis might well have considered, however, the hazards of campaigning without adequate means of returning the disabled to duty quickly. He would need every man, which meant he would need the best of medical facilities. But the winter at Winnsboro had just shown that he could not even count upon having adequate medical facilities. At best the army had only crude medical understanding; doctors still bled men dying from loss of blood, dirty fingernails inoculated against smallpox, and filthy rags served to clean instruments.

Bad as their methods were, the doctors were still generally preferable to no doctors. The Earl, however, never had enough doctors or elementary medical supplies. The shortage of medical help became apparent at the siege of Charleston, and continued to trouble the army all through 1780. "The situation of the mates of the general hospital is really pitiable," Dr. John McNamara Hayes, chief physician at Charleston, wrote in April. "They are not allowed a servant, as every other part of the army, nor when they get one, are they allowed provisions to support him. At a time their services are wanted, they are employed in their domestic concerns, nor can I with justice condemn them." [39] The situation had grown still worse when the Earl examined the Charleston hospital in the middle of July. He discovered "a most alarming deficiency of medicine, and a want of medical assistance, and of stores." [40] Although he asked Clinton for medical supplies, the commander in chief never sent them. By November the medical arrangements had deteriorated even further. "We have recd no stores from New York," Hayes told Cornwallis, "nor have the surgeon & mates required been sent. Our mates here have been all ill, and some so far reduced as to render a visit to Europe necessary to supply their places." [41] Charleston, nonetheless, possessed the best medical facilities for the British army in South Carolina. The Earl often shipped his sick down to the city because Hayes cured them and returned them to duty more quickly than did his own physicians.

If the problem of sickness assumed enormous proportions for a stationary army, would it not overwhelm the lieutenant general during a campaign to the north, when Charleston would be beyond the reach of his sick and when he would have few qualified men and fewer medical supplies for treating the disabled on the spot?

With all the problems he faced, could he, in fact, afford to move into North Carolina at all? Congress was reorganizing the shattered American army in the South. Thus if he moved north he would face not only larger numbers of Continentals but also better generals than he had faced before. Nathanael Greene had replaced Gates, and Daniel Morgan, whose fierce riflemen had tormented Burgoyne at Saratoga, served under Greene. Would the Earl's army be in shape to face them? It had never suppressed patriot activity, even in the halcyon days after Camden. The once-active loyalists had melted away after King's Mountain. Could he ever feed himself on the march, when only the gigantic and ruthless efforts of Commissary Stedman had kept him alive at Winnsboro? Would he be able to replace the clothes, arms, ammunition, salt, rum, medicines, and other provisions that a northern campaign would consume, when Balfour at Charleston had been unable to forward any more than the bare necessities to him at Winnsboro? North Carolina's rivers would present obstacles to cross rather than highways of transportation. Once he crossed those obstacles would he know where to find his enemy? Could he ascertain the enemy's troop strength and disposition in a country dominated by whigs, when he had been unable to secure such information in a more loyal province from people to whom he could promise and give protection? Lastly, did he really expect that North Carolina would be kinder to the health of his troops than South Carolina? If not, could he hope to cure his sick during a winter offensive, when he had not been able to cure them in winter quarters? These were weighty considerations indeed.

The Earl thought about them during his winter at Winnsboro, and thought about them deeply. Yet when the time for decision drew near, when action beckoned on the horizon and victory just beyond it, Cornwallis did not hesitate. Clinton would have hesitated — indeed, would probably have remained in South Carolina. Not Cornwallis. He weighed his obstacles against his possible gains and determined to move north. He would smash Greene.

CHAPTER 12

Cowpens
"The Late Affair
has almost Broke my Heart"

SEVERAL CONSIDERATIONS shaped his decision to pursue Greene early in January of 1781. First he had to think of Britain's friends to the north. True, bitter experience in South Carolina had moved him to term loyalist militia "dastardly" and "pusillanimous." But the loyalists in North Carolina had in the past shown their zeal and activity on some occasions — albeit prematurely and sometimes against Cornwallis' own express instructions. Furthermore, the loyalists' unreliability in combat did not necessarily rule out their usefulness in nonmilitary capacities: the offering of provisions, intelligence, guides, civil government, among the most important. The loyalists in North Carolina had originally been very numerous, more numerous, Stedman believed, than in any other colony.[1] But, dispersed throughout a thinly populated colony and "mixed in every district with people of opposite principles" who had "possessed themselves of the powers of government," they were, Cornwallis knew, at a great disadvantage. Their attempts to manifest their loyalty had often brought "fatal consequences" to themselves and their cause.[2] They and their families often suffered much, and the Earl felt deeply for the cruelties inflicted upon them by

their patriotic neighbors. He must afford them relief, even if
they proved as useless to the royal cause as their colleagues in
South Carolina.[3] In any event, the British government encouraged the move, based upon "repeated assurances they had received" that thousands of North Carolinians from all parts of
the province "would flock to the King's standard." [4]

Cornwallis had yet another reason for the northward move.
Beset by logistical problems in South Carolina, he thought he
could never master these difficulties so long as the Americans
had an army in being, and a rallying point for that army, in the
South. North Carolina sheltered Greene's forces, and the existence of Greene's forces had, the Earl believed, encouraged rebels
in South Carolina to harass British foraging parties, interrupt
communications, snipe at provision trains, and terrorize loyalists
into docile submission. Cornwallis could not hold South Carolina without controlling North Carolina, and he could not control North Carolina until he defeated Greene.

To defeat Greene meant first catching him — a difficult task.
The American had no intention of getting caught, and he had
proved his generalship in the past, in times of both triumph
and adversity. Nathanael Greene was the thirty-eight-year-old
son of a Rhode Island Quaker preacher. An ironmaster, he operated his father's forge and ironworks at Coventry on the
Pawtuxet River.[5] Thus when the war came, he almost literally
beat plowshares into swords. His occupation gave him great
muscular strength and an extremely solid look. Square of jaw
and full of determination, he had fought at Trenton, Germantown, Monmouth, Newport, and had suffered through the winter at Valley Forge. He became the new leader of the American
forces in the South, replacing the dishonored Gates. Cornwallis
found him a solid foe, but Greene also had a thorough respect
for his British adversary. To Anthony Wayne, the Quaker once
wrote: "Be a little careful, and tread softly; for depend upon it,
you have a modern Hannibal to deal with in the person of

Cornwallis." [6] Unfortunately for the "modern Hannibal," Greene was to prove a Fabius.

The Quaker determined to divide his army for the purpose of "desultory incursions in different, and nearly opposite quarters" and to alarm and harass the British outposts on the frontiers of South Carolina. He hoped also that his constantly moving army would supply itself more easily than if it remained stationary in a countryside already partly stripped of provisions. It would at the same time "infuse some spirit in the militia," whose help Greene needed.[7] He entrusted his light troops to Brigadier General Daniel Morgan and sent him by the heads of rivers to the western frontiers of South Carolina — there to threaten Ninety-Six. Morgan's command consisted of 300 infantry under Lieutenant Colonel John Eager Howard, 170 riflemen under Major Francis Triplet, and 70 light dragoons under Lieutenant Colonel William Washington.[8] Greene took the remainder of his army to the Peedee in order to alarm the country around Camden.

Cornwallis intended to challenge these arrangements and the man who organized them. But he would not act hastily or without proper planning. Haste had ruined the campaigns of friend and foe alike in the past and had indeed thrust Gates into disaster. The Earl would first secure his rear. He would march to catch Greene, but in the process he would not hazard the land or people already gained for the King. He left garrisons at Augusta, Savannah, Charleston, Camden, Ninety-Six, and other places. In all, they came to five thousand rank and file[9] whom he entrusted to Lord Rawdon.

Even with his rear secure, however, Cornwallis refused to move against Greene without further precautions. He knew he marched north against a wily foe, and he knew from previous experience that rebel militia who ran from an open fight with regulars delighted in attacking foraging parties, gobbling up supply trains, and intercepting dispatch riders. He could not, in

short, depend upon remaining directly in touch with the forces
he left behind. So he provided an alternate line of retreat,
should retreat become necessary, and an alternate line of supply.
He sent an expedition of about three hundred men under
Major James Craig to the Cape Fear River in North Carolina.
They sailed from Charleston on January 21.[10] It would be "a
serious business to go into the heart of N. Carolina," the Earl
explained to his subordinates, unless the British held the harbor
which commanded the approach to Wilmington.[11] But Cornwallis hoped that once Craig had established himself, he could
use the waterways of North Carolina to supply the British army
in the interior, as Balfour in Charleston had used those of South
Carolina.[12]

Finally, Cornwallis hoped to make his own task simpler by
making Greene's harder. Should Greene but miscalculate once,
as Gates had miscalculated, the British general could pounce
upon him and destroy him. If Greene not only had to worry
about the Earl's army to the south but also about another British
force to the north, he might make that miscalculation. Of
course, Cornwallis could not easily send a portion of his own
forces to the north of Greene, but Clinton could. And for once
Clinton cooperated. He dispatched an expedition under Benedict Arnold — now a British brigadier general and ferociously
sought after by the patriots — to Virginia to conduct harassing
raids during January of 1781.[13] Arnold planned to help Cornwallis in two ways: he would burn the Virginian stores that
supplied Greene, and he would try to entice Greene into divert-
ing some of his troops away from North Carolina toward Virginia.

These precautions taken, the Earl could lead his own force
after Greene. Including the 1900 men under Leslie who were
marching to join him, that force numbered about 3200 men —
450 Germans (Bose Regiment 347, Jagers 103), 700 provincials
(British Legion 451, North Carolina Volunteers 256), and
2050 British.[14]

They would march through an area liberally punctuated with rivers, all flowing in a generally southeasterly direction. Upstream, to the northwest, almost all of them fork, some of them more than once. Thus, whereas about eight major rivers — the Santee, the Peedee, the Cape Fear, the New, the Neuse, the Pamlico, the Roanoke, the Chowan — cut the coast of the two Carolinas above Charleston, when the British proceeded to the inland regions, they found that the number of major rivers and creeks multiplied to more than twenty. The Santee forked into the Congaree and the Wateree; the Congaree in turn split up into the Saluda, the Enoree, the Tiger, the Pacolet, and the Broad Rivers; and the Wateree branched to form the Catawba and Little Catawba Rivers. The Peedee River forked into the Great Peedee and the Little Peedee, and the former into the Yadkin and Little Rivers. Major branches off the Cape Fear included the South, the Black, the Northeast Cape Fear, the Deep, and the Haw Rivers. The Haw split into Ready Creek and Troublesome Creek. There were others as well.

Each of these represented an obstacle to both sides, especially to a pursuer with no boats and sometimes with none but the scantiest knowledge of the terrain and even of the location of fords. During the winter months, heavy rains made the Carolina backwoods a nightmare of mud and swollen streams. Men and horses alike sickened. Some died. Always there was yet another creek to cross. The streams did not lie passive — mere idle markings on a map. They grasped for all who came within their touch. The winter of 1781 brought torrents, on which they battened and grew strong. Greedy, they even left their natural bounds to claim more prey. Through such a land Cornwallis now planned to lead his men.

But before he could lead them, he had to bring them together. Circumstances, together with the activities of General Greene, combined to delay that junction. Although Cornwallis could not move decisively against his adversary until Leslie joined him, still he chose to order his major general to remain

several days at Camden. Cornwallis had received an ominous
report that the French had arrived at the Cape Fear before
Craig.[15] Until he ascertained the truth or falsity of the report,
he hesitated to commit himself too far to the North Carolina
venture. By detaining Leslie's corps at Camden, Cornwallis
avoided full commitment. He also held Greene "in suspense as
to his future movements." If the report should prove false (as it
did), the Earl hoped to leave Winnsboro on January 7. Leslie
could follow from Camden on the ninth.[16]

Cornwallis felt that once Leslie had joined him, he could
move in earnest against Greene. But Greene had at once simplified and complicated the Earl's job: he had split into two parts
the army that Cornwallis wanted to catch and destroy. By sending Morgan against Ninety-Six the Quaker had weakened himself greatly, thus rendering more certain his defeat if only the
British could bring him to battle. But at the same time the British commander could not ignore Morgan's threat to Ninety-Six.
Cruger might ordinarily have withstood an attack without reinforcements, but the present time found him particularly vulnerable. Militia Colonel Andrew Pickens had defected, taking
some men with him, because he considered the destruction of
his property by some tories a violation of the protection the
British had promised him in return for his oath.[17] Cornwallis
wanted to reinforce Cruger and to destroy the force threatening
him. Since that force comprised part of Greene's army anyway,
the American Quaker offered him a unique opportunity to
strike two blows at once. The destruction of Morgan would
open a campaign ultimately aimed at the destruction of Greene.

Cornwallis therefore decided to send Tarleton in pursuit of
Morgan. To help his subordinate and to reinforce Ninety-Six
later, the Earl also dispatched the 7th regiment. He ordered it
to take the Legion commander's baggage and a 3-pounder
gun to Brierly's Ferry. There it would join Tarleton, act with
him for so long as he judged useful, and then proceed to Ninety-

Six with his "old gun," also a 3-pounder.[18] The Earl ordered
Tarleton to keep on the left flank of the main British force and
to advance on either the east or west bank of the Broad River,
whichever he judged best from his own intelligence.[19] As distance widened between the Legionnaire and his commanding
general, communications between them became increasingly
spotty and unreliable, yet they usually managed to keep in
touch. On January 4 the Earl heard from Tarleton that "Morgan had retired" (abandoned the move toward Ninety-Six and
turned back north) and "was got too far to give any hopes of
overtaking him." By January 8, according to Cornwallis' best
information, Tarleton had arrived at the south side of the Enoree (the southernmost of three parallel tributaries of the
Broad), and Morgan had reached the Pacolet (the northern-
most of the three tributaries). Then heavy rains came to delay
Tarleton, who could not pass the swollen Enoree and Tiger (the
middle of the three tributaries) Rivers that intervened between
him and Morgan's men on the Pacolet.[20]

Meanwhile, the Earl broke camp and marched his men north.
His operations had reached a critical stage, with the forces that
he had intended to use against Greene now divided into three
parts — his own, Tarleton's, and Leslie's. The Earl had to join
Leslie soon, for the sake of both their armies. Until that junction, Cornwallis could do nothing. He could not send any more
aid to Tarleton because his own army was too small for further
detachment. Nor could he push ahead to try to stop Morgan's
retreat, since he could not spare a strong detachment to guard
his baggage and provisions. He needed Leslie badly, but Leslie
needed him just as badly. The major general, reduced to short
rations, toiled through swamps and mud, repairing a road as he
marched. Cornwallis even had to send four thousand pounds of
meat and some salt to Rocky Mount (northeast of Winnsboro)
for the use of Leslie's hungry men when they arrived there.
When the major general finally reached the neighborhood of

Rocky Mount on January 14, Cornwallis concerted his final
plans for a junction. It proved difficult, in an unmapped area,
to find reliable guides. Nor were the place names always clear.
Cornwallis carefully explained to Leslie how to get to Stewart's
New Cross Roads (not Stewart's Old Cross Roads), their place
of junction — providing, of course, that his own information
was correct.[21] The roads were very bad indeed. On January 16
the Earl arrived at Hillhouse's Plantation between Turkey and
Bullock Creeks. There he stopped, ordered meal to be ground,
and awaited Leslie's arrival.

The overriding urgency of the junction with Leslie necessarily meant that Cornwallis could not promise Tarleton anything.
He told as much to Tarleton and to two other subordinates,
Rawdon and Balfour. He slowed his own movements to facilitate the junction with Leslie, and he exerted himself to keep in
constant communication with the Legion commander. Tarleton's pursuit of Morgan, however, undoubtedly constituted one
of the least of the Earl's worries. The dragoon officer had a
large, disciplined force of regulars and provincials who ought to
scatter Morgan's ragged rabble at the first charge. Cornwallis
had good reason to hope that soon one of Lieutenant Colonel
Tarleton's infrequent dispatches would announce the welcome
news of a victory.

As the rivers fell Tarleton at last found himself able to continue his chase of General Morgan. On January 12 he resumed
his march. His force numbered about a thousand men, approximately half of them his own Legion of cavalry and infantry, the
other half regular British regiments (or remnants thereof) and
a meager artillery train of two 3-pounders.[22] This army, larger
than Cornwallis' own forces until Leslie's men joined, Tarleton
deemed sufficient to engage Morgan or at least to force him over
the Broad and into the arms of Cornwallis. The Legion commander crossed the Enoree and Tiger Rivers on the fourteenth
and two days later the Pacolet. Then only Thicketty Creek and

Morgan lay between Tarleton and the Broad River. The British officer roused his men early, for he sniffed action. They marched at three o'clock in the bitterly cold morning of January 17.[23] In the chill darkness they passed over Thicketty Creek. Then Tarleton learned that Morgan had halted and taken a position on the near side of the Broad River with the intent of giving action. All eager, Tarleton hurried forward.

Five months earlier Cornwallis had recommended the Legion commander for promotion in the regular army to lieutenant colonel (he was then a major of regulars although lieutenant colonel of the Legion) and had described him as "one of the most promising officers" he had ever known.[24] Typically, when Tarleton gained his promotion, he did not even mention it to Cornwallis, much less express his gratitude.[25] Hundreds of other people experienced Tarleton's "ungenerous" behavior, but he cared little for the opinion of others. Astride his horse, dressed in the handsome green of the Legion, he rode, so he thought, toward fame and glory.

Sir Joshua Reynolds' portrait of him shows a very handsome young man, who is saved from "prettiness" by the length of his nose and the strength of his chin. He is smallish, well-muscled, and compact of body. His face displays coldness, hauteur, self-assurance, and determination. Here, the viewer realizes, is a man who would suffer no pangs of doubt or qualms of conscience — one who would always act without hesitation. Significantly, he is grasping his sword as though to unsheath it.

He quickly taught the Americans to hate him, and his name in the South became synonymous for "butcher." His name also became a word of terror effective for quieting troublesome children. The carnage that followed Buford's surrender at the Waxhaws gave rise to the term "Tarleton's Quarters," an expression some of the over-the-mountain men used when they shot down Ferguson's surrendered men at King's Mountain. Tarleton's heart was virgin to the prompting of mercy, and he promised to "discriminate with severity" between friends and foes. "If warfare allow me," he once told Cornwallis, "I shall give these disturbers of the peace no quarter. If humanity obliges me to spare their lives, I shall convoy them close prisoners to Camden." [26] According to one story, Tarleton dined at the house of the widow of patriot Richard Richardson, then plundered and burned it. He also drove the cattle, hogs, and poultry into the barns before he set fire to the buildings. "This thing was done," the story concludes, "because he pretended to believe that the poor old general was with the rebel army; though, had he opened his grave before the door, he might have seen the contrary." [27] Many soldiers with Greene's army or Morgan's detachment would have given a week's ration of food and spirits to lay their hands on the young British officer of dragoons. Even his fellow officers felt no love for Tarleton. He had been known to commandeer their horses for his Legion, and many of them never got paid.[28]

One patriot critic wrote that Tarleton had acquired a "distinguished reputation, but he was greatly indebted for his military fame to good fortune and accident. In all his previous engagements [before Cowpens] he either had the advantage of surprising an incautious enemy — of attacking them when panick-struck after recent defeats — or of being opposed to undisciplined militia. He had gathered no laurels by hard fighting against an equal force. . . ." [29] While not entirely fair, the assessment strikes close to the truth. Tarleton welcomed additions to the ranks of the enemy opposing him: "The more difficulty, the more glory." [30] Difficulty did not always bring glory, however, as Tarleton discovered at Blackstock's against Sumter. Yet the Green Dragoon would not learn by his mistakes, indeed, would not even admit that he made mistakes. Seven years after his repulse at Blackstock's, when the whole world knew Sumter had beaten him, Tarleton still claimed it as his own victory. A critic wrote justly of Tarleton's account of his campaigns in America: "From too great attention to his own exploits, Lieutenant Colonel Tarleton pays not that decent regard to those of others, which historical truth indispensably requires." [31] Such was the man that Morgan turned to face at Cowpens on the morning of January 17.

Morgan was a very different sort of man. Rough and tough and ready with his fists, he had risen to command through sheer ability. Known to many as the Old Wagoner because he had driven a supply wagon for Braddock's army, he had been hit by an Indian bullet in the French and Indian War and lost all the teeth in his lower left jaw. For striking a British lieutenant he had received four hundred ninety-nine strokes of the lash, but miraculously survived. Morgan always asserted that the drummer boy had miscounted and that George III owed him one lash. The mass of scar tissue on his back inspired the men to whom Morgan showed it. Great waves of racking pain from rheumatism or sciatica periodically engulfed his body. Nonetheless, he carried on, fraternizing with the men, walking among them the night before he had decided to give battle, encouraging them.[32]

Morgan's militia, which he had previously dispersed to gather forage, had orders to meet their commander and his main army at the best gathering spot around, Hannah's Cowpens, on January 16. That night Morgan learned of the nearness of Tarleton's forces and knew he stood little chance of passing the Broad River (the nearest place to cross, Cherokee Ford, was seven miles distant) before being caught by the fast-moving British. Accordingly, the Old Wagoner determined to make his stand upon the spot. Against anyone but Tarleton, that decision might have been fatal for Morgan. Against anyone but Tarleton, Morgan might not have made his stand there.

Hannah's Cowpens provided no commanding ground for the

Americans. The surrounding countryside was all relatively flat, only slightly rolling. The approach to the battlefield lay almost in a plateau, with a view of the ridges to the northwest. The land sloped up just a little where the British would commence their charge. The open woods were free from underbrush. The terrain remained similar all the way to the Broad River, six miles to the rear of the American lines: it offered no shield to a retreating force pursued by cavalry. As Tarleton himself observed, the Cowpens offered "as proper a place for action" as he could desire. Indeed, he said, "America does not produce many [places] more suitable to the nature of the troops under his command." [33] In other words, it was cavalry ground, and Tarleton had a superiority of three to one in cavalry.[34] The Green Dragoon also had an overall superiority of five to four in numbers.[35] The Old Wagoner, seemingly, had chosen a bad place to fight and had boxed himself in.

Morgan's troop dispositions at first may have seemed as unwise as his choice of battlefield. He placed militia (known for their propensity to run) in the front line to take the first shock of the charge. Morgan reasoned, however, that since militia always broke and ran anyway, he would have them break and run on command, after firing a few rounds. The main line, composed of light infantry, of Maryland and Delaware Continentals, and of Virginia and Georgia militia, took position atop a small hillock one hundred fifty yards behind the first line. To the rear, behind the crest of a second hillock, waited the reserve, consisting of William Washington's cavalry and of mounted infantry under Lieutenant Colonel James McCall. Morgan placed one hundred fifty riflemen in advance of the front line of militia. They could pick off enough redcoats to dampen the British charge and then retire to the main line.

The Americans slapped their hands together to keep warm. "About sunrise the British line advanced at a sort of trot, with a loud haloo. It was the most beautiful line I ever saw," an Amer-

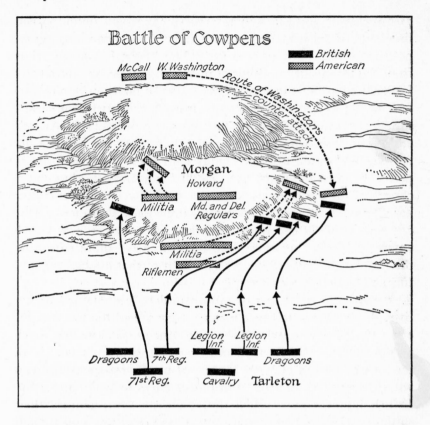

Battle of Cowpens

ican private wrote later. "When they shouted I heard Morgan say, 'They give us the British haloo, boys, give them the Indian haloo, by God.'" [36]

Although his men had been marching since 3:00 A.M., Tarleton was not one to halt and ponder once he saw the enemy. Like Murat and Custer of later times, he galloped to the sound of the guns. Hastily the dragoon spread out his line, anxious to charge. To form the center of his main line he sent his infantry — the 7th, Legion, and light infantry — strengthened by his two 3-pounders and by dragoons on either flank. More cavalry and the

71st regiment remained in reserve to the rear. Actually, the line had not fully formed and the reserve had not yet taken its position when Tarleton charged. The "view haloo" swelling from the throats of hundreds of men who had never hunted the fox or the hare or the stag aptly suited the occasion, for the attack was as ragged as a ride to hounds. Tarleton had not consulted the commandants of the regiments, Majors McArthur and Newmarsh, who were men of experience. He had not attempted to "soften up" the enemy with his artillery before exposing his men to enemy fire. He had not, indeed, obtained a clear view of the enemy's force and situation, for the riflemen kept him at a distance — his cavalry drew back after one American volley left fifteen horses riderless. But Tarleton attacked anyway with an "un-officer-like impetuousity" more suited to the hunt than the battlefield. The sight of that attack, "premature, confused, and irregular," [37] was for Morgan a good omen. The American front line of militia under Colonel Pickens delivered one or two telling rounds. They aimed for the officers' epaulets and then retired to the main line as ordered. Tarleton now scented an easy victory and pressed forward. But, characteristically, he had allowed McArthur no discretion to advance with the reserve when the front line pursued the militia. As the British infantry approached the American Continentals, they sustained a deadly fire. Their lines, already uneven owing to the loss of so many officers to militia bullets, grew more ragged. Before his infantry could make an impression upon the Continentals, Tarleton ordered forty of his cavalry to engage the enemy's left. They charged gallantly, but fire from Morgan's reserve, together with a countercharge by Washington's cavalry, drove them back with great loss. As the British wavered, Tarleton ordered his reserve into action. To the shrill and heady sound of bagpipes, the 71st Highlanders moved forward under McArthur. The British line steadied, and the American right now stood in danger of being outflanked.

Lieutenant Colonel John Eager Howard, in command of the

Maryland regulars and Virginia militia, attempted to ward off
the peril by changing the position of a company of Virginians on
the extreme right. He wished them to face to the left, forming a
right angle with the rest of the line, so as to confront the flanking 71st regiment. But the maneuver, as ordered, demanded
the Virginians to face about and then wheel in a quarter circle.
In the heat of the battle, misunderstanding and confusion resulted. "First a part and then the whole of the company commenced a retreat. The officers along the line seeing this, and
supposing that orders had been given for a retreat, faced their
men about and moved off." [38] Morgan began to worry, but
Howard noticed the orderliness of the retirement and assured
his superior that "men were not beaten who retreated in that
order." The Old Wagoner, with an intuitive grasp of tactics
and an inspired sense of battlefield expediency, planned the retreat to continue until the men reached the rising ground near
Washington's cavalry. Then, supported by the horse, they
would coolly face about, level their muskets, and pour a withering fire into their adversary's ranks.

Despite the good order of the American retreat, if British cavalry had struck hard at this critical moment they might well
have won the field. Tarleton later stated that he had sent an
order for the cavalry to charge. Whether or not he did, the
horses made no move. The infantry continued to pursue the
retiring Americans, no doubt thinking them routed, but —
tired from their long march — they could not overtake the
enemy. The consequent slowness of the infantry, together with
the absence of the necessary cavalry attack, gave the American
commander a chance to rally his men. On command they
formed line and charged with bayonets.

The unexpected move proved fatal to Tarleton's dreams of
glory. Sight of that advancing row of steel, their own favorite
weapon, unnerved the exhausted redcoats. No less than two
thirds of the British infantry officers had already fallen and
nearly the same proportion of private soldiers. "In disorder from

the pursuit, unsupported by the cavalry, deprived of the assistance of the cannon, which in defiance of the utmost exertions of those who had them in charge, were now left behind, the advance of the British fell back, and communicated a panick to others, which soon became general: a total rout ensued." [39] So utter was the rout that none of Tarleton's efforts availed to halt it. Some two hundred fifty British horsemen, who had not yet even joined battle, fled through the woods, riding down officers who opposed their flight. The Americans took the two cannons. The British infantry, too tired to run very fast or very far and "dispirited on many accounts, surrendered at discretion." [40]

After a brief personal encounter with William Washington, in which Tarleton had the further disappointment of seeing his pistol shot wound his adversary's horse rather than its rider, the Legion commander galloped off. Self-blame formed no part of any bitterness he felt. Several years later he explained that his disposition of troops "was planned with coolness, and executed without embarrassment." [41] With Tarleton rode fourteen officers and forty horsemen who, as their leader commented, were "not unmindful of their own reputation, or the situation of their commanding officer." [42]

The entire battle had lasted under an hour. At the end of those fatal fifty minutes, the British had lost eight hundred stand of arms, two 3-pound cannon, sixty Negro servants, one hundred horses, thirty-five supply wagons, and the colors of the 7th regiment. They had also lost something approaching eight hundred men: approximately one hundred killed, more than two hundred wounded, and more than four hundred captured unwounded.[43] The Americans reported only twelve killed and sixty wounded.[44] The Old Wagoner had more than repaid the British for the scars crisscrossing his back, and George III still owed him one lash.

While the surviving British fled through the woods to join Tarleton and the main army under Cornwallis, their less fortunate comrades remained upon the battlefield as prisoners of the Americans. Only with difficulty could Morgan's officers restrain their men from meting out "Tarleton's Quarters" to the tired and stunned captives now in their power. Indeed, according to Captain Duncanson of the 71st regiment, Tarleton's officers and men had orders to give no quarter and did not expect any for themselves. Thus it was that Captain Duncanson, after surrendering his sword to Colonel Howard, stood close beside his captor. When Howard mounted his horse, Duncanson almost unseated him by tugging at his saddle. Annoyed, Howard demanded an explanation. Then the captain blurted out the unpleasant nature of his orders and his expectations, his tongue loosened by the sight of some of Howard's men approaching. Howard put the British officer in charge of a sergeant so that he would suffer no ill use. Several years later, Colonel Howard received messages from Duncanson "expressing," as Howard said, "his obligation for my having saved his life." [45] Another officer among the prisoners, Major Archibald McArthur, concentrated his thoughts more upon the past than the future, but his thoughts were just as unhappy as those of his subordinate, Duncanson. Howard related that the major spoke very freely, declaring "that he was an officer before Tarleton was born; that the best troops in the service were put under *'that boy'* to be sacrificed; that he had flattered himself the event would have been different, if his advice had been taken, which was to charge with all the horse, at the moment" of the American retreat.[46]

McArthur, Duncanson, and the other unfortunate prisoners, who had been up since 2:00 A.M. and had been marching and then fighting since 3:00 A.M., had little time to rest, for Morgan marched from the Cowpens before noon heading toward the Broad River.[47] He had no wish for the British to recover their captured men, as had occurred after King's Mountain.

As Tarleton and his fifty-four loyal horsemen spurred through the woods away from the scene of their disaster, they came upon what Tarleton called "a party of the Americans." Actually the party consisted of about fifty loyalists who had served the dragoon as spies and guides. They were making off with some of the British baggage, "saving" it from the rebels. Hearing the headlong progress of horses, they feared the enemy and dove into the bushes. But the Legionnaires perceived the homespun-clad looters, ran them down, and sabered them. (Tarleton said they "were dispersed.")[48] The most charitable interpretation (though it may well be incorrect) is that the dragoons mistook the identity of the loyalists — but the consequence was that in the days after Cowpens, Lord Cornwallis found it impossible to obtain information of Morgan's whereabouts. His intelligence service, disintegrating before this incident, collapsed after it.

Tarleton continued on toward the Broad River, smarting from his defeat. Later he wrote that, while on this route, he "heard with infinite grief and astonishment, that the main army had not advanced beyond Turkey Creek." [49] Perhaps the dragoon leader already planned, as he rode away from his humiliation, to blame the lieutenant general for his own shortcomings. Perhaps he thought of attributing his loss to the Earl's failure to march to his relief with the main army. For Tarleton's apparent ignorance of Cornwallis' whereabouts, which he professed in retrospect, is otherwise difficult to comprehend. True enough, the impetuous young leader of the Legion had not received his superior's letter of January 16 which stated that Leslie would join the Earl's forces on the seventeenth or the day after and that the Earl proposed to march from Hillhouse's Plantation (between Turkey and Bullock Creeks) in three or four days to Beattie's Ford.[50] Nonetheless, Tarleton had, by his own admission, received Cornwallis' letter written from Bull Run on January 14, informing his subordinate that he would march to Hillhouse on the sixteenth.[51] Since this plantation, where Cornwallis would arrive on January 16, lay twenty-five miles from Cowpens and since Tarleton's light troops by means of a forced march beginning at 3:00 A.M. had only traveled five miles before they came up with Morgan at 8:00 A.M. on January 17, why did Tarleton assume, or pretend to assume, that Cornwallis must be nearby when the battle ended just fifty minutes after it had begun? Only gross ignorance of the geography of the border country of North and South Carolina could justify such an assumption, and Tarleton certainly never admitted ignorance of anything. But if he hoped to blame Cornwallis, he could plug this gap in his story by ignoring the letters from his chief and averring that the lieutenant general planned from the beginning to move his forces in support of Tarleton's. The dragoon later wrote that he had "requested his lordship to proceed up the eastern bank [of the Broad River] without delay, because such a movement might perhaps admit of co-operation, and would undoubtedly stop the retreat of the Americans." [52] He implied that his lordship agreed to the request but failed to comply with the agreement so that Cowpens turned into a disaster. Tarleton never recovered from his humiliation at the hands of Morgan. When he wrote his account of the Revolution after the war, he duped himself into believing that Cornwallis had agreed to cooperate with his scheme and, indeed, he even duped some later historians into believing the same thing.[53] While this wild tale could not absolve Tarleton from tactical failure, it neatly removed from him the onus for the disaster. Morgan was not caught and destroyed because Cornwallis did not live up to his bargain with Tarleton.

But if Cornwallis would have agreed to such a bargain, which is doubtful at best, he never received a letter from Tarleton proposing it. Indeed, before Cowpens he did not hear from Tarleton between January 11 (or 12 if Tarleton misdated his letter, as Cornwallis thought) and the day after the battle itself. Furthermore, the Earl's cooperation in such a plan would have required knowledge of where to find Morgan. As his own letters to Tarleton make clear, however, Cornwallis did not know Morgan's whereabouts and thought him well over the Broad River.

Perhaps Tarleton misread his superior's letter of January 14:
certainly he misquoted it. "I have not heard of Morgan's moving," Cornwallis wrote, "but conclude He will now cross Broad
River, as I hear it has fallen very much." [54] Why hurry to the
Broad if the Old Wagoner had already crossed it? Yet in Tarleton's *History* this letter metamorphosed into precisely the opposite of the original: "that he [Cornwallis] imagined the enemy
would not pass the Broad River, though it had fallen very
much." [55] If Tarleton believed before the battle what he wrote
six years after it, his disappointment becomes more understand-
able, and his error and carelessness even more incredible.

But even had Cornwallis known Morgan's whereabouts and
even had he received Tarleton's proposal, it is doubtful that he
would have agreed to it. The lieutenant general, after detaching approximately a thousand men under Tarleton, had remaining with him only about seven hundred men until joined
by Leslie's reinforcements. Waiting for Leslie, rather than taking the risk of being "beat in detail," made good sense. Somewhere out there in the woods lay the force of General Greene,
and in the shadow of King's Mountain, the Earl could not overlook the possible reappearance of the over-the-mountain men.
Even if his own force were safe enough, what of Leslie's exhausted men who had struggled through the swamps and re-
paired a road? They would be safer once they had formed a
junction with the "main" body under the lieutenant general.
Furthermore, not only did Cornwallis believe that Morgan had
got far ahead of Tarleton — "I fear Morgan has too much the
start of you," he wrote on January 16 — but also he naturally
did not expect Tarleton to suffer a defeat. The dragoon's numbers equalled or exceeded Morgan's and consisted of provincials
who were seasoned veterans, stiffened by regiments of regulars.
Morgan, not Tarleton, should have been the man in trouble.

Imagine, then, Cornwallis' incredulity and dismay when he

first heard of the Cowpens disaster! Initial word reached him
many long hours before Tarleton appeared the following day to
confirm the evil news.[56] The dark hours before dawn stretched
out interminably to the British general who waited with antici-
patory dread the arrival of the man who would tell him whether
these things were true. Tarleton's report on the morning of January 18 snuffed out any tremulous hope the Earl entertained.
An American prisoner in the British camp later declared that
he had witnessed the dragoon's report. According to the story
he told, Cornwallis "leaned forward on his sword as he listened
to his subordinate. Angered by what he heard, he pressed so hard
that the sword snapped in two, and he swore loudly that he
would recapture Morgan's prisoners no matter what the cost." [57]
Such a spectacle from the sternly self-disciplined lieutenant
general is difficult to imagine, but there can be no doubt of his
private feelings. "The late affair has almost broke my heart," he
wrote to Rawdon.[58]

Well might it break his heart. Tarleton had dealt his campaign a crippling stroke: the loss of the light troops was irreparable, and it lessened his effectiveness throughout all his subsequent moves. Indeed, one British officer present at Cowpens
went so far as to say that if Cornwallis had still had his light
troops, his victory at Guilford Courthouse would have been decisive rather than tenuous, and General Greene "could probably
have brought off as few of his army" as did Gates at Camden.
Furthermore, the officer added, the blockade at Yorktown
would never have occurred because the Americans would have
sued for peace.[59] Although wildly optimistic about what the
British might have accomplished with the light infantry intact,
the officer's comment reflects contemporary opinion (including
Clinton's) about the fatal effect of Cowpens on the outcome of
the southern campaign.[60] News of the British defeat also had a
bad effect upon the "minds of the Country People." After Cowpens, throughout all the arduous marches that eventually

brought his much-reduced army to Wilmington, Cornwallis got little accurate intelligence and little support from the inhabitants of North Carolina. If King's Mountain set his feet upon a fateful path, Cowpens made the path a stonier one.

Despite the military embarrassment and the personal grief that Tarleton's defeat had caused Cornwallis, the Earl neither publicly blamed nor privately reproached his dragoon officer. Whatever might have been his inmost thoughts, they remained just that. To Clinton, Germain, and others, he praised Tarleton generously. Not so some of Tarleton's colleagues. A few of the British officers who had been captured and paroled to Charleston angrily declared that the Cowpens disaster "was the consequence of trusting such a command to a boy like Tarleton." [61] Mutterings within the army itself and especially among the men of the 2d battalion of the 71st, who had lost their comrades-in-arms (the 1st battalion) at Cowpens, reached the dragoon's ears. Nor did officers hide their censure. Tarleton's popularity, never very high with his colleagues, sank yet lower. Chafing at the evident disapproval and the stage-whispered comments, Tarleton sought to save his pricked vanity. He took an ultimatum to his superior: Cornwallis should either express his approval of the Legion commander's conduct or give him permission "to retire till inquiry could be instituted" — that is until he could obtain a court martial on himself.[62] It was, in a sense, blackmail: whatever Cornwallis privately thought of Tarleton's conduct at the Cowpens, he now needed his dragoon more than ever to command the few light troops he could still muster.[63] Faced with the alternative of approving Tarleton's conduct or losing his services for what would probably be the duration of the campaign, Cornwallis did not hesitate to write his subordinate a letter expressing his approval. "You have forfeited no part of my esteem as an officer by the unfortunate event of the action of the 17th: The means you used to bring the enemy to action were able and masterly, and must ever do you honor. Your disposition was unexceptionable; the total misbehaviour of the troops could alone have deprived you of the glory which is so justly your due." [64] It is a curious letter, totally uncharacteristic of Cornwallis, and seems almost curt. But Tarleton was content and would stay. Now the British army could chase Greene.[65]

For Cowpens had been lost by Tarleton rather than won by Morgan, despite the great credit that must be given the Old Wagoner for his judicious arrangements, his cool head, and his quick adjustments to a changing battle. "During the whole period of the war," Stedman wrote later, "no other action reflected so much dishonour upon the British arms." [66] The passage of time scarcely alters that judgment, but some men, like Sir Henry Clinton, tried to shift much of that "dishonour" to Cornwallis. For Clinton saw Cowpens, like King's Mountain, as evidence of the folly of detaching too freely from the main army. In consequence, Cornwallis was beat in detail and all his plans ruined. Had he kept his entire force together, he could have held the South against any foe.[67]

Such reasoning by Clinton, who had never faced the perplexing problems of guerrilla warfare in the South but who, sitting in New York with his large army, could tell exactly how Cornwallis should have handled them, contains many fallacies. In the first place, the defeat of detachments from his regular army never hurt the Earl much, for in fact, he never sent out many detachments from his main force. Armies, not detachments, lost at King's Mountain and Cowpens. Cornwallis did establish posts in the interior but they usually held their own. Unfortunately, neither those posts nor his main army seemed to afford much protection to neighboring loyalists. Patriot militia usually beat loyalist militia in open fighting, but Cornwallis had little control over militia activity. His few detachments of regulars that failed to win their engagements — Weymss at Fishdam Ford and Tarleton at Blackstock's — only suffered loss after Ferguson's defeat at King's Mountain. But Ferguson's thousand men comprised an army, not a detachment, and a loyalist army, at that. In the second place, had Cornwallis any choice? The fully mobile patriots could hit and run within eight miles of any British force, whether it was a small group in a fixed post or three thousand men in a town. They struck terror into the loyalists. Such was the nature of warfare in the South. The numerous engagements of 1780 had demonstrated the fallacy of Clinton's theory that a united British army sitting immobile in South Carolina inside a few fixed posts would be sufficient to rally the loyalists and hold the province. If the Earl could not catch and defeat the patriot bands, he could never win the South, no matter how strong and well supplied his army. Ferguson had tried to quell the partisans and had been defeated. But he had had to make the attempt sooner or later, even if his commanding general might have preferred it later. After all, Ferguson had commanded an army of trained provincials, equal in number to their enemy and occupying a commanding position. If the loyalists could not beat the patriots at equal odds, no matter where the fight, they could not expect ever to win. For the patriots could make good their losses more easily than the loyalists, just as the Americans could recoup theirs more easily than the British. Put simply, Ferguson had to fight the mountain men sooner or later, and if he could not win, the British could not win. But what might a victory by loyalists — a victory Cornwallis had every right to expect — have accomplished? It might have cowed the rebels sufficiently to allow Cornwallis to hold North Carolina for several years, provided that no American army came down from Virginia.

But an American army did come down, and part of that army beat Tarleton at Cowpens. Tarleton's forces, like Ferguson's, were not a detachment. They were an army, larger even than the forces with Lord Cornwallis. Perhaps the Earl was foolish to divide his command, but what choice had he? Could he simply have allowed Morgan to ride and raid at liberty the Ninety-Six area? It was the most steadfastly loyal part of the Carolinas, and loss of the fort would have been disastrous to any hopes he might retain of encouraging loyalist support in South Carolina. Without such support he could not hold the province. Should he have taken his whole army after Morgan, leaving Greene free to assault Leslie or Rawdon? Neither alternative was palatable. In Cornwallis' eyes, neither was necessary. For Greene had made the foolish move, dividing his forces in the face of a powerful enemy. Why should not Tarleton with an army of veterans beat a force of the same size, half of it militia? After all, the Earl had destroyed, at much greater odds, an army which depended heavily on militia to make up its numbers. Before the battle of Cowpens, Greene rather than Cornwallis seemed in error. Tarleton would beat Morgan and reunite with Cornwallis. In the meantime, Leslie would have come up, and the combined forces could then crush the Quaker. Indeed, Greene had taken a tremendous risk. Nothing succeeds like success, but suppose Morgan had lost? What then would be the judgment of history on the generalship of Cornwallis compared to that of Greene?

CHAPTER 13

Guilford Courthouse
"A Bear with his Stern
in the Corner"

L ESLIE AND HIS TROOPS joined Cornwallis on January 18, the
day after Cowpens, only hours after Tarleton had made
his report. The Earl had much to think about, and though
Cowpens had cost him many fine soldiers, his thoughts cannot
all have been gloomy. Unlike Clinton, he was not one to brood
over the past. He now mustered about twenty-four hundred
men, including Leslie's and those of Tarleton's who had returned to the headquarters. Morgan, with his men — whom
Tarleton estimated at almost 2000 (six years later when he
wrote his *History of the Campaigns* he still reported Morgan's
men at 1920) — had a day's start, but could still be caught and
defeated. The Earl decided to chase the Old Wagoner and,
characteristically, wasted no time once he reached the decision.
At eight o'clock the following morning he marched his small
army toward their new adventure.[1] But that day and the next
he followed the wrong road (lack of adequate intelligence was
beginning to tell) and lost some precious time when he changed
direction.[2] By January 21, Cornwallis reached Buffalo Creek
(northeast of the Cowpens) where he learned that Morgan was

at Gilberton (now Lincolnton, north of Ramsour's Mills). "I shall march tomorrow with 1200 Infantry & the Cavalry," he wrote to Rawdon, "to attack or follow him to the banks of the Catawba." [3] Early rising and hard marching brought the army by the evening of January 24 to Ramsour's Mills on the Little Catawba, a branch of the Catawba that runs generally parallel to, and west of, the main river.

There the lieutenant general once again had to reach new decisions. Although he had tried to improve his pace by leaving behind most of his wagons and carts, Morgan had nonetheless crossed the Catawba River on the morning of the twenty-third, some thirty-six hours before Cornwallis' arrival at Ramsour's Mills. The victor of Cowpens had posted himself at Sherill's Ford on the east bank of the Catawba. Speed was now more than ever essential to the British, yet two things slowed them down: the hauling of their own baggage and guns and the late rains that had made the roads a mire and had swollen all the rivers and streams, rendering them swift and dangerous — difficult to cross. A week after the defeated Tarleton had rejoined him — and one day after his arrival at Ramsour's Mills — Cornwallis wrote to Rawdon (whom he had ordered to reinforce the threatened fort at Ninety-Six): "My situation is most critical. I see infinite danger in proceeding, but certain ruin in retreating. I am therefore determined to go on, unless some misfortune should happen to you, which God forbid." [4]

Cornwallis typically preferred advance to retreat despite the obstacles. The soundness of his judgment must be assessed in terms of the considerations that he had to weigh. His reasoning ran something like this: if he retreated, thereby failing to engage the American force, he might as well not be there at all. Worse, the dead of King's Mountain and of Cowpens would have fallen in vain and his own men would have endured for naught the rigors of the march to Winnsboro. The mere existence of a British force in the South was pointless: to be worthwhile it must do something to speed the reestablishment of royal government in America. This object could be attained in one or both of two fashions: by defeating the American regulars and militia or by rallying the loyalists to resist them. But the latter always depended on the former. Having observed for many months the zeal of the rebels and the pusillanimity of the loyalists in the Carolinas, Cornwallis had grown justifiably convinced that without some signal British victories there, the South would be irretrievably lost to the crown. Rather than invoke "certain ruin" he characteristically chose to face "infinite danger." [5]

Some of the danger stemmed from his own purposeful actions taken at Ramsour's Mills. Seeing that he could not at his present rate catch Morgan, Cornwallis determined to make of his whole army a fast-moving unit — in a sense a replacement for the light troops lost at Cowpens. In order to do this, however, he had to rid himself of his cumbrous impedimenta. Having reached a decision, he would now settle for no half measures — those he had already taken, to no avail, when he left much of his baggage behind on January 21. He ordered an immense conflagration. The Earl himself set the example by heaving onto it his own personal baggage and comforts, an action "which was followed by every officer of the army without a single murmur." Officers kept only that baggage which a few bathorses could carry.[6] Wagon after wagon fed the flames. When the destruction reached an end, but a few of them survived: those for the ammunition, salt, and hospital stores, together with four kept empty for later use by the sick and wounded.[7] Although some would later criticize this great bonfire as an important step in Cornwallis' downfall, his own subordinate, Brigadier General Charles O'Hara, had nothing but praise for the Earl, whose manner of executing the campaign, he said, "must ever do the greatest honor to Lord Cornwallis' military reputation, and to the gallant persevering spirit of his little army." [8]

But rapid pursuit of the Americans required more than just "a gallant persevering spirit" and a lightening of the army's load. The men would need shoes. At Ramsour's Mills the army found a supply of leather sufficiently large to allow each man to outfit himself properly. Cornwallis prudently ordered the company commanders to see to the soling and repairing of their men's shoes and directed every soldier to carry with him a pair of extra soles, "as the like opportunity may not happen for some time." [9] While baggage and wagons burned and the army shod itself, the commissary scoured the countryside for provisions.[10] Thus the pause at Ramsour's Mills for three days proved fruitful. A refreshed army took up the pursuit again.

Officers and men alike could now eagerly anticipate the future, feeling that at last they must come to grips with their hitherto-elusive foe. Now, finally, the will-o'-the-wisp whigs would have to materialize. While the officers might think with chagrin of their lost comforts — tents, beds, wine, clothing, etc. — the men felt a greater loss in being deprived of their single solace, rum. Yet they liked Cornwallis and had faith in him. They also knew that he would share their hardships. Nonetheless, although it is recorded that the army acquiesced with the greatest cheerfulness in the mass destruction at Ramsour's Mills, it is also recorded that a number of men deserted at that time — presumably those who preferred embracing the rigors of a frontier life to the distresses of making forced marches without the cheering comforts of rum at the end of the day.[11] It was certainly some consolation, however small, to the men when Lord Cornwallis ordered them an extra gill of rum on the afternoon of January 27. They also received two days' supply of meal. Henceforward the supply of rum would be "absolutely impossible" for a while, and that of meal "uncertain." [12] O'Hara described their predicament: "In this situation, without baggage, necessaries, or provisions of any sort for officer or soldier, in the most barren inhospitable, unhealthy part of North America, opposed to the most savage, inveterate, perfidious, cruel

enemy, with zeal and with bayonets only, it was resolved to follow Greene's army to the end of the world." [13]

The British marched on January 28 from Ramsour's Mills toward Beattie's Ford on the Catawba. Morgan, meanwhile, sat in
his camp at Sherill's Ford on the other side of the river. He kept
a wary eye on Cornwallis' activities while he waited for a reply
from Nathanael Greene, to whom he had sent a victory message
after the battle of Cowpens. The Rhode Islander received the
amazing news five or six days later, in his camp at Cheraw on the
Peedee River. When, after two more days, he learned that Morgan intended to wait for him at the Catawba for as long as he
found possible, Greene determined to send his army under
Huger northward to Salisbury, North Carolina, while he himself rode posthaste to join Morgan. Thus Greene left camp to
join his subordinate on the twenty-eighth, the same day Cornwallis left Ramsour's Mills. [14]

While Morgan waited, he watched the various fords of the Catawba. Starting at Island Ford (where a crossing had been
effected by the prisoners of Cowpens, whom Morgan had dispatched under guard of the militia, toward Salisbury) and proceeding southward, at intervals of approximately five miles each,
came Sherill's Ford, Beattie's Ford, and Cowan's (or McCowan's
or McGowan's) Ford. Morgan naturally knew that the British
would use one or more of these fords to cross the river, just as
Cornwallis naturally knew that the Americans would watch the
fords to bar his progress. So each tried to outmaneuver the
other, but as the ground for maneuvering was extremely cir-
cumscribed — limited to a few rutted quagmires on either side
of a rain-swollen torrent, passable if at all in but a few places —
the probability of a clash was high.

The Earl pushed his army, hoping not only to catch Morgan
but also to bring Greene to action before the latter could receive
reinforcements from Virginia. The men plodded on — the

thick red Carolina mud sucking hungrily at their new shoes and gaiters. Their light packs were, in a way, a blessing. On January 29 they camped at Fawney's Plantation six miles west of Beattie's Ford. They soon found the Catawba too high to cross but expected it to be passable in a day or two. Having left behind provisions and comforts so as to gain speed, Cornwallis' army chafed at the delay occasioned by the high waters. While they waited, the men dried their ammunition and cleaned their gear.[15] Their commanding officer used the time to plan a rapid march toward Salisbury, where Greene's army was approaching. He also planned a small deception. When the Catawba at last fell enough on February 1 to permit a crossing, the Earl put it into operation. He sent a strong column under Lieutenant Colonel Webster six miles upstream to Beattie's Ford to divert the attention of the Americans, while he led the main force across the river at Cowan's Ford.

The Catawba was a "broad, deep, & Rapid water, full of very large rocks." The place where the British crossed, the wagon ford, measured about half a mile across. On the opposite shore stood high, steep hills that hung down over the river and that were "cover'd with the largest timber." [16] Here General William Davidson of the North Carolina militia had posted some of his men but not his main force, for he had miscalculated. He had anticipated that the British would employ the horse ford, which was much shallower and smoother than the wagon ford they actually used and which came out about a quarter of a mile below.[17] Thus the main rebel force waited downstream of the place where the British crossed. All Davidson's men had lain down the night before with their guns. At daybreak all still slept soundly save one "who discovered the noise of horses in deep water." Apparently the tory guide had led the British slightly astray from the wagon ford into "swimming water." [18] Owing to a fog that hung over the water, the guard at the wagon ford did not actually see the redcoats until they had advanced nearly one hundred yards into the river. Meanwhile Davidson's men had grabbed up their guns, scrambled to their prechosen individual stands, and commenced firing upon the British now struggling through the water below them.

"Lord Cornwallis, according to his usual manner, dashed first into the river, mounted upon a very fine spirited horse." [19] Although a rebel bullet brought the horse down in midstream, the creature did not fall until it reached the shore and his lordship, who seems to have led a charmed life, escaped injury. Of course, since he had led the van of his little army, the Earl had crossed much of the river before the surprised whigs could measure their range accurately and bring all their firepower to bear. Firing grew hotter as his men followed their commander. Struggling after his lordship came the brigade of Guards, two 3-pounders, the regiment of Bose, the Royal Welsh Fusileers (23d Regiment), half the pioneers, and Tarleton's corps. The Catawba was swift, the bottom rocky, the water four feet deep, and the enemy fire increasingly severe.[20] "For a while," said a tory accompanying the redcoats, "I saw 'em hollerin and a snortin and a drownin — the river was full of 'em a snortin, a hollerin and a drownin. . . . " [21] The British struggled and cursed and stumbled through water up to their breasts with knapsacks on their backs and sixty or seventy rounds of powder and ball in each pouch "tied at the pole of their necks, their firelocks with bayonets fixed on their shoulders." Thus encumbered they were totally unable to fire a shot all the while that three hundred marksmen sniped away at them. Sergeant Lamb, stumbling across with his 23d regiment, watched the current carry some of the strongest men and even some of the horses downstream. The angry Catawba bore away General Leslie's horse, and General O'Hara's mount rolled with him down the swollen torrent for nearly forty yards. The river also swept off his feet the bombadier steering one of the 3-pounders and carried him "headlong" downstream. Immediate realization of the man's irreplaceability spurred Lamb to instant action. The sergeant, who had been "encouraging the men to hold fast by one another," let go his own hold and dove in. In nine or ten strokes he overtook the bombadier about forty yards away — so swift was the current. Although the soldier was exhausted from having been swept "heels over head" in the water, Lamb got him on his feet and led him back upriver to safety and his gun. "It was very remarkable," the sergeant later commented, "and taken particular notice of by the British troops, that during this transaction not one shot was fired at us by the Americans." Afterward, however, the firing intensified once more. Yet the whigs managed to inflict only a few casualties: one British officer and three privates killed, thirty-six wounded.[22]

At last the British reached the opposite shore, where they "dropped their setting poles, and brought their muskets and cartridge-boxes to their places, faced to the left, and moved up the narrow strip of low ground to make room for the succeeding section, which moved on in the same manner." Once out of the water they immediately faced a hill in front of them, "in many places so steep they had to pull up by the bushes." Nonetheless they advanced steadily, and a brisk exchange of fire ensued. Davidson ordered a slight withdrawal and arranged his men behind trees one hundred fifty yards to the rear. Then, as the British slowly advanced amidst a scattered fire, the American general received a ball through the heart and fell dead.[23] At that point "the rebels made straight shirt tails, and all was silent." [24]

The chase continued through a pouring rain. Many of the retreating whigs found the road to Salisbury clogged with baggage and provision trains and with retreating civilians frightened into running by the reverberations of the tremendous cannonade put up by Webster's diversionary force at Beattie's Ford. Tarleton and his Legionnaires galloped in pursuit. At Tarrant's Tavern, some ten miles from Beattie's Ford along the Salisbury Road, many of the fleeing rebels paused to refresh themselves.

There they mingled with civilian refugees who had also arrived in large numbers, their wagons loaded with personal possessions. Indeed, they so cluttered and packed the lane outside the tavern as to render it nearly impassable. In the midst of this jumble of people, wagons, and horses, the men carried out pails full of whiskey with which to revive their own flagging spirits. While so employed the cry suddenly went up, "Tarleton is coming!" Consternation fell upon the cold, wet, and thirsty men. Of all possible news, the arrival of the dread dragoon was the most unwelcome. Confusion held them undecided. Finally some crossed the fence to take a stand, as directed by Captain Nathaniel M. Martin, while others crossed the fence to disappear with the pails of spirits.[25] Then the green dragoons burst upon the scene.[26]

By his own account of the affair that followed, Tarleton encouraged his horsemen by adjuring them to "remember the Cowpens." Thus goaded, the Legionnaires charged down the lane into the clutter of wagons and men, brandishing their sabers. They dispersed the rebels, killing nearly fifty on the spot, Tarleton said — "but a British officer, who rode over the ground not long after the action" stated that "he did not see ten dead bodies of the provincials in the whole." [27] Several of these ten were unarmed old men who had come to the tavern in the general alarm. The horsemen also inflicted saber wounds upon a number of other Americans and upon several feather beds that left their downy contents in the muddy lane.[28]

The chase now continued toward the Yadkin River. Morgan and Greene crossed it at Trading Ford, about seven miles northwest of Salisbury. As the recent heavy rains had swollen the Yadkin enough to make it unfordable, they ferried themselves on boats that Greene had previously ordered to be ready.[29] Cornwallis did not know about the boats. He hurried on in pursuit of the rebels as fast as the muddy roads would permit.[30]

On February 3, Cornwallis sent O'Hara on ahead in an attempt to catch Morgan on the near side of the Yadkin. The Earl knew that the river would have grown high and turbulent from the rains, so he entertained hopes of trapping his elusive foes. Alas for his hopes, the boats so assiduously garnered by Greene had safely borne across the flood waters all save a few baggage wagons and about one hundred fifty militia. O'Hara bore down upon this small rear guard, which "after giving a few shots, in the language of this country, split and squandered, that is run away." [31] As dusk fell they disappeared, but the baggage remained with O'Hara. The main British force arrived at Trading Ford on the Yadkin on February 4 to discover the river quite unfordable and the Americans once again escaped. If whig sympathizers saw the hand of God in the rising of the waters, what must the mud-soaked redcoated soldiers have thought, seeing themselves deprived of their rum and also of a chance to take a whack at the rebels?

The frustrated British once again could do nothing but wait for the waters to fall or find another way across the river. Tired of the former method, they chose the latter. Above Trading Ford the Yadkin formed a bulging horseshoe and became convoluted so that it was a considerable distance to the next crossing point, descriptively named Shallow Ford. A crow flying on the west side of the Yadkin River would have to go almost twenty-five miles from Trading Ford upstream to Shallow Ford; the British army, lacking wings, had to march by a route forty miles long. While they negotiated the muddy back roads of the unfamiliar country, Greene's men under Morgan pushed along the main road that led northeast from Salisbury, across the Yadkin at Trading Ford, and on to Guilford Courthouse. Here they waited to be joined by General Huger, who had led Greene's chief force northward from the old camp at Cheraw, and by Greene himself, who had remained behind for a while to form a rear guard to watch Cornwallis at the Yadkin.

The Earl ordered his army to maintain the "Strictest Silence in getting off their Ground & during the March" northward to Shallow Ford.[32] He knew that Greene expected reinforcements from Virginia, and he still entertained hopes of catching the American general and forcing him to an action before the auxiliary troops could join him. To do so, however, he would have to outpace Greene and get between him and the fords across the Dan River — for the Dan (lower down called the Roanoke) was the last obstacle separating the rebels from Virginia, whence they could receive supplies and reinforcements.[33]

The lieutenant general and his small staff undoubtedly thought that at last a British rain was falling. Twice before, first at the Catawba and then again at the Yadkin, "American rains" had swollen the rivers so that the pursuing British could not cross. Now they hoped that the Dan would be too high for Greene and that the Americans would finally be trapped between, as it were, the devil and the deep blue sea. But the Quaker again deprived Cornwallis and his men of their opportunity to play the role of the devil, for he had cannily arranged for boats at both Irwin's and Boyd's ferries, downstream of the fords toward which Cornwallis headed. With these vessels Greene's army safely crossed the Dan, having previously formed a junction with Huger's force.[34] Despite his utmost efforts, the lieutenant general failed to reach the Dan until about twelve hours after the enemy's rear guard had stepped ashore on the northern bank of that river.[35]

While Greene scampered into Virginia to resupply and reinforce himself, Cornwallis halted his pursuit at the Dan River. He had driven the entire rebel force out of North Carolina and had pressed the Americans so closely as to make it impossible for them to raise the militia in North Carolina. But his own army now felt the effects of their rapid pursuit. Tired and ill-equipped, they were also hungry, for their speed of movement had for days at a time precluded foraging the countryside.[36] The Earl decided not to pursue Greene into Virginia but instead to turn back southward for the dual purpose of calling upon the support of the loyalists and of trying to supply the soldiers.

Accordingly the British marched to Hillsboro, then the capital of North Carolina. The town — which had recently served as the headquarters of the American army — lay near the northern boundary of the province, about forty-five miles east of Guilford Courthouse and about thirty-five miles (as the crow flies — no direct road) south of Boyd's Ferry over the Dan River. On February 22 (the forty-ninth birthday of General George Washington), "Lord Cornwallis with the usual formalities erected the King's Standard at Hillsborough, and invited all His Majesty's loving Subjects to take up arms and join his forces in defence of their civil libertys." [37] The surrounding area supposedly held a populace mostly devoted to the British cause who would flock to the colors. In London the government still dreamed of utilizing this solid core of pro-royal sentiment that it believed filled the breasts of these unschooled backwoodsmen. Cornwallis, himself, had long before lost faith in the reliability and efficiency of loyalist support. But he was a soldier and he would do his duty by giving the loyalists a rallying point. If he had expected none to come, however, he was wrong. Guards commander O'Hara described the events after the British arrival at Hillsboro:

The novelty of a camp in the backwoods of America more than any other cause brought several people to stare at us. Their curiosity once satisfied, they returned to their homes. I am certain that in our march of near a thousand miles, almost in as many directions, thro' every part of North Carolina, tho every means possible was taken to persuade our friends as they are called and indeed as they call themselves to join us, we never had with us at any one time one hundred men in arms. Without the experiment had been made, it would have been impossible to conceive that government could in so important a matter have been so grossly deceived. Fatal infatuation! When will government see these people thro' the proper medium? I am persuaded never.[38]

If at first the loyalists were reluctant to show themselves, they became almost invisible after the incident on the Haw River, sometimes called Pyle's Massacre.

Colonel John Pyle, a loyalist physician, had assembled a group of three or four hundred other loyalists and prepared to lead them to join Cornwallis. Tarleton had been dispatched from Hillsboro to offer them protection and at the same time to prevent repetition of a rebel raid carried out a few days before at Hart's Mill. So when Pyle's men were approached by a body of green-jacketed dragoons, they naturally, albeit disastrously, assumed them to be members of Tarleton's Legion. In fact, they belonged to "Light Horse" Harry Lee's Legion, and Lee had himself fathered the deception. A lieutenant colonel of cavalry at the age of twenty-five, Lee much resembled Tarleton in youth, spirits, boldness, and ruthlessness. Legend said he had come into the world "booted and spurred, his spurs made of the purest handhammered silver, twirling his saber over his head and shouting, 'Charge the bastards! · Ride them down boys.' " [39] Certainly his appearance did not discredit the legend. With his bright blue eyes and his long blond hair tied at the nape with an eelskin, he captivated the ladies around his family's plantation at Leesylvania. His good looks, however, had a somewhat imperious quality, perhaps a reflection of his ungovernable temper. All in all, he was, like Tarleton, the very image of an eighteenth-century cavalry officer — dashingly handsome, impatient of obstacles and delays, not easily brooking criticism. But whereas Tarleton's dark handsomeness gave him an air of impetuosity, Lee's blond handsomeness lent him an aura of cool aloofness. Certainly his better education (he graduated from Princeton), his interest in military history, his constant willingness to study and experiment in order to improve his command, his assiduity at gathering intelligence, and his unerring battlefield instinct made him a better officer than Tarleton. He had received a commission as a captain of a troop of cavalry in Bland's regiment of Virginia Light Dragoons at the outbreak of

the Revolution. Immediately, Harry acted as if he possessed an
independent command. He carefully chose the men for the
troop — all as young as himself — and when he found no more
action in Virginia than riding his stallion bareback and slashing
at targets with a weighted saber he took his troop, independent of
his regiment, off to join Washington's ragged army in its retreat
from Cornwallis in New Jersey. Veterans at first laughed at his
dandies in their blue uniforms, calf-length boots, and burnished
helmets with white dyed horsehair plumes. But the laughs
turned to cheers when Harry proceeded almost immediately to
raid a British supply train, bringing back twenty wagons loaded
with goods and food sorely needed by the hungry Americans. From then on he saw continuous service. Soon he rose to
major in the continental army and assumed command of a partisan cavalry force which operated as independently from the
American army as Tarleton did from the British. When Greene
took up the southern command, Lee received promotion to lieutenant colonel. At the same time the addition of infantry to his
cavalry allowed him to form a legion, the counterpart of Tarleton's, to act with Greene's army. Like Tarleton's, this corps
added verve to the struggle.[40]

Greene had sent Lee back into North Carolina to harass Cornwallis and dampen any loyalist resurgence. Lee soon got his
chance. He just missed surprising Tarleton at a farmhouse near
the Haw River, but he did capture two of Tarleton's officers still
putting their papers in order. Then he consulted Brigadier
General Andrew Pickens, whose militia operated with his own
corps. Both men agreed that Lee's command should pretend to
be part of Tarleton's Legion. To increase chances for the success of the deception, although most people in the area could not
tell one uniform from another, Lee forced Tarleton's officers to
march in front of him. When Light Horse Harry learned from
two farmers that Pyle was in the vicinity down a side road, he
sent word back to Pickens asking for support. Meanwhile he
approached the loyalists nonchalantly.

The loyalists, thinking themselves at last under British protection, happily drew up beside the road to allow the horsemen
to pass, a request which Lee, in the guise of Tarleton, had forwarded to Pyle by way of one of the farmers he had met. Soon
the tories found themselves virtually surrounded without being
in the least aware of their enemies' presence. Lee intended to
march along the tory column until he met Pyle at the head, at
which time he would reveal his true identity and demand submission. But just as Lee reached Pyle and started to shake his
hand, he heard firing behind him. The tories had at last recognized some of Pickens' men in the rear, apparently not by their
faces but by the green twigs they wore in their hats to identify
them as of the rebel militia.[41] The discovery came too late to let
them prepare. In a flash Lee's Continentals had their sabers at
work among the alarmed tories, many of whom still did not understand that they, rather than "Tarleton," had erred in recognition, for they persisted in marking themselves out for destruction by crying "Hurrah for King George!" When the affair
ended about a hundred loyalists lay dead and most of the others
wounded. Pyle himself, severely wounded, fled to a small pond
close by and, according to tradition, jumped into it and lay until
night with only his nose above the water. Then he crawled out,
walked home, and recovered. A tory sergeant, questioned by
Lee about the terrain, expostulated: "Well, God bless your soul,
Mr. Tarleton, you have this day killed a parcel of as good subjects as ever his Majesty had." To this the rebel leader retorted:
"You d——d rascal, if you call me Tarleton I will take off your
head. I will undeceive you: we are the Americans and not the
British. I am Lee of the American Legion, and not Tarleton."
The next day the rebels counted ninety-three bodies but
thought some had been carried off during the night.[42]

After this incident the loyalists of North Carolina naturally
regarded as less than totally reassuring the presence of British

troops. Furthermore, Greene had reentered North Carolina about the time of Pyle's defeat. Since the Rhode Islander had received reinforcements during his short stay in Virginia, his return allowed loyalists little peace of mind. The tories' ardor cooled yet further when Cornwallis, after slaughtering several of their draught oxen, left Hillsboro sooner by several days than he had announced when he raised the royal standard there.

The British had begun to go hungry. Their premature departure from Hillsboro as well as their resort to devouring the local draught animals were both occasioned by the great scarcity of food in the area — the rebels had long held a post there and had eaten most of the cattle nearby.[43] Whereas after their departure from Winnsboro they had sometimes lacked enough to eat, after Hillsboro hunger became their usual condition.[44]

The British marched from the capital on February 25 toward the Haw.[45] They crossed the river and camped near one of its tributaries, Alamance Creek, at a place descriptively named Stinking Quarter. "From that time to the 15th March," O'Hara noted, "the two armys were never above twenty miles asunder, they constantly avoiding a general action and we as industriously seeking it. These operations obliged the two armys to make numberless moves which it is impossible to detail." [46] The soldiers and officers of both armies suffered during this period from hunger, cold, wet, and fatigue. Cornwallis fared like a common soldier, allowing "no distinction." Sergeant Lamb recalled that "sometimes we had turnips served out for food, when we came to a turnip field; or arriving at a field of corn, we converted our canteens into rasps and ground our Indian corn for bread; when we would get no Indian corn, we were compelled to eat liver as a substitute for bread, with our lean beef. In all this his lordship participated, nor did he indulge himself even in the distinction of a tent; but in all things partook our sufferings, and seemed much more to feel for us than for himself." [47]

Neither Cornwallis nor his soldiers could foresee that the future held sufferings even worse than those they had hitherto known. For all of them, more immediate considerations came crowding in — the everyday problem of supplying food and the daily striving, by cunning or speed or both, to come up with the rebel force and bring it to action. While the private men eagerly anticipated a battle, the Earl himself was not merely spoiling for a fight. Rather he must have felt that the whole rationale of his campaign, as well as the losses and sufferings sustained by his army, demanded a battle — that is, a head-on confrontation of the full force of the rival armies, even if it had to be on the enemy's terms. Perhaps Cornwallis placed too high a value on saving face under all circumstances, but if so it was a lesson that his proud nation strove to teach all its soldiers. Nor is it certain that the Earl was wrong, for indeed his actions showed, if not strategic brilliance, at least strong internal logic. That is, if the campaign had been worth starting then it was worth carrying to a conclusion. As Cornwallis saw it, his actions were entirely consistent with waging an offensive war: it was Clinton whose inactions were foolhardy.

In New York, meanwhile, Clinton and the rest of the British could form no clear idea of the Earl's situation and his difficulties. During the early days of March they began to receive favorable news of Cornwallis. The Earl, it was said, had advanced into Virginia in pursuit of Greene and Morgan, who had retreated before him. Another account had it that Cornwallis had caught Morgan, defeated him, and released the prisoners the American had taken at Cowpens. Rebel troops now scurried toward Philadelphia. Greene was retiring, rumor had it, so as to facilitate a junction with the troops he expected from Washington, which "were certainly at Trenton the 28th of February." But these reinforcements could not possibly reach Greene "until his fate is determined." The British had "everything to hope and expect" from the success of Cornwallis' operations.[48]

If only Cornwallis could have had such a sanguine view of

events as had those so far from them. But the true situation did not match the one pictured by the garrison in New York. Before the middle of March, Greene received numerous reinforcements: a brigade of militia from Virginia under Brigadier General Robert Lawson, two brigades of militia from North Carolina under Colonel Pinketham Eaton and Brigadier General John Butler, a "considerable detachment" of regulars raised for eighteen months, and militia from the frontiers under Colonels William Campbell and William Preston.

Naturally the British had tried to intercept some of the reinforcements before they could join Greene. Indeed that endeavor, together with an unremitting search for food, accounted for most of the British movements between February 26 and March 1 when the reinforcements reached Greene. Of course the Earl wanted to catch the Americans and fight them, but he now was "totally destitute of information." [49] Greene, meanwhile, was trying to avoid confrontation until he had his additional brigades, so he constantly moved his camp, marching and countermarching in an erratic sweep. Always, however, he stayed within ten or twenty miles of Guilford Courthouse. Cornwallis did manage, despite the paucity of information, to force a clash with one of Greene's detachments, but there was no contact with the main army until Greene's reinforcements joined him.[50] At that time (March 14), the Quaker invited his adversary to attack him by taking up a position at Guilford Courthouse — a position he had chosen in advance. He now outnumbered the British two to one. His time had come.

News of Greene's stand reached Cornwallis the same day. As if to climax the two and a half months of waiting for the engagement, a bizarre episode had taken place the night before. A British escort, bringing along the Earl's baggage, had got lost in the dark woods, and Lee's Legionnaires, sent out in pursuit, had also got lost. Both British and Americans had been forced to dismount and wait for dawn before returning to camp.

Cornwallis heard of this episode via a young cornet from Lee's Legion who was sent the next day with a message from Greene to Cornwallis. The amiable cornet, whose name was Middleton, explained to Cornwallis that Lee had set out the previous night in pursuit of baggage and escort, "in the expectation of putting them in the right course." This idea so tickled the Earl that he burst into laughter and asked: "Well, why did he not do it?" Middleton explained that Lee had himself got lost. The Earl then turned to his aides and said: "You see I was not mistaken." [51]

Greene was not in so jovial a mood as his British counterpart, although he had picked his spot and chosen the time for battle. That night of the fourteenth he waited in the anxious hope that neither of the two things he dreaded most would occur — rain, which would render American muskets useless and give an undue advantage to British bayonets, and a night attack, which would terrorize his militia and unseasoned regulars. But the weather held fair, and Cornwallis did not attack during the night, for not until that night could he confirm reports that Greene lay at Guilford.[52] He determined to meet his foe the next day.

On March 15 the British marched at daybreak in two columns. Tarleton led the advance. The left column comprised the main body of the army and the artillery, while Hamilton's Carolinians and a few dragoons marched on the right with the baggage.[53] The redcoats had been at Guilford before, during their pursuit of the Americans in the preceding month. Cornwallis, however, had taken less particular note of the land than had Greene, who even then had chosen it for a future battle site. The British commander now regretted his omission, for intelligence once again failed him. Prisoners taken by Tarleton, the Earl later averred, "could give me no account of the enemy's order or position, and the country-people were extremely inaccurate in their description of the ground."[54] That ground offered, in fact, considerable advantages to a defender and corresponding disadvantages to an attacker. The surrounding countryside was gently rolling, green, and thickly wooded. The wild roses that scrambled over banks, a few cultivated fields, and several gullies occasionally broke the green. The denseness of the woods protected the American flanks from attack and also made artillery relatively ineffectual, particularly for the attackers. The Americans had taken up positions such that, while themselves protected by the woods, they could use the few cultivated plots to give them a fairly clear field of fire. Greene's army possessed yet another advantage — that of number. Much has been made of the fact that more than half of the American force consisted of militia, supposedly by definition inferior to regulars. Certainly Gates' raw levies had scattered before the grim discipline of Cornwallis' redcoats. But Greene's militia was not Gates' militia. Some of the irregulars from North Carolina and more of those from Virginia had tasted battle. Also present were the riflemen of Colonel Charles Lynch and those of Colonel William Campbell. The latter — the tough, hardened backwoodsmen who had brought disaster and death to Patrick Ferguson at King's Mountain — feared no man and no army of men, especially if they wore red coats. In addition, Greene commanded fifteen or sixteen hundred Continentals. Some of them were, to be sure, inexperienced recruits. But Continental training now matched British training, and seasoned Continentals could hold their own with British regulars. Greene brought into battle between four and five thousand men, including a great many regulars and campaign-hardened irregulars, riflemen with few peers and no superiors, and the best cavalry in North America.[55]

Against them the British could muster only between nineteen hundred and two thousand men. Ill-fed and ill-clothed, those who were not foot-weary were ill-horsed. Their chief sources of strength lay in their discipline and, closely associated with it, their long familiarity with unequal odds. At Guilford Courthouse they would need these strengths to face the tremendous advantages held by the Americans. Although most of the Earl's veterans undoubtedly felt in their hearts that familiar leap of eager anticipation, intermingled sometimes with the warm-cold thrill of danger, a few did not share the general enthusiasm. One in particular, a Captain Maynard of the Guards, grew gloomy and despondent during the approach to Guilford. The change became more noticeable to his comrades as Maynard naturally displayed a cheerful disposition. He had shown great gallantry in several previous actions. Thus it seemed strange when, shortly before the action began at Guilford, he confided to Colonel Norton that "he felt himself very uncomfortable and did not like the business at all." In vain Norton tried to laugh away the captain's forebodings. But Guilford Courthouse, in a thinly settled province thousands of miles from the British Isles, would prove to be Maynard's last battlefield.[56]

The first skirmishing — a colorful affair between opposing cavalry some three miles west of Guilford — gave little indication of the major battle to follow. Tarleton's advance guard ran into Lee, scouting like Tarleton ahead of his army. They met in a long lane and fought briefly. Although Lee claimed victory for himself, so did Tarleton.[57] In any event, neither side won any advantage from the skirmish. The Americans withdrew, and the British continued their advance. Tarleton had been injured, however. A rifle ball shattered the first and middle fingers of his right hand. Despite pain and danger, he rode weaponless and defenseless, his right hand in a sling, throughout the rest of the battle.

After this initial skirmish Cornwallis might well have halted. For he now moved toward a battle with a foe whose strength he did not know and upon ground which he remembered only vaguely. Yet he was determined to give battle, even if on

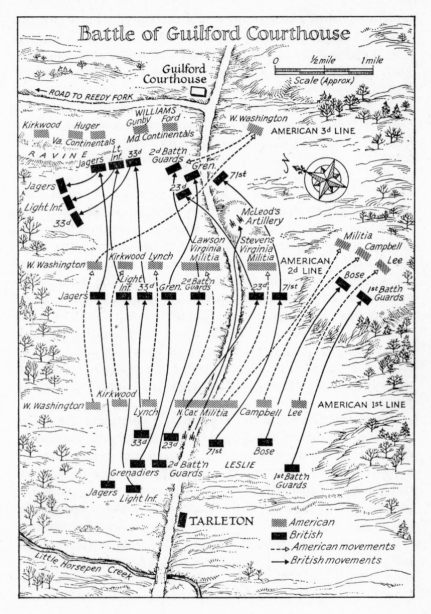

Battle of Guilford Courthouse

Greene's terms. Those terms would certainly be harsh, for the
Quaker had taken to heart the lessons of Cowpens. He had
drawn up his army in three parallel lines, facing approximately
west, whence the British would come down the road leading
from New Garden past Guilford Courthouse. In the first two
lines, which extended north and south across either side of that
road, Greene had placed his militia, North Carolinian in the
first and Virginian in the second. The American commander
intended that these mostly raw troops should fire their muskets
once or twice before they broke and ran — for such craven behavior was only to be expected of them. Besides, to be fair, they
could scarcely stand up to a British bayonet charge when they
had no such terrible weapon with which to meet their attackers.
In any event, Greene meant them to inflict telling losses upon
the British before his strongest troops, the Maryland and Virginia regulars whom he drew up in his third line, became engaged. In effect, the Americans had a tremendous reserve of
fresh troops. The third line waited on the north side of the road
— its right flank protected by the dense woods and its left flank
protected in the later stages of the battle by artillery on the road.
Approximately half a mile separated the American first and
third lines, with the second line slightly forward of a midway
position.

But Cornwallis could not immediately determine the entire
American disposition as he urged his troops forward. He at once
saw the road sloping downward in front of him until crossed by
a small stream — a tributary of Horsepen Creek unimagina-
tively named Little Horsepen Creek — from which point the
ground began to rise again. On either side he noted open fields,
but in the distance, at the top of the incline, he observed that
the road once again entered dense forest. Just in front of the
forest and protected by rail fences that enclosed the fields, he
could barely make out the North Carolina militia. But that
glimpse immediately showed him the deadly situation he faced.

Perhaps five to six hundred yards of open field lay between the North Carolina line and the bottom of the hill where the stream crossed the road. The open space in front of the Americans, across which their line extended and which their position commanded, was approximately one quarter of a mile wide. This area — uphill for a quarter of a mile through muddy fields with insecure footing — Cornwallis' men would have to traverse under fire. True, enemy muskets could pose little threat until the last eighty or one hundred yards, but the North Carolinians carried rifles, and on their right flank Greene had placed Lynch's riflemen and on their left flank Campbell's riflemen. Lee's Legion reinforced Campbell, while William Washington's cavalry and Kirkwood's company of light infantry supported Lynch. Those lethal rifles of Lynch, Campbell, and most of the North Carolinians had an effective range of up to three hundred yards and could kill at an even greater distance. Furthermore, the Americans had two 6-pounders astride the road trained upon the stream crossing. The guns had an effective range of six to eight hundred yards so that at least from the stream onward, in other words for six to eight interminable minutes, the British soldiers would come under fire.

As Cornwallis and his men came over the crest of the rise, the American artillery opened up. The detachment of Royal Artillery returned the cannonade with three guns. For some twenty or thirty minutes the artillery of both sides boomed at each other, not entirely harmlessly for an American round killed a British lieutenant in the first moments of the barrage. During the artillery duel the lieutenant general coolly planned his attack and deployed his forces. He placed the regiment of Bose and the 71st Highlanders on his right, under the command of Major General Leslie. The 1st battalion of Guards under Colonel Norton supported them. To Lieutenant Colonel Webster he gave command of the left wing, consisting of the 23d regiment and the 33d. Brigadier General O'Hara commanded the support for the left — the Grenadiers and the 2d battalion of Guards. The reserve consisted of the Jagers and the light infantry of the Guards, who remained in the woods to the left of the guns, and the cavalry under Tarleton, who took up a position on the road behind the guns.

At about half past one in the afternoon Cornwallis signalled the advance and the British line began to move. The North Carolina militia now observed the awesome spectacle of a long line of redcoats approaching with deliberation. The green jackets of the Jagers and the blue ones of the Bose made patches of contrasting colors.[58] The day's bright sun glittered on the inexorable row of bayonets, save where obscured by lingering puffs of black smoke from the recent artillery barrage. Down the hill and across the stream they came. But the North Carolinians stood firm. Greene (like Morgan at Cowpens) had earlier exhorted them to give "Two rounds, my boys, and then you may fall back!" They fired their first round on command when the British reached a point some one hundred fifty yards distant.[59] One thousand rifles speaking from so near tore large holes in the line of redcoats.[60] One William Montgomery, present at that first telling fire, said that "the part of the British line at which they aimed looked like the scattering stalks in a wheat field, when the harvest man has passed over it with his cradle." [61] Captain Dugald Stuart of the 71st said that "one half of the Highlanders dropped on that spot." [62] But the British soldier lived through months of foot-weary campaigning for just such a moment. The line staggered, then immediately re-formed and continued its advance.

When the British right flank arrived within musket range of the rail fence protecting the militia, the North Carolinians witnessed a sight that had terrified so many militia so many times before, in so many battles, and had rendered useless their superior numbers and often superior weapons. Leslie halted his line and barked out commands. Despite their losses, despite the murderous American fire, the redcoats on order deliberately presented their muskets as one man and loosed a tremendous volley. Then they gave a yell, the bloodcurdling yell of the Highlanders, and charged straight at the North Carolinians with fixed bayonets. Some of the militia in the left center, thoroughly terrified, broke and ran through the woods to their rear as fast as they could, throwing away rifles, knapsacks, and canteens. Yet Campbell's veteran riflemen had seen redcoats before, and they refused to budge. To some of the North Carolinians, greater safety seemed to lie with the grim, determined, frontiersmen than in panic-stricken flight, so they attached themselves to Campbell. These men and the Carolinians still holding the center delivered yet another, and very deadly volley, at the charging British when they came within thirty or forty paces (seventy-five or a hundred feet). Nearly one third of the remaining Highlanders fell and the Bose Regiment also suffered. Fighting grew bloody and desperate. But the desertion of most of the North Carolina militia and the cool competence of redcoats with their bayonets forced the American left to withdraw slowly into the woods.

The British left under Webster had sustained similar losses from the first American round. To save his men worse punishment the lieutenant colonel ordered a charge, naturally hoping to gain contact with the enemy before the latter could reload and fire again. Hitherto the British had advanced at the deliberate one hundred twenty paces per minute laid down by general orders.[63] Now they gave a yell and broke into a sharp run in good order. But "when arrived within forty yards of the enemy's line," Sergeant Lamb noted, "their whole force had their arms presented, and resting on a rail fence. . . . They were taking aim with the nicest precision." Even the battle-hardened British were not undaunted by the sight of the open end of all those rifle barrels. "At this awful period," the British sergeant observed, "a general pause took place; both parties surveyed each other a moment with most anxious suspense." But Webster, perhaps Cornwallis' best officer, whose flanking movement had helped rout the Americans at Camden, rode boldly forward in the front of the 23d and goaded his men forward. He shouted "with more than his usual commanding voice (which was well known to his brigade), 'Come on, my brave Fuzileers.' " Inspired by their leader, Lamb and his fellows "rushed forward amidst the enemy's fire; dreadful was the havoc on both sides." [64]

The militia had, for the most part, done what Greene had asked of them. Having delivered their two rounds, the rest of the center now gratefully took refuge in the second part of their order — the part allowing them to fall back. To be precise, they ran like scared rabbits, less from the savage mien of the enemy than from the awful sight of his fixed bayonet. Twenty-one inches of gleaming steel at the end of a four-and-a-half-foot Brown Bess filled most green troops with terror. At the second American line the Virginia militia parted ranks to admit the North Carolinians, apparently giving them a few jeers as they ran past.

The battle now left the cleared fields and carried on into the dense woods. Fighting became yet more fierce and very confused. Friend and foe even found it difficult to locate each other. The British suffered under additional handicaps: here among the trees they found it hard to use a bayonet; the musket was not a sharpshooter's weapon; and they were unskilled as woodsmen. Most if not all of their hidden foes had rifles and long experience as frontiersmen. But the British and their German auxiliaries doggedly came on.

By now Cornwallis had had to commit his entire reserve, save for the cavalry. For although the bulk of the North Carolina militia had broken and run, the flanks held firm. The American left flank, stiffened by Campbell's riflemen, still poured a destructive fire upon the advancing redcoats. The latter, finding their line enfiladed — that is, the enemy's fire sweeping the length of it rather than coming at right angles to it — had to meet the threat by pivoting their own wings to meet the Americans head on. Thus Leslie on the British right had to call up his support, the 1st battalion of Guards, and place them on his extreme right, beyond the 71st and Bose, so that they could oppose the American left, where Campbell's riflemen, reinforced by Lee's light infantry and cavalry, directed a devastating fire upon them. Webster on the British left "changed his front" to the left and called up his reserve force of Jagers and light infantry of the Guards. With their help the 23d and 33d swept the American right — composed of Lynch's riflemen, Kirkwood's company of regulars, and Washington's cavalry — back from its position. Meanwhile O'Hara moved his supporting force of the Grenadiers and the 2d battalion of Guards into the center area left vacant by the wheeling movement of the British wings. The battle progressed unevenly. In the confused fighting in the woods, some of the British forces at last swept all opposition before them and arrived at the second American line in one continuous movement; whereas in the case of the Bose and 1st battalion of Guards, on the extreme right, their opposition stubbornly held its ground, and they struggled savagely through their own private battle here in the woods for almost two hours, until at the end of the main engagement Tarleton's cavalry swooped down upon the American riflemen and drove them off. Here the struggle grew so intense that at the beginning of the action the Americans nearly routed the elite Guards. Cornwallis, who seemed everywhere at once, discovered the Guards' hesitancy. He hastily rode up and rallied them personally while American bullets shot his iron-gray horse from under him.[65] Undaunted, he managed to find a dragoon's horse and dashed off to encourage his left flank.

The American artillery during this fierce infantry struggle withdrew from the first line to the third — it did not halt at the second line since it would have been of little use in the woods.

For the same reason the British artillery, which moved along the road parallel to the army's advance, did not unlimber again after the initial barrage until it reached the third American line. The cavalry of both sides likewise could do little in the thick woods where the fight with the second rebel line occurred. Tarleton, who would later help the Bose, supported the advance of the artillery. Cornwallis had ordered him to keep his corps compact "and not to charge without positive orders, except to protect any of the corps from the most evident danger of being defeated." [66]

The second line of Virginia militia now awaited the British advance. Drawn up behind trees, they were divided into two brigades straddling the road — that of Stevens on the American left and Lawson on its right.[67] Lynch's riflemen had fallen back to the extreme right of the militia, and Kirkwood's company of light infantry and Washington's cavalry had joined them. Campbell's riflemen and Lee's corps would have supported the Virginian left, but they still fought their private war against the Bose and Guards. Like the North Carolinians, the Virginians carried rifles. Stevens had not forgotten the ignominy of Camden and determined that today Virginia would show its true mettle. He had posted sharpshooters in his rear ordering them to shoot "every man that flinched." [68]

Cornwallis, in effect, faced an untouched American second line with only part of his army. He left the Bose and 1st battalion of Guards behind to their bloody struggle and re-formed a new line to face the Virginians. The Highlanders and Fusiliers under Leslie composed the right of this new line — the Fusiliers having shifted to their right to support the Highlanders who had lost the aid of the Bose and 1st battalion of Guards. Webster led the much heavier left wing consisting of the 33d, Jagers, and light infantry supported by O'Hara with the Grenadiers and the 2d battalion of Guards. Although heavier, it also had to attack the stronger position of the enemy's second line, including their regular riflemen. As in the earlier assault, the British sustained heavy losses while the Americans "kept up for a considerable time a galling fire which did great execution." [69] Cornwallis, back from rallying the 1st Guards battalion, now rode into the scene of this major engagement and pushed the attack home.

Slowly his strong left began to force back the Americans. The Earl, satisfied with their progress, hastened to the right where his troops were meeting stiffer resistance. In the thickness of the woods, overhung with clouds of smoke from black powder, the situation confused men and officers. Cornwallis hoped to encourage his Highlanders and Fusiliers forward. But as groups of the Virginians made frequent stands in the woods, the lines were not clearly drawn. Sergeant Lamb, having pursued an American officer, found himself cut off from the Guards on one side and the Fusiliers on the other by parties of pursuing Americans. But the zealous British commander soon galloped into the same situation. Totally indifferent to the rifle fire and absorbed in the problems of command, Cornwallis paid no attention to his danger nor even noticed that the saddlebags on his borrowed horse had slipped under the creature's belly and dragged bumpingly along the heavy underbrush retarding his progress. "I immediately laid hold of the bridle of his horse," Lamb later recalled, "and turned his head. I then mentioned to him that if His Lordship had pursued the same direction he would, in a few moments have been surrounded by the enemy and perhaps cut to pieces or captured. I continued to run alongside the horse, keeping the bridle in my hand, until His Lordship gained the 23rd Regiment, which . . . were drawn up in the skirt of the woods." [70]

Even with their commander safely arrived to urge them on, the British right only with difficulty made headway against the

stubborn resistance of Stevens' Virginians. Samuel Houston
fought in Stevens' brigade. He and his comrades, Houston later
averred, withstood three bayonet attacks, each time yielding at
first and then driving the British back.[71] Even after some of Stevens' men carried their leader from the field with a bullet
through his thigh, the ranks held. Cornwallis, his nerves cool
and his mind clear despite his recent scrape, decided to commit
his cavalry. He ordered Tarleton to charge and the Virginian
left fell back.

The British left had meanwhile progressed more rapidly
against the American right. Their assault pushed back Lawson's
brigade steadily but unequally. The extreme American right
gave way most readily; and the left of the brigade, hard against
the road, held its ground longest. Indeed, the effect was as
though the British had pushed open a gate with its hinges on
their right hand. As they opened the gate wide, the Virginia
militia strung out along the road which then formed its line of
retreat. With the last barrier thus removed, the British poured
through the opening to engage the third and last American line.

Hard as the redcoats had fought, the bloodiest confrontation
of the entire battle still awaited them. For in this third line
Greene had placed his best men, four regiments of Continental
troops: two Marylander and two Virginian. On the far right of
the third American line stood the ubiquitous Kirkwood, who
had taken up that position after the distintegration of the second American line. Then came the two Virginia regiments of
Colonel John Green and Lieutenant Colonel Samuel Hawes,
under the command of Brigadier General Isaac Huger. Two 6-
pounders under Captain Samuel Finley strengthened the middle of the infantry line. On the left Colonel Otho Williams
commanded the 1st and 2d Maryland Regiments of Colonel
John Gunby and Lieutenant Colonel Benjamin Ford. Greene
had placed all of this third line on the north side of the New
Garden Road. The two 6-pounders that Captain Anthony Single-

ton had brought into position there after the opening barrage protected their left flank on the road itself. Behind the Americans lay another road running parallel to their line toward Reedy Fork, affording an escape route if needed. The courthouse that gave its name to the battle stood just across the latter road at its junction with the New Garden Road up which the British had advanced.[72] Greene's troops occupied a commanding position atop a hill, their line conforming more or less to the semicircular shape of the forward face of the hill. Below them lay a ravine through which a small brook ran in wet weather and which the British would have to cross under fire. Across the New Garden Road, on the American left flank, relatively open ground led across another small brook to another eminence, atop which William Washington, after he had withdrawn from the second line, had stationed his cavalry. All in all, Greene's third line held the most advantageous ground that the area afforded. The Quaker could await with justifiable confidence the outcome of the final encounter.

First of the British ranks to burst out of the woods into the open area in front of the Americans came the light infantry, closely followed by the Jagers and the 33d regiment — all under Webster.[73] Caught up in the madness of battle, Webster led his men in a charge without calculating the odds. The Continentals held their fire until the redcoats were but a hundred feet away, then hit them with a punishing volley. Immediately after the volley the 1st Maryland Regiment and Hawes' regiment of Virginians counterattacked with fixed bayonets. Exhausted and confused, Webster's force broke and ran back into the woods. Webster himself took a musket ball in his knee. Nonetheless, he held on and rallied his men to re-form and await reinforcements. The 1st Maryland returned to its place in the line.

The 2d battalion of Guards then swept forward on the right

of Webster's position and attacked the American left. The 2d
Maryland, a newly recruited regiment, took panic at the sight of
the redcoats' bayonets and fled back through the woods. The
Guards, now led by Lieutenant Colonel Stuart since O'Hara
had been wounded, pursued Ford's fleeing men. They captured
Finley's two 6-pounders only to abandon them when they reeled
under the impact of two almost simultaneous attacks: one upon
their left flank and another upon their rear. Colonel Gunby of
the 1st Maryland lost his horse and Lieutenant Colonel John
Eager Howard (of Cowpens fame) immediately took command
of the 1st Marylanders and started them in a bayonet charge
upon the Guards' left flank. Even before the Marylanders had
reached the Guards, William Washington gathered his cavalry
for a charge. The American horsemen, in their commanding
position at the top of the rise to the left of the American infantry line, had before them the best ground in the whole battlefield for a cavalry attack. From this point they hurled themselves at full tilt into the rear of the Guards, hacking right and
left with their sabers. Among Washington's horsemen rode a
giant and fearsome figure: Peter Francisco who stood six feet
eight inches tall. He wielded a huge five-foot sword which General George Washington had given him in response to his complaint that ordinary swords were too light.[74] According to Lieutenant Holcomb, a fellow combatant, Francisco slew eleven men
"with his brawny arms and terrible broadsword." At one time,
the story goes, a Guard pinned Francisco's leg to his horse with a
bayonet thrust. The young giant helped the soldier pull out the
steel, then as his enemy turned "he made a furious blow with his
sword and cleft the poor fellow's head down to his shoulders."[75]

Just after Washington's cavalry passed through the Guards'
ranks like a ravaging whirlwind, Howard's men arrived to de-
liver a staggering flank attack. Two combatants drew special
notice from those around them during this fierce action. Colonel Stuart who led the Guards and Captain John Smith of the

Marylanders. According to one account they had met previously and "had vowed that their next meeting should end in blood. Regardless of the bayonets that were clashing around them, they rushed at each other with a fury that admitted but of one result." [76] A brief and bloody personal conflict ensued. Small sword in hand, Stuart lunged at his foe. But Smith dodged the sharp point, and Stuart lost his footing when he stepped upon the arm of another man whom Smith had just felled. With a single backhanded blow to the head with his sword, Smith then dispatched the British colonel. Stuart's orderly sergeant continued his superior's attack, but Smith's sergeant in turn cut him down. Smith then felled another Guard before a bullet caught him in the back of the head. His men carried their captain from the field and to their delight discovered he had only been stunned. [77]

Even the Guards' experience and discipline could not forever stand proof against such an onslaught. They had plainly begun to get the worst of the fight and had begun to fall back when Cornwallis, who had arrived in time to observe their difficulties after barely escaping capture by Washington's wild cavalry attack, [78] resorted to a desperate measure. Fearing that the Guards might all be overrun, he resolved to stop the American advance in the only manner available to him. Lieutenant MacLeod had brought two 3-pounders along the road to a small eminence just beside it on the south side. Although not extremely high, the knoll offered an advantageous location for artillery, which from there could reach to the American line, the nearest portion of which lay but two hundred fifty yards distant. Cornwallis ordered MacLeod to load his guns with grapeshot and direct his fire into the midst of the human melange. O'Hara, who lay bleeding nearby in the road, supposedly "remonstrated and begged" his commander to spare the Guards, but Cornwallis repeated the order. "This is a necessary evil," he told the Guards commander, "which we must endure, to arrest impending destruction." [79] The carnage upon friend and foe alike was frightful, but it did serve its purpose. When the smoke cleared away, the surviving Guards had regained the safety of their own guns and those of Washington's and Howard's men who could still move had abandoned their pursuit and retired to their own lines.

Now more British troops came up and the battle was nearly over. For, unlike Cornwallis, who must push the fight to its limits, Greene dared not risk everything upon a last-ditch stand. While the wounded O'Hara exerted himself to rally his decimated 2d battalion of Guards, the Grenadiers and the 71st emerged from the woods on his right and the 23d on his left. Webster led the 33d and light infantry up again from the ravine. At the same time Tarleton appeared upon the road with some of the cavalry. The Earl re-formed his line and advanced. "The enemy were soon put to flight," he noted, "and the two 6-pounders once more fell into our hands; two ammunition-wagons and two other 6-pounders, being all the artillery they had in the field, were likewise taken." [80] Greene could not take his artillery with him because his artillery horses had all been killed. He waited for a while at Reedy Fork, three miles from Guilford, to collect stragglers and then marched all night to his former camp at the ironworks on Troublesome Creek, around fifteen miles from the battlefield.[81]

Cornwallis had won the field, but he might have inflicted much greater losses upon Greene had he then had the services of the light troops lost by Tarleton at Cowpens. As things stood, however, he could not pursue the retreating enemy, especially "as their cavalry had suffered but little." [82] Apart from the more than a thousand returned as missing (those who had run away), Greene's official casualty figures listed only 78 killed and 185 wounded.[83] Cornwallis estimated their losses at much more, saying that the Americans left between 200 and 300 dead upon the field, and that, in addition to the wounded who escaped and followed Greene's army, "the houses in a circle of six or eight miles round us are full of others." [84] The British destroyed some 1300 muskets and rifles left on the field by the Americans.

The Earl's heavy casualties amounted to 532, or more than one quarter of the number engaged. Of these 93 were killed outright, although some of the 413 wounded later died. Twenty-six were missing. Among commissioned officers, 5 were killed and 24 wounded, some fatally. The Guards had suffered the heaviest casualties, numbering among the killed and wounded 11 of their 19 officers and 206 of their 462 rank and file.[85]

The redcoats reeled from fatigue and hunger. They had not eaten anything for twenty-four hours, having consumed their last meal — four ounces of flour and the same amount of "very lean beef" — between 3:00 and 4:00 P.M. on the preceding day.[86] They had been under arms since 5.30 A.M., had marched twelve miles, and then had fought a fierce and bloody two hours' battle. Their hundreds of wounded lay scattered over a wide area and could not all be found and collected, much less tended, before nightfall. The sky had begun to cloud over near the end of the battle, and soon after the American withdrawal the skies opened and rain "fell in torrents." The British passed the rainy night shivering and soaking on the ground without food or tents. Perhaps as many as fifty of the wounded died during this ghastly night. Commissary Stedman called the scene one of "horror and distress." "The cries of the wounded and dying who remained on the field of action during the night," he said, "exceed all description." [87] One of the wounded, however, did attempt to describe his experiences:

I never did and I hope I never shall experience two such days and nights as those immediately after the battle. We remained on the very ground on which it had been fought, covered with dead, with dying and with hundreds of wounded, rebels as well as our own. A violent and constant rain that lasted above forty hours made it equally impracticable to remove or administer the smallest comfort to many of the wounded. In this situation we expected

310 *The Disastrous Drive North*

every moment to be attacked. There could be no doubt that the enemy must be very well informed of our loss, and whatever their loss might be their numbers were still so great as to make them very formidable. And they had only retired eighteen miles from us. Fortunately for us they did not, or even followed us when we marched but at a very respectable distance, or have ever fired a single shot since the affair of the 15th.[88]

For Charles, Earl Cornwallis, lieutenant general of His Majesty's forces in America, the night passed in the lonely vigil of command. If Cornwallis felt touched to the quick, he gave no sign, just as he had coolly fired artillery into his gallant Guards, although to do so must have wrenched his heart. What his men now needed was calm assurance, not hand-wringing.

Guilford Courthouse was a dearly bought British victory — so dearly bought that Cornwallis could never resume the offensive in the Carolinas. Yet perhaps no other senior commander the British sent to North America could have won it. His physical and moral courage, his drive, his persistence, his cool resourcefulness, and his leadership saved the British hopes in the South on that bleak day, the ides of March. He had gone into the fight with impossibly long odds against him, yet he had never wavered, never flinched, and by sheer force of will and character had chased the Americans off the field. Every critical moment of the battle found the Earl on the spot to direct his men. And after all the slaughter, exhausted as he must have been, he still had the resolve to form up his entire line and charge again. A lesser man would have faltered at the very beginning. At Guilford Courthouse, as at Camden the year before, Cornwallis' tactical leadership was at its best, and its best must be described as superb. It is perhaps not too much to say that had the Cornwallis of Camden and Guilford been in command, instead of Howe, over the large forces Howe led in the early years of the war, he would not merely have defeated Washington in battle, but would have utterly crushed him.

CHAPTER 14

Wilmington
"Our very Shatter'd Exhausted,
Ragged Troops"

FOR THE BRITISH GENERAL the immediate future meant caring for his own and the enemy's wounded, collecting captured arms, finding food for men and forage for horses, and writing dispatches to superiors. In camp he applauded his officers and soldiers for their "Extraordinary Valour," and in his dispatches he warmly praised them, saying that their actions and conduct "will do more justice to their merit than I can by words." [1] He did not relate, and it therefore did not appear in the *Gazette*, that "every part of our army was beat repeatedly on the 15th March, and were obliged to fall back twice." [2] The Earl sent his aide-de-camp, Captain Brodrick, home to England with the dispatches. Weeks later, when Brodrick and his news reached London (on June 5), the ministry and its detractors immediately saw the Pyrrhic nature of Cornwallis' victory. Charles James Fox remarked that "Another such victory would ruin the British army." [3]

Certainly the part of the army remaining to Cornwallis' command was for the time being ruined — unfit for action. The men had no food after the battle ended, and medical supplies for the wounded were limited.[4] Therefore, despite their great fatigue, the lieutenant general sent his men to attend to the wounded and to search for food and forage. In the latter endeavor the men had little success, for the surrounding countryside yielded but little sustenance. They did indeed have some wheat, but the mill they used to grind it broke down. On the seventeenth Cornwallis told the troops that he was "thoroughly sensible of the distress they suffer for the want of flower or meal" but that they could not yet move from Guilford since "their Continuing here at Present is Necessary for the Safety of their Wounded Companions." [5] Presumably this message referred only to those with the most dangerous wounds, for on that very morning Cornwallis sent off seventeen wagons loaded with some wounded — men who could not possibly either walk or ride a horse but whose "cases will admit of their being again with the army." [6] For the sake of the wounded who could not yet be moved, the army remained at Guilford one more day. The Earl ordered all the women except one per company to follow the wagons of wounded. [7]

Cornwallis and Greene, meanwhile, exchanged messages regarding the American wounded who lay upon the battlefield. On March 16 the British commander wrote to his enemy: "I have given orders to collect the wounded of your Army at Guilford Court House, where every possible Attention shall be paid to them, but as it is not in my power to give them sufficient Assistance I must recommend it to You to send immediately Surgeons to take care of them, & a Supply of Necessaries & Provisions." Greene, who had actually dispatched a surgeon before he received the Earl's letter, replied the next day to express his thanks to Cornwallis and to say that he would send an immediate supply of provisions and other necessaries for the hospital. [8] But this exchange — a normal and humane arrangement — gave rise to one of those durable myths with which the revolutionary period abounds. "A flag [of truce] came in," so goes the whig tale, "with a message from Cornwallis; and presently, putting their own interpretation upon it, the men declared that the British commander had summoned Greene to surrender, and that Greene had replied, 'I am ready to sell you another field at the same price.' " [9]

Before he could leave the battlefield Cornwallis also had to collect and arrange for the disposition of American weapons and prisoners. The British had captured four 6-pounders, mounted on traveling carriages with limbers and boxes, together with 2 ammunition wagons, 160 round shot, 50 case shot, and powder. They took the cannons and ammunition with them. They also captured 1300 stand of arms, some of which they distributed among the militia, and the rest they destroyed on the field.[10] American prisoners presented a greater problem. Cornwallis could neither destroy them nor give them to the militia, and he certainly could not take all of them with him when he marched from Guilford. About all he could do was guard them closely until the army left, keep a few particularly important or dangerous ones with him, and put the rest on their parole.

In connection with the disposition of prisoners, Cornwallis revealed some of those traits of leadership — personal acquaintance with the enlisted men, knowledge of their individual characters, openly expressed gratitude for their services — which endeared him to the rank and file of his army. A British sergeant had charge of the guard mounted over the prisoners, including an American captain who had committed "depredations" upon the loyalists. The provost marshal told the sergeant to take particular care to prevent the captain's escape, as Lord Cornwallis feared that he would again terrorize the loyalists if he regained his freedom. But the American captain bribed one of the sergeant's sentries and made good his escape. The Earl, "highly displeased," ordered the sergeant to appear before him. But when the man approached, the Earl's grim face suddenly "changed into a smile." He saw that it was Roger Lamb, whom he had employed to write duplicates of his dispatches during the

campaign, who may have saved his life at Guilford, and whom
he knew would not accept a bribe. Accordingly, Cornwallis directed his aide-de-camp to release Lamb to his regiment and to
confine the sentinel who had permitted the American to escape.[11]

On March 18, the day after the wagons left, the rest of the
British departed that field of suffering and death. They had with
them most of the wounded who had not gone in the seventeen
wagons the previous day. Those who could still sit a horse rode.
Others, the more severely hurt, were borne in horse litters, a
mode of transport seemingly designed by the devil for the express purpose of providing additional torture to those pain-
racked bodies. Surprisingly, many survived this rough treatment, including the badly injured O'Hara who had wounds in
the thigh and breast.[12] Yet it is perhaps not so surprising when
one considers that these were tough men who had endured great
hardship. Also, they were following a leader whom they loved
and trusted and for whom they would give their best.[13]

Sixty-four of the wounded, "the bad cases," had to stay behind. Cornwallis left them at the Quaker Meetinghouse in New
Garden, about five miles from Guilford Courthouse, under the
care of the surgeon, Mr. Hill, and of two surgeon's mates. Hill's
medical supplies consisted chiefly of the knife and saw, yet astonishingly, only eighteen or slightly over one quarter of these men
had died by April 6 when the surgeon wrote his report.[14] For
them, death must have been a welcome release after days of ago-
nizing pain. The survivors became Greene's prisoners.

The remainder of the army fell back by easy marches to Cross
Creek, a large settlement chiefly inhabited by Scots, at the head
of the Cape Fear River. They left behind an abject population
which had not responded to Cornwallis' proclamation, issued
March 18, announcing his complete victory over the rebel forces
and calling upon "all loyal subjects to stand forth & take an ac-

tive part in restoring order & government." The proclamation
even promised amnesty to all rebels, "murderers excepted," who
would "surrender themselves with their arms & ammunition at
headquarters or to the officer commanding in the district con-
tiguous to their places of residence on or before the 20th day of
April next. . . ." [15] But the rebels saw no reason to surrender
now that the redcoats were so obviously running — if not from
them, then from starvation. The loyalists who did come forward
remained but a few days. Although, as a Quaker resident of the
area explained, most people wanted to be reunited to the British, "they had been so often deceived in promises of support,
and the British had so often relinquished posts, that the people
were now afraid to join the British army, lest they should leave
the province, in which case the resentment of the revolutioners
would be exercised with more cruelty; that although the men
might escape, or go with the army, yet, such was the diabolical
conduct of these people, that they would inflict the severest punishment upon their families." [16] In other words, the conflict had
assumed ever more intensely the vicious characteristics usually
associated with civil war. If Cornwallis needed further proof of
the manner in which rebels had terrorized and cowed the populace with loyalist inclinations, he soon received it. The day before the British army reached Cross Creek, an unkempt scare-
crow of a man joined it. This unfortunate loyalist had been
forced to live for three years "in the woods, under ground" eating only what he could get from the woods, including acorns as a
substitute for bread.[17]

The British suffered another disappointment upon their arrival at Cross Creek. They had been informed that the Scots "to
a man" would join them and that supplies could reach them
easily along the river from Wilmington without "the least obstructions from the people of the country." These glowing reports, the irrepressible O'Hara remarked acidly, proved "false in
every particular. . . ." [18] Cornwallis expressed his disappoint-

ment with Cross Creek in more tactful terms in a dispatch to the
American secretary. "Provisions were scarce," he said, "— not
four days' forage within twenty miles — and to us the navigation of the Cape Fear River to Wilmington impracticable, for
the distance by water is upwards of an hundred miles, the
breadth seldom above one hundred yards, the banks high, and
the inhabitants on each side generally hostile." [19] So the Earl,
who had hoped to rest his army at Cross Creek, had to move
again.

The redcoats struggled down the west side of the Cape Fear
toward Wilmington encumbered with about four hundred sick
and wounded, barefooted, and "in the utmost want of necessaries
of every kind. . . ." [20] They cut a broad swath of devastation as
they went, for not only did the soldiers take all the food and
forage they could find, but also the camp followers plundered
houses and their inhabitants of any goods and valuables they
could lay their hands on.[21] In addition to a barren countryside,
the British left behind those of their number who did not survive the jolting wagon or horseback ride. Five officers died en
route to Wilmington, including the much-beloved Lieutenant
Colonel Webster of the 33d.[22] Cornwallis, according to Sergeant
Lamb, "was struck with such pungent sorrow" upon hearing of
Webster's death that he turned, looked at his sword, and "emphatically exclaimed, 'I have lost my scabbard.' " [23] Webster's
body was buried in Elizabethtown, a small community on the
Cape Fear, some forty miles upstream from Wilmington. After
the army's arrival at its destination, the Earl took upon himself
the painful task of writing to the Reverend Dr. Webster to inform him of his son's death.[24]

The tattered remnants of the army arrived in the environs of
Wilmington on April 7.[25] There Cornwallis took up headquarters in an elegant house that Major Craig had picked out earlier
when he had occupied Wilmington on orders from Cornwallis.

At last he might enjoy some rest and relaxation in comfortable quarters. John Burgwin, a former treasurer of the North Carolina colony, had built the imposing white frame house only ten years before. He lived in his mansion for but a few years and then, seeing the handwriting on the wall, went to England along with other loyalists. Soon thereafter the Revolution broke out, and he "broke his leg" — the usual excuse employed by those who did not wish to return. Judge Joshua Wright bought the house and was living in it when Major Craig arrived to take possession of Wilmington.

Cornwallis allowed the Wright family to stay in their house during the brief (two and a half weeks) time he and his staff occupied it. Judge Wright's daughters served them tea in the afternoon. In fact, one of the young British officers and one of the daughters fell so in love that they cut their initials together on a window in the house.[26] The Earl himself, however, had more weighty matters on his mind than the pleasures of a springtime dalliance. In that lovely Burgwin house he had to clear away past business and plan for the future — a future that would take him north to Virginia to another small village on another river.

Before he could concentrate on his future, however, he had to rest and resupply his men, tend the sick and wounded, write letters and dispatches, fill vacancies, and settle matters of promotion. He wrote to Clinton of the "distress" he felt over "having no power to gratify those whose zealous services, courage, & abilities have often relieved me in my most anxious moments." He therefore begged Sir Henry's helpful intervention in securing favor for those "whose services have been most meritorious & whose interest I have particularly at heart." [27] He made other requests of Clinton, some regarding promotion and one asking for a blank commission to indemnify a sergeant major, "a very old soldier," who wished to retire. Cornwallis urged that the granting of such commissions had been "very much the practice" recently and was the only way of preventing that "useful commission from being improperly disposed of." [28] He continued to press for promotion for Tarleton and wrote to both Germain and Lord Amherst for that purpose. He also tried his best to reward Lieutenant Henry Haldane, who had sometimes acted as his aide-de-camp, for his many services. Haldane wished to quit the engineers, and Cornwallis asked Amherst to recommend him to the King for a lieutenancy of Guards, or if His Majesty declined that, promotion to captain. Cornwallis had more success in his efforts for Tarleton than for Haldane. The King, because of the Earl's "very earnest recommendation," brevetted the Green Dragoon to lieutenant colonel, but he would not transfer Haldane to the Guards because he disliked the policy of engineers' changing their branch of service.[29]

Cornwallis also nearly completed the months' long negotiations with Nathanael Greene over an exchange of prisoners. The two had begun correspondence in December of 1780, but difficulties and dissension had delayed a settlement. Indeed, not until after he left Wilmington, on May 3, 1781, was a mutually satisfactory cartel agreed upon and arranged between representatives of the two armies at the house of Mr. Claudius Pegee on the Peedee River. The first delivery of American prisoners would embark at Charleston on or before the fifteenth of June and sail immediately to Jamestown on the James River, where the first delivery of British prisoners would then embark on or about the first week in July and sail for the nearest British port. Greene later interrupted the cartel, after a few exchanges, because of complaints of irregularities on Balfour's part in Charleston, including hanging a prisoner.[30]

While he rested and refreshed his army and cleared his desk of old business, Cornwallis turned his thoughts toward the future. What should he do? Staying in Wilmington would serve no useful end, and as the summer approached, heat and malarial mosquitoes would decimate the ranks of his men. Cornwallis had had experience of the Carolina summer and of its effects upon unaccustomed Britons — indeed, less than a year earlier, he himself had languished for weeks with a fever.[31] Should he then return south to Charleston to reinforce Rawdon in South Carolina? Or should he push north to join General Phillips, whom Clinton had sent with five thousand men to the Chesapeake Bay area in Virginia?

All his natural inclinations lay with the northern route, yet he knew that Greene's army had turned south and was even then advancing toward South Carolina. Cornwallis feared for Rawdon's safety. But if he himself returned south, could he arrive in time to assist Rawdon? Cornwallis thought not, but he was loath to cut himself off from all possibility of rendering aid to his second in command. Therefore, while he crystallized his ideas and gradually committed himself more and more to a junction with Phillips, he at the same time took steps that would permit him, up to the very last moment, to return to Charleston.

To Major General Phillips he wrote with the obvious hope of gaining support for his own favorite idea — a full-scale offensive carried to Virginia. At the very least, they must have no more stumbling around in the dark:

> Now my dear friend, what is our plan? Without one we cannot succeed, and I assure you that I am quite tired of marching about the country in quest of adventures. If we mean an offensive war in America, we must abandon New York and bring our whole force into Virginia; we then have a stake to fight for, and a successful battle may give us America. If our plan is defensive, mixed with desultory expeditions, let us quit the Carolinas (which cannot be held defensively while Virginia can be so easily armed against us) and stick to our salt pork at New York, sending now and then a detachment to steal tobacco, &c.[32]

But convincing Phillips was not enough. Cornwallis must also convince Clinton. He wrote the latter to much the same effect, although the words were of course more appropriate in tone to the exalted rank of commander in chief in America:

> . . . I am very anxious to receive your Excellency's commands, being as yet totally in the dark as to the intended operations of the summer. I cannot help expressing my wishes that the Chesapeak may become the seat of war, even (if necessary) at the expense of abandoning New York. Until Virginia is in a manner subdued, our hold of the Carolinas must be difficult, if not precarious. The rivers in Virginia are advantageous to an invading army; but North Carolina is of all the provinces in America the most difficult to attack (unless material assistance could be got from the inhabitants, the contrary of which I have sufficiently experienced), on account of its great extent, of the numberless rivers and creeks, and the total want of interior navigation.[33]

Finally, Cornwallis also wrote to the American secretary, Lord George Germain, urging the soundness of a major offensive in Virginia.[34]

Apart from his own strategic plan for an offensive in Virginia (Cornwallis was the only senior British general who had even formulated a strategic plan since Saratoga), the Earl had compelling reasons for not going south again. He had just traversed that land and knew the hazards and difficulties of trying it again, especially with so reduced a force: the many rivers that made travel a nightmare, the dearth of food and forage, the numerous enemies and lack of active friends (Greene's "continentals alone are at least as numerous as I am," he lamented). Furthermore, if Rawdon should defeat Greene, Cornwallis would not be needed; whereas should Rawdon lose to Greene, his own return would expose his men to great peril without much prospect of their being of real benefit to Rawdon in protecting the interior posts. After all, could less than fifteen hundred troops — all the men he mustered in Wilmington — really affect the decision in South Carolina? Probably Cornwallis could do nothing but sit out the rest of the war in Charleston, losing all chance for action and surrendering all influence over the course of the war. Thus everything seemed to recommend an attempt to join Phillips and conduct an active campaign in Virginia with their combined forces.

Cornwallis could not, however, turn his back on his friends to the south should they need him. Accordingly, he decided to postpone his point of no return until he learned of Rawdon's success or failure against Greene. On April 24 he ordered Balfour to send transports in case he needed them to return to Charleston. They would merely represent an insurance policy, however, in the event that his plans could not be consummated or in the event of an emergency demanding him in Charleston. If he did not use them, the transports could carry the sick and wounded and camp followers.[35] He determined to move from Wilmington into the interior as bait to lure Greene north, if possible.[36] His men rested and his plans completed, Cornwallis once again prepared to campaign against the Americans.

He left Wilmington on April 25 with one thousand four hundred thirty-five rank and file present and fit for duty,[37] but he kept in communication with Major Craig in Wilmington and prepared to return there if necessary. At one point, indeed, he almost did go back. On May 4 he told Craig: "I wrote to you yesterday to say, that when transports & provisions arrive in Cape Fear I will return to embark. Give me early notice and communicate this to Balfour immediately." [38] But then a week later, at Halifax on May 12, he heard "from all quarters" that Rawdon had defeated Greene at Hobkirk's Hill.[39] Since Rawdon therefore had no need of his help, Cornwallis turned north. On May 13 he crossed his Rubicon, the Roanoke River.

PART V

The War Ends

The Frustrated Commander

CHAPTER 15

*Virginia: The Last Campaign**

WHEN CORNWALLIS left North Carolina he must have had some idea that Clinton would not approve. Had he waited at Wilmington until Balfour had forwarded to him three dispatches from Sir Henry, he would have known for certain that his superior had no intention of making Virginia a major field of operations.[1] Yet Cornwallis acted on his own without awaiting orders. At the time, and later in retrospect, he pleaded as justification "the delay and difficulty of conveying letters, and the impossibility of waiting for answers." [2]

Phillips received Cornwallis' letter of April 24 on May 6, while on his way back to Portsmouth after a raid on Petersburg. He immediately about-faced to return and await the Earl. Meanwhile the latter zigzagged toward Petersburg over the Neuse and Tar rivers. On May 10 he reached Halifax. He heard from Phillips on the twelfth and crossed the Roanoke on the thirteenth.[3] The march itself was not particularly eventful, but it was not very pleasant either. Tarleton as usual forged ahead, capturing arms, boats, and meal,[4] but never enough of the last. The troops grew increasingly hungry and sickly as the march progressed. Even when they did find corn or wheat they often could not grind it into meal, for the streams had now become so drought-parched that they would not turn the mill wheels.[5] Nonetheless, Cornwallis' small force was still reasonably intact when he finally joined Phillips' army in Petersburg on May 20. To the Earl's sorrow, however, he found that his friend Phillips had died five days earlier of a fever. Benedict Arnold had taken command of Phillips' forces.[6]

What was Cornwallis now to do? Clinton had originally sent Arnold to Virginia with two thousand men to fortify a base at Portsmouth for the navy's ships and to harass the province with raids that would draw attention away from Cornwallis in South Carolina. In March Phillips had brought another twenty-five hundred men to Virginia and had taken over command. His instructions had been similar to Arnold's — to fortify a naval base other than Portsmouth if that place seemed unsuitable and to conduct harassing operations which would indirectly aid Cornwallis' campaign further south.

Shortly after the Earl reached Petersburg, yet more reinforcements came up the James River and the British army in Virginia now numbered over seven thousand effectives — about five thousand present and fit for duty.[7] Was such a large force still intended only to build a naval base and conduct raids? Cornwallis hoped otherwise, but now, for the first time in nearly a year, he felt the restraining hand of the commander in chief. He read Clinton's orders to Phillips, and was disconcerted. Obviously he would have to think about raids and naval stations rather than a grand offensive.

Almost immediately he concluded that Portsmouth would not serve the navy's purpose. Lieutenant Colonel Von Fuchs, of the Prinz Feld Infantry Regiment of Hesse-Cassel, whom Phillips had left in command at Portsmouth, wrote Cornwallis on May 23 that the works there were "but slender," and the sandy soil made daily repairs mandatory. Frequent desertions from the garrison owed primarily to the "severity of the duty" which re-

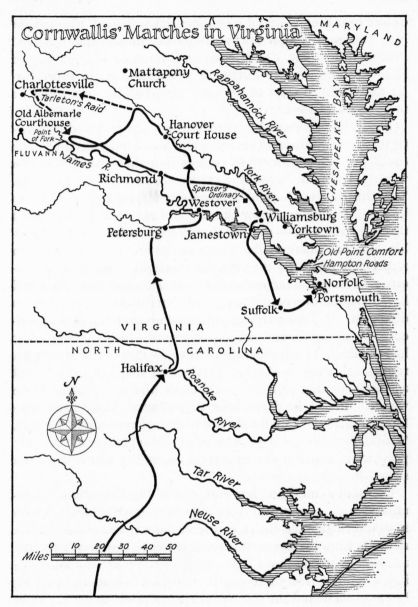

Cornwallis' Marches in Virginia

quired over four hundred men every day.[8] Arnold, who left for New York shortly after Cornwallis took command, had not liked Portsmouth either. The Earl wrote Clinton on May 26 that he favored Yorktown over Portsmouth because it could afford better protection to ships of the line, was healthier, and could be more easily fortified.[9]

But if the new commander in Virginia was prepared to investigate the possibilities of choosing and fortifying a naval base, he could not bring himself to believe that that was all Clinton would let him do. "From the experience I have had," he wrote, "and the dangers I have undergone, one maxim appears to me to be absolutely necessary for the safe and honourable conduct of this war, which is, — that we should have as few posts as possible, and that wherever the King's troops are, they should be in respectable force. By the vigorous exertions of the present governors of America, large bodies of men are soon collected; and I have too often observed that when a storm threatens, our friends disappear." [10] That statement summed up admirably his experience in the Carolinas — an experience of which Clinton never had the faintest comprehension. But now that Cornwallis had a respectable army in the key province of the South, he hoped against hope that Clinton would allow him to campaign as he wished. Indeed, he dared hope that Clinton would even reinforce his army. "I shall take the liberty of repeating," he said, "that if offensive war is intended, Virginia appears to me the only province in which it can be carried on, and in which there is a stake." [11]

Cornwallis could not, however, exceed Phillips' original commission without approval from the commander in chief. To do so would change the entire nature of the war and would depart radically from his assignment to reduce the Carolinas (although admittedly he had never felt it possible to do so without securing Virginia). He therefore reinforced Portsmouth, sending Leslie to command the garrison there, proposed to destroy mag-

azines and stores, as Phillips had done, and planned to chase the
Marquis de Lafayette (then commanding the only American
force of consequence in Virginia) away from Richmond. After
these operations he would retire toward Williamsburg to await
Clinton's reply to his letter pleading for an offensive. The former capital was "healthy," provident in "subsistence," and close
to Yorktown, which Clinton might prefer to Portsmouth.[12] At
Williamsburg Cornwallis could learn of Sir Henry's final intentions and act accordingly. If the commander in chief approved
the idea of reducing Virginia and agreed to reinforce his subordinate, the Earl would await the fresh troops. If Sir Henry
wished for something else, then Cornwallis could easily march
his army to Portsmouth and send it where Clinton desired as
soon as the navy provided the necessary ships. In May at least,
Cornwallis clearly took the only proper course he could take,
aware as he was of Phillips' orders but anxious at the same time
to reduce Virginia.

He now had a month to campaign, for he did not expect to
receive Clinton's response much sooner. His first and most obvious business lay with Lafayette.

The Marquis had gone to Virginia in March of 1781 with a
twofold mission: to catch and hang the traitor Arnold and, by
his very presence in Virginia, to inhibit British operations and
thus indirectly help Greene's campaign against Cornwallis in
the Carolinas. He had had little success in either venture.

Pursuit of Phillips brought Lafayette on April 29 to Virginia's new capital, Richmond. The Marquis then received a few
meager reinforcements, which brought his numbers to around
three thousand men. Although Phillips had gone, Lafayette remained there to protect the capital and in late May he awaited
Cornwallis' pleasure.[13]

"I shall now proceed to dislodge Lafayette from Richmond,"
the Earl wrote Clinton from Byrd's plantation at Westover on

May 26, "and with my light troops to destroy any magazines or stores in the neighborhood, which may have been collected either for his use or General Greene's army." [14] Cornwallis crossed the James River at Westover and pushed on to Hanover Court House on the North Anna, where he bivouacked on June 1. The march did indeed "dislodge" Lafayette, who left Richmond when the redcoats approached and who kept about twenty miles between himself and his opponents. The Marquis retreated north in order to meet, as soon as possible, a reinforcement of three regiments (about eight hundred men) of Pennsylvania Continentals under "Mad Anthony" Wayne, who were marching through Maryland toward him. On the same day that Cornwallis reached Hanover Court House, Lafayette camped at Mattapony Church.

The Earl now saw little hope of catching his adversary and gave up the fruitless chase. He did not feel the same necessity to seek out and fight the Marquis at all costs that he had felt toward Greene. His whole campaign did not, as in the Carolinas, depend on beating the American army, because Clinton had not yet allowed him a prolonged campaign. By his retreat Lafayette had left the western and southern parts of Virginia virtually defenseless, so Cornwallis turned to his second object, the destruction of magazines and stores. He commanded two units ideally suited for that purpose: the Queen's Rangers and the British Legion.

Both the Rangers and their leader, Lieutenant Colonel John Graves Simcoe, had colorful histories. As a military leader, Simcoe possessed a dash and gallantry similar to Ferguson's. He was more careful than the Scotsman, however, and steadier of purpose. Thus he survived the Revolution to become the first governor of Upper Canada. Scarcely a handsome man, he had a full face (equipped in later life with a double chin) that gave the impression of being round but was actually rather square. Save for his eyes, he would have looked like a complacent country gentleman. But those eyes belied the calm of the rest of his face, for they held the gleam of a restless energy and a joy of living. Indeed, Simcoe gave the appearance of a man who, had it not been for the accident of war, must still have found some release for his spirits.

He was seemingly destined for the military from birth. At Exeter Free Grammar School he had devoted himself to the study of ancient and modern literature and had "eagerly devoured every tale of war." From Exeter he had gone to Eton and then to Merton College, Oxford. He had continued to study military campaigns and before leaving Oxford had mastered "Tacitus and Xenophon, ever after his constant friends and companions, whether in the study or on the tented field." At age nineteen he obtained an ensign's commission in the 35th regiment, which went to America shortly after the outbreak of the Revolution. He later switched to the 40th and fought at Brandywine. Howe, pleased with his conduct, gave him command of the Queen's Rangers and promoted him to major. In due course Simcoe became a lieutenant colonel and he sailed with Arnold to Virginia. There he campaigned steadily, and was one of the first officers to greet Cornwallis when he joined Phillips' army and the first to tell Cornwallis the melancholy news about Phillips.[15]

The unit he commanded was one of the most flamboyant provincial regiments in the British service. First raised by Robert Rogers in 1776,[16] its ancestry went back to the famous Rogers' Rangers of the Seven Years' War. Although Rogers lost his command in the early years of the Revolution, the Rangers remained as flexible and as free and easy as their founder was accused of being. Uniformed in green like Tarleton's Legion, the regiment consisted mainly of light horsemen and companies of light infantry. On some occasions, Highlanders or Irish Volunteers attached themselves to the unit, which at its full strength mustered about six hundred loyalists.

Cornwallis now ordered the Queen's Rangers to Point of Fork, where the Rivanna River joins the Fluvanna to form the James. At the time, the Rangers could only muster about two hundred infantry and one hundred cavalry fit for duty. The Earl therefore reinforced them with two hundred men of the 71st Highlanders. Cornwallis had originally ordered the 71st to accompany Tarleton on a raid simultaneous with Simcoe's. Upon receipt of the order, however, the officers of that regiment "drew up a remonstrance, and presented it to lord Cornwallis, stating their unwillingness to serve under Tarleton, from a recollection of his conduct at the Cowpens," where the other battalion of the 71st fell prisoner to Morgan. As a result of this remonstrance, the Earl attached the Highlanders to the Rangers instead of to the Legion.[17] For artillery Simcoe took along a 3-pounder. Although fifty of his men had marched themselves barefoot already, the entire unit volunteered for the detached service. Their object at Point of Fork was twofold: to destroy stores; and, if possible, to catch Steuben, who was believed to command a force of two or three hundred militia (he actually had closer to a thousand).

From now on Simcoe enjoyed great success. Marching hard, sleeping at arms, he and his men swept up and kept prisoner every man they saw along the way to prevent any warning of their approach from reaching Steuben. Simcoe used every artifice in order to deceive and surprise his adversary. When Simcoe neared Point of Fork he learned from some prisoners that Steuben was hastily transporting stores and his army from the north to the south side of the Fluvanna. The lieutenant colonel captured a patrol of enemy dragoons, ordered his men to change uniforms with them, and sent his now-disguised Rangers ahead at a gallop to the only house on the point where, it was hoped, they might find and capture Steuben. But the Baron had gone. Upon learning that Steuben's command outnumbered his own, Simcoe tried yet another ruse. He attempted to fool the enemy into believing he was the advance guard of Cornwallis' entire army. He marched the only unit dressed in red, the 71st, to the banks of the Fluvanna, and to give the impression of large numbers, he dispersed the women and baggage in the woods on the summit of the hill above. Then, while the rest of his corps occupied the heights above the point, he ordered his 3-pounder to fire one round, for terror rather than for destruction (although Simcoe later averred that it killed the horse of one of Steuben's orderly dragoons).

The ruse worked. At daylight Simcoe discovered the opposite bank empty of Steuben's army. Some of his men swam across and sent back canoes, which the Baron, in his haste to leave, had not staved in. The Rangers also built a float and, one way or another, ferried themselves over to destroy or confiscate the stores Steuben had left — twenty-five hundred stand of arms, quantities of gunpowder, saltpeter, rum, brandy, carpenters' tools, entrenching tools, wagons, cloth, even a 13-inch mortar, five howitzers, and four 9-pounders which Cornwallis later used at Yorktown. The Earl, meanwhile, had moved the bulk of his army at a more leisurely pace and joined his active subordinate at Point of Fork on June 7. The army remained in the vicinity until the thirteenth, while the Rangers continued their raids, this time along the north bank of the Fluvanna, destroying tobacco and gunpowder.[18]

During this time, Tarleton had acted with equal vigor. Cornwallis had ordered his dragoon leader to "disturb" the Virginia assembly, then sitting at Charlottesville.[19] Disturb it Tarleton did. He dashed west with 180 dragoons and 70 mounted infantry, sprinted into the town on June 4, surprised the entire assembly, and seized some of its members. Indeed, he nearly caught the governor of Virginia. According to one account, Thomas Jefferson was entertaining the speaker of the assembly and other members when he learned of Tarleton's approach. A captain of the Legion had taken his men directly toward Monti-

cello, and they were actually climbing the winding road leading
to the mansion when a young American lieutenant spied them
and gave the alarm. Jefferson's family immediately bundled
into a waiting carriage and rumbled away, while the governor
himself jumped on a horse and galloped after them. Ten minutes later Tarleton's horsemen burst into Monticello. The
Green Dragoon had missed a prime capture, but he proceeded
to carry out his assignment to destroy stores. He then rejoined
the main force.[20]

With Tarleton's return, Cornwallis once more commanded a
united army, and he decided to keep it together. He did briefly
consider dispatching the Legion to raid Old Albemarle Court
House and to try to catch Steuben.[21] But he changed his mind
when he learned that Wayne had joined Lafayette on June 10,
which made the American force much more formidable. Detaching in the presence of this larger army might dangerously
weaken his own. Indeed, Wayne had brought seasoned Pennsylvania Continentals to join the Marquis near Raccoon Ford on
the Rapidan. The reinforcement meant that the American force
now opposed to Cornwallis was nearly his equal in numbers.
Almost half of that force consisted of Continentals,[22] and
many of the militia were veterans commanded by such experienced warriors as William Campbell of King's Mountain and
Edward Stevens, who had fought against Cornwallis throughout
the southern campaign. His confidence now increased by his increased strength, Lafayette inched ever closer to his adversary.

Cornwallis, having completed his raiding, retired toward Williamsburg. He moved down the James at a leisurely pace. Lafayette followed cautiously. He watched the British evacuate
Richmond. He watched them march down the river. He grew
continually more confident. Perhaps he really began to believe
that the Earl's parade toward Williamsburg was what it appeared to the country people — a British retreat before an army
of Continentals and militia. In any event, Lafayette grew so
bold that at one point he divided his force in the hopes of luring

Cornwallis into battle. Cornwallis, however, was not looking for a fight. Knowing as he did that his superior body of horsemen could prevent any surprise attack, he disregarded the Marquis almost contemptuously. He deemed it more important to reach Williamsburg and find out what Clinton had in mind for Virginia than to skirmish with the Frenchman. If Sir Henry permitted a systematic campaign, then he would deal with Lafayette once and for all.

On the twenty-fifth, the day that the British army reached Williamsburg, the young Marquis camped at Bird's Tavern, only ten miles away. Though he had failed to coax Cornwallis into battle, Lafayette still hoped to catch and destroy the British rear guard, which had not yet joined the army. So that day he sent an advance detachment under Colonel Richard Butler toward Spencer's Ordinary, about halfway between his own army and the British. Butler discovered the rear guard, consisting of Simcoe's Rangers and a party of Jagers. A hot fight ensued, distinguished by several individual acts of heroism. The engagement ended when the greatly outnumbered Rangers retreated toward Williamsburg. They had proceeded less than two miles when Cornwallis came up with the advance of his army. Simcoe then faced about and returned with his commander and this overwhelming force to the site of the battle. There the British recovered some of their wounded, whom Simcoe in his retreat had left under a flag of truce in the tavern (the Rangers lacked wagons to carry them off). The lieutenant colonel only admitted to losses of ten killed and twenty-three wounded, but Lafayette represented Butler to have killed sixty and wounded one hundred. Cornwallis discovered that Simcoe had taken three officers and twenty-eight privates prisoner, but he did not estimate American casualties.[23] The encounter had given Cornwallis his first opportunity to gauge the fighting mettle of Lafayette's forces.

*

After shepherding the Rangers safely into Williamsburg, the Earl had time to review his past and to plan for his future. He could look back on his raiding operations with reasonable pride. He had shaken the rebel legislature. He had burned American stores. Could he now capitalize on the situation and reduce Virginia? Even without reinforcements he had enough strength to challenge Lafayette. The prisoners taken at Spencer's Ordinary told him the approximate size of the Frenchman's force. With a free hand, Cornwallis felt more than capable of dealing with the Americans. But his freedom to act depended upon the wishes of his commander in chief. Sir Henry expressed those wishes in letters of June 11 and 15 which reached the Earl in Williamsburg on the twenty-sixth, the morning after his own arrival. They dashed his hopes.

Cornwallis' move from North Carolina into Virginia had appalled Sir Henry,[24] who had never contemplated any sort of major operations in the Chesapeake for the summer of 1781. On the other hand, the vigor of the Earl's campaign in the Carolinas had impressed the ministry. Lord George Germain inclined to support Cornwallis in his plea for an offensive in the Chesapeake that summer. Lord George, increasingly disenchanted with Clinton's sedentary war in New York, was coming to believe that an active general like Cornwallis might end the war in America with the troops already there. No more pestering the government for reinforcements. Clinton, of course, was aware, through Germain's letters, of the minister's attitude. The conviction grew within him that the ministry itched to give Cornwallis the supreme command in his stead. This consideration prompted Sir Henry, who was never very decisive in his written instructions to subordinates — he would seem to give five different orders all at once, some of them inconsistent with others — to treat Cornwallis almost as an equal in the directions he sent that summer. He implored him to do one thing or another, but only on rare occasions did he command him to a specific course of action. This attitude lessened the impact of his orders on the Earl, especially since the orders became increasingly contradictory.

Nonetheless, all through that summer, Clinton adhered basically to his belief that the army's main operations should focus on New York. He would permit harassing operations in Virginia to relieve the pressure on British arms in South Carolina and would push the construction of a naval station, but he would not allow a major campaign. Although neither Phillips nor Arnold nor Cornwallis had found the sort of station Clinton wished, although indeed they believed no suitable place could be found, Sir Henry clung to his idea. He realized that the British could not depend upon perpetual naval supremacy along the Atlantic Coast and that a French fleet in the Chesapeake might threaten any large British army in Virginia. Every summer for the past three years a major French squadron had appeared on the coast, and the previous year the French had taken Newport, Rhode Island, and turned it into a permanent base. Furthermore, Clinton had no faith in the British admiral commanding in North America, Marriot Arbuthnot. While this naval threat from France remained constant and while he reposed no confidence in the ability of the British navy to ward off that threat, Clinton naturally looked unfavorably upon Cornwallis' request for an active campaign in Virginia. But Sir Henry had a more immediate reason to refuse the southern adventure. On May 22 and 23, George Washington had conferred with the Comte de Rochambeau, commander of a French force of five thousand men that had gone to Newport the previous year to cooperate with the Americans. At Wethersfield, Connecticut, the two planned a combined operation of the French and American armies.[25] There Washington learned from Rochambeau that a large French fleet, commanded by the Comte de Grasse, had left France in March accompanied by transports with reinforcements for Rochambeau. The fleet would head for the West Indies, but vessels containing six hundred troops would separate at the Azores and sail directly to Newport. The French admiral, furthermore, had assured Rochambeau that after his tour in the West Indies he would sail to North America, probably in late summer, to assist operations there. At Wethersfield the American and French commanders discussed the possibility, based upon this momentous news, of an attack upon Cornwallis in the Chesapeake. Yet Washington insisted that they concentrate initially on New York. Plans might be changed later, depending upon the wishes and capabilities of Grasse when he actually appeared off the North American coast. Sir Henry learned of this meeting and guessed that he might be the target of a Franco-American attack. Under these circumstances he scarcely felt inclined to detach yet more from his forces to support a major offensive in Virginia. On the contrary, he wanted reinforcements from Cornwallis' army to help ward off the expected attack on Manhattan.

Although Clinton wrote several letters in the spring and early summer, only two reached Cornwallis by June 26: those of June 11 and 15. Both were of the same tenor. Sir Henry averred that Lafayette had only two thousand men to oppose the Earl's force of nearly eight thousand (Clinton always juggled figures to suit his opinions), while his own army of eleven thousand men at New York was threatened with a siege by a force twice that number. Cornwallis should fortify a post and send reinforcements, which, in consideration of the odds, he could easily spare. "I beg leave to recommend it to you," Sir Henry said, in his letter of June 11, "as soon as you have finished the active operations you may now be engaged in, to take a defensive station in any healthy situation you chuse (be it at Williamsburg or Yorktown). And I would wish in that case that after reserving to yourself such Troops as you may judge necessary for an Ample defensive, and desultory movements by water for the purpose of annoying the Enemy's communications, destroying Magazines

&c, the following Corps may be sent to me in Succession as you can spare them." Clinton then specified the units he wished: the equivalent of six regiments of infantry, all the Rangers, whatever cavalry the Earl still had from the detachment of the 17th dragoons, all the light cavalry, and all the artillery the Earl could spare. "You will immediately embark a part of the troops," Clinton reiterated in his letter of the fifteenth.[26]

Although he disapproved of his superior's orders, Cornwallis exerted himself to carry them out. On June 28 he took Simcoe and an escort of cavalry to Yorktown. After looking it over, he concluded that it, too, failed to answer the purposes Clinton had in mind. Simcoe then pointed out that if any of the points below Yorktown seemed suitable for a post, a garrison could move easily to them from the village. So as not to overlook any possibility, Cornwallis personally inquired about the alternate places Simcoe had suggested. He discovered that they, too, were unsuitable, for the water was too shallow to admit ships of war. During this survey, Americans annoyed him with artillery from Gloucester, an event which cannot have made him happier about the search for naval stations.[27] He finally completed his reconnaissance and returned to Williamsburg, planning to march from there to Jamestown, where he would cross the James River and proceed down to Portsmouth. There he had ordered such transports as were available to be ready to receive the troops that his chief had demanded as reinforcements.

On June 30, before breaking camp, he sent off another dispatch to Sir Henry. He recounted his operations against Lafayette and went on to offer some strategic opinions. "It is natural," Cornwallis stated, "for every officer to turn his thoughts particularly to the part of the war in which he has been most employed." Of course Clinton should think of New York, but it was equally natural for Cornwallis to think of the problems he himself had encountered in the South. "And as the security at least of South Carolina," the Earl continued, "if not the reduction of North Carolina, seemed to be generally expected from me, both in this country and in England, I thought myself called upon, after the experiment I had made had failed, to point out the only mode in my opinion of effecting it, and to declare that until Virginia was to a degree subjected we could not reduce North Carolina, or have any certain hold of the back country of South Carolina, the want of navigation rendering it impossible to maintain a sufficient army in either of these provinces at a considerable distance from the coast, and the men and riches of Virginia furnishing ample supplies to the rebel southern army." In that statement he once again summed up, for the benefit of Sir Henry, his entire experience in the South. He had defeated armies, he had sometimes pitted Tarleton effectively against partisans, but none of it had availed so long as Virginia remained a source of supply, comfort, and reassurance. But Clinton was the commander in chief. His opinions differed, and "to those opinions it is my duty implicitly to submit." In accordance with Clinton's instructions, Cornwallis had reconnoitered York and Gloucester as possible defensive posts and thought them both unsuitable. He had then ordered the few transports available at Portsmouth to prepare to receive part of his army. He promised to send off the other troops requested as soon as Clinton forwarded the necessary transports. When he saw Portsmouth he could better estimate the number of men needed to defend it (or another post, if he could still find one). He questioned, however, the utility of Portsmouth or any other small station. Certainly he would obey orders, but, he added: "I submit it to your Excellency's consideration, whether it is worth while to hold a sickly defensive post in this bay which will always be exposed to a sudden French attack, and which experience [certainly his own experience] has shown makes no diversion in favor of the southern army." If Sir Henry was determined to have the naval station, the letter concluded, would he permit his subordinate to return to Charleston? [28]

Thus Cornwallis had responded promptly to orders received and had prepared to carry them out punctually, despite his stated misgivings about their nature. Little more could be expected of him. If he did not seem overly concerned at that time with Clinton's worries for the safety of New York, the reason for his unconcern was easy to find. He had fought and marched with his army for a year, had seen it die from fever, suffer from hunger, shiver from want of clothes, and stumble from want of shoes, while Clinton had sat in New York to all intents and purposes warm and well fed and totally inactive.

On July 4 the Earl took his men down to Jamestown and prepared to cross the river. He had anticipated that Lafayette would "insult" his rear guard during the crossing and so had planned a surprise for the increasingly bold Marquis. By giving false intelligence to his enemies, he intended to divide and defeat Lafayette's force. He might indeed have destroyed the Marquis had not nightfall intervened to end the action. The battle at Green Spring, one of the least publicized in the Revolution, proved once again that, when at his best, Cornwallis as a tactician had no superior on either side in the Revolution.

Lafayette had fostered the notion that Cornwallis' return down the James from Richmond was a retreat from American forces. However false, the Marquis' picture of events bolstered up the faint-hearted who despaired for American fortunes. Also, Lafayette had managed to fish from the river the guns that Cornwallis had dumped there when he left Richmond. At Tyree's Plantation, twenty miles from Williamsburg, his army celebrated the Fourth of July. They fired off their artillery and held a grand review. Then Lafayette gave a dinner for his officers. He was in high spirits. Cornwallis was retiring and his own army by now equalled his opponent's in numbers, if not in discipline. The Marquis commanded 3 militia brigades of about 2180 men under William Campbell, Edward Stevens,

and Robert Lawson; three contingents of Continentals under
Peter Muhlenberg (800 New England and New Jersey soldiers), Anthony Wayne (750 Pennsylvanians), and Christian
Febiger (450 new Virginia levies); 50 Continental dragoons; 60
militia cavalry; and 300 artillerymen. [29] Cornwallis' "retreat"
beckoned him to glory. If he could stick close behind the redcoats and if the Earl were careless, he might cut up a part of the
British army.

On July 5 Lafayette moved his army to Chickahominy
Church. The next morning he sent Wayne ahead with five hundred troops (while he followed with the rest) to scout his adversary. If, as seemed probable, Cornwallis had already taken his
main body over the river, Wayne could strike a blow against the
rear guard. The hot-headed Pennsylvanian set off immediately.

"Mad Anthony" Wayne, whose nickname has been attributed
to various sources, had always been a soldier at heart. At school
he had shown more zeal for martial games then for Latin, and he
had frequented a local tavern in order to hear soldiers' talk. By
the age of nineteen Wayne had acquired most of the vices of an
officer and a gentleman — horseracing, whist, rum, wine, and
billiards. But he had also picked up a knowledge of mathemat-
ics, surveying, and astronomy — all subjects relevant to the military career he had already chosen for himself. When in 1776
Congress authorized a Continental army which would include
four Pennsylvania battalions, Wayne got a commission as colonel and command of one of the battalions. From that time on
he had fought steadily in the Revolution — in Canada, at Brandywine, Germantown, and Monmouth. Now a brigadier general, in July of 1781 at Green Spring he prepared to fall upon
the British rear guard.[30]

Cornwallis could not have hoped for a more impetuous man
than Wayne to lead the American van into his carefully planned
ambush. "Concluding that the enemy would not bring considerable forces within our reach," he later explained, "unless they

supposed that nothing was left but a rear guard, I took every means to convince them of my weakness." On July 4 he moved the bulk of his army to bivouac at Jamestown. That evening he sent the Queen's Rangers across the river to protect the army's baggage. The next day Cornwallis began shipping over most of his army's equipment (a task he estimated would require two days) but kept his men on the Jamestown side of the river.

The Earl camped his men northwest of Jamestown in a position extremely advantageous for himself and disadvantageous for an attacking force. On his right were several ponds. On his left a large morass reached to the James River. In front of him towards the northwest, connected to his position only by a narrow causeway, lay Green Spring Farm. Swampy woodland occupied the ground on either side of the causeway. To advance his men generally along a broad front, Wayne would have to send them struggling through the morass. If Cornwallis could entice Mad Anthony to move forward along the causeway and through the morass, he could outflank him and then, with his overwhelming numbers, cut him to pieces.

On the morning of July 6 Tarleton dispatched a dragoon and a Negro (several Negroes had followed the British army for deliverance from southern slavery) with false intelligence. Posing as deserters, they should tell Wayne that the main body of the British army had crossed the river and that only their own units — the Legion and a detachment of infantry — remained on this side of the river. Cornwallis, meanwhile, had posted pickets all across his front, supported by cavalry on his left, the area which Wayne's forces now approached. Behind the cavalry, hidden by the woods from Wayne's view, the Earl had drawn up his army in two lines. On the right he had placed some light infantry, the brigade of Guards, and the Hessians; and on his left the 76th regiment, the 80th, part of the 43d, the Legion, and more light infantry companies.

Wayne swallowed whole the false information the British had

fed him. He left the farm at about 3:00 P.M. and advanced impetuously toward his adversary. Cornwallis ordered his pickets to fall back slowly and steadily, luring Wayne onward. After two hours of skirmishing with the pickets, Wayne's five hundred men at last neared Cornwallis' army, still without the least suspicion of its presence. To embolden his attacker even more, Cornwallis left unattended, in his front, a single piece of artillery. The French major, William Galvan, who held a command under Lafayette, now dashed forward with some fifty or sixty light infantry to seize the gun. Wayne, his "broad face glowing with pleasure," rode after him and merely laughed as a bullet clipped the plume from his hat. Cornwallis chose this precise moment to begin his surprise assault: a barrage from artillery loaded with grape and cannister, followed by a charge. The Hessians, Guards, and light infantry on his right met such little opposition that they immediately threatened to outflank the American left. Wayne, who only a moment before had thought himself the easy victor over a small British rear guard, now found himself attacked by an overwhelming force in front and flank. But Mad Anthony lived up to his nickname. He instantly decided that he could save himself in one way only — by deceiving the British as to his real strength. He unlimbered the three field pieces he had with him and formed up his Continentals in a long line. Then he ordered them to charge bayonets. Such an audacious maneuver, he hoped, might check the British momentarily and give him time to retreat back across the morass to Green Spring Farm.

Lafayette, meanwhile, had arrived at the farm with the main body of his army and had watched with increasing horror Wayne's advance. He had walked to a point of land jutting into the river to the right of Green Spring, whence he had seen the entire British army waiting to spring upon his subordinate. Although he tried to warn Wayne and to rush up reinforcements, he was too late. Cornwallis personally led the 80th against the

Continentals. If Wayne's bayonets daunted him, they did so only momentarily. His men directed a "close, warm" fire upon the Continentals and made "a devil of a noise firing and huzzaing." Wayne's brave charge soon turned into a confused retreat and his well-formed line into a shambles. Men stumbled and fell as they plunged through the morass back toward the farm. Cornwallis' infantry pursued closely, and the Earl allowed his men to pick out and fire at individual targets. At such close range — Cornwallis charged when Wayne was only fifty yards away — the Brown Besses did terrible damage. The Continentals even had to abandon two field pieces because musket balls brought down the horses drawing them. Dashing forward in an attempt to rally his men, Lafayette himself lost two horses to British bullets. But, while he had badly mauled his enemy, Cornwallis could not continue the pursuit. His charge had come at dusk, and Wayne's men retreated in increasing darkness toward Green Spring Farm. The British commander now needed cavalry to gallop down upon the routed enemy, and cavalry simply could not gallop through woods and bogs in the darkness. So the Earl finally broke off the engagement. As he later wrote laconically to Balfour: "the darkness of the evening prevented me from making use of the cavalry, or it is probable the Pennsylvania line would have been demolished." [31]

Cornwallis lost only 5 officers wounded and 70 enlisted men killed and wounded, while Lafayette and Wayne lost about 145 killed, wounded, and missing, of whom 10 were officers. Tarleton, with his usual malice, later gave Cornwallis very little credit for his consummate skill. He preferred rather, in his *History of the Campaigns,* to castigate the Earl for not following up his victory and wiping out Lafayette's entire force. The next day the Green Dragoon took a patrol of two hundred cavalry and eighty mounted infantry across the swamp to pursue the enemy. He discovered the Marquis' army camped six miles away from the site of the battle and concluded that "they would have been an easy prey to a powerful detachment of the British, who could have marched into their rear by several roads, whilst the light troops amused them in front; or the infantry might have followed the route of the continentals in case they retreated, and the English dragoons and mounted infantry could have passed through the woods into their front, or on their flank, and have impeded and harassed them till the foot could force them into action." [32]

But Tarleton, who had conclusively demonstrated in a year of campaigning that he had none of Cornwallis' tactical sense, supposed the absurd. To presume that Lafayette, already well aware of his losses, would sit around and wait while the entire British force moved across the morass and causeway he had so recently vacated was to presume that he was unaware of his danger. Had Cornwallis advanced the next day, Lafayette most certainly would have retreated, and Cornwallis would then have been no more likely to catch him than during the previous month's campaign. Furthermore, Tarleton's scheme would have required Cornwallis, with his army on one side of the river and his baggage and best scouts (Simcoe's Rangers) on the other, to tear off in the hope that, after a night in which to recover, Lafayette would still be confused and disorganized. The Earl had, after all, only whipped Wayne's advance guard. The main force of Lafayette's army, almost equal in numbers to the British, had never even fought at Green Spring. They were fresher by far than Cornwallis' troops. And if Lafayette had stayed to fight, though the British would probably have won, it would have been a bloody battle. Wayne had shown the mettle of his Continentals, and in any fight now the Earl would suffer heavy casualties. Casualties, of course, would not help Clinton, who wanted reinforcements for the expected siege of New York. After all, he had emphatically told the lieutenant general to engage in no active campaign in Virginia and to send troops to New York, where they were needed, as quickly as possible. What matter if

Lafayette kept the field? The Earl had attempted a final ruse to beat him and, if possible, to wipe out his army. The ruse had succeeded in wiping out a part of that army. This limited success, however, did not give Cornwallis license to try, without baggage or guides, to catch up with the rest of the army. Even if he could have beaten the Marquis, he would have had to abandon the fruits of victory and send many of his troops to New York.[33]

The battle over and Lafayette humbled, Cornwallis took his main army across the James. But on July 8 at Cobham, across the river from Jamestown, he received a letter from Clinton dated June 28. It was the first of a series of contradictory orders from Clinton that plagued him during the rest of the summer. As the season wore on, Sir Henry grew increasingly obtuse. His plans became as "involved as his style. He wanted Cornwallis to attack Pennsylvania, to establish a post on the Chesapeake, to detach to New York. He was dallying with the idea of raiding Philadelphia himself. He was scheming to capture the French squadron at Rhode Island. He had so many irons in the fire that he could not concentrate on any one, and his varied and numerous plans give in sum the impression of planlessness." [34] Sir Henry's dispatch of June 28, for example, forgot the threat to New York which had seemed so imminent in his letters of the eleventh and fifteenth and now disclosed that the commander in chief intended to raid Philadelphia (an idea with which he had toyed before) and to destroy American stores collected there. He therefore requested Cornwallis, if he had not already dispatched to New York the troops named in the letters of the eleventh and fifteenth, to send instead a new force to Philadelphia including artillery, wagons, transports, and sloops. These units would join Clinton's army in New York after the raid.[35] Cornwallis opposed raiding Philadelphia and had said so in May. Now he once again protested Clinton's plans in a letter written the same day he received Clinton's new orders. A defensive post in Virginia, he argued, "cannot have the smallest influence on the war in Carolina, and . . . only gives us some acres of an unhealthy swamp, and is for ever liable to become a prey to a foreign enemy with a temporary superiority at sea: Desultory Expeditions in the Chesapeak may be undertaken from New York with as much ease & more safety, whenever there is reason to suppose, that our Naval Force is likely to be superior for two or three months." [36]

His objections made clear, Cornwallis now adjusted himself to his fresh orders. He forwarded this latest dispatch to Leslie at Portsmouth and ordered him to make all the necessary arrangements. He promised to give immediate orders about the artillery and stores and to continue to Portsmouth to await the arrival of transports. Cornwallis then marched toward Suffolk, slightly southwest of Portsmouth, planning to arrive there in four or five days.[37] In the meantime he sent Tarleton off on another raid toward Prince Edward Court House, to the west of Suffolk, with orders to destroy stores of every kind. Tarleton left the next day, marched hard, and achieved little. He discovered that most of the stores had already been shipped south to Greene's army.[38]

When Cornwallis arrived at Suffolk on July 12, he received Clinton's letters of May 29, June 8, and June 19. They fortified his sense of Clinton's purposelessness and hindered the establishment of any rapport with his commander in chief. The letter of May 29 told Cornwallis for the first time how entirely displeased Clinton had been with the move into Virginia and served to exacerbate the resentment Cornwallis now felt toward his chief. The letters of June 8 and June 19 informed the Earl how urgently Clinton needed all the troops and supplies Cornwallis could spare for the defense of New York: "the Enemy will *certainly* attack this Post," and "I am much in want of Howitzers &c I think your Lordship can spare some." [39] But, of course, neither Clinton's disapproval nor his fears for New York (which had by now mysteriously lessened) altered the situation of July 12. Now the Earl was engaged in carrying out an entirely different set of orders. "I have only now to inform your Excellency," Cornwallis wrote, "that every exertion shall be made to fit out the Expedition [for Philadelphia] in the completest manner without loss of time." [40]

During the next week he forwarded units to Leslie at Portsmouth and empowered his subordinate to equip and prepare the expedition. He himself retained for the use of his army only six boats for infantry and four for horses, allowing all the other vessels accumulated by the navy to be employed in the Philadelphia venture. While these preparations moved apace, Cornwallis dispatched more raiding parties like Tarleton's previous one to destroy stores destined for the Americans in South Carolina. [41]

By July 20 Cornwallis had completed his preparations and the troops had begun to embark for Philadelphia. The Queen's Rangers, in fact, had already boarded their transport when a message from Clinton arrived at 1:00 P.M. which stopped the sailing and countermanded all that had been done. Clinton's new instructions were the sharpest and most explicit of those he directed at his lieutenant general during that unprofitable summer:

I have received your lordship's letter of the 30th June [Clinton wrote] and the admiral has dispatched a frigate with his and my opinions in answer to it. I cannot be more explicit by this opportunity than to desire that, if you have not already passed the James River you will continue on the Williamsburg Neck until he arrives with my dispatches by Capt. Stapleton. If you have passed it and find it expedient to recover that station, you will please to do it and keep possession until you hear further from me. Whatever troops may have been embarked by you for this place [New York] are likewise to remain untill further orders. And if they should have been sailed and within your call you will be pleased to stop them. It is the admiral's and my wish at all events to hold Old Point Comfort which secures Hampton Road. [42]

These instructions took Cornwallis completely aback and, not surprisingly, roused him to fury. He had fought hard for a year, gone without food and clothes, marched and countermarched, all in a vain attempt to conquer the South. Although he had gone to Virginia without orders, once there he had obeyed every single directive Clinton had sent him. Now, when it seemed that he would be finished in Virginia, that his army would be broken up and most of it sent north and when, against his own better judgment, he had gone to considerable trouble to embark that army, had indeed actually put some troops aboard ship, he received an abrupt command to cancel everything. He was now to use his whole force merely to fortify a post. To Cornwallis, the command was both absurd and contradictory. He had never said he required an entire army to fortify a post, yet here he was ordered to keep one for that sole purpose. If he were to command an army, he wished to use it to reduce Virginia. But rank was rank, and orders were orders. Again, as before, Cornwallis did his best to obey his superior's commands.

Immediately upon receiving Clinton's message, Cornwallis told Leslie to halt the embarkation and ordered an engineer to survey Old Point Comfort for the purposes the commander in chief had in mind.[43] The next day, while awaiting the results of the survey, the Earl received yet another letter from Sir Henry, also dated July 11, urging the naval station in the Chesapeake Bay area and informing him that Admiral Graves, who had replaced Arbuthnot, agreed with him upon the necessity for the station. Cornwallis could fortify Yorktown, if he deemed it advisable so as to give additional security to Old Point Comfort. Clinton thought that his subordinate needed only three thousand men to hold the position, but would allow him to keep more if he really needed them. The Earl was "at full liberty to detain all the Troops now in Chesapeak . . . which very liberal concession will I am persuaded convince your lordship of the high estimation in which I hold a Naval station in Chesapeak." [44] Sir Henry represented that Cornwallis had argued in his letter of June 30 his inability to send off any men at all if he were also to establish a post capable of protecting ships of war. But in truth, Cornwallis had never, either in his letter of June 30 or in any other letter, argued as Clinton set forth. He had protested against establishing a defensive post but had never suggested that holding such a post required an entire army. Indeed, he thought Sir Henry's interpretation came close to lunacy and wrote to Graves a few days later implying as much. "He thought," Cornwallis said, "a secure harbour for line of Battle ships of so much importance in the Chesapeake, that he wished me to possess one even if it should occupy all the force at present in Virginia." [45]

The commander in chief, however, contradicted himself in the letter. For if one part of his instructions seemed to give Cornwallis an army, the other part took it away. Clinton stated that Cornwallis could not operate offensively during the summer (although in his letter of June 30 the Earl had already mentioned his offensive operations against Lafayette) and therefore directed his subordinate, after deciding how many men he needed for erecting works at Old Point Comfort, for covering Yorktown, and for "other Services" in the Chesapeake, to send Sir Henry "the remainder." [46] In other words, Cornwallis could keep and could not keep as many men as he wished. The situation had become ludicrous. Clinton had originally given one set of orders, and Cornwallis had obeyed them. Then Sir Henry had given a new set of orders, and Cornwallis had obeyed them. Now as the Earl proceeded to obey a third set of directions, his commander in chief, in a single letter, misinterpreted his subordinate's arguments and sent in reply two diametrically opposed orders.

Cornwallis resolved upon a course of action which, he hoped, would answer the spirit, if not the substance (for that was impossible), of Clinton's orders. Lieutenant Sutherland, the engi-

neer sent to survey Old Point Comfort, reported his findings
within the next few days: he found the ground totally unsuitable for erecting fortifications designed to protect naval vessels.
Men would have to transport soil from a great distance to build
ramparts and parapets. Once built, the fort would not protect a
fleet because there was no bay where ships could lie secure under
cover of the fort's guns. Indeed, an enemy fleet of superior
strength would probably maneuver between the weaker fleet
and the fort. Cornwallis wished to verify the report, so he personally visited the location, accompanied by the captains of the
British ships then lying in Hampton Road. They unanimously
disapproved of Old Point Comfort for the naval station.[47]

While he conducted these surveys, other letters from Clinton
reached him, all emphasizing the necessity for a station on the
Chesapeake and reiterating disapproval of the march to Virginia. Cornwallis, in turn, sent off another dispatch on July 26.
After recapitulating and justifying his past actions, especially
the march to Virginia, he explained his previous failure to fortify a post. He stated first that, until Clinton had authorized
him to keep an entire army if necessary for the purpose, he had
never really understood how much Clinton valued such a post.
Second, he maintained that there really were no locations adequate for Clinton's desires. But since Sir Henry was so determined to have a naval station, Cornwallis thought York and
Gloucester opposite it were the only feasible locations. They
were far from ideal — erection of works would require much
time and labor, they were "easily accessible to the whole force of
this province," and they did not command "an acre of ground"
— but they were the only places suitable for vessels requiring
deep water. The Earl would evacuate Portsmouth and fortify
York and Gloucester.

Since Clinton had permitted him to keep as many troops as he
wished for the work, Cornwallis now decided to use his entire
army. Three reasons compelled him to retain all his force.

First, York and Gloucester lay on such low ground, helped but little by nature, that unusually strong works would be needed to defend them. To build such strong fortifications in a short time required large numbers of laborers — laborers who could only be drawn from the ranks of the British army. Secondly, Cornwallis needed a large force because it would give him the necessary superiority in the field "to draw forage and other supplies from the country." Finally, only a large army could detach numbers of men to work on fortifications while still retaining a sufficient force to guard the working parties.[48]

Having explained himself — fully, he thought — Cornwallis rounded up his army and sailed for Yorktown in the boats and transports then at Portsmouth. The faithful Leslie he sent to replace Rawdon, now very ill in South Carolina. On August 2 his lordship began disembarking his men and immediately commenced fortifying Yorktown and Gloucester. At the same time he ordered O'Hara, who had replaced Leslie at Portsmouth, to destroy the works there and to evacuate the position. O'Hara accomplished this task by August 22.

Cornwallis spent that hot August of 1781 digging at Yorktown. Using every available Negro, pushing his own soldiers to the limit, and refusing to promise Clinton any troops until the works were finished, he struggled to entrench himself in a small town whose name, hitherto little known, would soon become famous.[49]

CHAPTER 16

The World Turned Upside Down*

A TRAIN OF EVENTS totally beyond Cornwallis' control now began its progress toward his isolated post. The combination of a French fleet in the Chesapeake and a Franco-American army would soon besiege him at Yorktown. Only Clinton could have prevented, or at least diverted, the allied army from hastening to Virginia. Only the British navy in the West Indies could have prohibited the French commander in those waters, the Comte de Grasse, from sailing to the Chesapeake, or at least have followed him with enough strength to keep him from bottling up the Earl. Both Clinton and the British navy failed.

In early July, Sir Henry labored under the conviction that Washington and Rochambeau designed to attack him. And, indeed, they intended precisely that during the first weeks of the month. Their combined armies remained outside New York and constantly reconnoitered the British position. Washington, however, had rounded up only six thousand of the ten thousand Continentals he wanted for the siege of Manhattan. With Rochambeau's five thousand men, the Franco-American force only equalled Clinton's. They were scarcely the superior forces needed for attacking an army that had been in New York long enough to fortify itself strongly. Furthermore, Clinton received German reinforcements the same month. Washington, in correspondence with Greene and Lafayette in the South, grew increasingly wary of assaulting Sir Henry. He had always kept Cornwallis in mind as an alternative target. News that reached the American commander on the afternoon of August 14 finally prompted him to choose that alternative. Rochambeau learned from Barras in Newport, who had the news from Grasse himself, that the latter had sailed toward the Chesapeake from the West Indies with twenty-nine ships of the line and three thousand troops. Rochambeau immediately sent this momentous information to Washington. Opportunity now beckoned. If Barras could leave Newport with support for Grasse and if Washington and Rochambeau could slip around Clinton, the allied army and the two French fleets could trap Cornwallis.[1]

Since Grasse had stipulated that he could stay in the Chesapeake no later than October 15, Washington hastily assembled his army and started it south on August 19. Clinton's spies, who had thoroughly infiltrated the American forces, now "deluged headquarters with reports." At the same time, evidence came to Clinton and Admiral Graves in New York that Grasse intended to sail from the West Indies. Yet Sir Henry sat immobile. Unperturbed, he let his enemies march away unmolested. When a subordinate suggested that he ought to follow Washington, Clinton rejected the notion "for fear that the enemy might burn New York in his absence." Days passed. As every day saw him farther and farther from the city, it became ever increasingly obvious that Washington had no designs upon New York. Still Sir Henry did nothing. "He had no anxiety about Virginia, where, he believed, 'the season prevented active operations.'" Yet what other destination could Washington have? The British commander evidently believed that his foes were practicing an elaborate deception to lure him away from his precious New York. "For days after his opponents had left for the

Chesapeake, in other words, he could see only the danger to Manhattan that no longer existed." [2] So Clinton whiled away the idle summer hours.

If Sir Henry seemed to lose not only his sense of urgency but also his common sense, the navy did little better. Despite Sir George Rodney's intelligence of Grasse's movements, his British West India fleet failed to intercept and fight the French ships. Furthermore, when Grasse took his entire fleet to the north, Rodney refused to believe it on grounds that the French admiral would not sail away and leave the French islands defenseless. Sir George insisted instead that Grasse took only a part of his squadron, perhaps fourteen ships of the line, to New York. So he dispersed his own fleet, even though it was initially smaller than Grasse's (twenty-three of the line against Grasse's twenty-seven plus a 50-gun ship). For reasons of health, Sir George turned over his command to Samuel Hood and then sailed for England in the 80-gun *Gibraltar*, which he considered the finest ship of her rank in the navy. He also sent two more ships of the line home with a convoy and posted six to various other duties. On his way to Europe he belatedly dispatched a frigate to Graves with news that the enemy had headed for the Chesapeake. To follow Grasse and reinforce Graves, Hood now had but fourteen sail of the line. Hood sailed on August 6, the day after Grasse, under orders from Rodney to make the Capes of Virginia, then the Delaware, and then Sandy Hook.

Graves, meanwhile, went haring off on his own from New York. He decided to search for an enemy convoy supposedly bringing supplies to the French in Rhode Island. In the middle of July he took his entire fleet out. The move was foolhardy, for although Graves at that time did not know Grasse was heading for the Chesapeake, he did know the Frenchman was at sea and that he would be making for North America, probably New York. Presumably Graves had it in mind, in addition to intercepting the convoy, to attack Barras' fleet at Newport and prevent its junction with Grasse. But he bungled everything. "His cruise cost him timely intelligence, postponed till too late the attack on Rhode Island, put him where he should not have been at the juncture, and cut down the strength of his squadron. In return for all this he did not have a glimpse of the convoy, but spent most of his time in a fog off Boston." [3] He went back to New York on August 16 with two of his ships so badly damaged that he had to lay them up for repairs. Although the situation now grew urgent, Clinton and Graves "behaved as if they had months at their disposal." By the middle of August when Graves returned from his fruitless cruise, Clinton had received from several sources intelligence that Grasse was making for the Chesapeake. One report gave the actual size of the fleet. Toward the end of the month overwhelming evidence told the British commander in chief that Washington had moved south. Yet, incredibly, Clinton and Graves still took no action. Their imaginations, inferior to the wings of Macaulay's ostrich, would not even allow them to run much less to soar. At the very least Graves might have sailed to the Chesapeake for a possible rendezvous with Hood (who indeed had reconnoitered the Capes on the twenty-fifth), and their combined fleets might either have tried to hold Chesapeake Bay against Grasse or have gone hunting Barras, who had left Newport on the twenty-fifth. Instead, Graves loitered for twelve days in New York, while Clinton listlessly followed the reports of Washington's progress.

On August 28 Hood arrived in New York with his fourteen sail of the line. He had not seen Grasse, but he knew he was coming and knew the necessity for immediate action, either against Barras at Newport or against Grasse (whom he yet believed to have a fleet not much larger than his own). But time and tide evidently stood still for the two British leaders. Hood, "alarmed by his new commander's nonchalance, immediately took a boat for the long pull to Denyses Ferry on Long Island, where Clinton and Graves were conferring. He burst in upon them with a home truth. 'Whether you attend the army to Rhode Island or seek the enemy at sea, you have no time to lose. Every moment is precious.' " [4]

Hood's admonition, of course, came too late. On August 31, the very day Graves finally sailed for the Chesapeake, Cornwallis beheld a chilling sight. "There are between 30 & 40 sail within the capes, mostly ships of war, & some of them very large," he wrote Clinton. During the next three days he discovered the appalling extent of his predicament. By September 4 he had learned that the fleet was Grasse's, that it was in the Chesapeake, that forty boats with troops had sailed up the James River on the first, and that four ships lay at the entrance to the York River.[5] The Earl's situation was suddenly more desperate than it had ever been before — soon, too, his salvation would be out of his own hands. His position at York and Gloucester was particularly vulnerable to the combination now against him. He had not fortified Old Point Comfort for what had seemed very good reasons — reasons strengthened by the opinion of an engineer and the naval officers. Yet Old Point Comfort would have given an outnumbered British fleet room to maneuver. Yorktown did not. Furthermore, an army at Old Point Comfort could have escaped by water in several directions. An army at Yorktown, with an enemy fleet holding the York River, would have to cut its way out by land.

Furthermore, Cornwallis had split his army. He had fortified Gloucester — a village of a dozen or so houses on level ground across the river — because control of that point was necessary to his position at Yorktown. The river narrowed considerably opposite his base. Without control of Gloucester he could not protect either the few ships he had or any other friendly ones which might approach. In addition, Gloucester offered an avenue of retreat from Yorktown, provided that he could gather enough small boats to ferry the bulk of his army across the river.

Should he await a siege? The works at Yorktown could not

yet withstand a determined foe, and those at Gloucester were even less advanced. On August 16 Cornwallis had observed that without a garrison of over a thousand men the Gloucester works were not safe against a *coup de main*.[6] Perhaps the Earl should have attacked Lafayette the day he spotted Grasse. With a victory over the Marquis, he could have led his men out of the trap. Yet he would have needed to assemble his army from both sides of the river and prepare it for battle in a few hours — for he could presume Grasse would send ashore reinforcements at once. At any rate, by September 4, when he learned the extent of those reinforcements, that option was no longer open to him. He could still take a chance, to be sure, against the increased forces now opposing him. He might indeed have done so, but he had no idea how much worse his odds would become, for he did not know that Washington and Rochambeau had begun a march toward Virginia. Letter after letter from Clinton gave him to understand that they still concentrated against New York. But even without Washington's army, a formidable combination already opposed his exit from Yorktown. After those forty boatloads of troops, consisting of three thousand French regulars under the command of the Marquis St. Simon, joined Lafayette, the combined force had moved to Williamsburg. Grasse could also land armed sailors; indeed, he had offered Lafayette eighteen hundred men if he would storm Yorktown immediately.[7] Even without French sailors, Cornwallis knew that he had to reckon with an enemy force of eight thousand. Against them he could bring only five thousand present and fit for duty.[8] In other words, Lafayette and St. Simon probably commanded more trained regulars than Cornwallis. They also had the support of large numbers of seasoned militia.

Between September 1 and 5, Cornwallis tried to gather intelligence which might help him reach a final decision. He sent patrols of the Legion cavalry to the shores of the James and the

York to report on the size, strength, and disposition of the enemy. On the fifth they brought back information that might prove immensely important. An English fleet was standing in toward the bay, and Grasse had warped his ships out to meet it.

Had help arrived to take a difficult decision out of Cornwallis' hands? Yes, but alas! It was not enough help. Graves and Hood had brought nineteen ships of the line to face Grasse's twenty-eight, with Barras somewhere in the offing. They had reached the Chesapeake still unaware of Grasse's strength and sublimely confident that they would beat him and then chop up Barras. Once they saw the true odds, however, their confidence evaporated. Nonetheless, on September 5 they engaged the French "in one of the least inspired and most decisive naval battles of the century." The battle, a tactical draw, was a strategic defeat. While Graves "ignored the chance of entering the Chesapeake and allowed himself to be inveigled into almost a week of maneuvering at sea," Barras "slipped unmolested into the bay." [9] The French thereby increased their fleet to thirty-six sail of the line, nearly double the number led by Graves and Hood. After his fruitless cruising, Graves reconnoitered the Capes, found the enemy safely anchored inside them, and on September 13 sailed for New York.

While Grasse engaged the British fleet, Cornwallis learned of Washington's approach.[10] A week later, by September 17, he also learned the outcome of the fight between Graves and Grasse and that Barras had joined the French fleet. Thus by the middle of September he knew help was unlikely by sea and that reinforcements were coming to Lafayette and St. Simon by land. Cornwallis now had one chance, and one chance only, to fight the French commanders before Washington arrived to make the odds impossible. The Earl again ordered out patrols. He told Tarleton to reconnoiter the positions of Lafayette and St. Simon, "and to use every expedient to obtain exact intelligence of their numbers." [11] Tarleton chose three officers and six men to help him scout Lafayette's army, which had camped near the College of William and Mary. The Legionnaires returned to Yorktown with their information at about the same time that a woman brought in a return of the French and Americans. According to Tarleton, her intelligence "suggested the feasibility of an attack." Cornwallis, apparently in consultation with his officers, decided to make an attempt to break out. He debated two alternative schemes. The first plan required the army to advance in column down the long straight road to Williamsburg before daybreak. Ravines cut the ground near the former capital, and by advancing at night the redcoats could make advantageous use of the terrain and darkness, exposing themselves far less than in daylight to enemy artillery. The second plan proposed sending an advance force of twenty-five hundred in small boats, protected by gallies and armed vessels, up the York River to Queen's Creek, a stream whose source lay above Williamsburg. The creek flowed past the town into the York River. The troops would sail up the stream to the rear of Williamsburg, while Cornwallis, with the main part of the army, advanced dircetly on the enemy's front. The British would then hit Lafayette simultaneously in front and rear. After mulling over the two schemes, the Earl chose the first instead of the second which required too nice timing and involved too many imponderables.

But as Cornwallis worked out the details of his attack, yet another event postponed the fateful decision. A dispatch, dated September 6, arrived from Clinton on the fourteenth. It promised relief. Of course, Clinton could not have known on September 6 of the outcome of the fight between Grasse and Graves. However, he did know, since Cornwallis had told him and since his letter acknowledged receipt of the Earl's message, the approximate size of Grasse's fleet.[12] Yet he seemed to imply that Grasse would be no obstacle. "By accounts from Europe," he said, "we have every reason to expect Admiral Digby on the coast." Clinton did not say how many ships Digby was bringing with him, but from his letter Cornwallis might naturally assume that Digby's fleet, in conjunction with Graves and Hood, would be powerful enough to force a way through to him. "I think," Sir Henry continued, "the best way to relieve you is to join you as soon as possible, with all the force that can be spared from hence, which is about 4,000 men. They are already embarked, and will proceed the Instant I receive information from the Admiral that we may venture, and that from other intelligence the Commodore and I shall judge sufficient to move upon. . . . I beg your Lordship will let me know as soon as possible your ideas how the troops embarked for the Chesapeak may be best employed for your relief, according to the state of circumstances when you receive this letter. I shall not however wait to receive your answer, should I hear, in the mean time, that the passage is open." [13]

Clinton's letter helped seal the Earl's fate. Because of that letter, Cornwallis decided to abandon his planned attack and to await relief. The decision to wait ensured his capture, for although this time Clinton exerted himself, relief did not reach Yorktown soon enough. In view of the circumstances, did Cornwallis' decision make sense?

After the war he argued that Clinton had held out uniform promises of relief which affected his decision. His statement was true, but somewhat misleading in that there was only a short period during which he really had a chance to break out. Once Washington's troops had followed their chief to Williamsburg, the overwhelming odds against the British rendered it virtually impossible for them to fight their way out. Cornwallis did try once, just before his surrender, to slip out by stealth and failed. But the significant fact was that he did hold a promise of relief during the brief but critical interval in which he had to decide whether to try to leave or to stay. That interval was the time between his learning of the British naval failure (September 17) and the time at which he could estimate Washington's troops would arrive in Williamsburg — a span of perhaps a week or more. Perhaps he should not have relied upon Clinton's promises, in view of their past differences and his distrust of his commander. In any event, relief would have to depend upon the size of Digby's reinforcement, information that Cornwallis lacked. Nor could he have been expected to assume that Digby's fleet would necessarily be too small because of Clinton's former parsimoniousness, since the force when it finally did come was sizable, consisting of twenty-five ships of the line, eight frigates, and seven thousand troops.

The Earl also argued later that he did not attack because Sir Henry's orders did not give him "the smallest particle of discretionary power, different from holding the posts that I occupied." [14] Here Cornwallis hedged. Clinton never once ordered him to stay and let his entire army be taken, nor would any sane commander in chief have given such an order. Furthermore, when Cornwallis marched to Virginia, he did so without awaiting orders from Sir Henry. The Earl's excuse resembles one used by Burgoyne, who also pleaded positive orders as a reason for his surrender. Like Burgoyne, Cornwallis wrote this explanation after the event. It is doubtful that he would have heeded any orders requiring him to stay at Yorktown, had he seen a good chance of breaking out with minimum losses.

But was there a good chance between September 17 (when he learned of the lack of naval success) and September 26 (when all of Washington's troops had arrived in Williamsburg)? Cornwallis would have faced an army superior in numbers and equal in discipline to his own. He would have had to desert the loyalists who had taken shelter with him. He would have had to abandon his numerous sick. He would have had to leave behind all the ships at Yorktown — several galleys and armed transports, three frigates and a sloop — along with their officers and men (perhaps a thousand sailors). He would have had to sacrifice his artillery, wagons, provisions, and stores — in short, most of his equipment. Presuming he had won his battle, he would then have had to abandon his wounded and would perhaps have marched away from Yorktown with no more men than he had commanded when he first entered Virginia. Then where would he have gone? Washington approached from the north. Should he have tried to march south without food, stores, or provisions and without a possibility of getting any? He was convinced that such a course would bring disaster to the British cause in America and obloquy to himself. Certainly Clinton would never have excused his risking an army and British fortunes on so desperate a gamble.

Cornwallis regarded waiting for the relief that Clinton had promised as far better than risking everything in a battle with Lafayette. If relief came soon, then the combined British armies might give Washington the decisive blow that would end the Revolution. Even if help did not come in time to save him, surrender of his army would probably be no more disastrous to the British cause than risking that army in an attack on Lafayette. On September 16 and 17 he made up his mind. "If I had no hopes of relief," he wrote to Clinton, "I would rather risk an action than defend my half-finished works. But as you say Admiral Digby is hourly expected, and promise every exertion to assist me. I do not think myself justifiable in putting the fate of the war on so desperate an attempt." [15] The Earl estimated that he had six weeks of provisions. As things turned out, he only needed a five weeks' supply.

Nicholas Creswell, the English traveler who visited America during the earlier years of the Revolution, described Yorktown as "a pleasant town situated upon York River which is navigable for the largest ships. Close to the town there are several very good Gentlemen's houses built of brick and some of their gardens laid out with the greatest taste of any I have seen in America." [16] That description still fits Yorktown today, preserved much as it was in Cornwallis' time. Inns, public buildings, and Georgian brick or frame houses with their gardens lined the main road of the village, which ran roughly northwest, above and parallel to the river. Below the main road on the waterfront were the wharves, warehouses, and grog shops. Although a small town, with not more than three thousand inhabitants in 1781, it contained its share of prosperous merchants, tobacco planters, shopkeepers, innkeepers, slaves, and indentured servants. Visitors besides Creswell found Yorktown a charming, prosperous, and tranquil community.

But in September of 1781 the sound of picks and shovels, grunting and swearing, and occasional musketry disturbed the tranquillity as British soldiers and Negroes sweated to complete the unfinished works. Cornwallis had started, and now hastened to complete, an outer and inner line of fortifications, running roughly in a semicircle from east of the village around to the west. The outer position, about half a mile in advance of the inner one, afforded some natural defenses. A ravine west of Yorktown extended from the river "nearly half way around the inner works." Behind it along the marshy ground ran Yorktown Creek. Another stream, Wormley Creek, began about half a mile to the west of the ravine and curved slightly northeasterly. Natural obstacles thus offered some protection to the flanks of Cornwallis' outer works.

The allied enemy army could advance along any of four major roads, all of them commanded by the outer works. One road came from Williamsburg along the river, approaching Yorktown from the west. But outside the town a second road branched off to the right and ran in a southeasterly direction to intersect another road, the Hampton Road, which ran almost due north into Yorktown and cut between the ravine and Wormley Creek. From the east, a fourth road came into Yorktown, past the house of a local merchant, Augustine Moore, into Yorktown. The Earl built small fortifications on his left near the head of Wormley Creek and a large redoubt — the Fusiliers' redoubt manned by the 23d — on his right near the river and to the right of the Williamsburg Road. Near the Fusiliers' redoubt he anchored several armed vessels to command and assist it. But he concentrated chiefly on the land between the ravine and Wormley Creek, where nature had not helped very much. Here he built three redoubts, one on each side of the inland fork of the Williamsburg Road and the third on the left of the Hampton Road.

His inner works needed yet closer attention, for few natural obstacles lay between the outer fortifications and the village itself. Around Yorktown, Cornwallis constructed ten redoubts. He put two on his right facing the river road from Williamsburg, three in the back of the town, and three along his left facing downriver. Two more, the most important of the siege, known as redoubts 9 and 10, stood in advance of the redoubts on his left as an additional strength to them. The ground here offered the best advantage to a besieging force which had penetrated the outer lines, so here Cornwallis wished to make himself the strongest. In the fourteen batteries along his earthworks he planted sixty-five guns. Unfortunately, he had nothing larger than 18-pounders, and to get some of them he stripped the navy.[17]

On the whole, Yorktown offered few advantages to the defender. The outer works could employ some natural defenses, but to be effective, they required considerably more troops than Cornwallis commanded. When the siege began in earnest, toward the end of September, the defending force present and fit for duty — officers as well as rank and file of the British, German, and provincial troops, both infantry and cavalry — numbered 5129 men.[18] In addition to the infantry and cavalry, the army had 632 officers and men from various small (or badly re-

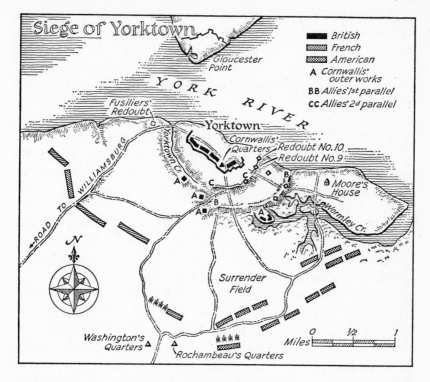

duced) units, including the guides and pioneers, artillery, and North Carolina Volunteers. Cornwallis could also call perhaps 800 sailors and marines from the British warships.[19] Against this rather modest army, Washington would bring to bear an overwhelming Franco-American force. The Continentals numbered over 5000, the militia over 3000, and the French about 8000.[20] In other words, the British were outnumbered two or three to one.

The Earl took up his headquarters in the house of Thomas Nelson (secretary to the former colony) — a structure that occupied commanding ground in the southeastern part of the village. Doubts beset him. From his headquarters he could see past the better houses, inns, and public buildings that lined the main road on the bluffs above the river to the point where the Williamsburg Road entered the village. Washington might come down that road, but if so he would probably not concentrate his force there. More than any other, that ground favored Cornwallis, guarded as it was by the Fusiliers' redoubt and by ships in the York River that commanded the approaches. To the Earl's left, south of the village, the position between the ravine and Wormley Creek seemed weaker. How long could the redoubts there hold off the allies? To the southeast, just ahead of his inner works, were redoubts 9 and 10. If they fell, could he hold Yorktown any longer?

It would make no sense, the Earl decided, to wait for the enemy to do his worst. Tarleton swept out to harass American militiamen who sniped away at the sweating British working parties. The navy sent fire ships against the French but caused them more fright than damage. All the while, the work continued: cutting trees, sharpening stakes, positioning artillery, and clearing woods to obtain a field of fire. Then on the morning of September 28 things changed. A picket in front of the working party on the right sent back word that the enemy was approaching. At last the waiting was over.

On September 17 Washington had boarded Grasse's flagship and persuaded the admiral to remain beyond his deadline of October 15. When the American commander returned to Williamsburg on the twenty-second, he found that his force, which had marched from New York to Head of Elk whence it had sailed in transports, had just arrived and begun to come ashore. They finished disembarking on the twenty-sixth. The next day Washington issued marching orders for 5:00 A.M. on September 28. The combined army filed out from Williamsburg in a single column — the French in advance of the Continentals — on the main road to Yorktown. Halfway there the army split into two segments: the French continued straight toward the western end of the British fortifications, while the Americans marched around to the right. The British picket which first raised the alarm, members of the light infantry commanded by Lieutenant Colonel Robert Abercrombie, had spotted French chasseurs and grenadiers.

Throughout that night and the following day, the allied force took up positions surrounding the Earl, from the York River on his northwest to Wormley Creek on his southeast. They deployed in a semicircle and divided between them the chores of the siege. The French took the western half of the semicircle, the Americans the eastern. Cornwallis let them encamp and establish their lines. But how long, he asked himself, should he hold his outer works against them? His enemies had not as yet brought forward their siege guns. Would they try to assault and carry the outer fortifications? The longer he held those works, the longer he could hold Yorktown. But sticking to them for as long as possible would cost many casualties and thus reduce his army's effectiveness for offensive action should help arrive. As the time arrived for the Earl to make another critical decision, once more, for the third time, external events decided matters for him.

On the evening of September 29 an express boat with another message from Clinton slipped by the French blockade. The commander in chief had met with his general officers and with Admirals Graves and Digby (the latter had reached New York on the twenty-fourth with three ships of the line). At that meeting, Sir Henry announced, it was "determined that about 5,000 men, rank and file, shall be embarked aboard the King's ships, and the joint exertions of the navy and army made in a few days to relieve you and afterwards co-operate with you. . . . There is every reason," he concluded, "to hope we start from hence the 5th October." [21]

It was that encouraging letter which prompted Cornwallis to

an act that gave the allies their first advantage. "I have this evening received your letter of the 24th," the Earl wrote Clinton on
the twenty-ninth, "which has given me the greatest satisfaction.
I shall retire this night within the works, and have no doubt, if
relief arrives in any reasonable time, York and Gloucester will
be both in possession of his Majesty's troops." [22] George Washington awoke on the morning of September 30 to find that his
enemy had abandoned his outer defenses without a fight. Had
the British general blundered terribly? Tarleton thought so. If
Cornwallis had held his outer line longer, Tarleton argued, he
might have bought himself enough time to hold out until Clinton's relief force arrived. Yet the Earl cannot have favored this
reasoning. He had a force of less than six thousand to hold a
position over two miles in circumference against almost treble
his numbers. To spread them out evenly invited Washington to
concentrate against a particular point. To concentrate them
meant weakening one part in favor of another. On the other
hand, with his preponderant numbers, Washington could
threaten all areas and at the same time mass enough troops to
break through any weak points. Even if the outer works held
for a few extra days, would not the Earl have such high casualties there that the inner defenses would fall so much the sooner?
Tightening his lines, especially with help due to arrive in a few
days, seemed the best way to keep his army intact until Clinton
sailed up the river. Yet Cornwallis would probably have fought
in his outer fortification, just as he would probably have fought
Lafayette and St. Simon, had not Clinton's messages promising
immediate help invariably arrived at exactly the crucial time
when a decision had to be reached.

On the same day the British abandoned the three redoubts of
their outer works between the ravine and Wormley Creek,
Washington's forces moved into them. But all was not jubilation for the American commander. Tarleton, eager for action,
ordered a lieutenant of his Legion to scout the Americans and

seize as many prisoners as possible. The lieutenant, moving along the abandoned redoubts, surprised Colonel Alexander Scammell of the light infantry reconnoitering with a small party. Tarleton said the Legionnaires, though fewer in number than the Americans, charged without hesitation and "brought off Colonel Scammell who was wounded in attempting the retreat." But the Americans held that Tarleton's butchers shot Scammell in the back. On the same day St. Simon's light infantry drove in Cornwallis' pickets in front of the Fusiliers' redoubt. Sharp skirmishing followed, but the 23d held its post without trouble.

Cornwallis knew the Americans and French would turn his abandoned outer works into an offensive line as soon as they could. They would collect sticks and shovel dirt to make gabions (baskets of earth) and fascines (bundles of brush and sticks). In the absence of natural cover, they would use these bundles to protect themselves while they dug trenches. Cornwallis could slow up their progress most effectively with his artillery. On the thirtieth he began to cannonade his enemy in earnest, and as September gave way to October, his fire grew fiercer. Surgeon James Thacher of the American army commented that during October 3 and 4 there came "a considerable cannonading from the enemy; one shot killed three men, and mortally wounded another. While the Rev. Mr. Evans, our chaplain, was standing near the commander-in-chief, a shot struck the ground so near as to cover his hat with sand. Being much agitated, he took off his hat, and said, 'See here, general.' 'Mr. Evans,' replied his excellency, with his usual composure, 'you had better carry that home, and show it to your wife and children.' " [23] Lieutenant Colonel St. George Tucker, of Lawson's Virginia militia, commented on October 2: "The Firing from the Enemies works was continued during the whole night at the distance of fifteen or twenty Minutes between every shot — By these means our works were interrupted altho' no Execution was done — Since Sunrise this Morning the firing has been much more frequent the Intermissions seldom exceeding five Minutes and often not more than one or two Minutes." [24]

The allies watched the British artillery. As soon as they saw a flash they stopped their work and dove for cover. But ceaseless cannonading during the first days of October cost Cornwallis precious ammunition. He could not very long continue the bombardment at the same rate, so he hit upon a device nearly as effective as firing off round after round. His artillerymen flashed a small bit of powder near the muzzles of their guns, "which is frequently mistaken for the fusing at the touch-hole." [25] Americans scattered when they saw the flash. The Earl also sent patrols out at night to disrupt the enemy's progress. These sorties inevitably brought some sharp and bloody skirmishing.

These tactics only delayed the allies, however, and as their work inexorably advanced, Cornwallis rearranged his forces. Tarleton's Legion, especially the cavalry, was of little use now that the allies had blockaded Yorktown so tightly. On the other hand, the enemy had not yet closely invested Gloucester: Tarleton could still meet the enemy there.

In early August Cornwallis had sent to Gloucester a force consisting of Simcoe's Rangers, a detachment of the 80th Infantry, a regiment of Hessians, light companies from the 23d and 82nd regiments, the Jagers, and the North Carolina Volunteers.[26] There they had built a line of entrenchments and four redoubts and had planted three batteries of artillery mounting nineteen guns. Simcoe, despite interference from General Weedon's Virginia militia, had been able to forage successfully beyond his lines. Late in September, Washington sent Weedon some reinforcements under the command of the Marquis de Choisy. They consisted of a force of eight hundred marines from the French fleet, together with the Duc de Lazun's legion of six hundred men, half infantry and half cavalry. Since they lacked the necessary artillery, they did not besiege Gloucester. But Choisy did interrupt foraging. Cornwallis thought that Tarleton's cavalry might still be used against Choisy. Besides, in Yorktown the Legion horses could do nothing but devour forage.

So during the evening of October 2 Tarleton took his men over to Gloucester in boats. The next morning Dundas sent out detachments from all units to forage in front of the works. Simcoe suggested that Tarleton should lead the operation, for he hoped that Lazun might mistake the Legion, fresh and strong, for the Rangers, now reduced in numbers. If Lazun attacked, Tarleton could ruin him. About three miles from Gloucester the British found corn and loaded it onto their wagons and bathorses. At 10:00 A.M. they finished and turned back toward Gloucester. Their route took them south down a long, narrow lane enclosed on both sides by fields. About half a mile before it reached the first British work, a small redoubt, the lane broadened to pass through an open field on its right and a woods on its left. Choisy moved his force south to invest Gloucester more closely at about the same time that the foraging party finished work. Lazun's cavalry (lancers armed with spears) served as an advance party. When they reached the long lane, a Legion lieutenant in command of a small rear guard observed their approach and reported it to his commander. Tarleton immediately faced about his entire command — the Legion and units of the Rangers and 17th — to dispute the passage with the French. But Tarleton, always impatient, refused to wait for his force to assemble and galloped ahead with a small group, eager to fight. He ran straight into a forest of lances. One of them plunged deep into the side of a horse next to Tarleton's. The beast fell against the Legion commander's mount, toppling both horse and rider. Tarleton scrambled to his feet looking anxiously for another horse. He might have been captured, but fortunately for him, by this time the rest of his cavalry had caught up and had attacked Lazun's. In the confusion Tarleton got hold of

another animal and charged again. But he and his men faced
cavalry just as good as themselves. They made no impression at
all upon the French (Tarleton asserted that it was because his
men forgot their training in a mad scramble to rescue him).
The dragoon leader soon ordered a retreat and managed to
reach the safety of his infantry, who faced about and deployed
on either side of the lane. Lazun's men galloped after the retreating Legionnaires straight into a withering fire from the
waiting British foot soldiers. The French, in turn, retreated to
their infantry, who had just reached the broader portion of the
lane. The Legion commander, now badly outnumbered, retired
beyond the British redoubt and into the Gloucester works.
Choisy then invested the town closely. In this, his last cavalry
action of the American Revolution, Banastre Tarleton had been
as brave, as dashing, and as foolish as ever.[27]

His spirit chafed at the prospect of prolonged inactivity, but
he did not have to take the physical punishment that soon befell
his comrades across the river. Cornwallis had bombarded his
opponents fiercely before Washington had been able to reply in
kind. Now, however, the American commander had brought
forward his own artillery. The guns had come by water from
Head of Elk and had landed at the James River. The gun
teams, however, had gone round to the peninsula by land. They
did not arrive fast enough or in sufficient numbers to suit Washington, who used his own baggage wagons and animals to haul
the artillery to Yorktown. He urged all officers to follow his example. By October 6 his cannons had reached the siege lines and
he could begin to return Cornwallis' fire with interest.

From that day on, the siege became a straightforward matter.
The art of the siege had been perfected, or at least systematized,
a century before by Vauban, in the service of Louis XIV. According to Vauban's method, the besieging force first surrounded the enemy fortress and then began to approach it by
means of a series of parallel lines. The "first parallel," or outer-

most one, was a trench dug parallel to the walls of the fort. When completed, it gave housing to the siege guns which, thus protected, could cannonade the defenders at close range and weaken their defense. At Yorktown, Washington concentrated his parallels on Cornwallis' left, because the ravine on the Earl's right inhibited such an operation. The allies' first parallel ran from a point near the British center for two thousand yards around to the York River. The distance of this trench from the Earl's lines varied from six hundred to eight hundred yards. The area of greatest separation was near the river, where redoubts 9 and 10 stood in advance of the British inner works. From the first parallel, the besieging force dug "approach trenches" toward the fortifications in a zigzag pattern, thus affording maximum protection from artillery and musket fire. From the approach trenches the attackers normally dug a second parallel and brought more heavy guns up to it. Washington's second parallel, between three hundred and five hundred yards in advance of the first, would be ineffective until it reached the river. It could not reach the river, however, until the allies captured redoubts 9 and 10, which stood directly in their line of advance. Once Washington carried those redoubts, his second parallel would move him close enough to fire his siege guns at point-blank range against the British defenses. Then the Yorktown works would quickly become a shambles. Cornwallis knew, for a century of warfare had proven it, that without relief no hope existed for him and his garrison once the siege began. Almost powerless, he had to watch the ineluctable approach of the deadly parallels, awaiting with resignation the breach of his lines and the moment of surrender. His only hope lay in prolonging the process until help arrived, and he could only do that by sorties against the allied working parties digging the trenches and parallels. He might chase them out of their works momentarily, fill in their ditches, and spike their guns. But sorties only delayed. Unrelieved, Yorktown must fall.

On the morning of October 7 Cornwallis arose to an ominous

sight. A long embankment, running from his center to the river on his left, had suddenly appeared. During the dark, rainy night of October 6, Washington had begun work on his first parallel, and the British had neither seen nor heard him. The embankment now gave cover to the Americans and French who labored at digging trenches and enlarging the parallel. To distract attention from this work, the French under St. Simon had constructed another parallel in front of the Fusiliers' redoubt. From that protection, allied artillery could threaten any attempts to break out in that direction and could fire on British ships in the river.

Cornwallis had not known precisely, but he had guessed, where Washington intended to dig the main parallels. He had kept up an artillery barrage all through the night of the sixth. Nonetheless, his gunners failed to do significant damage to the working parties. (The heaviest casualties he inflicted on the enemy were those suffered by the French under St. Simon, who had launched a false attack on the Fusiliers' redoubt.) Rain and darkness had worked, as so often in the past, to the Americans' advantage. Rain inhibited effective use of his artillery, and darkness prevented the Earl from spotting the working parties. He apparently directed most of his fire during the night of the sixth against the redoubts that he had abandoned and the Americans had taken over.

The Franco-American force now exerted itself to construct sites for batteries within the first parallel. By the logical rules of siege warfare, Cornwallis should have made sorties against these working parties. But he had resolved to preserve his force until relief came, so he kept his men within their lines. During the next two days the French and Americans advanced their construction far enough to bring up artillery, mortars, and stores. On the afternoon of the ninth, the first parallel was completed. The British, who had pounded the enemy ceaselessly, now prepared to receive their punishment.

At 3:00 P.M. Washington opened his bombardment. The allied guns which were superior in numbers and in weight of metal — Washington had 24-pounders — did terrible damage. They devastated Yorktown. The defenders, who a moment before had carried out their disciplined routine among ordered rows of tents, now scrambled wildly for safety. Stephen Popp and his comrades of the Anspach regiments hurled their tents into ditches. "The enemy," Popp said, "threw bombs, one hundred, one hundred fifty, two hundred pounders; their guns were eighteen, twenty-four and forty-eight pounders. We could find no refuge in or out of town. The people fled to the waterside and hid in hastily contrived shelters on the banks, but many of them were killed by bursting bombs. More than eighty were thus lost, besides many wounded, and their houses utterly destroyed. . . . Soldiers and sailors deserted in great numbers." [28] "I saw bombs," observed another Anspacher, "fall into the water and lie there for 5, 6-8 and more minutes and then still explode. . . . The fragments and pieces of these bombs flew back again and fell on the houses and buildings of the city and in our camp, where they still did much damage and robbed many a brave soldier of his life or struck off his arm and leg." [29] Nor did the barrage spare officers. Artillery rounds blasted to pieces the Nelson house, Lord Cornwallis' headquarters. He found limited personal security by building a bunker in the secretary's garden. For staff meetings he had to use a cave near the waterside.

The Earl won momentary respite for his men on the tenth, however, when he performed an act of mercy. He allowed Secretary Nelson to leave the beleaguered city and to take shelter with the allied forces, and while Nelson was crossing over, the Americans held their fire. That morning also brought another note from Clinton, who again promised relief, though at a more distant date. A small boat had slipped by the French fleet and arrived at Yorktown bearing Major Charles Cochrane with Sir Henry's latest dispatch. (Poor Cochrane two days later went to the lines with Cornwallis and fired off one of the guns. As he looked over the parapet to note the effect of his fire, an enemy cannonball, which narrowly missed the Earl, took off his head.) "Your lordship," Sir Henry wrote, "may be assured that I am doing every thing in my power to relieve you by a direct move." Clinton hoped to get out of New York by October 12 but did not promise it.[30]

In the afternoon, after Nelson had reached safety, the allies resumed their bombardment with increased fury. They had now opened two new batteries: a French one on their left, opposite the Fusiliers' redoubt, mounting ten 18- and 24-pounders and six mortars; and an American one of four 18-pounders and two mortars. The French fire was particularly effective. Their artillerymen poured red-hot shot into the frigate *Charon* and reduced it to a blazing hulk. They also destroyed a few transports and forced the others to take shelter across the river at Gloucester. Six boatloads of British troops, who tried to creep upriver on the Gloucester side beyond Choisy's right flank, returned hastily amid a shower of balls and mortars. The French and American barrage grew so destructive that it reduced the British artillery response to about six shots an hour.

Pressure mounted relentlessly. On the next day two more French batteries, holding six 24-pounders, went into operation. At noon Cornwallis scribbled off a note to Clinton. "Nothing but a direct move to York River, which includes a successful naval action, can save me. . . . We have lost about seventy men, and many of our works are seriously damaged. With such works, on disadvantageous ground, against so powerful an attack, we cannot hope to make a very long resistance." For the rest of the afternoon the Earl helplessly watched the bombardment rip apart his position. At 5:00 P.M. he added a postcript to his note: since writing at noon, he told Clinton, he had lost another thirty men.[31]

That night the allies began their second parallel. Cornwallis ought to have made sorties, and both the French and Americans expected an attack. But patrols only clashed, and the Americans derived more excitement from the shot and shells whirring over their heads from their own guns in the first parallel than from any activity by the British. Sometimes the allied artillerymen cut their fuses too short and their shells exploded over their own working party. But the Americans found time for humor amidst the brilliant fireworks. At dusk, Steuben's men, including the Pennsylvanians, carried out shovels, spades, hoes, and fascines to begin the parallel. Despite a wound in the left thigh, Wayne went with them. As he hobbled about, encouraging his men, a shell suddenly whistled by. Steuben, who had been closely supervising the work, threw himself into the half-dug trench, and Wayne stumbled in after him, missing his footing and falling upon the Baron. "Ah ha, Wayne," Steuben supposedly remarked, "you cover your general's retreat." [32]

Cornwallis was in no mood to joke when he looked out over his lines on the morning of the twelfth. The second parallel, now deep enough to cover the men working in it, had progressed amazingly. In some places only two hundred yards from the British guns, it had crept directly toward redoubts 9 and 10. Just a thousand feet from them the new trench ended in an epaulement, a breastwork which could hold a large number of men. As the allies worked to enlarge and strengthen this parallel, their batteries maintained an incessant barrage. "One saw men lying nearly everywhere," Anspacher Johann Doehla remarked, "who were mortally wounded and whose heads, arms, and legs had been shot off. Also one saw wounded continually dragged and carried down by the water. Likewise on watch and on post in the lines, on trench and work details, they were wounded by the terribly heavy fire; and soldiers and sailors were always digging in the sand by the water." [33] Yet Cornwallis could do nothing but watch. Many of his own guns had by now been silenced, and every time he showed the others, he invited a devastating fire. His men suffered horribly. The wounded increased hourly, but so too did the sick. According to Commissary Stedman, illness prostrated men as rapidly as American shot and shell.[34] Supplies — both of food and ammunition — were running short. The Earl determined, if his ammunition held out, to slaughter his horses and salt them for food.[35]

During the next three days the allies concentrated their fire on redoubts 9 and 10, which blocked the path of their second parallel to the river. Cornwallis had fortified these strongpoints heavily with fraise work (sharpened stakes driven into the earthwork and pointing upward) and abatis (trees felled lengthwise and entangled with each other, their branches in the direction of the enemy trimmed and sharpened). He had stationed a mixed force of Hessians and British, about one hundred twenty men, under Lieutenant Colonel Henry Johnson of the 17th to hold number 9. Major James Campbell of the 71st and about fifty men occupied number 10. Washington intended to carry both fortifications by direct assault and then incorporate them into his second parallel.

He chose the night of October 14 for this dangerous work. For the attack on number 10 he gave Lafayette command of four hundred American light infantry. The Marquis in turn gave Lieutenant Colonel Alexander Hamilton the honor of leading the storming party, the "forlorn hope." To Rochambeau fell the task of carrying number 9, and for the assault he selected four hundred men from the Gatinois and Royal Deux-Ponts Regiments. He placed them under the command of Major General the Baron de Vioménil, who entrusted the "forlorn hope" to Lieutenant Colonel the Comte Guillaume de Deux-Ponts, the brother of the colonel of the Deux-Ponts Regiment.

To the British redcoats crouched in redoubt 10 on the night of October 14, deliverance must have seemed far away. Their fortification stood directly above the river, and they could hear clearly the lapping of the tidal waters against the shore. Many of them must have searched the river day after day for the British fleet which never came. On that night, they may have been more tense than before, for they knew the allied assault upon their stronghold must come soon. Anxious hours passed. Suddenly a noise at the abatis alerted them. American sappers and miners had reached the obstruction and were struggling to clear it with axes. The redcoats rushed to the edge of the parapet and hurled down hand grenades. But they barely had time to level their muskets before the enemy swarmed over them. They could not run, because Lieutenant Colonel John Laurens had taken a party to the rear of the redoubt and cut off escape. They struggled briefly in the dark against a thicket of bayonets, and then they surrendered. The Americans, like Wayne's men at Stony Point, had charged with unloaded weapons.

Vioménil and Deux-Ponts had a bloodier struggle for number 9. Although artillery had damaged it less than Washington believed and although the obstacles in front of it were stronger than those around number 10, the French charged valiantly. A Hessian challenged them — "Wer da" — at one hundred twenty paces, but they hurried on. At the abatis they hesitated. Redcoats poured a withering fire into their ranks while their engineers strove to clear away the tangle of trees and branches. The obstructions removed, they scaled the earthworks and fired in at the defenders. No bayonet struggle ensued, for the British, outnumbered more than three to one, surrendered once the French reached the top and opened fire. Johnson, however, managed to escape to his lines. The two actions that night cost Cornwallis six officers and sixty-seven men taken prisoner, and twenty-six killed.[36]

On the morning of the fifteenth, Cornwallis saw the net drawing ever tighter around him. The allies had wasted little time in self-congratulation after taking the redoubts. Instead they had gone right to work turning 9 and 10 into part of the fortifications for their second parallel. The Earl now hurried off another dispatch, the last before his surrender. He informed Sir Henry of what had happened the previous night and concluded: "My situation here becomes very critical; we dare not show a gun to their old batteries, and I expect their new ones will open tomorrow morning. Experience has shown that our fresh earthen works do not resist their powerful artillery, so that we shall soon be exposed to an assault in ruined works, in a bad position, and with weakened numbers. The safety of the place is therefore so precarious, that I cannot recommend that the fleet and army should run great risk in endeavouring to save us." [37]

Cornwallis now planned his final defense. He knew that the enemy batteries, once mounted in the second parallel, might force his surrender in hours. A desperate sortie could postpone the awful moment. During the day, therefore, he selected the group to undertake such a venture: Lieutenant Colonel Robert Abercrombie and three hundred fifty men of the light infantry and Guards. Their task was to spike the enemy's guns — that is, block up the touchholes. A picture readily springs to mind of the Earl, tired and haggard, huddled in the cave beside the York River outlining to his subordinates their chances. Perhaps he told the lieutenant colonel that little hope remained, that Clinton probably would not come, indeed that he himself had advised the commander in chief not to take the risk. No glory would attach to Abercrombie if he succeeded, however brilliantly. At best he would purchase only a few days' reprieve for the beleaguered garrison. Some of his men would die, but the British army would probably have to surrender anyway.

Undaunted, Abercrombie crept out of the lines around 4:00 A.M. on the sixteenth. He slipped into the second parallel beyond the American position and turned westward to the area held by the French. There he surprised a small detachment of the Agenois Regiment, many of whom were asleep, and spiked

four guns of their battery. He then moved into the French communication trench near the first parallel. He halted momentarily, however, when he found close at hand another battery
which he could not identify. It was that of the American Captain Joseph Savage. Savage called out: "What troops?" Abercrombie shouted, "French," and his hesitation over, urged his
men forward. "Push on, my brave boys," he yelled, "and skin
the bastards." The lieutenant colonel managed to spike three
guns in the American battery before the Comte de Noailles,
close at hand with a party of grenadiers, heard the noise and
counterattacked. The Frenchman drove Abercrombie off, killing eight of his men and taking twelve of them prisoner.[38]

Unfortunately, the lieutenant colonel's gallant sortie had not
fulfilled its purpose. His troops had spiked the guns too hastily,
and within a few hours the allies had their batteries operating
again. Cornwallis, left to himself without Clinton's inhibiting
letters and no longer expecting relief to arrive, had tried a vigorous sortie. It had failed. Now he had only one more chance
— escape.

During the day of October 16, Abercrombie's failure became
apparent. The clamor of perhaps a hundred guns engulfed the
British in a pandemonium of sound. The boom of artillery was
punctuated by the crash of walls and roofs. The very earth
shook. Rest, indeed thought, became all but impossible. Only
the waterfront caves offered some slight relief from the worst of
the din. In the midst of this deafening uproar, Cornwallis
planned his last desperate gamble. Under cloak of darkness, his
army would steal across the river and the next day attack Choisy.
With luck and determination, it just might save them.

That night the Earl sent Lord Chewton, one of his aides-de-
camp, across the river with orders for Tarleton (now in command at Gloucester) to prepare to attack Choisy the next morning. Tarleton sent back boats to ferry over the British army.
Before eleven o'clock Cornwallis sent off the first wave of troops

— the light infantry, most of the Guards, and the 23d. Although allied artillery had destroyed many of his boats, he figured that he had enough — sixteen large vessels — to get his force across in three trips. Of course, he would have to leave behind all his artillery and stores, and he also intended to leave a detachment to surrender for the sick and wounded, and the townspeople.

All went well initially. The first group crossed the river and reached Gloucester around midnight. The boats returned and loaded the second wave. Then, as had happened so often before, the weather turned against Cornwallis. Well might the Americans be convinced that their cause had divine favor. A violent squall blew up. The boats could not take over the second group. The few that had already started were scattered downriver. Not until 2:00 A.M. did the weather begin to moderate. By then it was too late. The Earl could not ferry the rest of his army to Gloucester in time to prepare it for an attack on Choisy. Having part of his army on one side of the river and part on the other invited an immediate assault by Washington, an assault that could not fail and would bring the British heavy losses. So the lieutenant general ordered back to Yorktown the troops he had sent to the point, and they returned the morning of the seventeenth.

That morning the fire grew unbearable. "The whole peninsula," James Thacher observed, "trembles under the incessant thundering of our infernal machines." [39] "Our works," Cornwallis related, "were going to ruin, and not having been able to strengthen them by an abatis, nor in any other manner but by a slight fraizing, which the enemy's artillery were demolishing wherever they fired, my opinion entirely coincided with that of the engineer and principal officers of the army, that they were in many places assailable in the forenoon, and that by continuance of the same fire for a few hours longer, they would be in such a state as to render it desperate, with our numbers, to attempt to maintain them. We at that time could not fire a single gun; only one 8 inch and little more than 100 Cohorn shells remained." [40]

About 10:00 A.M. Cornwallis sent a drummer out to mount a parapet and sound the parley. No one could hear him over the din, but his uniform was unmistakable. Then an officer with a white handkerchief walked out in front of the British defenses. Firing ceased. An American ran forward to blindfold and escort him through the American lines to Washington. The British officer presented his commander's letter to Washington. It read:

> SIR;
>
> I propose a cessation of hostilities for twenty-four hours, and that two officers may be appointed by each side, to meet at Mr. Moore's house, to settle terms for the surrender of the posts of York and Gloucester. [41]

Charles, second Earl Cornwallis, had proposed a surrender that would virtually end all British authority in the thirteen former colonies. On the same narrow peninsula, only a few miles from Yorktown, lay Jamestown, where the English experience in America had begun. The proposal for surrender came on October 17, the anniversary of Burgoyne's surrender at Saratoga.

After some haggling — Washington first insisted on reading Cornwallis' proposals before granting a parley, and Cornwallis in turn forwarded some unacceptable conditions — both sides agreed that commissioners should meet on the eighteenth to work out terms of capitulation. All firing ceased and during the night of the seventeenth St. George Tucker remarked that "a solemn stillness prevailed — the night was remarkably clear & the sky decorated with ten thousand stars — numberless Meteors gleaming thro' the Atmosphere afforded a pleasing resemblance to the Bombs which had exhibited a noble Firework the night before, but happily divested of all their Horror." [42]

On the following day the Viscomte de Noailles, Lafayette's brother-in-law, and Lieutenant Colonel John Laurens, representing the Americans, met with Major Alexander Ross (Cornwallis' aide-de-camp) and Lieutenant Colonel Thomas Dundas of the 80th. They assembled at the Moore House, a handsome, two-story frame building, which commanded a fine view of the river down an avenue of trees. All afternoon and late into the night the commissioners sat working out the final details. At last they took their respective commanders rough drafts of the articles.

Washington had granted Cornwallis an honorable surrender. He allowed the Earl full use of the sloop *Bonetta* to carry troops and dispatches to New York, permitted British officers to retain their side arms, and let individuals keep their private effects. The garrisons of York and Gloucester were to be prisoners of the United States, the naval personnel to be prisoners of the French. Washington refused the Earl only one article — that "natives or inhabitants of different parts of this country, at present in York or Gloucester are not to be punished on account of having joined the British army." [43] Cornwallis naturally wanted to protect his loyalists, but the American leader would not accept that article on the grounds that loyalists were a matter for the civil government rather than the army.

So on the afternoon of October 19, British redcoats marched out to the surrender field and grounded arms. Many of them muttered or wept or cursed. A grand concourse of people flocked in from the surrounding countryside to watch the ceremony, carried on with all the pomp and pageantry of the eighteenth century.

Cornwallis, however, pleaded illness and remained in his headquarters. Perhaps the illness was psychological rather than physical. Certainly he, an English peer, had suffered a grand humiliation. A different humiliation was in store for his Legion commander. On October 23, as Tarleton rode through the streets of Yorktown, a Mr. Day claimed his horse and forced him to dismount then and there.[44] On the twenty-seventh, Cornwallis received George Washington formally at his headquarters (probably the fine house of Governor Thomas Nelson). Ironically, the Americans learned the following day that Clinton and Graves had finally arrived outside the Capes. They had left New York on the very day of the surrender, and were as ineffectual now as they had been in the past. They cruised offshore in heavy weather until their boats could confirm the loss of Yorktown. Then on October 29, they turned around and went back to New York.

Cornwallis gave the usual parole as a prisoner not to talk or to act against the United States until he had been exchanged and to report to whatever place the American commander in chief designated whenever required. In return, he had full liberty of movement — could even go to Europe if he wished. Since the terms of surrender had not allowed him to protect the loyalists in his army, he packed as many of them into the *Bonetta* as she would hold and sent her off. In New York they would be exchanged as prisoners of war.

The Earl completed a long dispatch to Clinton, recapitulating the events that had led to his surrender.[45] Then he cleared up other business and gathered together his papers and belongings. On November 4 he boarded the *Cochrane* and sailed down the York River toward New York and a meeting with Clinton.[46] Feeling the chill winter breath of defeat, he left behind him the Americans basking in their prolonged Indian summer. The passage was rough and stormy — they did not make New York until November 19 — but no rougher and stormier than the Earl's own thoughts. More than likely, he spent at least some of his time in sad and grateful tribute to the brave officers and men who had fought so willingly at his side. But soldiers must think of the future rather than the past. What would Clinton say? Far more important, what would the King and Parliament say when he returned to England? Was he, like Burgoyne and Howe, to face a parliamentary "inquiry"? Was obloquy to be his cup? As his ship rolled and heaved, he may already have begun pulling his thoughts into the body of a defense. For whom was it symbolic — for Cornwallis or for Clinton — that the *Cochrane,* after being in utmost danger of being lost, at last made a safe landing in a fog so thick that none could see land?

Notes
Select Bibliography

Notes

Prologue

(*pages 1-3*)

1. Edward M. Riley, ed., "St. George Tucker's Journal of the Siege of Yorktown, 1781," *William and Mary Quarterly*, 3d ser., V (July, 1948), 391–392, quoted in George F. Scheer and Hugh F. Rankin, *Rebels and Redcoats* (New York, 1957), p. 491.
2. According to St. George Tucker, Cornwallis built a "kind of grotto" for shelter at the foot of Nelson's garden. See "Tucker's Journal," *William and Mary Quarterly*, V, 386–387, in Scheer and Rankin, *Rebels*, p. 485.
3. Cornwallis actually had 5950 men, but only 4017 were fit for duty. See Public Record Office 30/11/103, f. 35: "State of the Army in Virginia under the command of Lieut. Genl. Earl Cornwallis, October 18, 1781." The Public Record Office 30/11 series comprises the Cornwallis Papers.
4. "Major Jackson's Mss.," Thomas Balch, ed., *Letters and Papers Relating Chiefly to the Provincial History of Pennsylvania, with Some Notice of the Writers* (Philadelphia, 1855), pp. 284–285: quoted in Scheer and Rankin, *Rebels*, p. 492.
5. The incident was recorded by Count Matheiu Dumas, *Memoirs of His Own Time*, 2 vols. (Philadelphia, 1839), I, 52n–53n: quoted in Scheer and Rankin, *Rebels*, p. 494. Modern scholars who have studied the Yorktown campaign in great detail question that the British ever played "The World Turned Upside Down." So many bands — French, British, German, and American — were at Yorktown that one would be

surprised if the tune, a very popular one, were not played sometime during the surrender ceremony. There is no reason to suppose British musicians did not play it, and, in any event, it was particularly appropriate. The American Revolution, to its participants, was full of symbolism. The authors themselves find some of the events striking and symbolic — the riderless white horse at King's Mountain, Cornwallis proposing to surrender on the anniversary of Saratoga. On that warm October day the world did turn upside down. The British knew it, and their musicians may well have expressed it.

Dumas' version of the surrender has also been questioned, especially the "never from such a good hand." However, Washington was the embodiment of eighteenth-century etiquette and followed precisely the traditional ceremonies involved in a surrender. Events may not have gone precisely as Dumas described them, but most eyewitnesses agreed on the general outlines of the ceremony, and it was sufficiently close to Dumas' picture to warrant our using his version.

Chapter 1

(*pages 7–16*)

1. Cornwallis to Henry Dunlas, Aug. 12, 1787: P.R.O. 30/11/150, ff. 34–37. When writing in a lighter vein to his son, Cornwallis conjured up a picture of the blue riband of the Garter, to which he had just been elected, stretched across his "fat Belly." See Cornwallis to Lord Brome, Dec. 28, 1786: Charles Ross, ed., *The Correspondence of Charles First Marquis Cornwallis*, 3 vols. (London, 1859), I, 247.

2. Charlotte Madan to Cornwallis, Jan. 22, 1791: P.R.O. 30/11/40, ff. 178–181.

3. Cornwallis to the Duke of York, Apr. 27, 1794: P.R.O. 30/11/277, ff. 41–42.

4. For the life of Sir Thomas see Leslie Stephen and Sidney Lee, eds., *Dictionary of National Biography*, 63 vols. (London, 1885–1900).

5. We are indebted for some of this information to Mrs. Christopher Storey, at the time of this writing the wife of the headmaster of Culford School. See also William White, *History, Gazeteer, and Directory of Suffolk and the Towns Near Its Borders* . . . (Sheffield, 1844), pp. 684–685.

6. John Nolen, ed., *The Art of Landscape Gardening by Humphrey Repton, Esq., Including His Sketches and Hints on Landscape Gardening and Theory and Practice of Landscape Gardening* (Boston, 1907), p.

192, has a diagram of Culford before and after the first Marquis'
alterations. More valuable is a letter from Charles Townshend to
Cornwallis, Feb. 18, 1790: P.R.O. 30/11/34, ff. 383–386. Townshend
describes the interior in detail.

7. The history of the Cornwallis family is taken mostly from G. E. Cokayne, *Complete Peerage of England, Scotland, Ireland, Great Britain
and the United Kingdom,* revised edition edited by Vicary Gibbs,
13 vols. (London, 1910–1949), III, 453–455. Kneller includes the
fourth Baron among his portraits of members of the Kit-Cat Club.
Letters from the first Earl to the Duke of Newcastle in 1745, 1747,
and 1750 are in British Museum, Additional Manuscripts 32, 704,
ff. 549–550; 32,713, ff. 20–21; and 32,720, ff. 19–20. Correspondence
concerning the borough in 1743 and 1758 may be found in P.R.O.
30/11/1, ff. 8, 11.

8. According to Basil Williams, *Whig Supremacy,* 2d ed. (Oxford, 1962),
pp. 22–23, between 1714 and 1760 the number of peers sitting in the
House of Lords remained almost constantly at 220. Of these aristocrats, 16 were representative peers from Scotland and 26 were bishops
of the Church of England.

Chapter 2

(pages 17–29)

1. Christopher Hollis, *Eton, A History* (London, 1960), p. 56.
2. R. E. Austen-Leigh, *Eton College Lists, 1678–1790* (Eton College,
1907), p. 52. In his *The Eton College Register, 1753–1790* (Eton,
1921), p. 127, Austen-Leigh becomes more definite. He asserts that
Brome entered in January of 1753 and remained at Eton until 1754.
3. Austen-Leigh, *Eton College Lists,* pp. xli–xlii.
4. Hollis, *Eton,* p. 130.
5. Martin Whish to the second Duke of Newcastle, 1768. Whish's memorandum is in the Newcastle Papers deposited at the University of
Nottingham, NeC 3922 (bundle 29, no. 26).
6. Hollis, *Eton,* p. 127.
7. Sir H. C. Maxwell Lyte, *A History of Eton College, 1440–1875*
(London, 1877), p. 303, and Hollis, *Eton,* p. 134.
8. Lyte, *History of Eton,* p. 297.
9. For the Eton Club see Herbert Harris to Cornwallis, Nov. 23, 1790,
and notice of Cornwallis' election, Feb. 9, 1790: P.R.O. 30/11/148,
ff. 128–130. Although Cornwallis loved Eton, he never tried to fool

himself in later years that life there had been easy, and he troubled
to warn his son that the boy might face some unpleasantness. In a
letter to Brome on Dec. 12, 1787, for instance, Cornwallis commented on his son's prospective promotion from the fourth form to
the remove. Once out of the fourth form Brome would no longer
have a six o'clock lesson. But, the Earl warned, "in my time the
remove was not a very agreable place." See P.R.O. 30/11/276, f. 18.

10. Lady Waldegrave, who wished to leave a gift to Eton, negotiated
through Cornwallis. See William George Freeman to Cornwallis,
Aug. 15, 1794: P.R.O. 30/11/277, ff. 52–53, and Elaine Waldegrave to
Cornwallis, Sept. 9 and Sept. 21, 1794: P.R.O. 30/11/234, ff. 92–95.
A printseller, R. Livesy, aware of the Earl's love of his alma mater,
solicited Cornwallis in 1790 to subscribe for some prints representing
an Eton festival in which Lord Brome would appear. See Livesy to
Cornwallis, July 26, 1790: P.R.O. 30/11/277, ff. 37–38.

11. First Earl Cornwallis to first Duke of Newcastle, July 15, 1758:
B. M., Add. MSS. 32,881, ff. 353–354.

12. Duke of Cumberland to first Earl Cornwallis, July 1, 1757: *Cornwallis Corr.,* I, 4.

13. Captain de Roguin to first Earl Cornwallis, Jan. 23, 1758: *ibid.,* I, 4–6.

14. Viscount Brome to Thomas Townshend, Sept. 2, 1758: *ibid.,* pp. 7–8.

15. *Ibid.*

16. First Earl Cornwallis to first Duke of Newcastle, July 15, 1758:
B. M., Add. MSS. 32,881, ff. 353–354.

17. First Duke of Newcastle to first Earl Cornwallis, July 18, 1758:
B. M., Add. MSS. 32,881, ff. 355–356.

18. Viscount Brome to Thomas Townshend, Sept. 2, 1758: *Cornwallis
Corr.,* I, 7–8.

19. Hotham Papers, Beverly, Yorkshire, DDHO 4/94, war diary of Sir
Charles Hotham.

20. *Cornwallis Corr.,* I, 3, and Hotham Papers, DDHO 4/95, war diary
of Sir Charles Hotham, Sept. 21, 1759.

21. *Cornwallis Corr.,* I, 3.

22. Neither of these engagements was decisive, but they were sharp,
bloody fights, which gave the young Charles his baptism of fire as a
regimental commander. Ross, the editor of the Cornwallis Correspondence, mistakenly believes (I, 8) that Brome returned to England
upon his promotion to captain and did not return to Germany until
June 26, 1761. Yet Brome was in Germany in the autumn of 1760,
at which time his father, in England, was attempting to secure a
promotion for him in a guards regiment. See first Earl Cornwallis to

first Duke of Newcastle, Aug. 5, 1760: B. M., Add. MSS. 32,910, ff. 286–287; Newcastle to first Earl Cornwallis, Aug. 28, 1760: *ibid.*, ff. 387–388; and Viscount Brome to Newcastle, from Geismar, Germany, Sept. 16, 1760: B. M., Add. MSS. 32,911, ff. 351–352. Brome was still in Germany in late December. See William Faucett to Lieutenant Colonel Hotham, Dec. 31, 1760: Hotham Papers, DDHO 4/11. Indeed, Brome did not return to England until the middle of April in 1761. See Elizabeth, Countess Cornwallis, to William Cornwallis, Apr. 18, 1761: Historical Manuscripts Commission, *Report on Manuscripts in Various Collections* (Dublin, 1909), VI, 297.

23. First Duke of Newcastle to second Earl Cornwallis, July 9, 1762: B. M., Add. MSS. 32,940, ff. 304–305.

Chapter 3

(pages 30–46)

1. On one occasion Cornwallis wrote from Grantham to his friend the third Duke of Portland: "You will be surprized to find a letter dated from hence, but I must remind your grace that I am a fox-hunter." See letter of Nov. 18, 1764, in the Portland Papers, University of Nottingham. Cornwallis was constantly pestered by the first Duke of Newcastle to come to Clermont for parties of one sort or another, and Cornwallis' mother noted to William Cornwallis that the second Earl had "a great deal of company at Culford." See Elizabeth, Countess Cornwallis, to William Cornwallis, Oct. 19, 1764: H. M. C., *Rept. on MSS. Var. Coll.*, VI, 308.

2. Cornwallis' bank account, preserved at Hoare's Bank, 37 Fleet Street, is the basis for our estimate of his finances. Mr. Winder, the archivist, kindly went over the Cornwallis accounts with us at the bank. Further information may be found in P.R.O. 30/11/290, paper 1; 30/11/286; 30/11/289, part 2, ff. 107, 110; and 30/11/285, f. 8. The Cornwallis rent-rolls provide yet another, although a confusing, source of information concerning the Cornwallis finances. These documents are in the possession of Lord Iveagh, and through the gracious permission of Lord Elveden we were able to examine them. Iveagh Manuscripts consulted were 12/15; 28/2; 12/7; 12/10; 28/17; 12/8; 12/9; 12/6; 12/11; and 11/9.

3. For the Cornwallis Island see Elizabeth, Countess Cornwallis, to William Cornwallis, Apr. 11, 1764: H.M.C., *Rept. on MSS. Var. Coll.*, VI, 309.

4. Before he left to fight in America Cornwallis maintained a house in

Jermyn Street. Later he moved to Mansfield Street. After his return from India Cornwallis lived at Charles and then lower Grosvenor Streets. See P.R.O. 30/11/280, ff. 18–19, 55b; 30/11/231, ff. 81–82; and 30/11/237 (in which bundle all of Cornwallis' letters are addressed from lower Grosvenor Street).

5. Henry Cornwallis, another brother, was actually older than James, having been born in 1740. But he died in 1761 of a "violent fever" contracted in Germany. Like the second Earl, Henry had chosen a military career, but the fatigues of campaigning in Germany had so ruined his constitution that the fever carried him away easily.

6. For Frederick see *D. N. B.* The first Earl's letters to Newcastle in 1745, 1747, and 1750 are in B. M., Add. MSS. 32,704, ff. 549–550; 32,713, ff. 20–21; and 32,720, ff. 19–20.

7. See Elizabeth, Countess Cornwallis, to first Duke of Newcastle, Aug. 3, 1763: B. M., Add. MSS. 32,950, ff. 33–34.

8. James Cornwallis, Bishop of Lichfield, to William Pitt, Jan. 26, 1788: P.R.O. 30/8/125, ff. 278–279.

9. She explained her efforts in letters to William during 1762–1764. See H.M.C., *Rept. on MSS. Var. Coll.,* VI, 300–305.

10. First Earl Cornwallis to William Cornwallis, June 27, 1761: *ibid.,* p. 298.

11. Second Earl Cornwallis to William Cornwallis, Oct. 18, 1764: *ibid.,* p. 308.

12. Molly's charming letters to her brother William are in *ibid.,* pp. 310–313. They cover the years 1769 and 1770.

13. Charlotte's letters are in P.R.O. 30/11/277, ff. 14–18; 30/11/270, ff. 100–103; 30/11/140, ff. 178–181. Although they date from a later period than the one discussed here, they give some insight into what her character must have been earlier.

14. P.R.O., Treasury 60/25, p. 292, order of July 30, 1782, shows his original date of appointment as lieutenant of the Tower as Nov. 5, 1760. Order in council of Jan. 23, 1771, P.R.O. 30/11/272, ff. 5–6, officially made him constable. But the King had appointed him to the office on Nov. 21, 1770. See Sir John Fortescue, ed., *The Correspondence of King George the Third,* 6 vols. (London, 1927–1928), II, 172.

15. A memorandum from the first Earl Cornwallis to the first Duke of Newcastle, B. M., Add. MSS. 33,055, f. 296, claims that the appointment of chief porter to the Tower (worth £150 a year at the time of the memorandum) had always been the prerogative of the chief constable. The first Earl therefore desired Newcastle's leave to ap-

point one of his younger sons to the position. The first Earl was appointed constable of the Tower on Apr. 13, 1761. See *George III Corr.,* I, 23.

16. James Cornwallis to William Cornwallis, Feb. 11, 1773: H.M.C., *Rept. on MSS. Var. Coll.,* VI, 313. Madan still held the "job" in 1780, but his total pay was only £89 6s., 8d. See P.R.O., Treasury 1/562, f. 61.

17. Cornwallis to Sir William Medows, Feb. 17, 1790: P.R.O. 30/11/174, f. 37.

18. Cornwallis to Lord Brome, Dec. 10, 1798: P.R.O. 30/11/276, f. 92.

19. It should be added at this point that Cornwallis had five sisters. Only three of them were living by 1762. We have followed the lives of Charlotte and Mary but have uncovered no trace in the Cornwallis Papers of Charles' relationship with the third sister.

20. P.R.O. 30/11/281, ff. 46–48.

21. The house sold for roughly half the total (£1430). See P.R.O. 30/11/281, ff. 1–45.

22. Jemima, Countess Cornwallis, to William Cornwallis, Sept. 3, 1778: H.M.C., *Rept. on MSS. Var. Coll.,* VI, 317.

23. Reynolds' porrtait, engraved by J. Watson and published in 1771, cost the Earl £73 10s.. See P.R.O. 30/11/280, ff. 1–6.

24. Junius, the savage polemicist, attacked Cornwallis in 1770 for continuing to support the government after he had formally withdrawn from it in 1768: "Where was the memory of this noble lord, or what kind of intellect must he possess, when he resigns his place, yet continues in the support of administration, and, to shew his independence, makes a parade of attending Lord North's levee, and pays a public homage to the deputy of Lord Bute! Where is now his attachment, where are now his professions to Lord Chatham; — his zeal for the Whig interest of England, and his detestation of Lord Bute, the Bedfords, and the Tories? Since the time at which these were the only topics of his conversation, I presume he has shifted his company as well as opinions. Will he tell the world to which of his uncles or to what friend, to Philipson or a Tory lord, he owes the advice which has directed his conduct? I will not press him farther. The young man has taken a wise resolution at last, for he is retiring into a voluntary banishment in hopes of recovering the ruin of his reputation." See letter to the printer of the *Public Advertiser,* March 5, 1770, in *Junius . . .,* 2 vols. (Philadelphia 1836), II, 310. Junius not only failed to understand Cornwallis' political outlook, but also he prob-

ably missed the Earl's reason for retirement. According to the *D.N.B.* Cornwallis probably retired from politics in order to devote time to his new wife and family.

25. *Memoirs of the Life of the Most Noble Marquis and Earl Cornwallis* . . . (London, 1806), p. 4. It is possible that jaundice as well as heartbreak contributed to her death. She wrote to her brother-in-law William on Sept. 14, 1778, that she was "as yellow as an orange," and felt "very ill." See H.M.C., *Rept. on MSS. Var. Coll.,* VI, 318.

26. Cornwallis to William Cornwallis, New York, Oct. 21, 1779: *ibid.,* p. 322.

27. The other four peers were Camden, Shelburne, Paulet, and Torrington. Chief Justice Lord Camden opposed it as illegal. The majority which voted for the Declaratory Act in the House of Lords numbered 125.

28. G. H. Guttridge, *English Whiggism and the American Revolution* (Berkeley, 1966), supports and elaborates upon this view. But Ian Christie, "Was There a 'New Toryism' in the Earlier Part of George III's Reign?," *Journal of British Studies,* V (November, 1965), 60–76, closely examines the internal developments of the 1760's and 1770's and effectively refutes Guttridge's views.

29. The role of George III in creating the political turmoil that surrounded his early years on the throne has been the subject of endless controversy. But nation states have usually unified themselves in time of danger to face a common foe and have enjoyed the luxury of internal dissent once the external danger has passed. There may be all sorts of particular explanations for Britain's following the pattern at this time, but follow it the country did. That Britain did not achieve the same unity during the War for American Independence is also not surprising. It was, to many Englishmen, a civil war. The country came together again later to face the forces unleashed by revolutionary France.

30. For Kinnoul see *D.N.B.* For his political relations with Newcastle see Sir Lewis Namier, *The Structure of Politics at the Accession of George III* (London, 1957), *passim.*

31. First Duke of Newcastle to Cornwallis, June 7, 1763: B. M., Add. MSS. 32,949, ff. 54–55.

32. Cornwallis to first Duke of Newcastle, July 29, 1763: B. M., Add. MSS. 32,949, ff. 436–437.

33. Elizabeth, Countess Cornwallis, to William Cornwallis, Sept. 17, 1763: H.M.C., *Rept. on MSS. Var. Coll.,* VI, 303.

34. Reports of the spies on Wilkes to the secretaries of state, Saturday, Nov. 12, 1763: William James Smith, ed., *The Grenville Papers Being the Correspondence of Richard Grenville, Earl Temple, K.G., and the Right Hon. George Grenville, Their Friends and Contemporaries,* 4 vols. (London, 1852–1853), II, 159.
35. Cornwallis to first Duke of Newcastle, Aug. 2, 1765: B. M., Add. MSS. 32,968, ff. 440–441; and Mar. 21, 1766: B. M., Add. MSS. 32,974, ff. 204–205.
36. See Rockingham Papers, Sheffield Public Library, R 53: "List of Members of House of Lords & how they voted in connection with repeal of Stamp Act & related matters 1766."
37. The salary of £1000 attached to this office helped the Cornwallis finances considerably. The Earl's lawyer, James Vernon, drew the salary when the need arose. From it Cornwallis paid his fire insurance on Culford and interest due on £6000 worth of mortgages. See P.R.O. 30/11/280, ff. 1–6.
38. Editorial note in *Cornwallis Corr.,* I, 10. See also P.R.O. 30/11/280, ff. 11–12.
39. P.R.O. 30/11/272, ff. 1–4, 5–6.

Chapter 4

(*pages 49–78*)
1. William B. Willcox, *Portrait of a General, Sir Henry Clinton in the War of Independence* (New York, 1964), p. 14.
2. *Ibid.*
3. See Charles Matthew Clode, *The Military Forces of the Crown; Their Administration and Government,* 2 vols. (London, 1869), II, Chap. XVI, esp. pp. 76–79.
4. In the dragoons, neither cavalry nor infantry, but originally mounted infantry and scarcely distinguishable from cavalry during the American Revolution, the cornetcy came to £1102 10s. and the lieutenant colonelcy to £5350. See Warrant of July 24, 1782, in P.R.O. 30/11/274, ff. 48, 50; and the printed "Prices of Commissions, &c. as apportioned and fixed by His Majesty's Regulations," dated War Office, 14 August, 1783: P.R.O. 30/11/8, f. 223. Prices did not change between 1772 and 1783.
5. "Memorandum relative to the general rules of Promotion, War Office, 10th April 1786": P.R.O. 30/11/8, ff. 219–221b.
6. An ensign in the guards earned 10s. 4d., an ensign in infantry

6s. 8d., daily. See Edward P. Curtis, *The Organization of the British Army in the American Revolution* (New Haven, 1926), pp. 158–159.

7. See the petition of Nicholas Cowes to the Earl of Northumberland, Mar. 16, 1765: Northumberland Manuscripts, vol. 41, f. 272. These manuscripts are on microfilm at the University of Michigan.

8. "General Officers to Rank in North America," Northumberland MSS., vol. 50, f. 235.

9. Cecil Woodham-Smith, *The Reason Why* (New York, 1960), p. 22. Though Woodham-Smith's is a "popular" history, the authors have yet to read a better social study of the army. The book deals with a period later than Cornwallis', but the army governed itself in essentials the way it had done in the Earl's time.

10. *Ibid.*

11. Clode, *Military Forces,* II, 62. The legally minded English tested the purchase system in the courts, but as early as 1682 the lord chancellor upheld it in chancery. Clode, *Military Forces,* II, 64, states that Parliament must have approved the system because it had increased the soldier's pay regularly but had not altered substantially that of officers up to the time he was writing, the middle of the nineteenth century. Purchase had been the usage for several years before a royal warrant of Charles II in 1683 dealt with purchase as an established system. See Clode, *Military Forces,* I, 70.

12. Christopher Ward, *The War of the Revolution,* ed. John R. Alden, 2 vols. (New York, 1952), I, 25.

13. See a typical enlistment oath in P.R.O., T. 1/572, p. 100.

14. See Clode, *Military Forces,* II, Chap. XV, esp. pp. 10–18.

15. Curtis, *Organization,* pp. 51–59, discusses the changing standards of recruitment.

16. Before the Revolution it had required a minimum height of five feet six and a half inches, a minimum age of eighteen, and a maximum age of thirty.

17. Usually the punishments ran between twenty-five and fifty lashes, but a thousand lashes was not unknown. See "General Orders by Major General the Honourable William Howe," *Collections of the New York Historical Society* (New York, 1884), XVI, 288.

18. A regiment usually consisted of one, but sometimes two, battalions. A battalion ordinarily had eight companies of regular infantry, one of light infantry, and one of grenadiers — around 500 men. Cavalry or dragoon battalions usually numbered 250 to 300 men. But the regiments rarely contained their "normal" complements of men.

The hurly-burly of recruiting, the creation of larger companies than normal, the creation of provincial regiments during the Revolution, regimental losses in the war never made good, detachments from several regiments to form a special unit, and many other factors reduced the "system" to chaos. By 1782 the service was in terrible "confusion." A war office memorandum of Nov. 9, 1782: P.R.O., W.O. 2/42, p. 55, notes: "Some battalions are still at 100 men pr. compy, some at 85, some at 70, some at 56, and some at 30. Some corps [battalions] have 12 companies, some have 10, some have 8, some 6, some 5, and some 3." Part of the confusion resulted from the use made of their formations in tactical operations during the Revolution. They might, as mentioned above, put together detachments from various units to form a single corps (a word much used by the generals and meaningless save as a description of any unit of men), they might mass the light infantry or grenadiers from several battalions together for a single operation, or in other ways break up the regimental and battalion organization. The provincial British Legion, for example, the unit first created by Clinton which Cornwallis invariably detached from his main army for swift marches and sudden attacks against the Americans, had as its colonel a captain of the 17th Dragoons, as its lieutenant colonel a captain in the Manchester Dragoons, as its major a captain in the 4th regiment, and two captains, one from the new levies, and one from the marines. See list of regular officers holding provincial commissions, 8 January 1779: Sir Henry Clinton Papers, William L. Clements Library, Ann Arbor, Michigan.

19. Robert Pringle to Edward Hughes, Sept. 18, 1718 (O.S.): P.R.O., W.O. 4/21, p. 187.
20. For examples of the King's orders, transmitted through the adjutant general's office, see P.R.O., W.O. 3/24, p. 147; 3/8, pp. 153, 192–193; 3/26, pp. 167–169; and 3/27, pp. 32, 109. General orders for Mar. 23, 1792 (W.O. 3/27, pp. 101–105), enjoined uniform adherence to a drill manual based on Colonel David Dundas' experiments with troops in Ireland. If officers cherished those individual differences that confounded army manuevering, they still generally followed patterns similar to those outlined in the major military treatises of the century, such as Bland's *Treatise on Military Discipline*. Regimental commanders familiar with them could usually form their units in accordance with the wishes of a general wishing to march or maneuver an army.
21. Clode, *Military Forces*, I, 107–108.
22. Several works describe army clothing. Curtis, *Organization*, pp. 14–

15, and Ward, *War of the Revolution*, I, 27, discuss uniforms during
the American Revolution. R. M. Barnes, *A History of the Regiments
& Uniforms of the British Army* (London, 1962), Chap. II, pp. 54–79,
offers color illustrations of the various types of uniforms for infantry,
cavalry, dragoons, etc. But the King constantly fiddled with uniform
patterns and changed them often, even during wartime. The best source
for discovering the standard uniforms in any given year is the War
Office 3 series in the Public Record Office.

23. Clode, *Military Forces*, I, 108.

24. In 1783 the King repeated all the past abuses and once more enjoined
officers to follow his "established regulations," not to "suffer the
smallest deviation" from them. See W. O. 3/26, circular order of Aug.
8, 1783.

25. Woodham-Smith in *The Reason Why* vividly describes the elegant
and stupid Lord Cardigan and details his attentions to the dress of his
regiment just before the Crimean War. Cardigan was an example of
the extremes to which an aristocrat would go in order to present a
glittering regiment. To supply a regiment, even without glitter, was
not an inexpensive undertaking. In 1767 Cornwallis spent £1086
15s. 8d. on his regiment for everything from coats and breeches to
lace, drumbells, slings, and fifes. Next year his costs went up £100.
See P.R.O. 30/11/274, ff. 1–5.

26. Curtis, *Organization*, p. 94.

27. See for example, W. O. 1/890, p. 134.

28. This aspect of the army administration in America is discussed more
fully in pp. 231–237.

29. Henry Fox, Lord Holland, as paymaster general made the fortune
that his son Charles tried to throw away at the gaming table.

30. Roger Lamb, *Memoir of His Own Life* (Dublin, 1811), pp. 64–65.

31. Curtis, *Organization*, discusses the pay system. See also W.O. 2/24,
p. 61.

32. Regiments were allowed six fictitious names on their rolls, "warrant
men," who "received" pay. Furthermore, the army usually allowed
each company three "noneffective" men, in reality nonexistent men,
on its rolls, whose pay went into a fund called the company, noneffective, contingency, or stockpurse. That the officers still abused
the public trust with doctored muster lists, the King's injunctions
against the practice as late as the 1780's testify. See the affidavits of
July, 1788, and the circular from the war office for July 22, 1788, in
P.R.O. 30/11/25, ff. 492–493. Doctored muster lists also help explain
why reliable army lists are hard to find.

33. See *Baroness Von Riedesel and the American Revolution: Journal and Correspondence of a Tour of Duty*, trans. by Marvin L. Brown (Chapel Hill, 1965), p. xxii, and John Burgoyne, *A State of the Expedition from Canada* (London, 1780), pp. 141, 171.

34. "Howe General Orders," *Coll. N.Y. Hist. Soc.*, XVI, 345.

35. "Return of Men, Women and Children of the British and Foreign Regiments, New Levies, and Civil Departments &c. victualed at New York and different Posts between the 22 and 29 August 1779," Clinton Papers.

36. Clode, *Military Forces*, II, 256.

37. *Ibid.*, II, 260. Clode discusses extensively military law and courts martial in both volumes of his work. For a summary see vol. II, Chap. XXVII, on the office of judge advocate general.

38. *Ibid.*, II, 336–337. The authors refer, of course, to the office of commander in chief of the armed forces, not commander in chief in America, a different and subordinate post held by the senior general there.

39. *Ibid.*, II, 316.

40. The best and most recent study of Germain only takes him through 1777 and reinterprets him more favorably than previous studies. See Gerald Saxon Brown, *The American Secretary, The Colonial Policy of Lord George Germain, 1775–1778* (Ann Arbor, Mich., 1963). Piers Mackesy, *The War for America, 1775–1783* (Cambridge, Mass., 1964), p. 16, often commends Germain's strategic conceptions and his dealings with the generals. He places a good share of the blame for British failures on the Admiralty and the generals in America. He particularly faults Burgoyne. But Alan Valentine, *Lord George Germain* (Oxford, 1962), offers the traditional, unfavorable view of Germain's policies.

41. Clode, *Military Forces*, II, 253.

42. *Ibid.*, II, 259.

43. War office and treasury records describe the secretary at war's duties. For the ones listed above see W.O. 1/890, p. 139; W.O. 2/42; W.O. 3/8, pp. 106–107; W.O. 3/11, pp. 2–6; W.O. 3/26, p. 88; T. 1/404, ff. 53–54; T. 27/29, p. 6; T. 27/30, p. 422; T. 29/30, p. 36. Olive Gee, "The British War Office in the Later Years of the American War," *Journal of Modern History*, XXVI (June, 1954), 123–126, describes Charles Jenkinson's work at the war office. She concludes that Jenkinson exercised very little power in army affairs during his tenure of office. He left patronage to Amherst, army discipline to regimental commanders, and medical appointments to Robert Adair, inspector general of regimental infirmaries. Jenkinson, Gee asserts, exerted

himself in the job of recruiting, maintained a judicious economy, and discouraged jobbery.

44. The war office, however, unlike many other administrative offices in the eighteenth century, expanded its staff as its duties increased. In 1720 the office had only nine clerks. See W.O. 26/16, p. 77. By 1782 the secretary at war supervised a staff including a deputy secretary, twenty clerks, two office keepers, three messengers, and two porters. See "Account of the Persons employ'd in the War Office, their business, salaries, and Perquisites, 20 July 1782": W.O. 2/42.

45. For a brief sketch of the history of these two departments and their relation to the ordnance see Clode, *Military Forces,* I, 265–267.

46. See "Establishment of the Royal Regiment of Artillery": P.R.O., S.P. 44/193, pp. 277–278.

47. Mackesy, *War for America,* p. 16.

48. See *Reports of the Commissioners of Military Inquiry, Appointed by Act 45 Geo. III, C. 47, to inquire into the Management of the Military Department, and into the Means of Preventing Abuses therein* (session 1806–1816), Session of 1808, vol. 5, p. 3. This report reviews past practices.

49. Curtis, *Organization,* p. 10.

50. Ward, *War of the Revolution,* I, 28–29, and Curtis, *Organization,* pp. 16–17, discuss the Brown Bess.

51. The British have been accused of being inflexible, unable to adapt themselves to the new type of fighting that North America required. Since they won nearly every battle they fought there during the Revolution the charge sounds hollow. Furthermore, they did adapt. Sir William Howe developed a new exercise for light infantry before he went to America. Seven companies practiced it at Salisbury in the summer of 1774. See Lamb, *Memoirs,* p. 89. The army abandoned some of its rigid and time-consuming exercises in face of the enemy when it began fighting in North America. After loading and priming, soldiers struck the breech of their rifle against the ground to jar the cartridge home down the barrel, instead of ramming it home as they had done in the past. The army, furthermore, shortcutted elaborate maneuvering and concentrated on priming, loading, firing a volley, and charging with the bayonets. See *ibid.,* p. 175.

52. E. B. O'Callaghan, ed., *Orderly Book of Lieut. Gen. John Burgoyne* (Albany, 1860), p. 3.

53. Lamb, *Memoir,* p. 104.

54. *Ibid.,* p. 105.

55. Roger Lamb, *An Original and Authentic Journal of Occurrences During the Late American War* (Dublin, 1809), p. 107.
56. Lamb, *Memoir,* p. 115.
57. Thomas Anburey, *With Burgoyne from Quebec,* ed. Sydney Jackman (Toronto, 1963), p. 160.
58. Baroness *Von Riedesel,* p. 58.
59. Dr. John McNamara Hayes, the chief physician of the British army in the South in 1780–1781, said of his hospital on James Island during the siege of Charleston: "The difficulty of procuring rice straw to fill bedding for the sick obliges me to request that you will be pleased to give orders to the commissary for forage & the quartermaster genl's department to furnish the hospital from time to time with that article and to be careful that no want of it should happen, by which the sick would experience great distress." See Hayes to John André, March 9, 1780: Clinton Papers.
60. *Madame Von Riedesel,* p. 61.
61. *Ibid.*
62. See the letters of Sir Jerome Fitzpatrick to various people describing in vivid detail conditions in 1798, which, during the Revolution, were as bad as, or worse than, those of the later period. Source P.R.O., Home Office 100/74, ff. 377–390.
63. Anburey, *With Burgoyne,* p. 22.
64. *Ibid.,* p. 89. The soldier, incidentally, received a reprimand only.
65. Lamb, *Memoir,* pp. 63–64.
66. General Orders of 23 Dec. 1777 in Rhode Island: W.O. 3/63.
67. "Howe General Orders," in *Coll. N.Y. Hist. Soc.,* XVI, 386.
68. *Ibid.*
69. Lamb, *Memoir,* p. 74.
70. One Isabella MacMahon, for instance, wife of soldier Thomas MacMahon, was tried along with her husband and found guilty of receiving stolen goods. The courts sentenced Thomas to 1000 lashes and Isabella to "100 lashes on her bare back, at the Cart's tail, in Different portions and the most Conspicuous Parts of the Town." See "Howe General Orders," in *Coll. N.Y. Hist. Soc.,* XVI, 288.
71. Thomas Anburey, *Travels Through the Interior Parts of America,* 2 vols. (New York, 1923), II, 24–25. Not in Jackman's edition.
72. Lamb, *Memoir,* pp. 181–183, records the story. Many years later the ex-sergeant Lamb, now a schoolteacher, encountered in Dublin the daughter who had been born in the wilderness.
73. See Frederick Mackenzie, *Diary of Frederick Mackenzie, Giving a*

Daily Narrative of His Military Services as an Officer of the Regiment of Royal Welsh Fusileers During the Years 1775–1781 in Massachusetts, Rhode Island, and Connecticut, 2 vols. (Cambridge, Mass., 1930), I, 6.

74. "Howe General Orders," in *Coll. N.Y. Hist. Soc.,* XVI, 285.

75. For songs of the British during the Revolution see John Tasker Howard, *The Music of George Washington's Time* (Washington, 1931), and Frank Moore, *Songs and Ballads of the American Revolution,* first published in New York in 1855 and reprinted in 1964.

76. Edward Howland Tatum, Jr., ed., *The American Journal of Ambrose Serle* (Los Angeles, 1940), p. 246.

77. James Phinney Baxter, ed., *Journal of Lieut. William Digby* (Albany, 1887), pp. 120–121.

78. *A Journal by Thomas Hughes* (Cambridge, Mass. 1947), p. 45.

79. Lamb, *Journal of Occurrences,* p. 196.

80. See Anburey, *Travels,* II, 3–4, and E. G. Schaukir, "Occupation of New York City by the British," *Pennsylvania Magazine of History and Biography,* X (1886), 434.

81. G. Damer to Lord George Germain, Sept. 27, 1781: H.M.C., *The Manuscripts of Mrs. Stopford-Sackville at Drayton House, Northamptonshire,* 2 vols. (London, 1904, 1910), II, 213.

82. Cornwallis to William Cornwallis, May 5, 1779: H.M.C., *Rept. on MSS. in Var. Coll.,* VI, 319.

83. Cornwallis to Lt. Col. Nesbit Balfour, Sept. 27, 1780: P.R.O. 30/11/80, ff. 48–51; to Lord Rawdon, July 15, 1780: P.R.O. 30/11/78, ff. 18–19; to Sir William Medows, Feb. 11, 1790: P.R.O. 30/11/174, ff. 27–30.

84. P.R.O. 30/11/274, ff. 45–47, and memorandum of Oct. 28, 1787 (in Cornwallis' hand): P.R.O. 30/11/194, ff. 3–5.

85. See for example Sir Archibald Campbell to Cornwallis, May 6, 1787: P.R.O. 30/11/8, ff. 80–90; memorandum of Oct. 28, 1787: P.R.O. 30/11/194, ff. 3–5; and Cornwallis to Sir William Fawcett, Dec. 11, 1795: P.R.O. 30/11/236, f. 161.

86. Cornwallis to Sir William Medows, Aug. 3, 1790: P.R.O. 30/11/174, ff. 105–107.

87. Cornwallis to Clinton, Dec. 17, 1767: Clinton Papers.

88. Time and again in India he showed his leniency. On one occasion he fumed against the "absurd" punishment of two thousand lashes. See his letter to Sir Archibald Campbell of Feb. 2, 1787: P.R.O. 30/11/159, ff. 37–38.

89. Lamb, *Memoir,* p. 90.

90. Sir William Fawcett to Cornwallis, Mar. 3, 1792: P.R.O. 30/11/270, ff. 84–86.
91. See Lt. Paris Bradshaw to Cornwallis, Apr. 27, 1793: P.R.O. 30/11/52, ff. 7–8.

Chapter 5

(pages 79–116)

1. See Germain to Cornwallis, Nov. 26, 1775: Germain Papers, William L. Clements Library. H.M.C., *Stopford-Sackville MSS.*, II, 19, calendars briefly and inadequately this letter. Germain consulted the Cabinet on the matter and told the King of its opinion that the Earl's presence would be "useful," "as his example will give credit & spirit to our proceedings against America." See Germain to the King, *George III Corr.*, III, 294–295, no. 1770. One panegyrist told a story in his *Memoirs of Cornwallis*, pp. 3–4, that when the Earl was "called on" to sail with his regiment for America, Lady Cornwallis applied to the Earl's uncle, the Archbishop of Canterbury, to secure from the King permission for Charles not to sail. The King agreed to the request, so the story goes, but Cornwallis from his "nice sense of honor" sailed anyway. The authors have found no support for this touching episode, either in the *Correspondence of George III* or elsewhere. Aside from the fact that Cornwallis' regiment was "called upon to embark" only after he had tendered his services and specifically requested that it accompany him, the action of Lady Cornwallis is totally alien to the conduct of eighteenth-century aristocratic wives, no matter how much they loved their husbands. Yet Thomas J. Fleming, *Beat the Last Drum: The Siege of Yorktown* (New York, 1963), p. 37, accepts the story as established fact.

2. For examples of the warmth between the two men see Germain to Cornwallis, Oct. 18, 1776: Germain Papers (ludicrously abridged in H.M.C., *Stopford-Sackville MSS.*, II, 44), and Cornwallis to Germain, Jan. 8, 1777: Germain Papers (repeated almost verbatim in H.M.C., *Stopford-Sackville MSS.*, II, 55–56). Germain's memorandum on Cornwallis' testimony is in Germain Papers.

3. Germain to Cornwallis, Dec. 6, 1775: Clinton Papers.

4. Willard M. Wallace, *Appeal to Arms, A Military History of the American Revolution* (Chicago, 1951), pp. 88–96, describes the operation briefly. Eric Robson, "The Expedition to the Southern Colonies, 1775–1776," *English Historical Review*, LXVI (October, 1951),

535–560, details the campaign. Willcox, *Portrait,* pp. 66–93, covers Clinton's role in the fiasco.

5. Phillips to second Duke of Newcastle, Saturday, n.d. [1775]: Newcastle Papers, NeC 2,727, Nottingham University.

6. Willcox, *Portrait,* pp. 77–78.

7. Cornwallis to Germain, Mar. 7, 1776: *Cornwallis Corr.,* I, 21.

8. Cornwallis to Germain, Apr. 18, 1776: *ibid.,* I, 22.

9. Clinton to Lord Percy, May 10, 1776: Northumberland MSS., vol. 50, ff. 228–229.

10. See for example Clinton to Cornwallis, June 1, 1776: Clinton Papers, copybook of letters commencing 11 January 1776.

11. Willcox, *Portrait,* p. 85.

12. See Cornwallis to Clinton, July 5 and July 6, 1776: Clinton Papers.

13. Most of the details of this fiasco come from Willcox, *Portrait,* pp. 87–93.

14. Carleton expected Cornwallis. Germain had written him on February 17, 1776, that the Earl would join him upon completion of the southern expedition. See B.M., Add. MSS. 21,697, ff. 130–131 (Haldimand Papers).

15. Howe to Germain, June 7, 1776: H.M.C., *Stopford-Sackville MSS.,* II, 35.

16. *Journal of Ambrose Serle,* p. 52.

17. Willcox, *Portrait,* p. 95, and Wallace, *Appeal to Arms,* p. 102.

18. Ward, *War of the Revolution,* I, 215.

19. Or so Sir Henry Clinton claimed in retrospect. See William Willcox, ed., *The American Rebellion, Sir Henry Clinton's Narrative of His Campaigns, 1775–1782, with an Appendix of Original Documents* (New Haven, 1954), pp. 40–41.

20. Ward, *War of the Revolution,* I, 211–230, summarizes the battle of Long Island. Willcox, *Portrait,* pp. 94–108, discusses Clinton's role. Troyer Steele Anderson, *The Command of the Howe Brothers During the American Revolution* (New York, 1936), pp. 125–128, does little with the battle, but painfully tries to excuse Howe's failure to attack the Brooklyn lines immediately. Anderson does not mention that Clinton suggested the flanking movement which assured Howe's success and was nearly turned down by the British commander with the incredibly stupid comment that "as the rebels knew nothing of turning a flank, such a movement would have *no* effect." See *Portrait,* p. 105.

21. See his testimony of May 6 in John Almon, ed., *The Parliamentary Register: or, History of the Proceedings and Debates of the House of*

Commons [*House of Lords*,] *1774–1880,* 17 vols. (London, 1775–1780), XIII, 2. See also pp. 8, 9, 11, 13, and 14.

22. According to Ward, *War of the Revolution,* I, 271–274, the Americans lost 146 iron and brass guns, 12,000 shot and shell, 2800 muskets and 400,000 musket cartridges at Forts Washington and Lee. For a brief description of the taking of the two posts see Wallace, *Appeal to Arms,* pp. 121–123, and Charles Stedman, *The History of the Origin, Progress, and Termination of the American War,* 2 vols. (Dublin, 1794), I, 246.

23. Cornwallis explained his reasons for stopping at New Brunswick in the parliamentary inquiry into Howe's conduct in 1779. See *Parliamentary Register,* XIII, 4, 9, and 16.

24. William S. Stryker, *The Battles of Trenton and Princeton* (Boston, 1898), p. 20, says: "Strange indeed does it appear that Cornwallis, with his large and well-equipped force, did not crush out with one blow this apology of an army, composed as it was, of men despondent, and many of them eager to seek safety in flight." Leonard Lundin, *Cockpit of the Revolution: The War for Independence in New Jersey* (Princeton, 1940), p. 151, states: "The explanations given by Howe and Cornwallis for loitering at New Brunswick when an energetic push might have trapped Washington's force against the Delaware and destroyed it, or at least inflicted irreparable damage upon it, seem extraordinarily feeble."

25. Howe to Germain, Dec. 20, 1776: *Cornwallis Corr.,* I, 24.

26. Stedman, *History of the American War,* I, 246–247. Even Clinton, who was not given to defending the Earl, believed in retrospect that only Howe's orders stopped him. See his *Narrative,* pp. 55–56.

27. Enoch Anderson, *Personal Recollections . . . (Papers of the Historical Society of Delaware,* no. XVI [Wilmington, 1896]), quoted in Ward, *War of the Revolution,* I, 283–284.

28. Stedman, *History of the American War,* I, 247.

29. Quoted in Stryker, *Battles of Trenton and Princeton,* p. 48.

30. Alfred H. Bill, *The Campaign of Princeton, 1776–1777* (Princeton, 1948), p. 85.

31. Bill, *Campaign of Princeton,* p. 88, states that Erskine said: "My Lord, if you trust those people tonight, you will see nothing of them in the morning." Ward, *War of the Revolution,* I, 310, gives Erskine's words as: "If Washington is the general I take him to be, he will not be found there in the morning." The substance is the same if the wording is different. Bill and Ward agree on the essentials.

32. Henry B. Carrington, *Battles of the American Revolution, 1775–1781:*

Historical and Military Criticism, with Topographical Illustration (New York, 1876), p. 286.

33. Quoted in Bill, *Campaign of Princeton,* p. 121.

34. Clinton, *Narrative,* p. 60.

35. Stedman, *History of the American War,* I, 314. See also Howe to George III, Apr. 25, 1777: *George III Corr.,* III, 44, no. 1993; and *London Gazette,* no. 11,776, June 3–7.

36. Lionel Smythe to Earl Percy, July 6, 1777: Northumberland MSS., vol. 52, f. 120. See also Ward, *War of the Revolution,* I, 327, and Carrington, *Battles of the Revolution,* p. 30.

37. Robert Mackenzie wrote to Lord Percy as early as Feb. 4, 1777, that: "Lord Cornwallis's situation in the Jersies has undergone no very material Change; frequent Skirmishes lessen his Numbers, and the Difficulty of getting Forage, which must daily encrease, exposes his Troops to great Fatigues — the Scarcity of this Article may prove very fatal to the early Operations of the Spring." See Northumberland MSS., vol. 51, ff. 89–90. Major General Charles Grey said before Parliament that Howe had to open his campaign late because of a lack of green forage, but that even so, he opened "earlier than I ever remember taking the field in Germany." See *Parliamentary Register,* XIII, 21. Anderson, *Command of the Howe Brothers,* p. 241, confuses Cornwallis' testimony with Grey's (Grey also served in Germany) and compounds his error by asserting that the Earl spoke at second hand about conditions in America in the spring of 1777 because "he did not arrive from England until the 5th of June (the day Grey testified he arrived)." Surely Howe's biographer ought to have known of the movements of one of Sir William's chief subordinates and realized that the Earl figured prominently in Howe's maneuvers of the spring. Cornwallis did not go home until late 1777, after the battle of Brandywine.

38. Willcox, *Portrait,* p. 143. So much has been printed about the Saratoga campaign there is little need to rehash it in any detail. The most recent and soundest analysis of it is in Mackesy, *War for American Independence,* pp. 114–125.

39. Quoted in Willcox, *Portrait,* p. 163.

40. For a description of the sailing and landing of the expedition see P. F. Thorne to Earl Percy, Aug. 31, 1777: Northumberland MSS., vol. 52, ff. 152–153.

41. Joseph Townsend, "Some Account of the British Army . . . and the Battle of Brandywine," *Bulletin of the Historical Society of Penn-*

sylvania, I, no. 7 (Sept. 1846), pp. 17–29: quoted in Ward, *War of the Revolution,* I, 350.

42. "Extracts from the Journal of Surgeon Ebenezer Elmer of the New Jersey Continental Line," *Pennsylvania Magazine of History and Biography,* XXXV (1911), 104–105: quoted in Hugh F. Rankin, *The American Revolution* (London, 1964), p. 155.

43. Ward, *War of the Revolution,* I, 350.

44. Detailed accounts of Brandywine are in Ward, *War of the Revolution,* I, 334–354, and Carrington, *Battles of the Revolution,* pp. 361–381. P. F. Thorne to Earl Percy, Sept. 29, 1777: Northumberland MSS., vol. 52, ff. 174–177, gives a contemporary British eyewitness account.

45. A writer whose name is crossed out in the document describes in great detail to Earl Percy in a letter of Dec. 11, 1777, the occupation of the river forts. See Northumberland Papers, vol. 52, ff. 217–218.

46. Howe to Germain, Dec. 13, 1777: H.M.C., *Stopford-Sackville MSS.,* II, 85–87.

47. See Cornwallis to Clinton, June 4, 1778: Clinton Papers.

48. Editorial note in *Cornwallis Corr.,* I, 31–32.

49. The entire series of correspondence relating to this event — the bailiff's and grand jury's memorials, Cornwallis' letter of Mar. 10, and treasury action — is in T. 1/452, ff. 209–216.

50. See T. 29/47, f. 35, minute of Apr. 15, 1778; board of works to treasury, June 26, 1778: T. 1/452, f. 202; and treasury secretary Robinson to board of works, July 24, 1778: T. 27/32, p. 192.

51. For the Earl's suite see: "Return of Servants &ca belonging to Headquarters and to General officers as victualled from 23d to 29th August 1779," Clinton Papers, Aug. 29, 1779. See also William Eden and Lord Carlisle to Lord George Germain, Apr. 11, 1778: H.M.C., *Stopford-Sackville MSS.,* II, 106, and Lord Carlisle to Lady Carlisle, Sept. 4 and Sept. 6, 1778: H.M.C., *Fifteenth Report, Appendix, Part VI, The Manuscripts of the Earl of Carlisle, Preserved at Castle Howard* (London, 1897), p. 364.

52. Carlisle, William Eden, and George Johnstone to Clinton, June 4, 1778: Clinton Papers.

53. See Willcox, *Portrait,* pp. 197–210.

54. Germain to Cornwallis, Apr. 12, 1778: *Cornwallis Corr.,* I, 33.

55. Cornwallis to Clinton, Mar. 12, 1778: Clinton Papers.

56. Clinton to [Edward Harvey?], Mar. 31, 1778: Clinton Papers.

57. Cornwallis to Germain, June 17, 1778: *Cornwallis Corr.,* I, 33.

58. *Ibid.*

59. Germain to Cornwallis, Aug. 6, 1778: *ibid.,* I, 34. "At present," Germain said in his reply, "he [the King] cannot dispense with your service in North America, especially as your lordship has a dormant commission to command all the forces there in case of the death of Sir Henry Clinton."

60. William S. Stryker, *The Battle of Monmouth,* ed. William Star Myers (Princeton, 1927), p. 90.

61. *Ibid.,* p. 42, and Appendix II, p. 279. Stryker closely examines Washington's forces and estimates their numbers as between thirteen and fourteen thousand men. He accepts, however, the grossly exaggerated figure of seventeen thousand men as the strength of the British force.

62. The most thorough and meticulous account of Monmouth is Stryker, *Monmouth.* Other accounts of the battle, which agree in broad outline, are Willcox, *Portrait,* pp. 233–236; Ward, *War of the Revolution,* I, 570–586; and Carrington, *Battles of the Revolution,* pp. 422–445.

63. Clinton to Germain, July 5, 1778: Clinton Papers.

64. Clinton, *Narrative,* pp. 92–95.

65. In September Clinton split his army into two divisions. He sent one of them under Cornwallis — about five thousand men — across the Hudson into New Jersey to cover foraging parties. There the Earl learned that a regiment of continental light horse, under Lieutenant Colonel Baylor, had assembled at the village of Old Tappan. A body of American militia had also gathered across the river at New Tappan. Both groups evidently intended to interrupt British foraging parties. Cornwallis determined to attack them both, simultaneously if possible, so that one group could not warn the other. He sent Lt. Col. Archibald Campbell, with whom he later worked closely in India, against the militia. Campbell failed. Boats did not arrive in time to ferry him across the Hudson so that he could pounce on New Tappan before word of the British approach filtered to the Americans from some of Campbell's deserters. The militia escaped but, characteristically, did not bother to warn Baylor. The other British column, under Major General Charles Grey, surprised the American dragoons completely. Grey's men stole quietly into the village and surrounded it. They silenced with bayonets a sergeant's guard of a dozen men near Baylor's headquarters. Then they hurled themselves into the three barns where the dragoons slept and fell upon the helpless men. Only thirty-seven Americans escaped the terrible carnage which followed. The laws of war at that time permitted an attacking force to refuse quarter to its foe during a night engagement on the assumption that darkness made

it impossible to distinguish friend from foe. Even so, the Americans considered Grey's action a terrible atrocity, albeit an effective one. It "struck such terror into the provincials that the British foragers were not afterwards interrupted." For the incident see Cornwallis to Clinton, Sept. 28, 1778: *Cornwallis Corr.*, I, 35; Clinton, *Narrative*, pp. 104–105; and Stedman, *History of the American War*, II, 44–46.

66. Germain to Clinton, Apr. 12, 1778: Clinton Papers.

67. Willcox, *Portrait*, pp. 261–262. Cornwallis, who cannot have harbored any illusions that the war would end soon, anticipated that Clinton would resign. He wrote on Nov. 24 that "I beg you will accept my most sincere wishes for your success, & for our meeting soon in England." On Jan. 22, 1779, he wrote from England that: "Government cannot send out a force that can tempt you to stay." Both letters are in Clinton Papers.

68. William Eden to Clinton, Jan. 23, 1779: Clinton Papers.

69. See Duncan Drummond to Clinton, Dec. 26, 1778, and Cornwallis to Clinton, Jan. 22, 1779: Clinton Papers.

70. Cornwallis to William Cornwallis, Dec. 22, 1778: H.M.C., *Rept. on MMS. in Var. Coll.*, VI, 319.

71. See Duncan Drummond to Clinton, Feb. 5, 1779: Clinton Papers.

72. Cornwallis to Clinton, Jan. 22, 1779: *ibid.*

73. William Musgrave, *Obituary Prior to 1880 (as far as Relates to England, Scotland, and Ireland)*, ed. Sir George J. Armytage, 6 vols., Publications of the Harleian Society, XLV-XLX (London, 1899–1901), II, 139, lists her death as Feb. 14. Cokayne, *Complete Peerage*, III, 456, mistakenly believes she died on April 14 and was buried at Culford on April 16. William Eden, on Feb. 13, predicted she would die soon. See his letter of that date to Clinton in Clinton Papers.

74. Duncan Drummond to Clinton, Mar. 3, 1779: Clinton Papers.

75. Cornwallis to William Cornwallis, Oct. 21, 1779: H.M.C., *Rept. on MSS. in Var. Coll.*, VI, 322.

76. Cornwallis to Clinton, Apr. 4, 1779: Clinton Papers.

77. Same to same, Apr. 9, 1779: *ibid.*

78. Cornwallis to William Cornwallis, May 5, 1779: H.M.C., *Rept. on MSS. in Var. Coll.*, VI, 319.

79. For his testimony see *Parliamentary Register*, XIII, 1–16.

80. See Walpole to Sir Horace Mann, May 31, 1779: W. S. Lewis, ed., *The Yale Edition of Horace Walpole's Correspondence*, XXIV (New Haven, 1967), 482.

Chapter 6
(pages 119–148)

1. Clinton to Germain, Aug. 20, 1779: Clinton Papers.
2. Quoted by Willcox, *Portrait*, p. 114.
3. Cornwallis to first Duke of Newcastle, July 29, 1763: B. M., Add. MSS. 32,949, ff. 436–437
4. Willcox, *Portrait*, p. 160.
5. Clinton to Germain, Aug. 20, 1779: Clinton Papers.
6. See Willcox, *Portrait*, pp. 281–283.
7. Clinton, *Narrative*, p. 144.
8. For the discussions between Clinton, Cornwallis, and Arbuthnot about the expedition see the box containing Clinton Papers, Sept. 16–26. Other pertinent material in the Clinton Papers concerning the expedition includes: "Autograph notes of Orders to Cornwallis, 2pp. and Answers to queries by Lord Cornwallis;" Governor Dalling to Clinton, Aug. 11, 1779; Cornwallis to Clinton, Sept. 27, 1779; and Clinton to William Eden, Oct. 10, 1779.
9. Willcox, *Portrait*, pp. 293–299, discusses the planning of the Charleston expedition.
10. See for example, Robert Walker to Thomas Tonken, Dec. 10, 1779: Clinton Papers.
11. David Ramsay, *The History of the American Revolution,* 2 vols. (Philadelphia, 1789), II, 156, states that five thousand people — militia, garrison and all male adults — surrendered at Charleston. He avers, however, that the garrison of Continentals numbered only twenty-five hundred. "The precise number of privates in the Continental army was 1977, of which 500 were in the hospitals." The officers included one major general, six brigadiers, nine colonels, fourteen lieutenant colonels, fifteen majors, eighty-four captains, eighty-four lieutenants, and thirty-two second lieutenants and ensigns.
12. Paul H. Smith, *Loyalists and Redcoats* (Chapel Hill, 1964), pp. 127–128, considers Clinton's stripping Georgia of troops "Britain's first error in the South." "Success in the southern colonies," Smith argues, "depended, above all, upon Britain's ability to protect the loyal inhabitants, and Clinton's opening move implied casualness about their safety. The withdrawal proved to be a bitter lesson to many Loyalists and undermined the confidence of many backcountry settlers, who

were completely at the mercy of rebel bands which now fearlessly
raided to within a few miles of Savannah."

13. Willcox, *Portrait,* p. 317.
14. For Clinton's orders to Cornwallis, dated April 23, 1780, see Clinton
    Papers.
    See also "Diary of Lieu. Anthony Allaire," in Lyman C. Draper, *King's
    Mountain and Its Heroes* . . . (Cincinnati, 1881), p. 492; and Corn-
    wallis to Clinton, Apr. 24, 1780: Clinton Papers.
15. For the relations between Clinton and Cornwallis during the Charles-
    ton campaign see Willcox, *Portrait,* pp. 300–319.
16. Clinton gave Cornwallis no credit at all for his work in the siege. Sir
    Henry claimed that the Earl had in no way contributed to cutting
    American communications. He had not suggested the move, "did not
    answer a word 'till it had succeeded," and did nothing to make it suc-
    ceed. "The Business of shutting the door was effectually done," Sir
    Henry said, "before I sent him to take the command." See Clinton to
    second Duke of Newcastle, May 14, 1780: NeC 2,631 (bundle 9, no 33).
17. For the correspondence relative to the two posts see Arbuthnot to Lord
    George Germain, May 15, 1780: H.M.C., *Stopford-Sackville MSS.,* II,
    161–165; Captain Charles Hudson to Clinton, Apr. 28, 1780: Clinton
    Papers; and the exchanges between Cornwallis and Clinton, April 26
    through May 5, in both Clinton Papers and in P.R.O. 30/11/2, ff. 5–30,
    and P.R.O. 30/11/73, ff. 1–7.
18. Benjamin Smith to his wife, Apr. 30, 1780: quoted in Stedman, *History
    of the American War,* II, 201n.
19. See Tarleton's letter to Clinton, Apr. 15, 1780: Clinton Papers. Corn-
    wallis' action was limited to a walk along the siege lines once Clinton
    had prepared them. On April 10 his aide-de-camp, Lieutenant Fitzroy,
    was slightly wounded by a cannonball. See James Bain, ed., "The Siege
    of Charleston: Journal of Captain Peter Russel, December 25, 1779 to
    May 2, 1780," *American Historical Review,* IV (April, 1899), 497.
20. "Allaire's Diary," in Draper, *King's Mountain,* p. 493.
21. See Cornwallis' very colorful account of Tarleton's action in his letter
    to Clinton of May 6: Clinton Papers.
22. Cornwallis to Clinton, May 7, 1780: *Cornwallis Corr.,* I, 43.
23. Clinton to Phillips, May 25, 1780: Clinton Papers.
24. Clinton to second Duke of Newcastle, May 14, 1780: NeC 2631 (bundle
    9, no. 33). But he told Phillips eleven days later that the Earl "will be
    of great use to us." See letter of May 25: Clinton Papers.
25. See Cornwallis to Clinton, May 30, 1780: Clinton Papers; Cornwallis

to Clinton, June 2, 1780: *Cornwallis Corr.*, I, 44; Tarleton to Cornwallis, May 30, 1780: *Cornwallis Corr.*, I, 45; and Clinton to Germain, June 5, 1780: Clinton Papers.

26. Instructions from Clinton to Cornwallis, June 1, 1780: P.R.O. 30/11/61, ff. 3–6. See also "Memorandums for the Commandant of Charleston & Earl Cornwallis," June 3, 1780: Clinton Papers.

27. For a discussion of the provincial regiments see Smith, *Loyalists and Redcoats,* pp. 33–36, and 63–78.

28. Troop figures for any century are deceptive and especially so for the eighteenth century. One can rarely be sure of the exact troop strength of a commander, and one set of figures should if possible be set against another and against the comments of observers. Our estimates come from various sources, the most important of which is the "State of the Troops under the Command of Lieut. General Rt. Honorable Charles Earl Cornwallis," dated June 15, 1780, and signed by Oliver DeLancy, Adjutant General: Clinton Papers. Frederick Mackenzie, Clinton's Deputy Adjutant General in New York also kept a running account of Cornwallis' forces. His returns of June 1, July 15, August 1, September 1, and November 15, 1780, are in the Mackenzie Papers, Clements Library. The commandant of Charleston also forwarded a return on June 13, 1780, which is in the Mackenzie Papers. P.R.O. 30/11/2, f. 2, lists the forces at Ninety-Six in August of 1780. P.R.O. 30/11/103, ff. 2b–3, is a return of Rawdon's troops at Camden in August of 1780. P.R.O. 30/11/103, f. 16, lists Rawdon's forces on Jan. 15, 1781, while P.R.O. 30/11/103, ff. 27b–28, lists the Earl's forces at Wilmington, North Carolina, on Apr. 15, 1781. By early 1781, of course, Cornwallis had been reinforced by Leslie. Contemporary writers agree that Cornwallis had only four thousand men in South Carolina. David Ramsay, who had no wish to underestimate the British numbers, attributed four thousand troops to Cornwallis. See *The History of the Revolution of South Carolina, from a British Province to an Independent State,* 2 vols. (Trenton, 1785), II, 114. Stedman, *History of the American War,* II, 216, and Lamb, *Journal of Occurrences,* p. 302, give Cornwallis about four thousand men. Banastre Tarleton, who published his *A History of the Campaigns of 1780 and 1781, in the Southern Provinces of North America* (London, 1787), on pp. 86–88, estimates the Earl had about fifty-four hundred men in South Carolina and one thousand in Georgia. Tarleton, however, nursed some sort of a grievance against Cornwallis and certainly condemned his generalship in his study. Thus he might have deliberately attempted to give Cornwallis more troops than he had

to make his failure seem all the more unjustified. Even so, Tarleton
is closer to the truth than some later writers. C. T. Atkinson, "British
Forces in North America, 1774–1781: Their Distribution and Strength,"
Journal of the Society for Army Historical Research, XVI, no. 61
(Spring, 1937), p. 20, gives Cornwallis 5103 officers and men present
and fit for duty in "Carolina" in September of 1780. Although Atkinson used Colonial Office and War Office records, neither his figures nor
indeed some of his units tally with other works and the authors'
sources. Willard Wallace, *Appeal to Arms*, p. 211, gives Cornwallis
eight thousand men, double the number he had in South Carolina
and more than he had in the entire South capable of active service.
Howard H. Peckham, *The War for Independence, A Military History*,
p. 139, estimates that Cornwallis had about six thousand troops for his
field army, for the garrisons at Charleston and Savannah, and for his
minor posts. Peckham, obviously, is much closer. Both Peckham and
Wallace are excellent works.

29. Cornwallis to Clinton, June 30, 1780: *Cornwallis Corr.*, I, 500, and
Tarleton, *A History of the Campaigns*, pp. 86–88.

30. *Ibid.*, pp. 87–88.

31. Cornwallis to Arbuthnot, Aug. 10, 1780: P.R.O. 30/11/79, f. 21.

32. Balfour to Cornwallis, Sept. 20, and Sept. 27, 1780: P.R.O. 30/11/64,
ff. 83–88, 112–113.

33. At least the Earl said it "blew a hurricane" in a letter to Balfour of
Sept. 3, 1780: P.R.O. 30/11/80, ff. 1–4. For examples of the difficulties
the rains put in the way of movement see Cornwallis to Rawdon,
Aug. 1, 1780: P.R.O. 30/11/79, ff. 8–11; Major Weymss to Cornwallis,
Aug. 2 and 4, 1780: P.R.O. 30/11/63, ff. 7–8, 17–18.

34. See Cornwallis to Rawdon, July 6, 1780: P.R.O. 30/11/78, ff. 7–9.

35. Cornwallis to Balfour, June 20, 1780: P.R.O. 30/11/77, ff. 16–17.

36. *Ibid.*

37. "An account of arms, ammunition & stores taken from the rebels &
now in the possession of the Commissary at Ninety Six, 19th June
1789," P.R.O. 30/11/2, f. 173.

38. Stedman, *History of the American War*, II, 215n.

39. Tarleton especially helped himself when he routed the American
dragoons at Monck's Corners. Before that he was "badly mounted."
See Ramsay, *Revolution of South Carolina*, II, 64–65.

40. When he first occupied Camden in June, for example, Cornwallis took
"a quantity of wheat & flour," twenty-one tierces of rice, three and a
half hogsheads of indigo, eighteen barrels of Indian cornmeal, one hogs-

head of rum, ninety hogsheads of tobacco, tea, sugar, coffee, bacon, ham, butter, and linen. He also rounded up nearly one hundred head of cattle and some sheep in and around the town. See Stedman, *History of the American War*, II, 215n.

41. As early as November of 1780 the want of money became "very hard" on the Charleston garrison, and as the months progressed the shortage became desperate. See Balfour to Cornwallis, Nov. 5, 1780: P.R.O. 30/11/4, ff. 27–34, and to Clinton in April, May, and June of 1781: P.R.O. 30/11/109, ff. 26, 32–33, and 36. Cornwallis wrote Clinton on Dec. 22, 1780: "The want of specie in this province puts us under the greatest difficulties. . . . the sum actually in the province is so inadequate for the necessary demands, that we have scarcely been able to pay the subsistence of troops." See *Cornwallis Corr.*, I, 75.

42. Clinton had originally created the first of these offices in July of 1779 and later seethed when Parliament credited Cornwallis with the office and the economies it produced. Over and over again, in marginal comments on Stedman's *History of the American War*, in comments on Tarleton's *A History of the Campaigns*, in memoranda, and in letters to Cornwallis which he never sent, he proved to himself that he originated the commissary of captures and as a result saved the crown the cost of nearly a million rations at the siege of Charleston. See his marginalia in the Clements Library's copy of Stedman; and, for example, "Abstract of fresh meat & rice issued to His Majesty's troops by the commissaries of captures, between 24th Feby & 16 March 1780;" "Sketch of instructions for commissioners of captures, July 1779;" Clinton to Cornwallis, n.d. but probably 1782 — all in the Clinton Papers. Clinton unquestionably created the office, but it is doubtful if he saved the crown a million rations. Sir Henry had a lot of good points, but he scarcely practiced economy. Furthermore, he gave Cornwallis no specific orders about the commissary before he left Charlestown, either in his instructions of June 1 or in his supplemental memorandum of June 3, in which he was deliberately vague about captures, simply asserting that "All interests are attended to and represented by the Orders I have given." Indeed, according to his commissary, Major Hay, Sir Henry had shied away from the whole question when it had come up at a meeting of general and field officers before he left for New York. Clinton feared for his personal financial solvency if he continued the office. The commissary granted receipts for appropriated property. The army eventually honored these receipts in cash if the person whose goods had been seized could prove his loyalty. This method of

operation might prove a terrible burden to Sir Henry when the time of reckoning came. Someone at the meeting suggested that Hay be given the right to sell for cash all rebel property taken in the past and to be taken in the future, the proceeds of such sales to go to the army as prize money. This procedure might not guarantee supplies for the troops, but it would certainly enrich them. The attorney general protested that if Clinton allowed such a practice he would be "ruined with law suits when he came to England, for that he would become liable for all Major Hay's receipts and transactions." From that time on Sir Henry "would have nothing to do" with the office of commissary, "nor give any orders relating to it." See Hay Manuscripts, Scottish Record Office, courtesy of Professor Arthur Bowler, University of Buffalo.

43. See Charles Stedman to Clinton, December, 1779, and Clinton's marginal notes on p. 5 of Stedman's *History of the American War*. Stedman is in *D.N.B.*

44. See, for example, instructions for the commissary of captures, Sept. 30, 1781: P.R.O. 30/11/6, ff. 387–388, and "Memorial of William Ancrum, late of Charlestown, S.C.," read at the treasury in July of 1783, P.R.O., T. 1/581, ff. 64–65.

45. Lieutenant Colonel Alexander Innes of the provincials found thirty thousand bushels of Indian corn and quantities of tobacco, wheat, and flour along the Congaree River. He methodically accounted for the stores but refused to turn them over to the man who claimed he had authority from Cornwallis to collect them.

46. Cornwallis received lists of "bad men," that is rebels, whose property should be seized. See P.R.O. 30/11/3, f. 18.

47. Tarleton, *A History of the Campaigns,* p. 90.

48. Patrick Ferguson to Cornwallis, July 4, 1780: P.R.O. 30/11/2, ff. 360–361.

49. Tarleton, *A History of the Campaigns,* p. 88.

50. Cornwallis did not commission the officer until after he left Charleston, but he planned it there and the commissioner, John Cruden, would be closely associated with the city.

51. Clinton had appointed a board of police for Charleston and allowed Cornwallis to make similar arrangements in other towns and villages. The Earl later enlarged upon the powers Clinton had given the Charleston police. See Clinton's memorandum in Clinton Papers.

52. P.R.O., T. 1/571, copy of Cornwallis' commission to John Cruden, Sept. 16, 1780.

53. See the copy of Cornwallis' proclamation of September in Tarleton, *A History of the Campaigns*, p. 186.
54. See, for example, Cornwallis' letter to Stedman on Dec. 15, 1780: P.R.O. 30/11/7, ff. 8–9. He instructed the commissary to apply in "all cases of the sequestered estates to Mr. Cruden . . . whom you are required to assist on every occasion, and by no means to counter act."
55. See memorandum in Clinton Papers: "That he [Cornwallis] requested he might also be appd commissioner with powers to restore civil govt. when he should judge proper, but this was not approv'd."
56. James Simpson to Cornwallis, July 30, 1780: P.R.O. 30/11/2, f. 393.
57. Martin to Cornwallis, July 28, 1780: P.R.O. 30/11/2, ff. 379–381.
58. Tarleton, *A History of the Campaigns*, p. 89.
59. James Simpson to Cornwallis, July 22, 1780: P.R.O. 30/11/2, f. 339.
60. Balfour to Cornwallis, July 12, 1780: P.R.O. 30/11/1, ff. 15–18.
61. Cornwallis to Balfour, Aug. 24, 1780: P.R.O. 30/11/79, ff. 35–36, and to Rawdon, Dec. 7, 1780: P.R.O. 30/11/83, ff. 29–30.
62. Cornwallis to Major General Smallwood, Nov. 10, 1780: P.R.O. 30/11/92, ff. 9–10.
63. P.R.O. 30/11/3, f. 28.
64. Balfour to Rawdon, Oct. 26 and 29, 1780: P.R.O. 30/11/3, ff. 289–290, 309–310.
65. Ramsay, *Revolution of South Carolina*, II, 288–289.
66. Conditions cannot have been much better for the Americans in the Camden jail under the care of a "stupid, drunken" provost. See Lt. Col. George Turnbull to Cornwallis, Sept. 11, 1780: P.R.O. 30/11/64, ff. 42–43.
67. By May 19, 1781, over four hundred Americans had enlisted in the Duke of Cumberland's regiment of Carolina Rangers. See Lt. Col. Odell to Cornwallis, May 19, 1781: P.R.O. 30/11/6, f. 91; and S.P. 41/26, "Recruiting list of the continental prisoners of war taken at the surrender of Charlestown . . . and at Gates' defeat at Camden." Interestingly enough, thirty-two of the Continentals were from England. Although the majority of the men came from the South, some came from Germany, the West Indies, Rhode Island, and New Jersey. Ramsay, *Revolution of South Carolina*, II, 288–289, says that 530 men eventually enlisted for the British service in the West Indies.
68. Ramsay asserts that at one time fifty-six people, white men and women, Negroes, felons, state prisoners, whores, two women of "amiable characters" and "respectable connexions" were all crowded together in the Provost. See *Revolution of South Carolina*, II, 264–265. The Provost

has been reconstructed on its old site in Charleston, and a stroll through it conveys the sense of hopelessness and helplessness that some of the prisoners must have felt.

69. Cornwallis to Clinton, Sept. 3, 1780: P.R.O. 30/11/72, ff. 51–52.

70. *Ibid.*

71. The text has given scant attention to Georgia and Florida, primarily because the Earl gave them scant attention. Yet civil and military officers approached him, as the commanding general in the South, with problems of one sort or another. Cornwallis sent orders occasionally, but he had on the whole to let things run as they would and hope for the best. See, for example, Lt. Col. Allured Clarke to Cornwallis, Aug. 20, 1780: P.R.O. 30/11/63, ff. 50–55; Governor Tonyn of East Florida to Cornwallis, Aug. 24, 1780: *Ibid.*, ff. 64–65; Clarke to Cornwallis, Jan. 2, 1781, and Apr. 6, 1781: P.R.O. 30/11/5, ff. 25–27, 171–173; and James Wright to Cornwallis, July 3, 1780: P.R.O. 30/11/2, ff. 237–238.

Chapter 7

(pages 149–165)

1. The phrase is Carrington's, *Battles of the American Revolution*, p. 334. Carrington is violently hostile to Gates.

2. Opinions of Gates' generalship have differed over the years. We recommend Samuel W. Patterson, *Horatio Gates* (New York, 1941), to anyone who wishes to see Gates in a more favorable light than we have presented here. *D.A.B.* outlines his career. Whatever his abilities at Saratoga, and they are disputed, it is hard to see how any American general, regular or militia, could have done worse than Gates did at Camden. Scheer and Rankin, *Rebels*, pp. 251–254, explains the situation between Schuyler and Gates.

3. Cornwallis to Clinton, Aug. 10, 1780: *Cornwallis Corr.*, I, 54–55.

4. Stedman, *History of the American War*, II, 215n.

5. Thomas J. Kirkland and Robert M. Kennedy, *Historic Camden*, 2 vols. (Columbia, 1905), I, 274.

6. Stedman, *History of the American War*, II, 227–228.

7. Cornwallis to Germain, Aug. 21, 1780: *Cornwallis Corr.*, I, 506. Sumter managed to capture the escort and redoubt on the fifteenth, but could not capitalize on his gains after Cornwallis' decisive victory. See Ramsay, *Revolution of South Carolina*, II, 145, and Tarleton, *A History of the Campaigns*, p. 102.

8. Information on Camden comes from a variety of works. Most important is Kirkland and Kennedy, *Historic Camden*. Volume I, *passim*, gives Camden's history in the revolutionary period. See also David Ramsay, *The History of South Carolina from Its First Settlement in 1670 to the Year 1808*, 2 vols. (Charleston, 1809), I, 597; and Richard J. Hooker, ed., *The Carolina Backcountry on the Eve of the Revolution: The Journal and Other Writings of Charles Woodmason, Anglican Itinerant* (Chapel Hill, 1953).

9. Stedman, *History of the American War*, II, 215n. Stedman says (*ibid.*, 220n) that at least until the first of July the British army in Camden was "wholly supported by supplies from the neighboring district."

10. P.R.O. 30/11/103, ff. 2b–3, lists 756 as sick. It is the official return of the troops at Camden on Aug. 13, the day Cornwallis arrived.

11. Cornwallis to Germain, Aug. 21, 1780: *Cornwallis Corr.*, I, 506.

12. Tarleton, *A History of the Campaigns*, p. 103.

13. "A Narrative of the Campaign of 1780, by Colonel Otho Williams, Adjutant General," Appendix B of William Johnson, *Sketches of the Life and Correspondence of Nathanael Greene . . . Compiled Chiefly from Original Materials*, 2 vols. (Charleston, 1822), I, 491.

14. Tarleton, *A History of the Campaigns*, p. 103.

15. Cornwallis to Germain, Aug. 21, 1780: *Cornwallis Corr.*, I, 506.

16. Lieutenant Colonel H. L. Landers, of the historical section of the Army War College, studied the battle closely in this century and estimated that "allowing for a due proportion of officers, noncommissioned officers, and other, the total strength fit for duty was about 3,700." See H. L. Landers, *The Battle of Camden* (Washington, 1929), p. 28.

17. Quoted in *ibid.*, p. 6.

18. *Ibid.*, p. 11.

19. "A Narrative of the Campaign," Johnson, *Sketches of Greene*, I, 487, 494.

20. *Ibid.*, p. 494. The most pertinent and most colorful sections of Williams' narrative, insofar as it relates to Camden, are printed in Hugh Rankin, *The American Revolution* (New York, 1964), pp. 249–250, 251–254. Rankin drew his material from Johnson, *Sketches of Greene*, I, 485–497.

21. Extract of a letter from an officer of the Volunteers of Ireland to his friend at Glasgow, dated Camden, Aug. 25, 1780: *London Chronicle*, Oct. 26, 1780, 131 vols. (London, 1757–1822), XLVIII, 398.

22. Stedman, *History of the American War*, II, 233.

23. For Ross' sailing and arrival see Cornwallis to Captain Henry, the naval

officer commanding at Charleston harbor, Aug. 21, 1780: P.R.O.
30/11/79; Balfour to Cornwallis, Aug. 31, 1780: P.R.O. 30/11/63, ff. 87–
88; Germain to Cornwallis, Nov. 9, 1780: P.R.O. 30/11/65, ff. 7–10;
and *London Gazette Extraordinary*, Oct. 9, 1780. The Countess Cornwallis wrote to William Cornwallis, Nov. 11, 1780 (H.M.C., *Rept. on
MSS. in Var. Coll.*, VI, 326): "Your brother, with about 1,500 troops,
has completely beat Gates, who had 6,500. It is impossible for anybody
to have gained more honour than he has done; nobody talked of anything else for a fortnight." Lord Pembroke wrote to Lord Herbert on
Oct. 14, 1780: "Is not Cornwallis's affair a brilliant one? It does him
great credit." The news even filtered to Vienna from where Sir Robert
Keith wrote to Lord Herbert on Oct. 25, 1780: "What a noble fellow
Cornwallis is; may every commander by sea & land follow his example
and all will go well with us still." See Lord Herbert, ed., *Pembroke
Papers (1780–1794), Letters and Diaries of Henry, Tenth Earl of
Pembroke and His Circle* (London, 1950), pp. 47, 56.

24. Our account of the battle of Camden comes from a variety of works,
both primary and secondary. The most important primary works in-
clude: Cornwallis to Lord George Germain, Aug. 21, 1780: *Cornwallis
Corr.*, I, 506–508; Stedman, *History of the American War*, II, 227–233;
Tarleton, *A History of the Campaigns*, pp. 102–109; Lamb, *Journal of
Occurrences*, pp. 303–306, and *Memoir*, p. 290; *London Chronicle*,
Oct. 26, 1780, XLVIII, 398; "A Narrative . . . by Williams," Johnson,
Sketches of Greene, I, 485–497, partially printed in Rankin, *American
Revolution*, pp. 249–250, 251–254. Ramsay's *Revolution of South
Carolina*, II, 147–150, counts as neither a secondary nor primary
work. Ramsay lived at the time the battle took place and knew some
of the participants involved. But he was not present at the battle and
gathered his knowledge at second hand. We prefer to call his history
a contemporary account. Secondary works include Wallace, *Appeal to
Arms*, pp. 212–215; Carrington, *Battles of the American Revolution*,
pp. 513–518; Kirkland and Kennedy, *Historic Camden*, I, 154, 169, 187;
Landers, *Battle of Camden;* and Ward, *War of the Revolution*, II, 712–
730.

Chapter 8

(*pages 169–193*)

1. David George to Cornwallis, Dec. 11, 1780: P.R.O. 30/11/66, ff. 33–34.
George had been preparing three wagons and teams to take to Charles-

ton when armed rebels appeared, stole his horses and wagons, plundered him of other goods, and carried him away prisoner. "I fear they will ruin me totally soon," George moaned, "if there is not a stop put to their coming among us and I am afraid to offer to move away, for if I was to offer to move off & the rebels was to hear of it they would follow me and take of everything I possess."

2. Turnbull to Cornwallis, June 5, 1780: P.R.O. 30/11/2, ff. 158–159.

3. O'Hara to the Duke of Grafton, Jan. 6, 1781: Bury St. Edmunds Record Office, Grafton Papers, Ac. 423/95. Ramsay's *Revolution of South Carolina*, II, *passim*, gorges the reader with tales of cruelty and horror, although, because Ramsay is a patriot, most of the cruelty is perpetrated by the loyalists. Stedman, *History of the American War*, II, 386n, 387n, and 388n, on the other hand, describes loyalist distress vividly.

4. Cornwallis to Clinton, Aug. 6, 1780: *Cornwallis Corr.*, I, 54.

5. Balfour's comments of May, 1781, sound strikingly like his superior's of August, 1780: "Indeed, I should betray the duty I owe to your excellency, did I not represent the defection of this province so universal, that I know of no mode, short of depopulation, to retain it." See Balfour to Clinton, May 6, 1781: P.R.O. 30/11/109, f. 34.

6. Smith, *Loyalists and Redcoats*, p. 141.

7. Keaty Simons to Cornwallis, Aug. 11, 1780: P.R.O. 30/11/63, ff. 36–37.

8. Gates to Cornwallis, Aug. 1780: P.R.O. 30/11/90, ff. 1–2.

9. Greene to Cornwallis, Mar. 16 and 17, 1781: P.R.O. 30/11/90, ff. 3–8.

10. Cornwallis to Cruger, Sept. 24, 1780: P.R.O. 30/11/80, ff. 5–6.

11. See Proclamation of Sept. 15, 1780: P.R.O. 30/11/3, f. 41.

12. Lamb, *Memoir*, p. 261.

13. Cornwallis to Cruger, Sept. 24, 1780: P.R.O. 30/11/80, ff. 5–6.

14. Cornwallis to Turnbull, June 16, 1780: P.R.O. 30/11/77, ff. 11–12.

15. Tarleton to Cornwallis, Dec. 26, 1780: P.R.O. 30/11/4, f. 404.

16. James Ferguson, *Two Scottish Soldiers, a Soldier of 1688 and Blenheim, a Soldier of the American Revolution, and a Jacobite Laird and his Forbears* (Aberdeen, 1888), p. 79.

17. Lt. Col. G. Nesbitt to Cornwallis, Sept. 8, 1791: P.R.O. 30/11/45, ff. 425–426.

18. William Dobein James, *A Sketch of the Life of Brig. Gen. Francis Marion and a History of His Brigade, from Its Rise in June of 1780 until disbanded in December, 1782, with Descriptions of Characters and Scenes Not Heretofore Published* (Charleston, 1821), Appendix, pp. 3–7, quoted in Rankin, *American Revolution*, pp. 243–245.

19. Tarleton to Cornwallis, May 30, 1780: *Cornwallis Corr.,* I, 45.
20. Tarleton came as close as he dared to telling the Earl of his intention to spare no rebels in a letter of August 5, 1780: "I have promised the young men who chose to assist me in this expedition," he said, "the plunder of the leaders of the faction. If warfare allows me, I shall give these disturbers of the peace no quarter. If humanity obliges me to spare their lives, I shall convey them close prisoners to Camden. For a confiscation must take place in their effects. I must discriminate with severity." See P.R.O. 30/11/63, ff. 19–20.
21. Cruger to Cornwallis, Sept. 28, 1780: P.R.O. 30/11/64, ff. 116–117.
22. Weymss to Cornwallis, Sept. 20, 1780: P.R.O. 30/11/64, ff. 91–92.
23. Ramsay, *Revolution of South Carolina,* II, 156.
24. Rawdon to Cornwallis, Dec. 5, 1780: *Cornwallis Corr.,* I, 514–516, and Rawdon to Rugeley, July 1, 1780: P.R.O. 30/11/95, f. 9.
25. Cornwallis to Cruger, Aug. 18, 1780: *Cornwallis Corr.,* I, 56–57.
26. The altered missive is in P.R.O. 30/11/95, f. 10.
27. See Washington to Clinton, Oct. 16, 1780: P.R.O. 30/11/2, ff. 235–236; and Clinton to Washington, Oct. 23, 1780: *Cornwallis Corr.,* I, 60.
28. Cornwallis to Clarke, July 2, 1780: P.R.O. 30/11/78, ff. 1–2.
29. Balfour to Cornwallis, June 12, 1780: P.R.O. 30/11/2, ff. 137–140.
30. The best and most recent analysis of the ministry's and army's relations with the loyalists is Smith, *Loyalists and Redcoats,* from which we have taken this summary.
31. *Ibid.,* p. 131.
32. *Ibid.*
33. Rawdon to Cornwallis, July 7, 1780: P.R.O. 30/11/2, ff. 252–255.
34. See Cornwallis to Balfour, June 11, 1780, and to Clinton, June 30, 1780: *Cornwallis Corr.,* I, 46, 500. For brief discussions of the proclamations' effects see Smith, *Loyalists and Redcoats,* pp. 130–133; and Willcox, *Portrait,* p. 321. Contemporaries on both sides, British and patriot, agreed on the adverse effects of the Clinton proclamation. Ramsay discusses it on pp. 111–123 and prints it in full on pp. 441–442 of *Revolution of South Carolina,* II. Stedman, *History of the American War,* II, 220–221, condemns the June 3d proclamation equally harshly.
35. Cornwallis to Arbuthnot, June 29, 1780: *Cornwallis Corr.,* I, 48.
36. See Cornwallis to Brigadier General Pattison, June 10, 1780: P.R.O. 30/11/77, ff. 3–4; and to Clinton, June 30, 1780; *Cornwallis Corr.,* I, 499–500. Part of the letter to Pattison is printed in *Cornwallis Corr.,* I, 46.
37. Cornwallis to Clinton, Dec. 4, 1780: *Cornwallis Corr.,* I, 72–73.

38. Major George Hanger, who served Tarleton's Legion in the South, remarked on the mobility of patriot militia. "The crackers and militia in those parts of America are all mounted on horse-back, which renders it totally impossible to force them to an engagement with infantry *only*. When they chuse to fight, they dismount, and fasten their horses to the fences and rails; but if not very confident in the superiority of their numbers, they remain on horse-back, give their fire, and retreat, which renders it useless to attack them without cavalry: for though you repulse them, and drive them from the field, you never can improve the advantage, or do them any material detriment." See *An Address to the Army; in Reply to Strictures by Roderick M'Kenzie, (Late Lieutenant in the 71st Regiment) on Tarleton's History of the Campaigns of 1780 and 1781* (London, 1789), p. 82.

39. Ferguson to Cornwallis, Aug. 29, 1780: P.R.O. 30/11/63, ff. 81–82.

40. For a closer analysis of the handicaps under which the loyalists labored see William H. Nelson, *The American Tory* (Oxford, 1961). Wallace Brown, *The King's Friends* (Providence, 1965), analyzes the loyalists state by state.

41. Turnbull to Cornwallis, Oct. 4, 1780: P.R.O. 30/11/3, ff. 178–180.

42. Balfour to Rawdon, Oct. 29, 1780: P.R.O. 30/11/3, ff. 309–310.

43. Balfour to Cornwallis, June 7, 1780: P.R.O. 30/11/2, ff. 101–102.

44. See Wallace, *Appeal to Arms*, pp. 241–242. Edward McCrady, *The History of South Carolina in the Revolution, 1780–1783* (New York, 1902), *passim*, details Browne's activities.

45. See Cornwallis to Browne and Wright, July 21, 1780: P.R.O. 30/11/78, ff. 36–38; and Wright to Cornwallis, Aug. 20, 1780: P.R.O. 30/11/63, ff. 49–50. Wright offered in his own defense that he had enlisted prisoners only from the Savannah prison ships who were inhabitants of Georgia and of them only fifty.

46. For an account of this engagement as told to the British see Rawdon to Cornwallis, June 22, 24, and 30, 1780: P.R.O. 30/11/32, ff. 179–182, 189–190, and 218–220. Wallace, *Appeal to Arms*, p. 212, estimates that about four hundred on each side participated in the battle. In his detailed account Ward, *War of the Revolution*, II, 706–708, credits the patriots with four hundred men and the tories with eight hundred, about seven hundred of whom fought in the battle. J. B. O. Landrum, *Colonial and Revolutionary History of Upper South Carolina* (Greenville, S.C., 1897), on pp. 147–166 outlines in detail this "comic opera" engagement.

47. Cornwallis to Rawdon, June 29, 1780: *Cornwallis Corr.*, I, 49.

48. Cornwallis to Germain, Sept. 19, 1780: P.R.O. 30/11/76, ff. 17–20.
49. Innes to Cornwallis, Sept. 5, 1780: P.R.O. 30/11/64, f. 29.
50. For a discussion of provincial regiments see Smith, *Loyalists and Red-coats*, pp. 33–36, 63–78.
51. Innes to Cornwallis, July 28, 1780: P.R.O. 30/11/2, ff. 373–374.
52. Turnbull to Cornwallis, June 14, 1780: P.R.O. 30/11/2, ff. 147–148.
53. Yet Stedman, *History of the American War*, II, 500, claims that between twenty-five and thirty thousand loyalists served in provincial regiments during the war.
54. Clinton to Cornwallis, May 20, 1780: Clinton Papers.
55. Clinton to Ferguson, May 22, 1780: *Ibid*. British stores would supply the loyalist militia with arms and ammunition, but if the men wished to serve on horseback instead of on foot they would do so at their own expense. "On every occasion," the instructions concluded, "you will pay particular attention to restrain the militia from offering violence to innocent and inoffensive people, and by all means in your power protect the aged, the infirm, the women and children of every denomination from insult or outrage." But since Ferguson was also to endeavor "as much as possible to subsist your men and supply their wants at the expense of the known and obstinate enemys of the king and constitution alone," it was nearly inevitable that a militia, full of hate for its opponents, and with its opponents' examples before it, would offer violence to all kinds, including the "innocent and inoffensive" people.

    When Cornwallis took command he made a few additions and changes. As sections of the interior of South Carolina submitted to British rule, he appointed field officers for militia, investing them with civil and military power. Then he divided the militia into two classes. The first class, consisting of men over forty with a certain amount of property or with a family or with a record of past service, he appointed for patrol duty only in their own neighborhoods. They could not be called out for anything beyond home duty save to help quell insurrection or turn back an invasion of the province. The second class, composed of younger men, would assist in home duties, but they would also be liable for six or twelve months' service in the Carolinas or Georgia. See Clinton to Cornwallis, May 20, 1780 and Clinton to Ferguson, May 22, 1780: Clinton Papers. See also Cornwallis to Clinton, June 30, 1780: *Cornwallis Corr.*, I, 499.
56. Ferguson to Cornwallis, Aug. 29, 1780: P.R.O. 30/11/63, ff. 81–82.
57. DePeyster to Cornwallis, Oct 11, 1780: P.R.O. 30/11/3, ff. 210–211.
58. Ramsay gives some idea of the punishment of war in his claim that the

savagery around Ninety-Six created some fourteen hundred widows and orphans. See *Revolution of South Carolina*, II, 275.

59. The Americans considered Ninety-Six so vital that Greene laid regular siege to it in the spring and early summer of 1781. Yet today the casual visitor, if unacquainted with its historical importance, would not even find the fort or, rather, what remains of it. It lies to the south of the sleepy town of Ninety-Six not far from a marker erected by the D.A.R. to commemorate the first settlers of the town. But it can only be reached by challenging one's car to travel the Carolina red clay road, impassable after a rain, which runs past the earthworks. They are scarcely recognizable after more than a century of neglect. But the explorer willing to brave the dense stand of poison ivy can still walk along the ramparts which defied the patriots for so long. For descriptions of the works constructed by Cruger see Major James Weymss to Lord Rawdon, Oct. 29, 1780; and Rawdon to Cruger, Oct. 31, 1780: P.R.O. 30/11/2, ff. 307, 332; and Roderick Mackenzie, *Strictures on Lt. Col. Tarleton's History "of the Campaigns of 1780 and 1781, in the Southern Provinces of North America"* . . . (London, 1787), pp. 142–143. Wallace, *Appeal to Arms*, p. 242, and McCrady, *History of South Carolina in the Revolution*, pp. 278–300, detail Greene's siege.

60. The most recent biography of Marion is Robert D. Bass, *Swamp Fox* (London, 1960). The book is intended for public rather than scholarly consumption, although the author cites sources for individual chapters. We are skeptical of several of the verbatim conversations quoted in the book, but Bass' work is a readable account of Marion's career.

61. Cornwallis to Clinton, Dec. 3, 1780: *Cornwallis Corr.*, I, 72.

62. Cornwallis to Clinton, July 15, 1780: P.R.O. 30/11/72, f. 30. Ward, *War of the Revolution*, II, 708–709, gives a brief account of the affair which he took from Edward McCrady, *The History of South Carolina in the Revolution*, pp. 594–599.

63. Ward, *War of the Revolution*, II, 709, gives a brief account of the affair. See also "Allaire's Diary" in Draper, *King's Mountain*, p. 502. Robert Bass, *Gamecock* (New York, 1961), pp. 63–66, enters into considerable detail.

64. Rawdon to Cornwallis, July 31, 1780: P.R.O. 30/11/2, ff. 399–400.

65. Ward, *War of the Revolution*, II, 709–711, and Bass, *Gamecock*, pp. 68–73, detail this affair.

66. Major James Weymss to Cornwallis, July 28, 1780: P.R.O. 30/11/3, ff. 377–378; Cornwallis to Clinton, Aug. 6, 1780, and to Germain, Aug. 29,

1780: *Cornwallis Corr.*, I, 53, 505. Bass, *Swamp Fox*, p. 35, mentions the incident.
67. Cornwallis to Clinton, Aug. 6, 1780: *Cornwallis Corr.*, I, 54.

Chapter 9

(*pages 194–216*)

1. Cornwallis to Clinton, Aug. 29, 1780: *Cornwallis Corr.*, I, 58.
2. Mackenzie, *Strictures*, pp. 42–49, estimates Cornwallis' force at about fifteen hundred regulars and half as many militia. Ward, *War of the Revolution*, II, 738, argues that Hamilton's five hundred North Carolinians marched with Cornwallis, but Mackenzie claimed they remained behind to protect Camden. Militia figures, in any event, are unreliable.
3. Cornwallis to Clinton, Aug. 23, 1780: *Cornwallis Corr.*, I, 58.
4. Smith, *Loyalists and Redcoats*, p. 147.
5. For the skirmish see Ward, *War of the Revolution*, II, 738.
6. For Hanger's life see Colonel George Hanger (fourth Baron Coleraine), *The Life, Adventures, and Opinions of Col. George Hanger, Written by Himself*, 2 vols. (London, 1801). This autobiography, so colorful in many places, often wanders off for page after page into the author's view of life, to the neglect of important events in that life during the American Revolution. Considering the paucity of British contemporary accounts of the Revolution, it is too bad Hanger did not give his readers more facts and less philosophy. Robert Bass, *The Green Dragoon* (New York, 1957), pp. 85–88, sums up Hanger's career.
7. Major Joseph Graham, whose account is printed in full in David Schenck, *North Carolina, 1780–1781* (Raleigh, N.C., 1889), pp. 106–112, is the main source for the skirmish at Charlotte. Hanger, *Address to the Army*, pp. 55–60, gives his version of the affair, while Stedman, *History of the American War*, II, 239, quotes Cornwallis' words. Each account differs a little from the others.
8. Ferguson, *Two Scottish Soldiers*, p. 61.
9. *Ibid.*, pp. 66–67.
10. Lamb, *Journal*, pp. 308–309.
11. Ferguson, *Two Scottish Soldiers*, pp. 62–63. Ferguson's biography comes from this work.
12. Draper, *King's Mountain*, p. 73.
13. *Ibid.*, pp. 151–153.
14. *Ibid.*, p. 198.

15. For this incident see Stedman, *History of the American War*, II, 203, and 203n–204n; "Deposition of Lady Colleton and Miss Elizabeth Giles, witnessed by Patrick Ferguson and Banaster Tarleton, Monck's Corner, April 15, 1780," Clinton Papers; and Clinton's ordering of a court martial for May 23, 1780, in a letter from Francis Skelly to John André: Clinton Papers.

16. Cornwallis to Balfour, Sept. 13, 1780: P.R.O. 30/11/80, ff. 20–21.

17. Cornwallis to Balfour, July 3, 1780: P.R.O. 30/11/78, ff. 3–4.

18. There is little point in recounting all the backwoods skirmishes, such as Cedar Spring, Thicketty Fort, and Wofford's Ironworks, in South Carolina. Draper, *King's Mountain*, and Landrum, *Colonial and Revolutionary History of Upper South Carolina*, narrate them in detail.

19. Cornwallis to Clinton, Aug. 29, 1780: *Cornwallis Corr.*, I, 59.

20. A month after Camden he wrote to his commander: "It appears to me of some importance to settle this corner through which alone, the backwater plunderers can infest S. Carolina, or the Georgians either communicate with them or North Carolina." See Ferguson to Cornwallis, Sept. 9, 1780: P.R.O. 30/11/64, ff. 81–82.

21. These brief sketches come from Draper, *King's Mountain*; Landrum, *Upper South Carolina*; and Schenck, *North Carolina*.

22. Quoted in Draper, *King's Mountain*, p. 169.

23. Ferguson to Cornwallis, Oct. 3, 1780: P.R.O. 30/11/3, ff. 176–177.

24. Ferguson to Cornwallis, Oct. 5, 1780: *Ibid.*, ff. 189–190.

25. Ferguson's failure to erect fortifications revealed his injudicious contempt for the rebels, for he had certainly proved his engineering skill to Sir Henry Clinton. Ferguson wrote a long treatise on fortifications which he sent to Clinton in March of 1779, and Clinton mentioned the major's "skill as an engineer" in a letter to Germain in 1780. See Ferguson to Clinton, Mar. 13, 1779, and Clinton to Germain, May 13, 1780: Clinton Papers.

26. Ferguson to Cornwallis, Oct. 5 and 6, 1780: P.R.O. 30/11/3, ff. 191–192.

27. Quoted in Draper, *King's Mountain*, p. 211.

28. Draper, *King's Mountain*, p. 227, gives the following figures: Campbell's men 200; Shelby's 120; Cleveland's 110; McDowell's 90; Winston's 60; Lacey's 100; Williams' 60; Graham's and Hambright's 50; making a total of 910 men. The men on foot included a party of Georgians who joined either Williams' or Chronicle's South Fork men.

29. Robert Henry and David Vance, *Narrative of the Battle of Cowan's Ford, February 1st, 1781, and Narrative of the Battle of King's Mountain* (Greensboro, N.C., 1891), pp. 21–26: in Rankin, *American Revolution*, p. 159.

30. James P. Collins, *Autobiography of a Revolutionary Soldier* (Clinton, Louisiana, 1859), pp. 51–54: in Rankin, *American Revolution*, p. 263.
31. Henry and Vance, *Narrative*, pp. 34–36: in Rankin, *American Revolution*, p. 262.
32. Thomas Young, "Memoir," *The Orion*, III (1843), 86–87: in Rankin, *American Revolution*, p. 261.
33. Collins, *Autobiography:* in Rankin, *American Revolution*, p. 263.
34. DePeyster to Cornwallis, Oct. 11, 1780: P.R.O. 30/11/3, ff. 210–211; and Allaire's Diary": in Draper, *King's Mountain*, p. 510.
35. Collins, *Autobiography*, pp. 51–54: in Rankin, *American Revolution*, p. 263.
36. DePeyster to Cornwallis, Oct. 11, 1780: P.R.O. 30/11/3, ff. 210–211.
37. Most of our narrative of King's Mountain, as previous notes make abundantly clear, comes from Draper's magnificent *King's Mountain*. In our opinion it is one of the finest contributions to the historical literature of the military phase of the American Revolution. Thoroughly researched, detailed, and well written, it is an exciting, living account of the hilltop fight, which perhaps more than all the other battles of the Revolution catches the imagination.

Chapter 10

(pages 217–229)

1. Collins, *Autobiography*, p. 263: quoted in Rankin, *American Revolution*, p. 263.
2. Ward, *War of the Revolution*, II, 742–743.
3. DePeyster to Cornwallis, Oct. 11, 1780: P.R.O. 30/11/3, ff. 210–211.
4. Allaire's account in *Royal Gazette*, New York, Feb. 24, 1781: printed in Draper, *King's Mountain*, p. 518.
5. Cornwallis to William Smallwood, Nov. 10, 1780: *Cornwallis Corr.*, I, 67. Draper's patriotic zeal in *King's Mountain* justifies the hangings with the same logic (or lack of it) that loyalists used to justify their own deeds of a similar nature. Draper does not, however, excuse the hanging of Mills.
6. Depositions by Lts. John Taylor and William Stevenson of the New Jersey Volunteers: P.R.O. 30/11/4, f. 254; and "Allaire's Diary," Draper, *King's Mountain*, pp. 511–515.
7. *Ibid.*
8. See, for example, the conversation which Draper records between tories and whigs at the home of Robert Henry shortly after the battle in *King's Mountain*, pp. 365–367.

9. *Ibid.,* p. 367.
10. Gray to Cornwallis, Sept. 30, 1780: P.R.O. 30/11/64, ff. 130–131.
11. Weymss to Cornwallis, Sept. 20, 1780: P.R.O. 30/11/3, ff. 80–81.
12. Weymss to Cornwallis, Sept. 30, 1780: P.R.O. 30/11/64, ff. 134–135.
13. See Bass, *Swamp Fox,* pp. 59–70.
14. Cruger to Cornwallis, Oct. 13, 1780: P.R.O. 30/11/3, ff. 220–221.
15. For the shortage of flour see Cornwallis to Turnbull, Oct. 5, 1780: P.R.O. 30/11/81, ff. 21–22. For an example of a militia report see Major Zachary Gibbs to Cornwallis, Oct. 12, 1780: P.R.O. 30/11/3, ff. 212–213.
16. Major Hanger described rebel harassment vividly. "I will aver, that when collecting forage, I myself have seen situations near that town [Charlotte], where the woods were so intricate, and so thick with underwood, (which is not common in the southern parts of America) that it was totally impossible to see our videtts, or our centries from the main body. In one instance particularly, where Lieutenant Oldfield, of the Quartermaster General's department, was wounded; the enemy, under cover of impervious thickets, impenetrable to any troops except those well acquainted with the private paths, approached so near to the whole line of the British infantry, as to give them their fire before they were perceived. Charlotte Town itself, on one side most particularly, where the light and legion infantry camp lay, was enveloped with woods. Earl Cornwallis himself, visiting the pickets of these corps (which from Tarleton's sickness I had the honour of commanding at that time) ordered me to advance them considerably further than usually is the custom, and connect them more closely one with the other." See Hanger, *Address,* pp. 68–70. See also Stedman, *History of the American War,* II, 240 and 240n.
17. Cornwallis to Turnbull, Oct. 5, 1780: P.R.O. 30/11/81, ff. 21–22; and to Maj. Gen. Alexander Leslie, Nov. 12, 1780: *Cornwallis Corr.,* I, 69.
18. Stedman, *History of the American War,* II, 240 and 240n.
19. His fever did not come upon Cornwallis "suddenly," as Draper says in *King's Mountain,* p. 369. His aide, Lieutenant Money, had noticed the Earl's indisposition from a cold as early as Oct. 10. See Lt. John Money to Balfour, Oct. 10, 1780: P.R.O. 30/11/81, f. 31. See also Rawdon to Turnbull, Oct. 19, 1780: P.R.O. 30/11/3, ff. 241–242.
20. Cornwallis to Balfour, Nov. 1, 1780: P.R.O. 30/11/82, ff. 1–2.
21. Stedman, *History of the American War,* II, 247–250. The commissary comments on a practice begun here that soon spread throughout the army. Soldiers adopted the militia practice of punching holes in their

tin canteens with a bayonet. The canteen then served as a rasp to grind corn.

22. *Ibid.*, pp. 248–249, and 249n. Stedman praised the loyalist militia for their efforts. Militia also scouted for and procured the provisions the army used when it camped at night. They drove in the cattle, gathered up crops, and fought off patriots. To reward them for these efforts, the men of the quartermaster general's department beat them and hurled abuse at them. When he recovered, Cornwallis would remember this treatment and add it to the score he had to settle with the quartermaster general.

23. Hanger, *Life*, II, 179.

24. Stedman, *History of the American War*, II, 247–250.

25. Lieutenant Stark's account is in a letter to Cornwallis of Nov. 9, 1780: P.R.O. 30/11/4, f. 81. See also Cornwallis to Balfour, Nov. 10, 1780: P.R.O. 30/11/82, ff. 18–19; Cornwallis to Cruger, Nov. 11, 1780: *Cornwallis Corr.*, I, 68; and Cornwallis to Clinton, Dec. 3, 1780: *Ibid.*, p. 511. Sumter dashed off an account to Nathanael Greene on November 9. See Greene Papers, volume II, Clements Library. Stedman, *History of the American War*, II, 252, and Bass, *Gamecock*, pp. 97–99, sum up the battle.

26. Bass, *Gamecock*, pp. 102–111, details the battle. See also Tarleton to Cornwallis, Nov. 22, 1780: P.R.O. 30/11/4, ff. 173–174.

27. Cornwallis to Clinton, Dec. 3, 1780: *Cornwallis Corr.*, I, 513.

28. See for instance the Earl's letter to Money on Nov. 11, 1780: P.R.O. 30/11/4, f. 92.

29. Major Archibald McArthur to Cornwallis, Dec. 1, 1780: P.R.O. 30/11/4, ff. 269–270.

30. See Rawdon to Cornwallis, Dec. 1 and 2, 1780: P.R.O. 30/11/4, ff. 263–264, 271–272. See also Ramsay, *Revolution in South Carolina*, II, 187–188.

31. As late as November 12 the Earl still talked about advancing to meet Leslie at Cross Creek, but he finally abandoned the idea by November 21. See his letter of that date to Leslie in P.R.O. 30/11/82, f. 75.

32. See Clinton, *Narrative*, p. 227; Clinton Papers, one of three boxes of memoranda; and Clinton's marginal comments on p. 215 of vol. II of Stedman's *History of the American War*.

33. For the sequence of exchanges, see Ferguson to Cornwallis, Sept. 30, 1780: P.R.O. 30/11/64, ff. 128–129; Cornwallis to Ferguson and to McArthur, Oct. 5, 1780: P.R.O. 30/11/81, ff. 18–20; Ferguson to Cornwallis, Oct. 3, 1780: P.R.O. 30/11/3, ff. 176–177; and Cornwallis to Ferguson, Oct. 6, 1780: P.R.O. 30/11/81, f. 23.

34. Mackenzie, *Strictures,* pp. 57–60.
35. Cornwallis to the Bishop of Lichfield and Coventry, Dec. 12, 1788: *Cornwallis Corr.,* I, 316.
36. Cornwallis to Ferguson, Oct. 6, 1780: P.R.O. 30/11/81, f. 23.

Chapter 11

(pages 230–248)

1. Cornwallis to Rawdon, Nov. 18, 1780: P.R.O. 30/11/82, ff. 61–62.
2. See Cornwallis to Major England, Sept. 20, 1780: P.R.O. 30/11/80, ff. 31–32; Cornwallis to Balfour, Aug. 31, 1780: P.R.O. 30/11/79, ff. 47–48; Turnbull to Cornwallis, Nov. 8, 1780; Balfour to Cornwallis, Nov. 5, 1780; and A. Knecht to Cornwallis, Nov. 24, 1780: P.R.O. 30/11/4, ff. 27–34, 61, and 198–199.
3. Cornwallis to Tarleton, Jan. 7, 1781: P.R.O. 30/11/64, ff. 29–30.
4. Cornwallis to Balfour, June 20, 1780: P.R.O. 30/11/77, ff. 16–17.
5. We are indebted for much of our knowledge of the wagon service to Professor Arthur Bowler, Department of History, University of Buffalo. See also the "Seventh Report of the Commissioners Appointed to Examine, Take, and State, the Public Accounts of the Kingdom," *Journals of the House of Commons,* XXXVIII (1803), 1069.
6. "We get plenty of good strong draft horses for ten or twelve pounds apiece, but mostly under ten," Cornwallis noted in November. "Now as government is charged fifteen I cannot help thinking there is still a fair profit left. Besides that, I cannot think Britain engaged in this war merely for the enrichment of the Qr. Mr. Genl." The Earl also refused to grant a warrant of 451 guineas to one captain in the department who had used up £2000 of the army's money with few measurable benefits to the army. See Cornwallis to Balfour, Nov. 16, 1780: P.R.O. 30/11/82, ff. 46–47; and Cornwallis to Major England, June 20, 1781: P.R.O. 30/11/87, ff. 11–12.
7. "You will hardly believe," Cornwallis declared to Balfour ten days following the Camden victory, "that after all our successes the Qr. Mr. Genl. can furnish only 26 teams, which he calls fit for service, except those attach'd to the regiments." See Cornwallis to Balfour, Aug. 29, 1780: P.R.O. 30/11/79, ff. 45–46.
8. Stedman, *History of the American War,* II, 249.
9. Cornwallis to Balfour, Sept. 3, 1780: P.R.O. 30/11/80, ff. 1–4.
10. Cornwallis to Balfour, Nov. 10, 1780: P.R.O. 30/11/82, ff. 18–19.

11. "Seventh Report of the Commissioners," *Commons Journals*, XXXVIII, Appendix 33, p. 1109.
12. Cornwallis to Tarleton, Jan. 7, 1781: P.R.O. 30/11/84, ff. 29–30.
13. Cornwallis to Balfour, Jan. 7, 1781: *ibid.*, ff. 25–26.
14. He testified against the abuses of this department in 1782 before the parliamentary commissioners investigating the department.
15. Stedman, *History of the American War*, II, 228n, 229n.
16. *Ibid.*, 354n, 355n.
17. Samuel Mathis to Henry Haldane, Nov. 21, 1780: P.R.O. 30/11/71, ff. 9–10.
18. Cornwallis to Stedman, Dec. 15, 1780: P.R.O. 30/11/83, ff. 46–47.
19. P.R.O. 30/11/110, ff. 4b–10 records Cruden's long and painful story. It contains his narrative before the board of police and the decisions of that body in 1781 and 1782. See also P.R.O. 30/11/7, ff. 8–19, "Copies of letters, from Earl Cornwallis, Lord Rawdon and others, likewise of a memorial, letters &c respecting the business of the sequestered property as well real as personal &c &c &c."
20. Balfour to Rawdon, Oct. 20, 1780: P.R.O. 30/11/3, ff. 289–290.
21. Balfour to Cornwallis, Nov. 5, 1780: P.R.O. 30/11/4, ff. 27–34.
22. Cornwallis to Balfour, Nov. 10, 1780: P.R.O. 30/11/82, ff. 18–19.
23. Cornwallis to Tarleton, Nov. 10, 1780: *ibid.*, ff. 20–21.
24. Cornwallis to Balfour, Nov. 17, 1780: *ibid.*, ff. 55–56.
25. See "Abstract of Cloathing received from New York by the Three Brothers Store Ship, Captain Lock, for the use of his Majesty's Provincial Forces in Carolina," Charleston, Nov. 30, 1780: P.R.O. 30/11/103, f. 11; and "Invoice of Camp Equipage &c Shipped on board the Brigg Experiment . . . ," *ibid.*, f. 8.
26. See Balfour to Cornwallis, Nov. 5, 1780: P.R.O. 30/11/4, ff. 27–34. Several letters in the Cornwallis Papers relate to this supply route. See, for example, Rawdon to Cornwallis, Nov. 16, 1780, and Balfour to Cornwallis, Nov. 3, 1780: *ibid.*, ff. 139–140, 252–253.
27. Cornwallis to Balfour, Nov. 27, 1780: P.R.O. 30/11/82, ff. 111–112.
28. See Cornwallis to Rawdon, Nov. 28, Dec. 1, Dec. 3, and to Balfour, Dec. 9, 1780: P.R.O. 30/11/82, ff. 119–120; P.R.O. 30/11/83, ff. 1–3, 7–8, and 31–32.
29. Cornwallis to Tarleton, Dec. 18, 1780: *Cornwallis Corr.*, I, 74.
30. Cornwallis to Rawdon, Nov. 16, 1780: P.R.O. 30/11/82, ff. 53–54.
31. Rawdon to Cornwallis, Nov. 29, 1780: P.R.O. 30/11/4, ff. 234–235.
32. Rawdon to Cornwallis, December, 1780: P.R.O. 30/11/66, ff. 25–26.

33. David George to Cornwallis, Dec. 30, 1780: *ibid.*, ff. 44–45.
34. Cornwallis to Leslie, Jan. 14, 1781: P.R.O. 30/11/84, ff. 59–60.
35. Balfour to Cornwallis, July 17, 1780: P.R.O. 30/11/2, ff. 317–318.
36. Weymss to Cornwallis, Aug. 4, 1780: P.R.O. 30/11/63, ff. 17–18.
37. Cornwallis to Balfour, Sept. 13, 1780: P.R.O. 30/11/80, ff. 20–21.
38. Cornwallis to Major England, Sept. 20, 1780: *ibid.*, ff. 31–32.
39. Hayes to John André, Apr. 13, 1780: Clinton Papers.
40. Cornwallis to Clinton, July 16, 1780: P.R.O. 30/11/ 72, f. 32.
41. Hayes to Cornwallis, Nov. 5, 1780: P.R.O. 30/11/4, ff. 134–135.

Chapter 12

(*pages 249–273*)
1. Stedman, *History of the American War,* II, 369.
2. Cornwallis to Sir James Wright, Bart., President, and the members of the board of agents for the American Loyalists: P.R.O. 30/11/94, ff. 9–10.
3. Only after his arrival upon the spot — for a longer period than the brief experience at Charlotte — did he reluctantly conclude that the long series of oppressions and persecutions had finally broken the spirits of the loyalists before the British appeared in North Carolina. "We had been too sanguine on both sides," he would later explain, "for expectations had been too high of cooperation & assistance, and our friends had expected too much from the appearance of a British army in the Province." See Cornwallis to Wright: P.R.O. 30/11/94, ff. 9–10.
4. Colonel Charles O'Hara to the Duke of Grafton, Apr. 20, 1781: Grafton Papers Ac. 423/191, Bury Record Office, Bury St. Edmunds.
5. For details of Greene's life see Thayer, *Greene.*
6. Quoted without footnote in Burke Davis, *The Cowpens–Guilford Courthouse Campaign* (Philadelphia and New York, 1962), p. 69.
7. Stedman, *History of the American War,* II, 353.
8. *Ibid.* gives these figures. Theodore Thayer, *Nathanael Greene, Strategist of the American Revolution* (New York, 1960), p. 297, credits Morgan with 620 men. See also Don Higginbotham, *Daniel Morgan, Revolutionary Rifleman* (Chapel Hill, N.C., 1961). Chapter VIII details Morgan's activities before the battle of Cowpens.
9. "State of the Troops left in South Carolina under the Command of the Right Honorable Colonel Lord Rawdon," Jan. 15, 1781: P.R.O.

30/11/103, f. 16. Of these almost half were provincials, the rest British and Germans.

10. Balfour to Lt. Col. George Campbell, Jan. 25, 1781: P.R.O. 30/11/109, ff. 5–6.

11. Cornwallis to Balfour, Jan. 1, 1781: P.R.O. 30/11/84, ff. 1–2. See also Cornwallis to Rawdon, same date: *ibid.*, ff. 3–4.

12. Actually Lt. Col. Robert Gray of the Cheraw militia had suggested the expedition to Cape Fear at the end of September, 1780. Gray reasoned that the British could never form an effective loyalist militia in the Cheraw area unless redcoats held the Cape Fear. Although Cornwallis by 1781 worried more about getting supplies than about getting loyalist help, Craig's expedition would hopefully answer both needs. See Robert Gray to Cornwallis, Sept. 30, 1780: P.R.O. 30/11/64, ff. 130–131.

13. For Arnold's account of his activities see P.R.O. 30/11/99, ff. 23–26.

14. The British regulars included: the elite Brigade of Guards (690); the 7th regiment (167); the 3d Company of the 16th regiment (41), the 23d regiment (286); the 33d regiment (286), the 1st battalion of the 71st regiment (249), the 2d battalion of the 71st (237), and the light company of the 71st (69). See "State of the Troops that marched with the Army under the Command of Lieut. General Earl Cornwallis": P.R.O. 30/11/5, f. 134. The figures quoted are rank and file present and fit for duty on Jan. 15, 1781. Leslie's men, who are included in the return, had not yet joined Cornwallis. Leslie brought the Guards, Bose, Jagers, some light horse, the North Carolina Regiment of Volunteers, and two pieces of artillery. See A. R. Newsome, ed., "A British Orderly Book, 1780–1781," *North Carolina Historical Review*, IX (1932), pp. 180, 278. As Leslie marched to meet him, Cornwallis made some alterations in the major general's forces, ordering Leslie to leave some units with Rawdon and to bring other forces from Rawdon's command.

15. Cornwallis to Rawdon, Dec. 30, 1780: *Cornwallis Corr.*, I, 77. Cornwallis said that the report "frightened" him, for if true, it "would greatly embarrass our operations, and engage us in a naval expedition, which I fear we are but ill prepared for."

16. Cornwallis to Rawdon, Jan. 1, 1781: P.R.O. 30/11/84, ff. 3–4. Greene knew, of course, that Cornwallis planned to march north and that he only awaited the junction with Leslie's reinforcements before moving. But Camden lies east of the direct route from Charleston (where Leslie had landed his men) to Winnsboro. Thus by ordering Leslie to Camden, Cornwallis "rendered precarious any calculations Greene might make as

to the time of commencing his movement toward Virginia" and also the route by which he would march. Had Leslie moved directly to Winnsboro an upper route north would have been indicated, thereby relieving Greene of apprehensions for himself and causing him to concentrate on affording relief to Morgan. On the other hand, Leslie's going to Camden seemed to indicate a lower route. See Henry Lee, Jr., *The Campaign of 1781 in the Carolinas, with Remarks Historical and Critical on Johnson's Life of Greene* (Chicago, 1962), p. 90. This book is a reprint of the work which first appeared in Philadelphia in 1824. For Cornwallis' plans for Leslie see Cornwallis to Balfour, Jan. 5, 1781: P.R.O. 30/11/84, f. 14.

17. For Pickens see McCrady, *South Carolina in the Revolution, 1780–1783*, pp. 18–22.

18. Cornwallis to Balfour and Rawdon, Jan. 1, 1781, and to Tarleton, Jan. 3, 1781: P.R.O. 30/11/84, ff. 1–4, 39.

19. Cornwallis to Tarleton, Jan. 5, 1781: P.R.O. 30/11/84, f. 15.

20. Cornwallis' letters to Rawdon, Balfour, Leslie, and Tarleton, P.R.O. 30/11/84, give a day-to-day account of his own movements and his intelligence of the movements of others during January of 1781. Leslie mentions his road repairs in a letter to Cornwallis on Dec. 26, 1781: P.R.O. 30/11/4, f. 398.

21. Cornwallis to Leslie, Jan. 14, 1781: P.R.O. 30/11/84, ff. 59–62. For Cornwallis' letters to Tarleton on the fourteenth and sixteenth, informing him of his own plans, see *ibid.*, ff. 63 and 76. Tarleton later said that he expected Cornwallis to march fast enough to trap Morgan. Yet the Earl had clearly outlined his own intended movements.

22. As with almost all troop returns for the army or ship returns for the navy in the eighteenth century, there is a certain amount of confusion evident in the accounts of Tarleton's force. According to Tarleton's own account of the *Campaigns*, pp. 210–212, he had 550 cavalry and infantry of the Legion, 200 infantry of the 1st battalion of the 71st regiment, 200 infantry of the 7th regiment, and 50 dragoons of the 17th. But Tarleton's account is in so many particulars in error that the authors sought confirmation of his troop figures, and have not been entirely satisfied. For example, the state of the army under Cornwallis, P.R.O. 30/11/5, f. 134, does not list the 17th Dragoons at all and places the numbers of rank and file of the British Legion at 451. Furthermore, it lists 69 from the light company of the 71st, and 41 from the 3d company of the 16th. Yet we know Clinton left 60 men of the 17th Dragoons in Charleston in June of 1780. Perhaps the men from the

light company of the 71st and 3d company of the 16th made up what Cornwallis referred to as the "corps annexed" to Tarleton's Legion. See Cornwallis to Clinton, Jan. 18, 1781: *Cornwallis Corr.*, I, 82. All accounts agree sufficiently, as far as number is concerned, in making 1000 a very close approximation. Morgan wrote Greene that the British "confess" to having fought with 1037 men. See M. F. Treacy, *Prelude to Yorktown, the Southern Campaign of Nathanael Greene* (Chapel Hill, 1963), p. 111.

23. Tarleton, *A History of the Campaigns,* pp. 213–214.
24. Cornwallis to Lord Amherst, Aug. 21, 1780: P.R.O. 30/11/79, ff. 29–30.
25. "You say nothing to me about your rank of Lieut. Colo.," Cornwallis wrote, "which if it is true that you have it, I take very ill, as you must be convinced that it is an event in which I feel myself much interested." Cornwallis to Tarleton, Nov. 8, 1780: P.R.O. 30/11/82, ff. 12–13. On Nov. 11, Tarleton informed the Earl of his promotion. See his letter of that date quoted in full in Bass, *Green Dragoon,* p. 113.
26. Tarleton to Cornwallis, Aug. 5, 1780: P.R.O. 30/11/63, ff. 19–20. The story of his name being used to hush children appears in Ferguson, *Two Scottish Soldiers,* p. 78.
27. Letter from Governor Rutledge, Dec. 8, 1780: quoted in Ramsay, *Revolution in South Carolina,* II, 159–160. Johnson, *Greene,* II, 471, attributed to Rawdon the very same burning of widow Richardson's property that Ramsay had attributed to Tarleton and cited the same source, a letter of Governor Rutledge of December 8. Bass, *Green Dragoon,* p. 111, attributes the deed to Tarleton.
28. Mackenzie, *Strictures,* pp. 39–40.
29. Ramsay, *Revolution in South Carolina,* II, 200.
30. Tarleton to Lieutenant Haldane, Dec. 24, 1780: P.R.O. 30/11/4, ff. 383–384.
31. Mackenzie, *Strictures,* pp. 26–27.
32. For Morgan's character and leadership see Higginbotham, *Morgan.*
33. Tarleton, *A History of the Campaigns,* p. 221.
34. Mackenzie, *Strictures,* pp. 95–96, says Morgan had about 100 cavalry and Tarleton 350. Treacy, *Prelude to Yorktown,* p. 94, gives Morgan 80 cavalrymen and 50 mounted infantrymen.
35. Morgan wrote Greene on January 19 that he fought with 800 men. See Treacy, *Prelude to Yorktown,* p. 111. Higginbotham, *Morgan,* p. 142, says that Morgan had "fewer than 1,000 troops opposing Tarleton's 1,100." Tarleton believed or pretended to believe that Morgan had 1922 men. See *A History of the Campaigns,* p. 216.

Cornwallis wrote Clinton on January 18, *Cornwallis Corr.*, I, 82, that Morgan's forces, by the best accounts he could obtain, consisted of 1200 or 1300: 500 Continental and Virginia state troops, 100 cavalry, and 600 or 700 militia. The militia, he explained, "is so fluctuating that it is impossible to ascertain its number, within some hundreds, for three days following." Even allowing, however, for the uncertain number of militia, Cornwallis' figures do not square with those of Morgan, who said that two thirds of his 80 were militia. If Morgan's account is accurate, he cannot have had more than 300 regulars, including the cavalry. Yet Treacy, *Prelude to Yorktown*, pp. 84 and 94 respectively, gives Morgan 290 Marylanders and 80 cavalry. The authors have accepted Morgan's figure as being closest to the total number involved, partly because Mackenzie, who fought at Cowpens under Tarleton, accepts Ramsay's statement that Tarleton had a superiority of five to four. See Mackenzie, *Strictures*, pp. 88ff. Even so, Mackenzie later confuses the issue by saying, on p. 95, that Morgan had 1000 men, two thirds of them militia, 100 cavalry, and the rest Continentals. Stedman, *History of the American War*, II, 360, says that the British were superior in numbers and that Morgan had 540 Continentals (including cavalry presumably) and the rest militia.

36. Thomas Young, "Memoir," *Orion*, II, 100; in Rankin, *American Revolution*, p. 270.
37. Mackenzie, *Strictures*, pp. 106–118, gives a detailed account and criticism of the action at Cowpens, particularly valuable because Mackenzie served in the engagement.
38. John Eager Howard, *Magazine of American History*, VII (1881), 279: in Rankin, *American Revolution*, p. 271.
39. Mackenzie, *Strictures*, pp. 99–100.
40. *Ibid.*, pp. 100ff.
41. Tarleton, *A History of the Campaigns*, p. 221.
42. *Ibid.*, p. 218.
43. Treacy, *Prelude to Yorktown*, p. 111, cites the material losses. Tarleton, *A History of the Campaigns*, p. 218, admitted some but not all of these losses. Higginbotham, *Morgan*, p. 142, says the Americans took 70 Negroes and 2 regimental flags (the other one perhaps that of the 71st). His evidence comes from the diary of a revolutionary officer in the Draper Papers of the State Historical Society of Wisconsin. According to Cornwallis' troop returns, P.R.O. 30/11/5, f. 134, Cowpens took 784 men away from the British. Treacy, *Prelude to Yorktown*, p. 111, states that the Americans killed 100, took 229 wounded,

and captured 400 unwounded, while Higginbotham, *Morgan,* p. 142, says the Old Wagoner killed 110 British and captured a total of 702 men.

44. These figures for American losses appear in Stedman, *History of the American War,* II, 359, and in all other accounts which the authors have seen. Information on the battle of Cowpens comes from a variety of works. The main ones include Tarleton, *A History of the Campaigns;* Stedman, *History of the American War,* II; Mackenzie, *Strictures;* Treacy, *Prelude to Yorktown;* Higginbotham, *Morgan;* and Bass, *Green Dragoon.* Kenneth Roberts, the eminent historical novelist, devoted a short book, *The Battle of Cowpens: the Great Morale Builder* (New York, 1958), entirely to this one engagement. Although interesting, and sometimes exciting, it can only be called semi-historical. Roberts, for example, put words into the mouth of Daniel Morgan without producing any evidence that Morgan ever said the words or even thought them. Perhaps the novelist deserves greater license than the historian in a work of history. But Roberts' main — indeed only — thesis about the significance of Cowpens seems ludicrous. He asserts, without any supporting evidence, that Cowpens served only to build flagging American morale and awaken the North to the problems of the South. "The true value of Morgan's victory at the Cowpens was its enormous effect on Northern morale, and its awakening of public opinion in the North to the need of giving Greene the military assistance he so richly deserved." (p. 103) Such an assessment overlooks completely the loss of all of Cornwallis' light infantry, which crippled him so severely at the beginning of the campaign against Greene, that had the Quaker general received neither a penny nor a trooper from Congress, Cornwallis might still have ended up disastrously.

45. Quoted in Lee, *Campaign of 1781 in the Carolinas,* p. 98n.

46. *Ibid.*

47. Treacy, *Prelude to Yorktown,* p. 113.

48. This incident is related in a number of places. See, for example, Landrum, *Revolutionary History of Upper South Carolina,* pp. 288–289. Landrum states that the Legionnaires recognized the loyalists before they attacked. Tarleton's story is in *A History of the Campaigns,* p. 218.

49. Tarleton, *A History of the Campaigns,* p. 218.

50. P.R.O. 30/11/84, f. 76.

51. See Tarleton, *A History of the Campaigns,* pp. 213, 219; and P.R.O. 30/11/84, f. 63.

52. Tarleton, *A History of the Campaigns,* p. 213.

53. See, for example, Ward, *War of the Revolution,* II, 763.

54. P.R.O. 30/11/84, f. 63.

55. Tarleton, *A History of the Campaigns,* p. 219.

56. Hanger, *Address to the Army,* p. 79, says that "many officers" arrived "that same day," but does not explain how they knew where to find Cornwallis, since Tarleton supposedly did not know. Ward, *War of the Revolution,* II, 764, says Cornwallis learned of Cowpens that evening by means of "a hard-riding courier on a well lathered horse," but again does not explain how the courier could arrive so far in advance of Tarleton. Higginbotham, *Morgan,* p. 147, says that Cornwallis "had heard rumors of Tarleton's disaster the night after the battle."

57. Higginbotham, *Morgan,* p. 147. Higginbotham cites McJunkin's memoir, Draper Papers, 23VV193, State Historical Society of Wisconsin.

58. Cornwallis to Rawdon, Jan. 21, 1781: P.R.O. 30/11/84, f. 78.

59. Mackenzie, *Strictures,* pp. 88–89.

60. See Clinton Papers. Patrick Ferguson, two and one half years earlier, had written a memorandum on the need for more light troops, since the infantry line was unsuited for the pursuit necessary to follow up successes. His remarks seemed in some instances almost to predict Cowpens. See his memorandum of Aug. 1, 1778, in Clinton Papers.

61. McCrady, *South Carolina in the Revolution, 1780–1783,* p. 53. McCrady quotes the *Memoirs* of General Moultrie, II, 256–257.

62. Tarleton, *A History of the Campaigns,* p. 222.

63. The authors must reject the suggestion of Treacy, *Prelude to Yorktown,* pp. 127–128, that Tarleton's demand constituted blackmail in the more direct sense; i.e., in the sense that Cornwallis feared an investigation into his own conduct. Cornwallis had no such fear, and the reason given by Treacy, the Earl's slowness of movement, does not apply. The authors have shown that Cornwallis had his own good reasons for his actions. More importantly, a court martial would have made public all letters and exchanges relative to the Cowpens campaign. Tarleton had much more to fear from such an exposure than Cornwallis.

64. Tarleton, *A History of the Campaigns,* p. 252.

65. It is interesting to speculate what might have been the course of events in the Carolinas and Virginia in 1781 if, months earlier, Tarleton had been in New York (rather than on board the *Romulus* sailing in Clinton's expedition to South Carolina) to receive a letter from the adjutant of the 79th regiment, ordering Tarleton to "take the Earliest opportunity" of joining his regiment at Jamaica. Naturally, he received the news when he arrived in South Carolina, but by then he had be-

come actively involved in Clinton's campaign, and Sir Henry kept him in South Carolina. What might have happened if Tarleton — the only British officer commanding British regulars to lose a major engagement to the Americans in the open field — had been in Jamaica rather than North America? See Timothy Russel to Tarleton, Jan. 23, 1780: Clinton Papers; and Bass, *Green Dragoon,* pp. 77–78.

66. Stedman, *History of the American War,* II, 359–360.
67. See Willcox, *Portrait,* p. 353. Willcox supports Clinton's judgment of Cornwallis in this instance, though not in other matters.

Chapter 13

(*pages 274–310*)

1. "British Orderly Book," *N.C. Hist. Review,* IX, 284–285.
2. At least Thayer, *Greene,* p. 307; and Higginbotham, *Morgan,* p. 147, assert that Cornwallis followed the wrong road.
3. Cornwallis to Rawdon, Jan. 21, 1781: P.R.O. 30/11/84, f. 78. That night Cornwallis ordered the Legion, the Guards, and the 33d to be ready to march the next morning at 6:30. See "British Orderly Book," *N.C. Hist. Review,* IX, 285.
4. Cornwallis to Rawdon, Jan. 25, 1781: P.R.O. 30/11/84, ff. 83–84.
5. Cornwallis' reasoning, though it may have been faulty, was consistently along these lines. After the war, when he engaged in an acrimonious pamphlet controversy with Clinton over who was to blame for the disaster at Yorktown, he repeated the same arguments to the public that he had used privately to justify his movements in North Carolina. See *An Answer to that Part of the Narrative of Lieutenant-General Sir Henry Clinton, K.B. which relates to the Conduct of Lieutenant-General Earl Cornwallis, During the Campaign in North America, in the Year 1781* (London, 1783): in B. F. Stevens, *The Campaign in Virginia, 1781: An Exact Reprint of Six Rare Pamphlets on the Clinton-Cornwallis Controversy* (2 vols.; London, 1888), I, 65–67.
6. O'Hara to Grafton, Apr. 20, 1781: Grafton Papers, Ac. 423/191.
7. There is some discrepancy as to what supplies Cornwallis retained. In his letter to Rawdon on the day of the bonfire, Cornwallis specifically enumerated rum, salt, ammunition, and hospital stores as items that he kept. See letter of note 4 above. In his letter to Germain dated from Guilford on Mar. 17, 1781, two days after the battle, he said that he kept only the wagons loaded with salt, ammunition, and hospital stores, and four "reserved empty in readiness for sick or wounded." See *Cornwallis*

Corr., I, 517. O'Hara wrote to Grafton (see letter of note 5) that "the only carriages that remained exclusive of the canon and ammunition were a few waggons for salt. Even the hospital waggons were destroyed." The discrepancy as to rum may be explained if Cornwallis at first kept the rum and later decided to dispense with it. The dates of his two letters make this suggestion a possible one. But the discrepancy as to the survival or destruction of the hospital wagons is less easily resolved, since both Cornwallis' letter to Germain and O'Hara's to Grafton were written well after the event — in other words, after any alteration of decision would have occurred. Stedman, *History of the American War,* II, 362 and 363n., says that no wagons were kept except those loaded with hospital stores, salt, and ammunition, and four empty ones for the sick and wounded.

8. O'Hara to Grafton, Apr. 20, 1781: Grafton Papers, Ac. 423/191.
9. "British Orderly Book," *N.C. Hist. Review,* IX, 287.
10. *Ibid.,* p. 286; Thayer, *Greene;* and *Cornwallis Corr.,* I, 517, mention collecting provisions. Cornwallis specifies flour.
11. Both Cornwallis (see letter of note 8) and O'Hara (see letter of note 5) mentioned the cheerfulness. Treacy, *Prelude to Yorktown,* p. 124, says there was a reduction of 227 men in Cornwallis' force "although no battle was fought and no epidemic occurred." But there were losses at Cowan's Ford. Treacy's figure of 227 is merely the difference between Cornwallis' "State of the Troops" for Feb. 1 and Mar. 1, respectively 2440 and 2213. See P.R.O. 30/11/5, f. 134. Davis, *Cowpens–Guilford Courthouse,* p. 73, also speaks of desertions but uses the same argument and figures as Treacy.
12. "British Orderly Book," *N.C. Hist. Review,* IX, 289.
13. O'Hara to Grafton, Apr. 20, 1781: Grafton Papers, Ac. 423/191.
14. The account of Greene is taken from Thayer, *Greene,* pp. 308–311.
15. "British Orderly Book," *N.C. Hist. Review,* IX, 291.
16. Description of Cowan's Ford comes mostly from O'Hara to Grafton, Apr. 20, 1781: Grafton Papers, Ac. 423/191. Lamb, *Journal of Occurrences* says the Catawba was about half a mile wide where the British crossed, but Schenck, *North Carolina,* p. 238, says four hundred yards.
17. Schenck, *North Carolina,* p. 239.
18. Henry and Vance, *Narrative:* in Rankin, *American Revolution,* p. 276.
19. Lamb, *Journal of Occurrences,* p. 343.
20. *Ibid.,* pp. 343–344.
21. Quoted by Rankin, *American Revolution,* p. 277.
22. Lamb, *Journal of Occurrences,* pp. 343–345. Schenck, *North Carolina,*

pp. 246–247, states that thirty-one were killed and thirty-five wounded.
23. Schenck, *North Carolina*, pp. 241–242.
24. Quoted by Rankin, *American Revolution*, p. 277.
25. See Schenck, *North Carolina*, pp. 243–246.
26. Tarleton later described the militia as "vigilant" and "prepared for an attack." See Bass, *Green Dragoon*, p. 166; and Tarleton, *A History of the Campaigns*, p. 226.
27. Stedman, *History of the American War*, II, 366 and 366n.
28. Schenck, *North Carolina*, p. 246.
29. Perhaps these boats were made from the boards that Greene had in late December ordered to be sent from all nearby sawmills to Haly's Ford, or Haley's Ferry, about fifty-five miles downstream (that is, generally southwest) from Trading Ford on the Yadkin. See Greene to Col. Thomas Wade, Dec. 19, 1780: Greene Papers, William L. Clements Library. In an endeavor such as boatbuilding Cornwallis suffered a distinct disadvantage. Even if he could control the sawmills, he would not know where to collect his boats, for he could not predict where the pursuit would take him. He certainly could not carry boats with him, having burned even most of his provisions on January 25. In fact, not only did he lack boats, but he also lacked information that Greene had a small fleet of them waiting.
30. On the night of February 1 the British camped at the crossroads to Salisbury. They marched early the next morning, but as the army passed by Tarrant's Tavern, some with marauding spirits — British or provincial — sneaked out of rank to burn the tavern along with several houses. Cornwallis issued a stern rebuke, calling the burning "a Disgrace to the Army" and promising to "punish with the Utmost Severity any person or persons who shall be found Guilty of Committing so disgraceful an Outrage." Well might he be wrathful, since each such act made the British plans more difficult and pacification of the countryside more remote. See "British Orderly Book," *N.C. Hist. Review*, IX, 293.
31. O'Hara to Grafton, Apr. 20, 1781: Grafton Papers Ac. 423/191.
32. "British Orderly Book," *N.C. Hist. Review*, IX, 295.
33. Cornwallis based his calculations on the assumption that Greene would not stand and fight. This assumption was correct, mainly because Greene's officers had earlier persuaded him not to take the offensive actions that he himself wanted. It seems to the authors that Thayer hedges the point in his *Greene*, p. 296, when he says that "Greene apparently sounded out Morgan on the advisability of offensive action

on the enemy's flank and found him opposed." The Greene Papers in
the Clements Library make it manifestly evident that Greene strongly
desired offensive action against Cornwallis and that only the unqualified
objection of all his ranking officers dissuaded him from it. Greene
wrote to Gen. Thomas Sumter, from his camp at Charlotte, on Dec. 12,
1780: "I proposed to Generals Smallwood & Morgan the attack upon
Lord Cornwallis. They are both pointedly against it as being impracticable. I am not altogether of their opinion; and therefore wish you
keep up a communication of intelligence and of any changes of disposition that may take place." Two days later, on December 14, Greene
wrote to the North Carolina Board of War — the Clements has a photo-
static copy of this letter, the original is in the New York Public Library
— "in the present state of things it is almost impossible to carry on any
offensive operations even upon the partizan scale much less with the
whole troops. When ever we move near the enemy, which is much my
wish; and which every officer of rank for want of a greater force of
more permanent arrangements now opposes; it will be necessary to
have our supplies regular."

34. This junction took place at Guilford Courthouse, between the Yadkin
and Dan Rivers. Huger reached Guilford Courthouse on February 8.
Colonel Otho Williams with the light cavalry and Greene with the
remainder of the force left Guilford Courthouse on February 10,
traveling their different routes. While Greene headed for Irwin's Ferry,
Williams was to head toward the upper fords of the Dan to deceive
Cornwallis. While the British pursued Williams, Greene crossed the
Dan on February 14, and Williams' light cavalry soon also crossed.
See Schenck, *North Carolina*, pp. 254–259; and Thayer, *Greene*, pp.
315–319.

35. O'Hara to Grafton, Apr. 20, 1781: Grafton Papers Ac. 423/191.

36. Their severe march had reduced to shreds the shoes newly made the
month before. Cornwallis wrote to Rawdon merely that "the fatigue
of our troops and the hardships which they suffered were excessive."
See Cornwallis to Rawdon, Feb. 21, 1781: *Cornwallis Corr.*, I, 85.

37. O'Hara to Grafton, Apr. 20, 1781: Grafton Papers Ac. 423/191.

38. *Ibid.*

39. Noel Gerson, *Light Horse Harry* (New York, 1966), p. 1.

40. Most of the information on Lee comes from *ibid., passim.*

41. Another version has it that the rebel militia at the rear of Lee's column
did not know his plans and opened fire once they had identified Pyle's
men as tories by the strip of red cloth in their hats.

42. Tarleton's Legion was apparently but a mile or so away in the woods at the time of Pyle's defeat, and Lee maintained that the attack had never been intended. Rather his plan had been to order Pyle's men either to throw down their arms and disperse to their homes or, if they preferred, to join the American cause. Then Lee would have continued with his original mission, which was to search out and engage Tarleton's corps. Once the initial cry of alarm had been raised, however, tenderness toward the enemy became out of the question. Some of the loyalists may have had time to discharge their muskets, but they certainly had no opportunity to reload. For such close work the sabers of the dragoons were a much surer weapon. Perhaps the military situation did not actually require the killing of almost one hundred men, but how is one to assess these matters? On the evidence Lee seems to stand acquitted of the charge of butchery. For Lee's account of the affair see Henry Lee, *Memoirs of the War in the Southern Department of the United States* (Washington, 1827), pp. 154–157. Benson J. Lossing, *The Pictorial Field-Book of the Revolution . . .* , 2 vols. (New York, 1885), II, 387, describes "Pyle's Pond." See also Schenck, *North Carolina,* pp. 278–282.

43. Cornwallis had promised the inhabitants not to slaughter their few remaining cattle (mostly draught oxen) unless it became absolutely necessary. Not only did that course of action become necessary, but also the British had to kill some of their own best draught horses. Nor was that the worst: the redcoats found themselves reduced to such straits that their commissary general even had to take a file of men and go from house to house to get food. See Lamb, *Journal of Occurrences,* p. 348; and Stedman, *History of the American War,* II, 373.

44. Part of that hunger owed to the failure of another of the Earl's projects. He had hoped to feed and supply himself using the waterways of North Carolina as he had used those of South Carolina. While at Hillsboro he had intended to establish a communication with the British fleet in the Cape Fear River and to bring supplies from loyalists at Cross Creek. Cross Creek was about sixty-five miles south of Hillsboro (more when one allows for the twists and turns of the road or river, whichever route is followed). The settlement lay on one of the northern branches of the Cape Fear River, eighty-five or ninety miles upstream from Wilmington. The river at Cross Creek, however, bore the name of North West River, and farther upstream still it became the Haw River. Cornwallis did not succeed, however, in opening up communications with Cross Creek, much less with Wilmington.

45. "British Orderly Book," *N.C. Hist. Review,* IX, 376.

46. O'Hara to Grafton, Apr. 20, 1781: Grafton Papers, Ac. 423/191. The movements can, however, be followed in detail in "British Orderly Book," *N.C. Hist. Review*, IX, 376–387.

47. Lamb, *Journal of Occurrences*, p. 381. The weary march soon began to tell, however, on both the soldiers and their commander. Desertions increased, and the Earl ordered more frequent roll calls. With the shortage of regular rations, the men turned to plundering on an increasingly grand scale. They stole, not only from the countryside, but from their fellows, and their women camp followers equalled or even surpassed them in thievery. The lieutenant general grew so exasperated, after repeated injunctions against plundering, that he repeated a general order he had first issued at Charlotte, explaining that they only hurt their own cause by robbing the very people they were supposed to help. His subordinate O'Hara soon lost all patience with the women, who constantly left the ranks in search of loot. He ordered them to be present at all roll calls. Any women absent were to be whipped and drummed out of his brigade, and in order for them to understand what a whipping meant, he required them to witness all punishment. See "British Orderly Book," *N.C. Hist. Review*, IX, 378–381.

48. See *New York Gazette and the Weekly Mercury* (New York, 1752–1781), Mar. 5, 1781; and Mackenzie, *Diary*, II, 478–480, entries for Mar. 3, 4, and 5, 1781.

49. Cornwallis to Germain, Mar. 17, 1781: *Cornwallis Corr.*, I, 519. This unfortunate ignorance of the enemy's position, which he said lost him "a very favorable opportunity of attacking the rebel army," undoubtedly owed in part to the activities of Tarleton. A few days after Pyle's Massacre a group of tories had approached to offer their services to the British cause. When they failed to give the password for the day, the redoubtable dragoon did not pause to ask questions. He charged them, killing or wounding those who could not manage to escape into the woods. The survivors did not make a reappearance, even when an enlightened Tarleton went looking for them. See Treacy, *Prelude to Yorktown*, pp. 162–163; Thayer, *Greene*, p. 325; and Davis, *Cowpens–Guilford Courthouse*, p. 133.

50. Despite the paucity of information about the main American army, the Earl did succeed in forcing a brush with one of Greene's detachments, under Otho Williams, at Whitsill's (or Wetzell's) Mill on Reedy Fork. The sharp but brief encounter on March 6 was remarkable chiefly for the "almost miraculous escape" of Lieutenant Colonel Webster who escaped injury although fired at thirty-two or thirty-three times, at

"point-blank range," by a select party of marksmen armed with rifles. See Schenck, *North Carolina*, pp. 290–291.

51. Lee, *Memoirs*, pp. 167–168n.
52. See Cornwallis to Germain, Mar. 17, 1781: *Cornwallis Corr.*, I, 516–520, 520–523; and Thayer, *Greene*, p. 327.
53. "British Orderly Book," *N.C. Hist. Review*, IX, 387.
54. Cornwallis to Germain, Mar. 17, 1781: *Cornwallis Corr.*, I, 521.
55. Thayer, *Greene*, pp. 326–327, gives Greene only forty-two hundred. Schenck, *North Carolina*, pp. 295ff. discusses Greene's army and concludes the American had over five thousand men. Stedman, *History of the American War*, II, 374, gives Greene over five thousand men.
56. Stedman, *History of the American War*, II, 384n.
57. See Lee, *Memoirs*, pp. 169–170; and Tarleton, *A History of the Campaigns*, p. 271. To a certain extent, the accounts are confused, for while Lee may have beaten Tarleton, he himself sustained losses from the Guards, advancing behind Tarleton, before the action at Guilford became general.
58. For the German uniform see Charles M. Lefferts, *Uniforms of the American, British, French and German Armies in the War of the American Revolution, 1775–1783* (New York, 1926), pp. 264–265. On p. 253 Lefferts has a color picture of the Jagers.
59. Both Tarleton and Stedman asserted that the Americans delivered their first round when the British were 150 yards distant. Schenck, *North Carolina*, pp. 343–344, carefully explains why 150 yards seems the acceptable and most likely distance between the British and the Americans when the latter opened fire.
60. The authors fail to understand why Thayer, *Greene*, p. 328, asserts that the North Carolina volley at four hundred feet was "too far to do much damage." Indeed, Thayer apparently accepts at face value Greene's own condemnations of the hapless North Carolinians. See pp. 328–329.
61. Schenck, *North Carolina*, p. 352; quoting from Caruther's *Sketches*, 2d series, p. 134.
62. Schenck, *North Carolina*, pp. 349–350.
63. See P.R.O., W.O. 3/26, p. 147. An order from the adjutant general's office, Mar. 20, 1784, repeats this order as the standard pace, which it must have been during the Revolution.
64. Lamb, *Journal of Occurrences*, pp. 361–362.
65. Schenck, *North Carolina*, pp. 360–361.
66. Cornwallis to Germain, Mar. 17, 1781: *Cornwallis Corr.*, I, 521.

67. Ward, *War of the Revolution,* II, 790; and Davis, *Cowpens–Guilford Courthouse,* p. 149, both have Stevens on the right and Lawson on the left. But Schenck, *North Carolina,* p. 362, *passim;* and Sir John Fortescue, *A History of the British Army,* 13 vols. (New York, 1899–1930), III, 377, have Stevens on the left and Lawson on the right. The latter are undoubtedly, considering the way the battle progressed, correct. Part of Ward's and Davis' confusion may arise from a misreading of Lee, a participant in the battle. Lee states that Stevens' right flank and Lawson's left flank rested on the great road. But, obviously, such an arrangement would place the brigade of Stevens to the left of Lawson. See *Memoirs,* p. 171.

68. Lee, *Memoirs,* p. 172; and Treacy, *Prelude to Yorktown,* p. 182.

69. Ward, *War of the Revolution,* II, 790.

70. Lamb, *Journal of Occurrences,* p. 362.

71. Schenck, *North Carolina,* p. 362, gives Houston's account.

72. On his map facing p. 321, Schenck, in *North Carolina,* shows Hunting Creek running roughly halfway between the third American line and the road to Reedy Fork and roughly parallel to both.

73. Most authorities who have studied the battle, and they are supported by Lee, *Memoirs,* p. 174, agree that the very first attack, an unsuccessful one, was led by Webster. After being repulsed he waited for more of the British line to move forward, and the next to appear were the 2d battalion of Guards. It is not clear whether Cornwallis deliberately omitted to mention the unsuccessful initial charge of his own 33d, among the others led by Webster, or whether, writing so soon after the event, perhaps in some hurry, he neglected to mention it. It scarcely seems probable that he was not informed of it, although to be sure Webster received a fatal wound during the battle. In any event, Cornwallis stated in his letter to Germain on Mar. 17, *Cornwallis Corr.,* I, 521–522, that the 2d battalion of Guards "first gained the clear ground near Guilford [*sic*] Courthouse. . . ." Stedman, *History of the American War,* II, 378, agrees with Cornwallis that Stuart and the 2d Battalion of Guards first reached the open ground at Guilford.

74. Davis, *Cowpens–Guilford Courthouse,* pp. 160–161, says that Francisco had been reared in Virginia after being found a castaway, "discovered in expensive clothing on the seashore as an infant." He had become a blacksmith and was by repute the strongest man in Virginia. He had fought in the northern campaigns and had several times refused an officer's commission on grounds that he had not enough learning.

75. Schenck, *North Carolina,* pp. 365–366; quoting from Foote's, *Sketches of North Carolina,* p. 278.

76. Johnson, *Sketches of Greene*, II, 12.
77. Samuel Mathis to William R. Davie, June 26, 1819: *American Historical Record* (1873), II, 109; quoted in Rankin, *American Revolution*, pp. 287–288.
78. Lee, *Memoirs*, p. 175.
79. Schenck, *North Carolina*, p. 366; and Lee, *Memoirs*, p. 177.
80. Cornwallis to Germain, Mar. 17, 1781: *Cornwallis Corr.*, I, 522.
81. Accounts of the battle — for example, of which specific units took part in a particular portion of the action at a given time — vary. The authors have tried to use firsthand British accounts whenever possible, supplementing them wherever they were obviously abbreviated by the use of American sources and of standard secondary works on the battle. Although many errors of detail may thus have been introduced into this account, the authors are convinced that the general outlines of the struggle will not be found in error.
82. Cornwallis to Germain, Mar. 17, 1781: *Cornwallis Corr.*, I, 522.
83. See Carrington, *Battles of the Revolution*, pp. 563–564. Ward, *War of the Revolution*, II, 793; and Treacy, *Prelude to Yorktown*, p. 187, give slightly different figures.
84. Cornwallis to Germain, Mar. 17, 1781: *Cornwallis Corr.*, I, 522. If the American figures are correct, then many of those whom Cornwallis counted as dead must have been wounded, and many of those in the houses round about must have been "missing" rather than wounded. However, if Cornwallis' figures are more nearly accurate, it seems apparent that Greene maligned a great many men by reporting them missing when in fact they were dead or wounded.
85. Stedman, *History of the American War*, II, 383; and Ward, *War of the Revolution*, II, 793.
86. Stedman, *History of the American War*, II, 384–385.
87. *Ibid.*, 385.
88. O'Hara to Grafton, Apr. 20, 1781: Grafton Papers Ac. 423/191.

Chapter 14

(pages 311–321)

1. See "British Orderly Book," *N.C. Hist. Review*, IX, 388; and Cornwallis to Germain, Mar. 17, 1781: *Cornwallis Corr.*, I, 522.
2. O'Hara to Grafton, Apr. 20, 1781: Grafton Papers, Ac. 423/191.
3. Quoted in Rankin, *American Revolution*, p. 291.
4. Ward, *War of the Revolution*, II, 795, says that the British had no food for forty-eight hours, i.e., from the evening of Mar. 14 to the

evening of Mar. 16, and then only four ounces of flour and four ounces of lean beef.

5. "British Orderly Book," *N.C. Hist. Review,* IX, 389.
6. *Ibid.,* pp. 388–389.
7. *Ibid.,* p. 389.
8. The three letters — Cornwallis to Greene Mar. 16, 1781 and Greene to Cornwallis Mar. 16 and 17, 1781 — are in P.R.O. 30/11/90, ff. 3–4, 5–6, and 7–8.
9. George Washington Greene, *The Life of Nathanael Greene,* 3 vols. (New York, 1871), III, 206. G. W. Greene states that he got the anecdote from Nathanael Greene Foster, whose father served under Nathanael Greene.
10. "Return of Ordnance, Ammunition and Arms taken at the Battle of Guilford 15th March 1781": P.R.O. 30/11/103, f. 23.
11. Lamb, *Journal of Occurrences,* pp. 436–437.
12. Mackenzie Papers, Clements Library.
13. The old picture, still held as an article of faith by many people, showed a well-fed, well-clothed British army, puffed up with pride and insolence, with so little staying power that the loss of their rum caused mass desertions. G. W. Greene's biography of *Nathanael Greene,* III, 165–166, illustrates this view well. Greene solemnly states that the British army was "well clothed, provided with good shoes for marching, and good blankets for sleeping, and a full allowance of good food." That author, apparently not noticing the self-contradiction, goes on to declare in volume III, p. 189, that "long marches, hunger, cold, and nakedness, were sacrifices which they found it hard to make. Desertions became frequent, even from the Guards, who claimed for themselves the superiority over all the regiments in the service." Other writers — for example Davis, *Cowpens–Guilford Courthouse,* p. 73; and Treacy, *Prelude to Yorktown,* p. 124 — repeat the same theme. Davis has no footnotes, but Treacy cites Johnson, *Sketches of Greene,* I, 407–408, and Ward, *War of the Revolution,* II, 765. Ward says that it "may have been partly because of" the destruction of provisions, especially rum, that "during those two days at Ramsour's many Hessians and some few British soldiers deserted, perhaps 250 in all." Both Davis and Treacy aver that in the month after the conflagration at Ramsour's Mills the British returns show a reduction of 227 men not accounted for by battle casualties or outbreak of epidemic; and both say that the Guards were reduced by one-eighth. This magical figure of 227 one assumes to be the difference between Cornwallis' figures of the rank and file present and fit for duty on Feb. 1, 1781 (2440) and on

Mar. 1, 1781 (2213), and the one-eighth reduction in the Guards from the same set of figures for the same dates, which show a decline from 690 to 605. These figures are in P.R.O. 30/11/5, f. 134. They do not appear in *Cornwallis Corr.*, I, but are printed without citation in Carrington, *Battles of the Revolution*, p. 565. According to the set of official figures that *is* printed in *Cornwallis Corr.*, I, 87 — it appears in P.R.O. 30/11/103, f. 17 in more complete form — 97 enlisted men, including sergeants, were killed or wounded in various actions in North Carolina preceding the battle of Guilford. This figure includes 70 Guards killed and wounded, leaving unaccounted for only 15. The authors consider sickness at least as probable an explanation as desertion.

14. In the account of the location of the hospital and in the lists of wounded and dead there are, as usual for most accounts of most Revolutionary events, inconsistencies. It seems almost certain that the hospital was situated at the Quaker Meetinghouse in New Garden — as Cornwallis himself says in his letter to Balfour, Apr. 5, 1781: P.R.O. 30/11/85, ff. 21–22 — rather than in the "New Garden Meeting House" as the surgeon Hill says in his report: P.R.O. 30/11/5, ff. 117–118, 179–180. Hill's roll of wounded and dead also shows contradiction, for the report at ff. 117–118 lists only seventeen as having died, and does not include among the wounded John Hill of the 23d regiment. Yet Hill appears in f. 180 as having died shortly after the battle, on March 19.

15. Various drafts of the proclamation appear in the Cornwallis Papers in P.R.O. 30/11/101, ff. 24–31. The proclamation is printed in *London Chronicle*, June 7, 1781, XLIX, no. 3825. Both the Cornwallis Papers and the *Chronicle* state the deadline for rebels to surrender as Apr. 20, not Apr. 12, the date given in an editorial note in "British Orderly Book," *N.C. Hist. Review*, IX, 391n.

16. Stedman, *History of the American War*, II, 386–387n.

17. *Ibid.*, II, 387–388n.

18. O'Hara to Grafton, Apr. 20, 1781: Grafton Papers Ac. 423/191.

19. Cornwallis to Germain, Apr. 18, 1781: *Cornwallis Corr.*, I, 92. Cornwallis had written similar news, expressing his "great mortification," to Clinton on Apr. 10. See P.R.O. 30/11/5, ff. 209–212.

20. Cornwallis to Balfour, Apr. 5, 1781: P.R.O. 30/11/85, ff. 21–22.

21. For a patriot account of the destruction left in the wake of the army see William Dickson to Rev. Robert Dickson, Nov. 30, 1784: *The Dickson Letters* (Raleigh, N.C., 1901), pp. 15–16, quoted in Rankin, *American Revolution*, p. 290.

22. The other four officers who died included Captains Schutz and Maynard

of the Guards and Captain Wilmouski and Ensign deTrott of the Bose. See Stedman, *History of the American War,* II, 391–392.

23. Lamb, *Journal of Occurrences,* p. 360.
24. The letter, written from Wilmington on Apr. 23, 1781, is printed in *Cornwallis Corr.,* I, 93.
25. It is difficult to say how many troops Cornwallis had when he arrived at Wilmington. To be sure, various sets of figures for different dates are available, and presumably one can arrive at a fair approximation of his strength by deducting or adding, as the case may be, for killed and wounded or for newly joined. According to Cornwallis' own figures, at Guilford on March 15 before the battle he mustered 1638 rank and file present and fit for duty (1924 total present and fit). See P.R.O. 30/11/103, f. 19, for a more detailed breakdown of these figures than appears in *Cornwallis Corr.,* I, 86. The next official set of figures, dated Wilmington, Apr. 15, shows Cornwallis with 1829 rank and file present and fit for duty (2186 total present and fit). The second set of figures represents a considerable increase over the Guilford set, including as it does the North Carolina Volunteers (201 rank and file, 238 total), who had presumably been with the baggage during the battle of Guilford Courthouse and then rejoined Cornwallis' army afterward; the 82d regiment (174 rank and file, 213 total) whom Cornwallis presumably joined at Wilmington; and a mysterious *increase* in the 33d regiment despite casualties (formerly 213 rank and file, 234 total; later 241 rank and file, 273 total). See P.R.O. 30/11/103, ff. 27b–28. If these 403 rank and file who were not at Guilford — 201 from the North Carolina Volunteers, 174 from the 82d, and 28 from the 33d — are subtracted from the 1829 rank and file at Wilmington on Apr. 15, the figure for rank and file *who had fought at Guilford Courthouse* and yet arrived "fit for duty" at Wilmington comes to 1426, 212 fewer than were present before the battle. Yet this decrease is scarcely in keeping with the severity of casualties at the battle which totalled 503 rank and file. If one takes the 212 difference between the Guilford figure and the "adjusted" Wilmington figure and subtracts from it the number of dead on the battlefield (88) and the number who died at the Quaker Meetinghouse hospital (17), one is left with a mere 107. This figure, logically, should represent the number of rank and file who upon Cornwallis' arrival in Wilmington had wounds severe enough to prevent their being counted "fit for duty." The figure seems ridiculously low and becomes totally absurd when a further deduction is made from it of the 40 rank and file of Royal Artillery and the 78 rank and

file of the Jagers who appear in the Guilford return but who are not included in the Wilmington rank and file figure of 1829 (they were listed in the Wilmington return in a different group as on detached service). For these and other similar reasons, the authors cannot believe that even the most official lists are reliable. Nevertheless, they would hazard a guess that Cornwallis arrived in Wilmington with approximately 1400 rank and file "present and fit for duty." This figure includes, of course, those who rejoined the army after the battle of Guilford.

26. Information on the Wright House comes from Richard Pratt, *Houses, History & People* (New York, 1965). The authors arrived in Wilmington on the weekend when the house was closed and so did not see the initials with their own eyes.

27. Cornwallis to Clinton, Apr. 24, 1781: P.R.O. 30/11/76, ff. 49–50.

28. Cornwallis to Clinton, Apr. 10, 1781: P.R.O. 30/11/72, f. 78.

29. Cornwallis to Amherst, Apr. 18, 1781: P.R.O. 30/11/85, ff. 36–37; Cornwallis to Germain, same date, *Cornwallis Corr.*, I, 91; and Amherst to Cornwallis, June 19, 1781: P.R.O. 30/11/71, ff. 23–24. The Earl received Amherst's letter in New York on November 19, a month after Yorktown.

30. Final articles of the cartel are in P.R.O. 30/11/91, ff. 58–59.

31. Cornwallis' returns from the middle of April through the middle of August dramatically illustrate the unhealthiness of the climate. The sick increased from 405 on April 15 to 497 on May 1, and 555 on May 15. By June 1, when admittedly the Earl's forces had been greatly augmented by the junction with Phillips' army (who must have contributed some sick of their own), the figure had soared to 881. From that time onward the sick list climbed steadily and rapidly, reaching 934 on June 15, 973 on July 1, 1044 on July 15, 1163 on August 1, and 1222 on August 15. See "Return of the Troops under Earl Cornwallis in South Carolina": Clinton Papers.

32. Cornwallis to Phillips, Apr. 10, 1781: *Cornwallis Corr.*, I, 88.

33. Cornwallis to Clinton, Apr. 10, 1781: *ibid.*, pp. 87–88.

34. Cornwallis to Germain, Apr. 18, 1781: *ibid.*, I, 90–91.

35. Cornwallis to Balfour, Apr. 24, 1781: P.R.O. 30/11/85, ff. 49–50.

36. Cornwallis' letter to Phillips, Apr. 24, 1781: *ibid.*, ff. 53–54, spells out the Earl's plans in detail.

37. "State of the Troops that marched with the Army under the command of Lieut Genl. Earl Cornwallis": P.R.O. 30/11/103, f. 29.

38. Cornwallis to Craig, May 4, 1781: P.R.O. 30/11/86, ff. 5–6. He wrote

this letter at Reeves' Plantation, eight miles from Dickson's Ford on the Neuse.

39. Cornwallis to Craig, May 12, 1781: *ibid.,* ff. 27–28. Tarleton's detractors show curious discrepancies in their reports of what Tarleton said with regard to Cornwallis' move north. According to Stedman, *History of the American War,* II, 394n, Tarleton proposed to Cornwallis that he (Tarleton) be allowed to march his cavalry back through the country to Charleston, which proposition the Earl "very judiciously rejected." On the other hand, Mackenzie, *Strictures,* pp. 122–123, says that Tarleton claimed to Col. John Hamilton on the march to Virginia "that *this march was a child of his own,* and that he gloried in it." Mackenzie further says that according to "general report," Tarleton said that Cornwallis might as well order the throats of his horses to be cut as to order a return to South Carolina. Yet Tarleton himself said in his *History,* pp. 283–284, that he was not among those who advised the march to Virginia. As usual, the dragoon covered himself with controversy.

Chapter 15

(pages 325–353)

*The exchanges between Cornwallis, Clinton, and Phillips during the spring and summer of 1781 — exchanges which finally brought the Earl to Yorktown — have been printed in several places but most completely in Stevens, *Clinton-Cornwallis Controversy,* I and II. In this and the following chapter, however, the authors cite the unpublished Cornwallis Papers and Ross' edition of Cornwallis' correspondence as their sources. We do this not because of inaccuracies in Stevens' work — he printed correctly most of the important letters — but because during the writing of this biography we had permanently available to us our notes from the Cornwallis Papers and Ross' edition of the Cornwallis correspondence. Stevens, on the other hand, we could only secure at intervals on a temporary basis.

1. See Willcox, *Portrait,* pp. 386–387.
2. Cornwallis to Clinton, Apr. 23, 1781: *Cornwallis Corr.,* I, 94. See also *Clinton-Cornwallis Controversy,* I, 68. Charles O'Hara surmised as early as Apr. 20 that Cornwallis would junction with Phillips at Petersburg. See his letter to Grafton of Apr. 20 in Grafton Papers, Ac. 423/191.
3. Cornwallis' route can be followed roughly in the map of Henry P.

Johnston, *The Yorktown Campaign and the Surrender of Cornwallis,
1781* (New York, 1881), p. 27. Various letters in the Cornwallis Papers,
P.R.O. 30/11/86, give a day-by-day account of his progress. See particularly Cornwallis to Tarleton, May 10, and to Craig, May 12, 1781:
P.R.O. 30/11/86, ff. 25–28. Tarleton, *A History of the Campaigns,* pp.
286–291, also describes the march.

4. See Tarleton to Cornwallis, May 8, 1781: P.R.O. 30/11/6, f. 69.
5. Cornwallis to Balfour, May 3, 1781: P.R.O. 30/11/86, ff. 1–2.
6. See Willcox, *Portrait,* pp. 385–386.
7. For Phillips' instructions see Clinton to Phillips, Apr. 5, 11, and 13,
   1781; and "Substance of Several Conversations with Major General
   Phillips on the Subject of Operations in the Chesapeak before his Embarkation on his Expedition thither,": P.R.O. 30/11/95, ff. 15–17, 18–
   21, 22–23, and 28–31 respectively. For the size of the Earl's army see
   "State of the Troops in Virginia under the Command of Lieutenant
   General Earl Cornwallis, 15th July 1781": Clinton Papers. This muster
   list includes the alterations since the previous return.
8. Von Fuchs to Cornwallis, May 23, 1781: P.R.O. 30/11/6, f. 102.
9. Cornwallis to Clinton, May 26, 1781: *Cornwallis Corr.,* I, 101.
10. *Ibid.,* I, 101–102.
11. *Ibid.,* I, 102.
12. *Ibid.,* I, 101–102.
13. For a summary of Lafayette's movements see Ward, *War of the Rev-
    olution,* II, 870–873; and Louis Gottschalk, *Lafayette and the Close of
    the American Revolution* (Chicago, 1942), pp. 208–238.
14. Cornwallis to Clinton, May 26, 1781: *Cornwallis Corr.,* I, 101.
15. The summary of Simcoe's life is taken from D. B. Read, *The Life and
    Times of Gen. John Graves Simcoe . . .* (Toronto, 1901). See also
    Simcoe's Military Journal . . . (New York, 1844), p. 209.
16. Smith, *Loyalists and Redcoats,* p. 70.
17. Stedman, *History of the American War,* II, 432n.
18. *Simcoe's Military Journal,* pp. 212–223.
19. Cornwallis to Clinton, June 30, 1781: P.R.O. 30/11/74, ff. 18–21.
20. This exciting narrative is cited by Johnston, *Yorktown Campaign,* p.
    44n. Tarleton, *A History of the Campaigns,* pp. 295–297, describes his
    raid. "The attempt to secure Mr. Jefferson," he remarks casually,
    "was ineffectual; he discovered the British dragoons from his house,
    which stands on the point of a mountain, before they could approach
    him, and he provided for his personal liberty by a precipitate retreat."
21. His orders to Tarleton of June 11 are in P.R.O. 30/11/87, ff. 5–6.

22. Ward, *War of the Revolution,* II, 874–875, estimates that Lafayette had
    about 4500 men. These included his original force of about 800
    Continentals and the 750 Pennsylvania Continentals Wayne brought;
    three brigades of Virginia militia totaling about 2100; new Virginia
    Continentals numbering 425; 200 men of the 2d and 4th Continental
    Artillery Regiments with 8 or 10 guns; 60 regular cavalry; and 60 volun-
    teer dragoons.

23. The main accounts of Spencer's Ordinary come from *Simcoe's Military
    Journal,* pp. 227–237; Gottschalk, *Lafayette,* pp. 258–260; Johnston,
    Yorktown Campaign, pp. 55–56; and Ward, *War of the Revolution,* II,
    874–875.

24. The following summary of British strategy and of Clinton's attitude,
    his plans, and his relations with the British government and the navy
    come from a variety of works. Most important are Clinton's own com-
    ments in his pamphlets (reproduced in Stevens, *Clinton-Cornwallis
    Controversy,* I), his *Narrative,* edited by Willcox, and his letters and
    memoranda in the Clinton Papers. It is a vast mass of material, and
    while the authors have examined much of it, they have found that its
    essence has been distilled admirably by William B. Willcox in several
    works: his comments in his edition of *Clinton's Narrative;* his article,
    "The British Road to Yorktown: A Study in Divided Command," *Amer-
    ican Historical Review,* LII (October, 1946), 1–35; and most impor-
    tantly his biography of Clinton, *Portrait of a General.* More critical
    of Clinton and less so of Cornwallis in discussing the events of the
    summer of 1781 is Mackesy, *War for American Independence,* pp.
    415–430. While the authors naturally tend to favor Cornwallis over
    Clinton, and thus Mackesy over Willcox, Willcox has studied the matter
    more thoroughly than Mackesy.

25. For the heads of this discussion see John C. Fitzpatrick, ed., *The
    Writings of George Washington,* 30 vols. (Washington, 1931–1944),
    XXII, 105–107. Douglas Southall Freeman, *George Washington,* 7 vols.
    (New York, 1948–1957), V, 286–290, discusses the meeting in detail.

26. Clinton to Cornwallis, June 11 and 15, 1781: P.R.O. 30/11/68, ff. 14–17,
    22.

27. *Simcoe's Military Journal,* pp. 237–238.

28. Cornwallis to Clinton, June 30, 1781: *Cornwallis Corr.,* I, 103–104.

29. Gottschalk, *Lafayette,* p. 263.

30. Information about Wayne comes from Harry Emerson Wildes, *Anthony
    Wayne, Trouble Shooter of the American Revolution* (New York, 1941).

31. Accounts of Green Spring come from Cornwallis to Balfour, July 16,

1781: P.R.O. 30/11/88; to Clinton, July 8, 1781: P.R.O. 30/11/74, ff. 30–36; Ward, *War of the Revolution,* II, 875–877; Gottschalk, *Lafayette,* pp. 264–267; Tarleton, *A History of the Campaigns,* pp. 353–354; Johnston, *Yorktown Campaign,* pp. 60–66; and Wildes, *Wayne,* pp. 252–257.

32. Tarleton, *A History of the Campaigns,* p. 356.

33. Willcox, *Portrait,* p. 404, concludes that Cornwallis "had the opportunity for a decisive blow at Lafayette. He let the chance slip, on the odd ground that his instructions were so positive and pressing that he could not pause to destroy the enemy." He cites as evidence Gottschalk's *Lafayette* and Tarleton's *A History of the Campaigns.* Nowhere have the authors found that Cornwallis stated positive and pressing instructions as his reason for failing to pursue. In letters both to Balfour and Clinton he blamed the darkness. That he could have annihilated Lafayette the next day, as Tarleton believed, is open to grave doubt, as we have shown.

34. Clinton, *Narrative,* xlii.

35. Clinton to Cornwallis, June 28, 1781: P.R.O. 30/11/68, f. 28.

36. Cornwallis to Clinton, July 8, 1781: P.R.O. 30/11/74, ff. 30–36.

37. Cornwallis to Leslie, July 8, 1781: *Cornwallis Corr.,* I, 106.

38. Cornwallis to Tarleton, July 8, 1781: P.R.O. 30/11/88, ff. 7–8; Tarleton, *A History of the Campaigns,* pp. 358–359; and Cornwallis to Clinton, July 17, 1781: P.R.O. 30/11/74, ff. 41–46.

39. Clinton to Cornwallis, June 8 and 19, 1781: P.R.O. 30/11/68, ff. 11–13, 25–27.

40. Cornwallis to Clinton, July 12, 1781: P.R.O. 30/11/74, ff. 38–40.

41. Cornwallis to Clinton, July 17, 1781: *ibid.,* ff. 41–46.

42. Clinton to Cornwallis, July 11, 1781: P.R.O. 30/11/68, f. 50.

43. Cornwallis to Leslie, July 20, 1781: *Cornwallis Corr.,* I, 107, and P.R.O. 30/11/88, ff. 42–43.

44. Clinton to Cornwallis, July 11, 1781: P.R.O. 30/11/68, ff. 43–45.

45. Cornwallis to Graves, July 26, 1781: P.R.O. 30/11/88, f. 50.

46. Clinton to Cornwallis, July 11, 1781: P.R.O. 30/11/68, ff. 43–45.

47. For the engineer's report see Lieutenant Sutherland to Cornwallis, July 25, 1781: P.R.O. 30/11/74, ff. 55–56. The opinions of the naval captains are enclosed in Cornwallis to Clinton, July 26, 1781: *ibid.,* ff. 59–60.

48. Cornwallis to Clinton, July 26, 1781: *Cornwallis Corr.,* I, 108–110 (misdated by Ross as July 27); P.R.O. 30/11/74, ff. 48–50, includes the whole letter, parts of which Ross did not print.

49. For Cornwallis' account of the progress of construction see his various letters in August to Clinton, O'Hara, and Leslie, printed in *Cornwallis Corr.,* I, 112–118.

Chapter 16

(pages 354–388)

*Several secondary works — ranging from the old but still useful Johnston, *Yorktown Campaign,* to volume V of Freeman's meticulously detailed *Washington,* to popular works such as Fleming's *Beat the Last Drum* — describe the siege of Yorktown. Several participants in the siege, most of them Americans, also kept diaries or journals recording their experiences. Because the outlines of the siege are so well known and have been so often described, the authors footnoted this chapter only when they quoted a person directly in the text or discussed a crucial event or introduced matter over which there is some disagreement.

1. For Washington's plans see Freeman, *Washington,* V, 297–310.
2. All quotations in this paragraph come from Willcox, *Portrait,* pp. 418–419.
3. *Ibid.,* p. 414.
4. *Ibid.,* p. 421.
5. See Cornwallis' four dispatches to Clinton on Aug. 31, Sept. 1, Sept. 2, and Sept. 4, 1781: P.R.O. 30/11/74, ff. 78–85.
6. Cornwallis to Clinton, Aug. 16, 1781: *ibid.,* ff. 68–69.
7. Gottschalk, *Lafayette,* p. 297.
8. See "State of the Troops in Virginia under the Command of Lieutenant General Earl Cornwallis, 15th August 1781": Clinton Papers.
9. Willcox, *Portrait,* p. 424.
10. Cornwallis to Clinton, Sept. 8, 1781: *Cornwallis Corr.,* I, 118–119.
11. Tarleton, *A History of the Campaigns,* p. 365.
12. See Clinton to Cornwallis, Sept. 6, 1781: *Cornwallis Corr.,* I, 119–120. Ross printed only parts of this letter. For entire letter see P.R.O. 30/11/68, ff. 81–82.
13. *Ibid.*
14. Stevens, *Clinton-Cornwallis Controversy,* I, 75.
15. Cornwallis to Clinton, Sept. 12, 1781: *Cornwallis Corr.,* I, 120.
16. *The Journal of Nicholas Creswell,* forward by Samuel Thornley (London, 1925), p. 206.
17. See, for example, Cornwallis to Captain Hudson, Aug. 9, 1781: P.R.O.

30/11/89, ff. 13–14. He requested six 12-pounders for the Gloucester works.

18. "State of the Army in Virginia under the Command of Lieut. General Earl Cornwallis, 1st October 1781": Clinton Papers.

19. Johnston, *Yorktown Campaign*, p. 111.

20. *Ibid.*, pp. 108–117.

21. Clinton to Cornwallis, Sept. 24, 1781: *Cornwallis Corr.*, I, 121.

22. Cornwallis to Clinton, Sept. 29, 1781: *ibid.*, I, 121–122.

23. James Thacher, *Military Journal During the American Revolutionary War, from 1775 to 1783* (Hartford, 1854), p. 280.

24. "Tucker's Journal," *Wm. and Mary Qtly*, V, 382.

25. *Ibid.*, p. 384.

26. *Simcoe's Journal*, p. 248; and P.R.O. 30/11/103, f. 35, "State of the Army in Virginia under the Command of Lieut. Genl. Earl Cornwallis, Oct. 18, 1781."

27. For accounts see *Simcoe's Journal*, pp. 251–252; Tarleton, *A History of the Campaigns*, pp. 377–378; and Lee, *Memoirs*, pp. 357–359.

28. Stephen Popp, "Journal, 1777–1783," *Pennsylvania Magazine of History and Biography*, XXVI (1902), 41; in Scheer, *Rebels*, pp. 484–485.

29. Johann Conrad Doehla, "The Doehla Journal," trans. Robert J. Tilden, *Wm. and Mary Qtly*, 2d ser., XXII (July, 1942), 251. Especially important for more details of the siege are pp. 241–274.

30. Clinton to Cornwallis, Sept. 30, 1781: P.R.O. 30/11/68, ff. 91–92.

31. Cornwallis to Clinton, Oct. 11, 1781: *Cornwallis Corr.*, I, 125. Ross is inaccurate in places and omits part of the letter. For the original see P.R.O. 30/11/74, ff. 101–102.

32. Quoted in Wildes, *Wayne*, p. 266.

33. "Doehla Journal," *Wm. and Mary Qtly*, XXII, 251.

34. Stedman, *History of the American War*, II, 460.

35. At least according to *London Chronicle*, L (July 3 to December 29, 1781), 512.

36. Both British and American sources agree on the number of prisoners taken, but they differ on the number of killed. We have taken our figures from Lee, *Memoirs*, p. 362. Lee was at the siege but did not participate in the storming.

37. Cornwallis to Clinton, Oct. 15, 1781: *Cornwallis Corr.*, I, 125.

38. This account comes from Johnston, *Yorktown Campaign*, pp. 148–149; and Freeman, *Washington*, V, 373–374.

39. Thacher, *Military Journal*, p. 286.

40. Cornwallis to Clinton, Oct. 20, 1781: *Cornwallis Corr.*, I, 129.

41. Cornwallis to Washington, Oct. 17, 1781: *ibid.,* I, 523.
42. "Tucker's Journal," *Wm. and Mary Qtly,* V, 391.
43. Article X of the capitulation.
44. The incident is recorded in many places. See, for example, "Tucker's Journal," *Wm. and Mary Qtly,* V, 394.
45. Cornwallis to Clinton, Oct. 20, 1781: *Cornwallis Corr.,* I, 127–131.
46. Mackenzie, *Diary,* II, 698, describes the sailing and arrival.

Select Bibliography

So extensive is the literature of the American Revolution that an exhaustive bibliography of all the works we consulted to compile this biography would be inordinately long. We offer, therefore, the following select bibliography of the works which we found most useful. For further details the chapter notes may be consulted.

Unpublished Sources

The most important source is, of course, the Cornwallis Papers. The Public Record Office houses 291 bundles of Cornwallis Papers, P.R.O. 30/11 series. For the Cornwallis family papers see P.R.O. 30/11/268–281 and 284–285. Cornwallis papers dealing with America are P.R.O. 30/11/1–7, 58, and 60–110. Of great importance also are the Sir Henry Clinton Papers in the William L. Clements Library at Ann Arbor, Michigan. We consulted, in addition, a wide variety of other unpublished sources, none of them so valuable as the Cornwallis and Clinton Papers. These include the Cornwallis rent-rolls at Elveden Hall in Surrey; the Cornwallis bank records at Hoare's Bank, 37 Fleet Street; the Newcastle Papers (Additional Manuscripts 32,679–33,201) in the British Museum; the Grafton Papers in the West Suffolk Record Office; the Newcastle and Portland Papers on deposit at the University of Nottingham; the Rockingham Papers at the Central Library at Sheffield; the Hotham Papers in the East Riding County Record

Office at Beverly in Yorkshire; the Germain Papers at the William L. Clements Library; and the Nathanael Greene Papers at the Clements Library. We were also able to use the manuscripts of the Duke of Northumberland on microfilm in the library at the University of Michigan. The Public Record office contains the War Office Records, and we consulted several volumes in the War Office 3 and War Office 4 series for information about Cornwallis, about his regiment, and about the British army generally. Also in the Public Record Office are Colonial Office 5/135–240, the military dispatches from America from 1771 to 1782.

Published Sources

We made use of several of the volumes of papers published by the Historical Manuscripts Commission, but the most important were *Report on Manuscripts in Various Collections*, VI (Dublin, 1909); the Manuscripts of Cornwallis Wykeham–Martin, of the Hill, Purton, Wilts, Esquire. The Cornwallis Wykeham–Martin Papers are essentially those of Admiral William Cornwallis, and many letters pertaining to the family are contained in them. Another report of the commission, *Report on the Manuscripts of Mrs. Stopford Sackville, of Drayton House, Northamptonshire*, vol. II (London, 1910), catalogs the letters of Lord George Germain. A few of Cornwallis' subordinates published works of one sort or another relating to the southern campaign and these proved valuable to the book. James Ferguson, *Two Scottish Soldiers* (Aberdeen, 1888), includes some letters of Patrick Ferguson. George Hanger, fourth Baron Coleraine, printed two works. *The Life, Adventures, and Opinions of Colonel George Hanger, Written by Himself*, 2 vols. (London, 1801), is disappointingly thin on the Revolutionary War, while his *An Address to the Army; in Reply to Strictures by Roderick M'Kenzie (Late Lieutenant in the 71st Regiment) on Tarleton's History of the Campaigns of 1780 and 1781* (London, 1789) defends Tarleton sometimes at the expense of accuracy. Roger Lamb also wrote two works, *Memoirs of his own Life* (Dublin, 1811) and *An Original and Authentic Journal of Occurrences During the Late American War* (Dublin, 1809). The second is by far the most informative. Roderick Mackenzie was wounded at Cowpens and never forgave Tarleton for the disastrous battle. He later criticized Tarleton and defended those whom Tarleton had attacked in a pamphlet with an impossibly long title: *Strictures on Lt. Col. Tarleton's History "of the Campaigns of 1780 and 1781, in the Southern Provinces of North America," wherein Military Characters and Corps are Vindicated from*

Injurious Aspersions, and several Important Transactions Placed in their Proper Point of View, in a Series of Letters to a Friend, by Roderick Mackenzie, late Lieutenant in the 71st Regiment (London, 1787). John Simcoe's memoirs of the Virginia campaign are included in *Simcoe's Military Journal: A History of a Partisan Corps called the Queen's Rangers, Commanded by Lieut. Col. J. G. Simcoe, During the War of the American Revolution; Illustrated by ten Engraved Plans of Actions, &c. Now First Published, with a Memoir of the Author and Others* (New York, 1844). Charles Stedman, *The History of the Origin, Progress, and Termination of the American War,* 2 vols. (Dublin, 1794), is important for an understanding of Cornwallis' logistic problems. Banastre Tarleton, *A History of the Campaigns of 1780 and 1781, in the Southern Provinces of North America* (London, 1787), is of course an extremely important source. One must, however, remember that Tarleton hoped to clear himself of any fault for the misadventures in America. In order to do so he often attacked others without justification and warped events to suit his purposes. He should always be checked against other sources.

The American opponents of Cornwallis also recounted, in letters or memoirs, their experiences in fighting him. John C. Fitzpatrick, ed., *The Writings of George Washington,* 39 vols. (Washington, 1931–1944), provides many letters of the American commander concerning his Yorktown operations. Volumes 22 and 23 are the most important. George Washington Greene, *The Life of Nathanael Greene,* 3 vols. (New York, 1871); William Johnson, *Sketches of the Life and Correspondence of Nathanael Greene . . . Compiled Chiefly from Original Materials,* 2 vols. (Charleston, 1822); and Charles Caldwell, *Memoirs of the Life and Campaigns of the Hon. Nathanael Greene* (Philadelphia, 1819) — all quote copiously letters or accounts from Greene and others involved in the southern campaign. Another valuable source is Henry Lee, *Memoirs of the War in the Southern Department of the United States* (Washington, 1827).

Perhaps the single most valuable printed work, however, which includes pamphlets by Clinton and Cornwallis and quotes many of the letters between them, is Benjamin Franklin Stevens, *The Campaign in Virginia 1781. An exact Reprint of Six Rare Pamphlets on the Clinton-Cornwallis Controversy with very numerous important Unpublished Manuscript Notes by Sir Henry Clinton, K.B., and the Omitted and Hitherto Unpublished Portions of the Letters in their Appendixes added from the Original Manuscripts with a Supplement Containing Extracts from the Journals of the House of the Lords. A French Translation of Papers laid before the House and a Catalogue of the Additional Correspondence of Clinton and of Corn-*

wallis in 1780–1781: about 3456 Papers Relating to the Controversy or Bearing on Affairs in America, 2 vols. (London, 1888). Volume I contains the pamphlets and arranges chronologically correspondence between May 17, 1780, and May 31, 1781. Volume II arranges correspondence chronologically from June 4, 1781, to Dec. 27, 1781. It also includes extracts from the Journals of the House of Lords, correspondence of Lord George Germain, and a catalog of additional correspondence.

Clinton wrote a memoir of his view of the events in America, and it has been edited by William Willcox, *The American Rebellion, Sir Henry Clinton's Narrative of his Campaigns, 1775–1782, with an Appendix of Original Documents* (New Haven, 1954). Cornwallis left no memoir, but many of his important letters were arranged for publication by Charles Ross, ed., *Correspondence of Charles, First Marquis Cornwallis*, 3 vols. (London, 1859). Only about the first third of volume I deals with the American period.

We used, of course, many more sources than the ones cited, such as newspapers, parliamentary records, and accounts of events by British, German, and American participants, but any study of Cornwallis in America, and especially in the South, must refer to the works cited above.

Secondary Works

For purposes of simplicity we have divided the works we found most useful into three sections: biography; works devoted to special aspects of the Revolution; and general works dealing with the Revolution.

Biography

Anderson, Troyer Steele. *The Command of the Howe Brothers During the American Revolution.* New York, 1936.

Bass, Robert D. *The Green Dragoon.* New York, 1957.

———. *Gamecock.* New York, 1961.

———. *Swamp Fox.* London, 1960.

Freeman, Douglas Southall. *George Washington.* 7 vols. New York, 1948–1957. Volume V is particularly important.

Gerson, Noel B. *Light-Horse Harry.* New York, 1966.

Gottschalk, Louis. *Lafayette and the Close of the American Revolution.* Chicago, 1942.

Higginbotham, Don. *Daniel Morgan, Revolutionary Rifleman.* Chapel Hill, 1961.

Partridge, Bellamy. *Sir Billy Howe.* New York, 1932.

Patterson, Samuel W. *Horatio Gates.* New York, 1941.

Read, D. B. *The Life and Times of General John Graves Simcoe, Commander of the "Queen's Rangers" During the Revolutionary War, and First Governor of Upper Canada Together with Some Account of Major André and Captain Brant.* Toronto, 1901.

Thayer, Theodore. *Nathanael Greene, Strategist of the American Revolution.* New York, 1960.

Wildes, Harry Emerson. *Anthony Wayne, Trouble Shooter of the American Revolution.* New York, 1941.

Willcox, William B. *Portrait of a General: Sir Henry Clinton in the War of Independence.* New York, 1964.

Special Aspects of the Revolution

Bill, Alfred Hoyt. *The Campaign of Princeton, 1776–1777.* Princeton, 1948.

Curtis, Edward P. *The Organization of the British Army in the American Revolution.* New Haven, 1926.

Davis, Burke. *The Cowpens–Guilford Courthouse Campaign.* New York, 1962.

Draper, Lyman C. *King's Mountain and Its Heroes: History of the Battle of King's Mountain, October 7th, 1780, and the Events Which Led to It.* Cincinnati, 1881.

Johnston, Henry P. *The Yorktown Campaign and the Surrender of Cornwallis, 1781.* New York, 1881.

Landers, H. L. *The Battle of Camden.* Washington, 1929.

Landrum, J. B. O. *Colonial and Revolutionary History of Upper South Carolina.* Greenville, S.C., 1897.

Lefferts, Charles M. *Uniforms of the American, British, French and German Armies in the War of the American Revolution, 1775–1783.* New York, 1926.

Lowell, Edward J. *The Hessians and Other German Auxiliaries of Great Britain in the Revolutionary War.* New York, 1884.

Myers, William S., ed. *The Battle of Monmouth by the Late William S. Stryker.* Princeton, 1927.

Ramsay, David. *The History of the Revolution of South Carolina from a British Province to an Independent State.* 2 vols. Trenton, 1785.

Schenck, David. *North Carolina, 1780–1781*. Raleigh, N.C., 1889.

Smith, Paul H. *Loyalists and Redcoats*. Chapel Hill, 1964.

Stryker, William Scudder. *The Battles of Trenton and Princeton*. Boston and New York, 1898.

Treacy, M. F. *Prelude to Yorktown, the Southern Campaign of Nathanael Greene*. Chapel Hill, 1963.

General Works Dealing with the Revolution

Alden, John Richard. *The American Revolution, 1775–1783*. New York, 1954.

Carrington, Henry B. *Battles of the American Revolution, 1775–1781: Historical and Military Criticism, with Topographical Illustration*. New York, 1876.

Fortescue, Sir John. *History of the British Army*. 13 vols. London, 1899–1930. Volume III deals with the Revolution.

Lossing, Benson J. *The Pictorial Field-Book of the Revolution; or Illustrations, by Pen and Pencil, of the History, Biography, Scenery, Relics and Traditions of the War for Independence*. 2 vols. New York, 1885. Volume II was the most valuable for our study.

Mackesy, Piers. *The War for America, 1775–1783*. Cambridge, Mass., 1964.

Peckham, Howard H. *The War for Independence: A Military History*. Chicago, 1958.

Rankin, Hugh F. *The American Revolution*. London, 1964.

Rankin, Hugh F., and Scheer, George F. *Rebels and Redcoats*. New York, 1957.

Robson, Eric. *The American Revolution in its Political and Military Aspects, 1763–1783*. New York, 1955.

Wallace, Willard M. *Appeal to Arms, A Military History of the American Revolution*. Chicago, 1951.

Ward, Christopher. *The War of the Revolution*, edited by John R. Alden. 2 vols. New York, 1952.

Index

Index

Index

Abercrombie, Lt. Col. Robert, 369, 382

Agenois Regiment, 382

Alamance Creek, N.C., 289

Albemarle Court House, Va., 334

Alien and Sedition Acts, 207

Allaire, Lt. Anthony, 215, 218–219

American army: in battle of Camden, 154, 158–164; in battle of Long Island, 87–90; British prisoners of, 314; compared with British, 53, 55, 64; defeat at Camden, 162–164; losses at Guilford Courthouse, 308–309; at Monmouth Courthouse, 111–112; poor health of, 155; uniform and clothing of, 56. *See also* American prisoners; Continental army

American civilians, in Charleston occupation, 146–147

American colonies: British politics and, 40–42; "state of rebellion" in, 171

American prisoners: in battle of Camden, 164; in battle of Guilford Courthouse, 313; British recruiting of, 186; Cornwallis on, 146; release of in South Carolina, 182–183

American Revolution: British and American troops compared in, 53, 55, 64; British mistakes in, 62; as civil war, 169; in career of Cornwallis, 24; price of British commissions in, 50; total risk of revolutionaries in, 185

Americans, in British army, 135–136

Amherst, Jeffrey, Baron, 60, 107

Anbury, Capt. Thomas, 68

André, Maj. John, 129

Arbuthnot, Adm. Marriot, 124–125, 127, 131, 138, 182, 350

aristocracy: in British army, 56, 64; at Eton, 19; as ruling class, 9, 17

Armer's Ford, S.C., 228

25; in Geneva and Cologne, 27; as aide-de-camp to Marquis of Granby, 28; as lieutenant colonel, 28; years at Eton, 18–22, 29; family background, 30–38; sobriety, 30; attachment to family, 31–38; income, 31–32; as Lieutenant of the Tower, 37; aid to brothers and sisters, 32–38; courtship, 38–39; wife's death, 40; votes with Rockingham whigs, 41; early politics, 41–43; religious affiliation, 42; loyalty to Newcastle, 43; meeting with Wilkes, 44; aide-de-camp to King George, 45; on eve of American Revolution, 46; as privy councillor, 46; opposes government policy, 45–46; as lieutenant general of Army of North America, 46, 51–52, 62; culpability of, 74; loyalty of army to, 74; diligence as commander, 74–75; administrative skill, 75–76; as army "reformer," 76; concern for British private, 77; honesty and patriotism of, 77; discipline, 77–78; justice and compassion, 78; asceticism, 78; volunteers to fight in America to suppress rebellion, 79; embarks for North Carolina, 80–82; attack on Charleston, 84–85; in New York (August, 1776), 86; at battle of Long Island, 87–90; in New York campaign, 90–91; pursues American army from Fort Lee, N.J., 91–93; misses opportunity at New Brunswick, 94; march toward Trenton, 95–96; at battle of Princeton, 96; "at worst" in Trenton-Princeton campaign,

98; contradictory qualities in, 98; and Philadelphia campaign, 101–104; returns to England (January, 1778), 105; and Tower hamlets, 105–106; returns to America (spring, 1778), 107; second in command under Clinton, 107; rift with Clinton, 108; attempts to resign, 108–109; at battle of Monmouth Courthouse, 110–111; thirsts for action, 113; resigns and again returns to England (November, 1778), 113–114; wife's illness and death, 114–115; return to America (April, 1779), 115; recovers strength and resolve, 116; break with Clinton, 119–123; to New York (July, 1779), 123; at siege of Charleston, 130–131; first "taste of independence" after Charleston, 133; lack of support from Clinton, 135; troop strength of, 136; southern campaign of, 137–138; supply difficulties, 139–142; food problems, 140–142; seizes rebel supplies and Negro slaves, 142–143; reestablishes civilian participation in government, 143–144; rebellion problem faced by, 145–146; and prisoners of war, 146; in battle of Camden, 149–165; learns of rebel plans at Camden, 153–154; after victory at Camden, 164–165; and loyalist militia, 169–193; "straight dealing" of, 171; distaste for cruelty and dishonesty, 171; loyalist support of, 172; his compassion, 173; in civil war, 173; treatment of rebels, 174; his clemency, 174–177;

THE FRENCH
ATLANTIC
AFFAIR